Racial Violence in Kentucky, 1865 – 1940

GEORGE C. WRIGHT

Racial Violence in Kentucky

1865–1940

Lynchings, Mob Rule, and "Legal Lynchings"

LOUISIANA STATE UNIVERSITY PRESS

Baton Rouge and London

Copyright © 1990 by Louisiana State University Press
All rights reserved
Manufactured in the United States of America

Louisiana Paperback Edition, 1996
05 04 03 02 01 00 99 98 97 96   5 4 3 2 1

Designer: Laura Roubique Gleason
Typeface: Trump Mediaeval
Typesetter: G&S Typesetters, Inc.
Printer and binder: Thomson-Shore, Inc.

LIBRARY OF CONGRESS CATALOGING-IN-PUBLICATION DATA

Wright, George C.
    Racial violence in Kentucky, 1865–1940 : lynchings, mob rule, and
"legal lynchings" / George C. Wright.
        p.   cm.
    Includes bibliographical references.
    ISBN 0-8071-1536-3 (cloth)   ISBN 0-8071-2073-1 (pbk.)
        1. Lynching—Kentucky—History.   2. Capital punishment—Kentucky—
History.   3. Afro-Americans—Kentucky—Crimes against—History.
4. Discrimination in criminal justice administration—Kentucky—
History.   5. Kentucky—Race relations.   I. Title.
HV6465.K4W75   1990b
364.1'34—dc20   89-38651
                                                                        CIP

The paper in this book meets the guidelines for permanence and durability of the
Committee on Production Guidelines for Book Longevity of the Council on Library
Resources. ∞

TO
My mother, Amanda Wright Knox
The memory of my father, Scott J. Wright (1926–1972)
and
My parents-in-law, Ida L. and William H. Ellison

Contents

Illustrations

Tables

Acknowledgments

One of the most enjoyable aspects of writing a book is to thank all of the people who have contributed in some way. My research began during the 1983–1984 school year at Harvard University, where I held an Andrew W. Mellon Faculty Fellowship. The late Nathan I. Huggins, W. E. B. Du Bois Professor of History and at that time director of Afro-American Studies, made office space and supplies available to me.

My research, especially the time-consuming but very necessary chore of tabulating the number of lynchings and legal executions, was greatly assisted by the following research assistants: Andrew Drozd, Laura Mayhall, Danalynn Recer, and Victoria Seligman. A number of librarians, especially those at Harvard University, the Manuscript Division of the Library of Congress, the Division of Special Collections and Archives at the University of Kentucky, the Kentucky Department for Libraries and Archives, and the office of Interlibrary Loans at the University of Texas, made my task easier. Special mention must be made of James M. Prichard, archivist at the Kentucky Department for Libraries, who brought to my attention a number of important documents. Additionally, Prichard graciously researched several different files for me and mailed numerous photocopies.

Several scholars assisted this study by offering their comments and by sharing various sources with me. Marion Lucas, professor of history at Western Kentucky University in Bowling Green, made me aware of resources at the National Archives in Washington, D.C., and shared his note cards on the Reconstruction period with me. Dr. James Klotter, general editor of the Kentucky Historical Society and the leading scholar on the history of Kentucky, read the manuscript and made invaluable suggestions. Klotter also sent me numerous articles and references. My good friend from graduate school, Albert S. Broussard of the Department of History, Texas A & M University, also read the manuscript, making his usual helpful suggestions. Albert is the person I can always turn to for encouragement, reassuring me that what I am doing is significant. On several occasions, Kentucky scholars who heard me lecture on racial violence sent me information about a particular lynching or incident I would not have found on my own. I am extremely thankful to these scholars for sharing their research with me.

In many different ways, the completion of this study has been assisted by Terry L. Birdwhistell, university archivist at the University of Kentucky. Every time I traveled to Lexington, Terry made available to me the many resources of the Divison of Special Collections and Archives. Several times he rechecked newspapers and census data and mailed articles and other materials to me. Terry and I have traveled throughout Kentucky in researching this project. He too read the manuscript and made useful suggestions. Furthermore, while in Lexington I could always count on being fed and entertained at Terry's home by his gracious wife, Janice, and their daughter, Jessica.

My research project, which required spending considerable time in archives in Atlanta, Washington, and Kentucky, would have been impossible without financial support. Early on, I received a grant from the American Association for the Study of State and Local History, which financed several research trips. Grants from the University of Texas Research Institute, African and Afro-American Research Center, and Department of History's Dora Bonham Fund helped pay for travel and research materials.

In addition, Betty Nunley, administrative associate in the Afro-American Center, read the manuscript, pointing out any number of errors. Dorothy Motton, senior office assistant, counted the charts dozens of times, made numerous phone calls, and kept me organized.

As I discovered several years ago when completing my first book, the people associated with Louisiana State University Press are great to work with. From the very first time I mentioned this proposed book to her, Beverly Jarrett, former associate director and executive editor, gave me encouragement. Also, Catherine Barton, former managing editor, is to be commended for suggesting numerous editorial changes that undoubtedly made this a better book.

In dedicating this book to my parents and in-laws, I am making a public acknowledgment to four people who have aided me in more ways than they know.

Finally, my family has made it easier for me to devote much of my time and energy to writing this book. Rebecca Ellison Wright, my daughter, has always helped my perspective on things, making me realize the importance of sometimes not working but spending time with her. My spouse since our undergraduate days in college, Valerie Ellison Wright, has patiently listened to me talk about this study and has made any number of comments about the book. In addition to pursuing her own very demanding career, she somehow finds the time and the will to help me in all my endeavors. I will always be grateful to Valerie for what she has contributed to me.

Racial Violence in Kentucky, 1865–1940

Kentucky, divided into seven regions

Region 1
Jackson Purchase
1. Ballard
2. McCracken
3. Marshall
4. Graves
5. Carlisle
6. Hickman
7. Fulton
8. Calloway

Region 2
Western Kentucky
1. Union
2. Henderson
3. Daviess
4. Hancock
5. Breckinridge
6. Meade
7. Hardin
8. Larue
9. Taylor
10. Green
11. Hart
12. Grayson
13. Ohio
14. McLean
15. Webster
16. Hopkins
17. Crittenden
18. Livingston
19. Lyon
20. Caldwell
21. Muhlenberg
22. Butler
23. Edmonson
24. Barren
25. Warren
26. Allen
27. Simpson
28. Logan
29. Todd
30. Christian
31. Trigg

Region 3
Louisville Metro
1. Oldham
2. Jefferson
3. Bullitt

Region 4
Central Kentucky
1. Shelby
2. Franklin
3. Scott
4. Harrison
5. Nicholas
6. Bourbon
7. Fayette
8. Woodford
9. Anderson
10. Spencer
11. Nelson
12. Washington
13. Mercer
14. Jessamine
15. Clark
16. Madison
17. Garrard
18. Boyle
19. Marion

Region 5
Northern Kentucky
1. Trimble
2. Carroll
3. Gallatin
4. Henry
5. Owen
6. Grant
7. Boone
8. Kenton
9. Campbell
10. Pendleton
11. Bracken
12. Mason
13. Robertson
14. Fleming
15. Lewis

Region 6
Eastern Kentucky
1. Montgomery
2. Bath
3. Rowan
4. Carter
5. Greenup
6. Boyd
7. Lawrence
8. Elliott
9. Morgan
10. Menifee
11. Powell
12. Wolfe
13. Magoffin
14. Johnson
15. Martin
16. Pike
17. Floyd
18. Breathitt
19. Lee
20. Estill
21. Rockcastle
22. Jackson
23. Owsley
24. Perry
25. Knott
26. Letcher
27. Leslie
28. Clay
29. Laurel
30. McCreary
31. Whitley
32. Knox
33. Bell
34. Harlan

Region 7
South Central Kentucky
1. Casey
2. Lincoln
3. Pulaski
4. Adair
5. Russell
6. Wayne
7. Clinton
8. Cumberland
9. Metcalfe
10. Monroe

Region 2

Region 3

Region 4

Region 5

Region 6

Region 7

Region 1

Kentucky Violence, Severe
and Long Lasting

This study of racial violence in Kentucky is an outgrowth of my book on Louisville blacks from 1865 to 1930. That study centered on the concept of "polite racism," a form of oppression that extended a few concessions to Afro-Americans as long as they accepted their "place" and remained at the bottom of society. Polite racism proved to be effective, for it tended to lull both Afro-Americans and whites into believing that conditions in Louisville were not as bad as they were elsewhere. While doing the research on Louisville blacks, I came across stories of lynchings that had occurred in the smaller towns in the state. I quickly realized that except for Louisville and Lexington, the state was similar to the Deep South in its attitude and its actions toward Afro-Americans. Furthermore, in Kentucky's larger cities, the police—an important symbol of white authority—were not above using force to ensure that blacks acted the way whites thought necessary. It became clear that racial violence, the reverse of polite racism, also existed in Kentucky and was probably more prevalent than the polite racism found in Louisville.

Although poor, young, uneducated blacks were the primary victims of white violence, no black person within Kentucky was immune from attacks by whites. Furthermore, the entire legal system upheld white violence by refusing to apprehend, charge, and convict white offenders of blacks, thus ensuring that all Afro-Americans were at the mercy of whites. Racial violence in Kentucky would be evident in many forms: in the whipping of blacks by their former slaveowners or by local police officials, in the destruction of black schools and property, in forcing all blacks in certain areas to leave the community, in the denial to blacks of right to fair trials, and in the cold-blooded murder of blacks, often at the hands of lynch mobs.

A full understanding of the racial violence in Kentucky requires a look at the black experience immediately at the end of the Civil War. As Leon Litwack explains, the mere fact that blacks had been slaves—someone's property—had protected them from the worst abuses of hostile whites. With emancipation, however, Afro-Americans had become vulnerable to attacks from whites. Another scholar of southern history, Otis A. Singletary, writes, "When the definitive account of the South during Reconstruction is finally written, it will contain deep and depressing undertones of violence. . . . Reconstruction was pre-eminently a period of violence."[1] White Kentuckians responded to the social, political, and other changes with unheard of violence, even by Kentucky standards. With state officials refusing to aid blacks or to prevent outbreaks of violence, the federal government extended the Freedmen's Bureau to Kentucky in January, 1866. Kentucky was the only slave-holding state that had remained loyal to the Union that also had the bureau, which further aroused the hostilities of many embittered whites toward their former slaves. Violence made life extremely hazardous for agents of the bureau. Moreover, this white violence became so widespread that many of the northern freedmen's aid societies that operated in other former slave states, helping the blacks in the transition from bondage to freedom, avoided Kentucky for fear of the lives of their workers.

The white violence in Kentucky during Reconstruction was most often directed at, and had its most devastating effect on, the freedmen. Upon returning home from fighting in the Union army, black soldiers were attacked by roaming white bands. As a report submitted to the Freedmen's Bureau explained, "Lawless men have recently seized several colored men who were former soldiers and abused them most brutally. The occasion of this is some meetings of the Colored people in Union League Meetings. The 'rebs' have resolved to break them up and as a means have commenced a series of brutal whippings and beatings."[2] On several occasions, groups of blacks petitioned the United States Congress for protection from white mobs, citing instances of lynchings and other lawless acts. Violence was so wide-

1. Leon Litwack, *Been in the Storm So Long: The Aftermath of Slavery* (New York, 1979), 275; Otis A. Singletary, *Negro Militia and Reconstruction* (Austin, 1957), 3.

2. John G. Fee in Camp Nelson to "The Officers of the Bureau" in Lexington, March 25, 1868, in Record Group 105, General Records of the Bureau of Refugees, Freedmen, and Abandoned Lands, National Archives (hereinafter cited as Freedmen's Bureau).

spread in Mason County that a number of the freedmen refused to sign a petition, fearing that their churches and property would be destroyed as a result of their complaints.[3] Although the Freedmen's Bureau failed to prevent most of the violence, blacks were rightfully concerned about the bureau leaving the state. As an Owensboro black explained, "The Bureau is our only protection in Kentucky. The civil laws of the State deprive us of our every right. Every black man is threatened in the State by every rebel . . . upon the removal of the Bureau. . . . He shall be paid up for daring to assert his manhood before that institution."[4]

Most often, blacks were limited in how they could respond to the violence of whites. Seeking protection in black communities, many rural former slaves began moving to Kentucky's cities, especially Louisville and Lexington. Although their exact number is difficult to determine, many decided to quit the state altogether. Under the best of circumstances, the Bureau of the Census tended to undercount the number of Afro-Americans in the United States. Also, if a person moved into an area but stayed only a short period of time, he was probably not counted in the population for that area. Despite limitations in giving an accurate count of the number of blacks, the census data clearly show that the percentage of blacks in Kentucky declined steadily over the decades (Table 1). In 1860, blacks accounted for 20.4 percent of the total population; they reached their lowest point in 1950, when they constituted less than 7 percent of the population. From 1860 to 1900, the state's black population increased by only 48,539, from 263,167 to 284,706, while the white population more than doubled, reaching 1,862,309 by the start of the new century.

The first part of this study, covering the Reconstruction period, will end with 1874. This period is especially significant because all aspects of racial violence in Kentucky—lynchings, "legal lynchings," and mob rule—were a part of black life by the mid-1870s. More than one-third of all the lynchings that would take place in Kentucky occurred between the years 1865 and 1874.

Lynchings—a brutal phenomenon that started during Reconstruction—would most surely continue in Kentucky in the years after 1875. Writing at the turn of the twentieth century, James E. Cutler

---

3. C. J. True to R. E. Johnston, July 2, 1867, Freedmen's Bureau.
4. William Sykes to T. D. Eliot, December 27, 1867, Freedmen's Bureau.

TABLE 1   Kentucky's Black and White Population, 1860–1950

Year	White	Black	% Black in Total Population
1860	919,484	236,167	20.4
1870	1,098,692	222,210	16.8
1880	1,377,179	271,451	16.5
1890	1,590,462	268,071	14.4
1900	1,862,309	284,706	13.3
1910	2,027,951	261,656	11.4
1920	2,180,560	235,938	9.8
1930	2,388,364	226,040	8.6
1940	2,631,425	214,031	7.5
1950	2,742,090	201,921	6.9

SOURCES: U.S. Census Bureau, *Negro Population in the United States, 1790–1915* (Washington, D.C., 1918), 92–98, 142, 780; U.S. Census Bureau, *Bulletin 8, Negroes in the United States* (Washington, D.C., 1904), 102, 282; U.S. Census Bureau, *Fifteenth Census of the United States, 1930* (Washington, D.C., 1932), III, Part 1, p. 893; U.S. Census Bureau, *Seventeenth Census of the United States, 1950* (Washington, D.C., 1952), II, Part 17, p. 26.

described lynching as "a criminal practice which is peculiar to the United States. The practice whereby mobs capture individuals suspected of crime, or take them from the officers of the law, and execute them without any process at law, or break open jails and hang convicted criminals, with impunity, is to be found in no other country of a high degree of civilization." A more recent scholar, James R. McGovern, explains that "the key to the phenomenon is community approval, either explicit, in the form of general participation by the local citizenry, or implicit, in the form of acquittal of the killers without a trial."[5] Scholars of lynching seem to agree that the total number of recorded lynchings falls short of the actual number. In Kentucky and elsewhere, several highly publicized lynchings, witnessed by thousands, occurred over the years. Yet a number of lynchings in rural

5. James Elbert Cutler, *Lynch-Law: An Investigation into the History of Lynching in the United States* (1905; rpr. Montclair, New Jersey, 1969), 1; James R. McGovern, *Anatomy of a Lynching: The Killing of Claude Neal* (Baton Rouge, 1982), x.

areas were not, for whatever reasons, reported by the newspapers. The Chicago *Tribune* and New York *Times,* both excellent sources on lynchings between 1882 and 1918, failed to report several lynchings that occurred in Kentucky. Some lynchings probably still remain hidden from scholarly scrutiny because of source limitations. Folk traditions tell of people who were murdered in isolated counties and dumped into rivers and creeks, or who—according to biased white newspapers—escaped from the authorities and simply disappeared. In other words, this uniquely American phenomenon probably occurred to a degree far greater than we can ever document.

Most sources have indicated that at least 205 people were lynched in Kentucky, placing it ninth among states with the largest number of mob murders. By contrast, my findings reveal that at least 353 people were lynched in the Bluegrass State.[6] A comparison of my figures for Kentucky with the number of lynchings for other states means, at least on the surface, that only three states had more lynchings than did Kentucky. This, of course, simply is not correct. It does suggest, however, that just as 205 lynchings for Kentucky is much too low a figure, the lynchings in Georgia, Mississippi, Texas, and elsewhere in the South have also been greatly undercounted. Further research in local newspapers and county histories, which proved to be invaluable sources in documenting 353 lynchings in Kentucky, should provide similar corrections for other states, especially in the number of lynchings that occurred prior to the mid-1880s. When discussing a lynching in their particular area, local newspapers gave all of the grisly details and, significantly, would often point out that the lynching was not the first one that had happened in their area. In December, 1896, after a black man was lynched in Mayfield, the local newspaper noted:

6. See, for example, Harry A. Ploski and Roscoe C. Brown (eds.), *The Negro Almanac* (New York, 1967), 212–15. My research has uncovered several lynchings in the state prior to the Civil War. In Louisville in May, 1858, four black slaves, having been found not guilty of murdering a white family, were seized by a mob. Three died by hangings and the fourth committed suicide, cutting his throat with a razor rather than die at the hands of the lynchers. Details on the case can be found in the Louisville *Daily Democrat,* December 23–29, 1856, and in *Frank Leslie's Illustrated Weekly,* June 13, 1857. William Barker, a white man, was lynched for the murder of another white man in Lexington in July, 1858. See *Harper's Weekly,* July 31, 1858. These mob murders have not been included in my estimate of 353 lynchings in the Bluegrass State.

The hanging of [Jim] Stone is the first lynching for a similar crime that has occurred in the county since 1870, when six negroes were hanged by masked mobs in and near the city. One was lynched in Bullock's grove, one near the Primitive Baptist Church, one a short distance south of where Mr. William McDonald now lives, one at the old Conner orchard, two at Kess Creek on the Paris Road, and one other in the same locality. This stopped the crime until the past few years, and Stone is the first one to suffer the penalty since twenty-five years ago.

In March, 1886, a black was lynched in Russellville for the attempted rape of a twelve-year-old white girl. The Louisville *Courier-Journal* (which documented lynchings that happened all over the state) explained in a matter-of-fact manner that Handy Woodward was hanged from a "large sycamore tree, the same from which the notorious Sambo Bailey was swung into eternity at the hands of a mob about two years ago." When describing, in 1889, the lynching of a black in Paris, the *Courier-Journal* informed its readers that "a negro was hung here in 1867, in broad daylight in the Court-yard, for raping an eleven year old daughter of a Mr. Doolin." In February, 1902, Tom Brown died at the hands of a lynch mob in Jessamine County after being accused of rape. The local newspaper took the occasion to inform its readers that another black man had been lynched in the county for rape in August, 1874.[7] Thus, news of one lynching often led to a search in the earlier newspapers from that county or region for details about another lynching.[8]

7. Mayfield *Monitor*, December 23, 1896; Louisville *Courier-Journal*, March 11, 1886, July 27, 1889; Jessamine *Journal*, February 7, 1902. Unfortunately, except for the Louisville *Leader*, which was published from 1917 to 1950, the dozens of Kentucky black newspapers that existed from the 1870s to the 1940s have not been preserved. Several out-of-state newspapers—the New York *Globe* (which became the *Freeman* in 1884 and the *Age* in 1887) and the Indianapolis *Freeman* being the best examples—often contain stories on racial violence in the state during the late 1800s. Accounts of some lynchings in Kentucky in the early twentieth century can be found in the Tuskegee Institute Newspaper Clippings. But for the most part, scholars, when consulting newspapers as one source for information on lynchings and other acts of racial violence in Kentucky, are forced to rely on accounts published by contemporary whites. Needless to say, the white newspapers must always be used with caution, keeping in mind the racial bias of the writers.

8. In July, 1894, Louis Lafordette was lynched in Boone County. The local newspaper, the Boone County *Recorder*, explained, "Lafordette makes the eighth man who has been lynched in this county in the last twenty years, and Boone county has a national reputation as the abode of the lawless and the lynchers." However, I was able to

Such details were vital to the documentation of lynchings in Kentucky prior to 1882. The Chicago *Tribune* started coverage of lynchings that year, showing how many people were killed and giving the reasons for those deaths. With the statistics of the *Tribune* in mind, a number of able scholars have speculated on why the lynchings of Afro-Americans increased dramatically in the last two decades of the nineteenth century. In his brilliant study of race relations in the American South, Joel Williamson explains that by the 1880s southern whites were convinced that blacks had broken free from the restraining influences of whites that had dominated their lives during slavery. Furthermore, he notes that the depression of the 1890s produced psychological effects on southern white men of the Victorian era, who saw themselves as the "providers and protectors in their families." The rage of white men toward the black beast rapist (which, of course, was their own creation) "was a kind of psychic compensation." Pursuing this point, Williamson states, "If white men could not provide for their women materially as they had done before, they could certainly protect them from a much more awful threat—the outrage of their purity, and hence their piety, by black men. What white men might have lost on one side in affirming their sense of self, they might more than compensate for on the other. Bread for their women was important, but it was nothing alongside their purity."[9]

In an important study on crime and justice in the American South, Edward Ayers points out that whites had long associated blacks with sexuality; therefore, he says, something else led to the increased violence of the 1880s. The lynching crisis, he concludes, "was a by-product of a new generation of southern whites and blacks who had grown to adulthood without close intimate contact of each other." He then adds, "At the time the lynching crisis hit the South no man under 30 years old, white or black, would have any memory of slavery at all—only of racial distrust, conflict, and bloodshed. Since most 'criminals' and most violent men have always been young, . . . it is safe to assume that most lynchers and lynching victims came from

---

find evidence on only three lynchings that took place in Boone County prior to the lynching of Lafordette. I have, therefore, counted only four lynchings, not eight, for Boone, which illustrates once again how the number of recorded lynchings is undoubtedly considerably lower than the number that actually happened.

9. See Joel Williamson, *The Crucible of Race: Black and White Relations in the American South Since Emancipation* (New York, 1984), 111–39.

this new generation. These men feared each other with the fear of ig-
norance. They saw each other dimly, at a distance."[10]

However, the findings cited herein clearly show no sudden or dramatic increase in Kentucky's lynchings in the 1880s or 1890s. Indeed,
the number of lynchings remained steady in the last two decades
of the nineteenth century when compared with the decade immediately after slavery. At least 117 were lynched within the state between 1865 and 1874. In other words, one-third of the total number of
lynchings in Kentucky happened in the decade after emancipation. In
the period highlighted by Ayers, Williamson, and other scholars,
lynchings seemed more sensational, with many victims burned to
death and their bodies shamelessly mutilated. Many "respectable"
whites condoned the acts of the mob, speaking out bluntly on what
steps should be taken to end the "negro problem" in southern society.
These actions made a strong impression and, coupled with the yellow
journalism of that day, contributed to the prominence given to lynchings in the newspapers. A modern-day parallel can be drawn with how
the American public has become aware of family violence, especially
child abuse. Much media attention has been given to the subject in
the last decade. Dramatic court trials have made national news. Practically every community can point to its own awful example of a par-
ent or babysitter sexually abusing a child. Yet, as a recent book by
Elizabeth Pleck shows, family violence is not a recent phenomenon.
During the years from 1874 to 1890, for example, in response to a
number of highly publicized cases of assault on children, concerned
reformers created organizations with the goal of ending family violence.[11] It is highly possible, given the huge amount of publicity and
the tough stance that law enforcement agencies have adopted in the
1980s, that the incidence of child abuse might actually be lower now
than in an earlier period when these awful events were more than
likely covered up. So, too, with lynchings. In short, my figures show
that more lynchings occurred in the fifteen-year period from 1865 to
1880 than during any other fifteen-year period, even the years from
1885 to 1900, which most scholars and contemporary observers called
the heyday of lynching.

10. See Edward Ayers, *Vengeance and Justice: Crime and Punishment in the 19th
Century American South* (New York, 1984), 223–65.
    11. See Elizabeth Pleck, *Domestic Tyranny: The Making of Social Policy Against
Family Violence from Colonial Times to the Present* (New York, 1987), 69–121.

If scholars agree that it is extremely difficult to account fully for all of the lynchings that occurred in the period beginning in the 1880s, then it is almost impossible to have anything close to an accurate count of the number of Afro-Americans lynched from 1865 to 1880. Several newspaper stories from the early 1870s give details of raids in various parts of the state by the Ku Klux Klan or the Regulators during which, according to these accounts, more than one hundred blacks were lynched. Since I could not obtain any corroborating evidence for these astonishing figures, they have been omitted from my count. Furthermore, in small communities newspaper editors who denounced the lawless white bands for attacking Afro-Americans ran the risk of bodily harm. This led others to remain silent about lynchings. Many Kentucky whites, because they wanted the Freedmen's Bureau removed from the state, had yet another reason to cover up the number of blacks being lynched. The slave narratives must also be used with caution when attempting to document lynchings and other racial violence. A former slave, Richard Miller, informed an interviewer about the lynching, in Danville, of the wife of George Bland by the Ku Klux Klan during the Reconstruction years. According to Miller, the Klan members, after killing Bland's wife, forced him to view the body. "He asked them to let him go back to the house to get something to wrap his wife in; thinking he was sincere in his request, they allowed him to go. Instead of getting a wrapping for his wife, he got his Winchester rifle, shot and killed fourteen of the Kluxers. The county was never bothered with the Klan again. However, George left immediately for the North." In all probability, this account is fictitious, especially the part about Bland killing fourteen members of the Klan. Therefore, the lynching of his wife has not been included in my tabulation.[12] If this study will encourage scholars of Georgia, Mississippi, Texas, and South Carolina—as well as the other states in which the number of lynchings greatly exceeded those in Kentucky— to investigate the period prior to the 1880s, then it will have achieved one of its purposes. Only then can we have a better understanding of the extent of this brutal form of oppression on Afro-Americans.

While the conclusions of Williamson, Ayers, and other scholars regarding the dramatic increase in lynchings in the late 1880s might be

12. George P. Rawick (ed.), *Alabama and Indiana Narratives* (Westport, 1972), 135–36, Vol. IV of Rawick (ed.), *The American Slave: A Composite Autobiography*, 19 vols.

questioned, these scholars are correct when saying that the ultimate reason for the rise of the "lynching bee" was the same reason that has always led to white violence on blacks. Afro-Americans were lynched for getting out of the place assigned them by white society. On more than one occasion, whites pinned a note to the body of a lynch victim as a warning to other blacks that the same would happen to them unless they changed their ways, returned to work, quit agitating for their rights, and in general left whites alone.[13] Immediately after the Civil War, whites sought to maintain control over blacks through force. Not surprisingly, most of the blacks were lynched not for rape but for being involved in politics. During the 1880s and 1890s, many white observers lamented the passing of the loyal Negroes that slavery had produced. In their place were "New Negroes," who, without the civilizing influence of whites, were actually regarded by whites as retrogressing to their "barbaric" African condition. In Louisville, Atlanta, New Orleans, and other southern cities, this attitude led to increased police brutality toward blacks; in the small towns and rural communities, it led to lynchings. The lynching and burning of one black became a vivid and violent reminder to all Afro-Americans of the dire consequences of getting out of their places. As Williamson clearly explains, "Thus symbolically, the lynching was often seen as an act against the whole black community and not merely the execution of one or more criminals."[14]

Like lynching, mob rule was also an effective tool for the control of Afro-Americans. However, unlike lynchings, which singled out individual blacks for summary punishment, riots directed violence toward all blacks (and especially their property). The most surprising aspect of my research on racial violence in Kentucky concerns the numerous instances of whites forcing blacks to leave their homes and land. Scholars have often failed to connect the practice of running blacks off their lands with lynching, but both were forms of oppression used by whites to keep blacks "in their place." Furthermore, a thorough knowledge of this whitecapping activity in Kentucky shows, far more clearly than does lynching, that most of the violence blacks experienced resulted from economic activities, not from al-

13. See, for example, the Mount Verna *Signal,* February 15, 1901; Tuskegee Clippings, Reel 22, Frame 72; Louisville *Courier-Journal,* August 2, 1908.

14. Williamson, *The Crucible of Race,* 187.

leged attacks on white women. To justify the wholesale removal of Afro-Americans, whites often proclaimed that Afro-Americans were involved in criminal activities, especially stealing livestock. Yet, as white newspapers and local police records clearly show, whenever blacks were guilty of criminal offenses, even minor violations, they were dealt with quickly and severely by the law; in Kentucky, for a black to be merely suspected of an offense would have been grounds for immediate action to be taken against him. When whites decided to rid their area of Afro-Americans, therefore, it was not because of supposed criminal activities but rather because of economic and social ones. In short, blacks who were prosperous or independent threatened the entire system of white supremacy.

Yet despite the lynchings and other acts of oppression, Kentucky blacks did not willingly submit to the whims of the white majority. They formed organizations, appealed to state officials, and on several occasions armed themselves to protect their property or prevent lynchings. Indeed, during the 1870s and again in the early 1900s, blacks challenged mobs by arming themselves and guarding the jailhouses to protect the lives of blacks accused of rape or murder. After a lynching in Georgetown in August, 1891, blacks resorted to arson to extract a measure of revenge, sending whites into a panic.[15] On several occasions after a lynching, whites grew so concerned about blacks arming themselves that curfews were instituted and the militia called out. Obviously, Kentucky blacks were far from passive or impotent. Although not always successful, they nevertheless consistently adopted measures to defend themselves.

Kentucky always had a handful of whites committed to ending racial violence. The state's first Republican governor, William O. Bradley, was influential in Kentucky passing its first comprehensive antilynching law. He constantly berated county officials for allowing lynchings to occur and for refusing to prosecute members of lynch mobs. Bradley even offered rewards for information leading to the arrests and indictments of members of lynch mobs. Two other Republican governors also attempted to end mob rule within the state. Elected to office in 1907, Augustus E. Willson sent the state militia to western Kentucky in an attempt to end the violent reign of the Night

15. Louisville *Courier-Journal*, September 5, 1874; Tuskegee Clippings, Reel 221, Frame 112; Georgetown *Times*, August 26, September 2, 1891.

Riders. During the early 1920s, Edwin Morrow spoke out against the continuation of lynch law and was responsible for the passage of another antilynching law. Governor Morrow became very active with the Commission on Interracial Cooperation, a group that worked to end racial unrest in the South. As governor, he urged white Christians, on a specially designated "Interracial Sunday," to discuss the religious, moral, physical, and educational needs of the state's black citizens.

The efforts of Afro-Americans, concerned state officials, and organizations like the National Association for the Advancement of Colored People led to a drastic decline in the number of lynchings in the state by 1930. This was, of course, consistent with the national trend. Another factor, however, also accounts for the decline in the number of lynchings within the state: Whites manipulated the legal system, ensuring that the vast majority of blacks accused of rape or murder received the death penalty, the same punishment meted out by the lynch mob. In his book on lynchings, Arthur Raper touches on the subject of "legal lynchings": "In the efforts to prevent a lynching, or to prevent further mob outbreaks after a lynching, peace officers and leading citizens often make promises which virtually preclude impartial court procedure. It is not incorrect to call a death sentence secured under such circumstances a 'legal lynching.' Except in rare cases, the presence of a mob defeats the end of impartial justice, either by lynching the accused person or by forcing the courts to summary and perhaps unjust convictions."[16]

On several occasions, white authorities and community leaders pleaded with the mob to allow the law to take its course, and in cases wherein a black was accused of rape or murder, "justice" was swift, sure, and painful. From the end of the Civil War until the 1940s, if indeed not later, countless numbers of black men were tried in hostile environments with judges and juries convinced of their guilt before hearing any evidence. Some of these cases took less than an hour from start to finish, with the jury not even leaving the courtroom to deliberate on the fate of the defendant. It is not difficult to imagine what would have happened to the members of the jury if they had returned a verdict of not guilty or had called for leniency. The matter of

16. Arthur Raper, *The Tragedy of Lynching* (Chapel Hill, 1933), 19.

such "legal lynchings" is often one of definition and is extremely difficult to prove because such activities were carried out "by the book" and had the sanction of the law behind them.

Perhaps more astonishing than the law discriminating against Afro-Americans are the many statements by whites denouncing the law for not adequately punishing criminals. Editorials in newspapers all over the state, even in the highly respected *Courier-Journal*, reached the conclusion, in the late 1800s, that the courts were too soft on crime and thereby contributed to the lawlessness of criminals. The lynchings performed by well-meaning whites, these editorials concluded, were necessary to protect the rights of law-abiding citizens. Obviously, the writers assumed that because much of the lawlessness in the state, particularly in eastern Kentucky, went unpunished, the law must have been lenient toward blacks as well. But as Frederick Douglass explained when commenting on blacks and the law:

> Whatever may be said of their weakness when required to hold a white man or a rich man, the meshes of the law are certainly always strong enough to hold and punish a poor man or a negro. In this case there is nei-ther color to blind, money to corrupt, nor powerful friends to influence court or jury against the claims of justice. All the presumptions of law and society are against the negro. In the days of slavery he was presumed to be a slave, even if free, and his word was never taken against that of a white man. To be accused was to be condemned, and the same spirit pre-vails to-day.[17]

Nearly all scholars acknowledge that only rarely—if indeed ever—did Afro-Americans receive anything approaching fair trials in the South. Yet few have closely investigated this phenomenon.[18] This study of Kentucky indicates how "legal lynchings," in conjunction with lynchings and mob rule, operated to ensure that Afro-Americans knew "their place" and remained at the bottom of society. As Jimmie

17. See the Louisville *Courier-Journal*, June 14, 1887, January 11, 1895. Frederick Douglass, "Lynch Law in the South," *North American Review*, CLV (July, 1892), 20.

18. In addition to the work of Edward Ayers, see the following: Litwack, *Been in the Storm So Long*; Howard Rabinowitz, *Race Relations in the Urban South, 1865–1890* (New York, 1978); Jimmie Lewis Franklin, *Journey Toward Hope: A History of Blacks in Oklahoma* (Norman, 1982); Roberta Sue Alexander, *North Carolina Faces the Freedmen: Race Relations During Presidential Reconstruction, 1865–67* (Dur-ham, 1985).

Franklin notes in his study on Oklahoma blacks, "One cannot escape or ignore the relationship between mob violence and the existing political system that maintained and reinforced the social order of the times."[19]

Richard Hofstadter, perhaps more than any other scholar, suggested the extent to which racial violence exists in our nation. His essay "Reflections on Violence in the United States" points out that violence, especially racial and ethnic violence, has always been part of American culture. "What is most exceptional about the Americans is not the voluminous record of their violence, but their extraordinary ability, in the face of that record, to persuade themselves that they are among the best-behaved and best-regulated of peoples." Hofstadter makes the point that lynchings—"open public murders conceived and carried out more or less spontaneously by a mob"—are a distinctively American institution. The primary function of lynchings, Hofstadter strongly argues, was to make sure that Afro-Americans understood their place:

> The lynching of blacks, although apparently spontaneous, seemed also to manifest a desire to establish beyond any doubt the point that the caste system of the South could not be challenged. In this respect there is a suggestive psychological similarity, even if no easily established historical affiliation, between the psychology of lynchings and the pattern of suppression of slave revolts. . . . By and large, slaves under the American slave system were deemed entitled to a trial, but where rebellions, real or imagined, were concerned, the law was swift, and the punishment was often harsh or even barbarous. From the beginning whites seemed to be determined, through the brutality of reprisals, to impress upon slaves the futility and the extraordinary danger of rebellion or otherwise resisting slavery.[20]

In Kentucky, even in spite of the harsh reprisals awaiting their attempts to improve their situation in life, some blacks—to be sure, always small in number—challenged the status quo. Indeed, the story of George Dinning is revealing if for no other reason than that he was an exception to what generally happened to Kentucky blacks. Dinning, born a slave, illiterate his entire life, the father of twelve children,

19. Franklin, *Journey Toward Hope*, 151.
20. Richard Hofstadter and Michael Wallace (eds.), *American Violence: A Documentary History* (New York, 1970), 1–22.

somehow saved enough money to purchase a farm. Indeed, by the time he was forty, Dinning had accumulated enough land and animals to arouse the envy of his white neighbors. Around eleven o'clock on the evening of January 27, 1897, twenty-five heavily armed white men knocked on Dinning's door and issued a warning, telling him that he had ten days to leave Simpson County. Their rationale was that Dinning had stolen chickens and hogs. Dinning denied being a thief, saying that the leading white citizens of the area could vouch for his good character. Members of the mob, who were already prepared for trouble, became indignant over Dinning's comments and started shooting into the house, wounding the black farmer twice. He somehow reached his gun and fired into the crowd, killing Jodie Conn. The men then fled the scene. Fearing their return, Dinning left his home; the next morning, he turned himself in to the authorities in Franklin, the largest city in Simpson County. After learning that Dinning was in police custody, the mob went back to his farm, drove off his family even though it was a bitterly cold winter day and one of the children was gravely ill, took what possessions they wanted, and burned his house to the ground.[21]

Concerned for Dinning's life, the sheriff of Franklin had him removed to Bowling Green, and eventually to Louisville, for safekeeping. Determined that Dinning would not be lynched, Governor Bradley sent a squad of state troops to protect Dinning during the trial in Simpson County. The reporter for the New York *Times*, like many observers, speculated that even though Dinning was a black man on trial for the murder of a white, his case would be one rare instance where a black would be found innocent. "The interesting feature of

---

21. An invaluable source is the Kentucky Governors' Papers, 1792–1926, Pardons and Rejected Petitions, located at the Kentucky Department for Libraries and Archives, Frankfort. Information on the Dinning case can be found in the William O. Bradley Papers within this collection (hereinafter cited as Bradley Papers). Pardons and Rejected Petitions contains information on the people given prison sentences and condemned to death. By law, if a governor decided to consider commuting a sentence or pardoning a prisoner, he was required to place notices in the community where the trial had taken place. Citizens would then write to the governor, expressing their opinions about whether or not a pardon should be given. Also, when trying to decide whether to grant a pardon, the governors often reviewed the transcript of the trial. Therefore, within these papers are often the only transcript in existence of a particular trial. In short, this entire collection—comprising more than one thousand boxes—is an invaluable source.

the case is that Dinning, on the face of the facts, cannot be convicted, as he was defending himself. . . . No witnesses can appear against him without admitting that they were members of the Kuklux band." Nevertheless, given the nature of "lynch law" in Kentucky, Dinning was found guilty of manslaughter on the testimony of the mob members who had been with Conn. The jury apparently ignored the fact that Dinning was on his own property and had been wounded by someone from the mob. He was sentenced to seven years of hard labor.[22]

The day after the trial, the governor's office began receiving letters calling for a full and complete pardon for Dinning. Many of the letters, not surprisingly, came from black churches, organizations, and political clubs, but an even greater number of letters came from whites, a few of whom identified themselves as former Confederates. Nearly all the whites expressed a strong belief in the law of self-defense, the right of a man—even a black man—to defend his home from invaders. Attorney Augustus E. Willson, who would serve as governor in the early 1900s, urged Bradley to free Dinning immediately. Willson concluded that Dinning's action made him a hero, one man who had stood up to a lawless mob. On July 17, after Dinning had been in prison for ten days, Governor Bradley made known his decision concerning a pardon. A reading of the transcript of the trial, he declared, proved that the twenty-five white men were not on a "peaceful mission" as some of them had testified in court. Members of the mob had fired first, the governor pointed out. It was a shame that no indictments had been made against any of them for attacking Dinning and his family and for returning the next day and destroying his home. In perhaps the key passage in his statement, Bradley said: "In protecting himself he did no more than any other man would or should have done under the same circumstance; and instead of being forced to wear a convict's garb he is entitled not only to acquittal but to the admiration of every citizen who loves good government and desires

22. *Commonwealth of Kentucky* v. *George Dinning*, Simpson Circuit Court (1897); New York *Times*, June 27, 1897. In the Bradley Papers, see the long letter Dinning sent to the governor, June 19, 1897, describing the incident and pleading that he not be returned to Simpson County to stand trial, and the letter from his wife, Mary, to the governor, May 11, 1897. She also gave details on the raid and the destruction of their home.

the perpetuation of free institutions." The governor ordered Dinning released from prison immediately. Upon being freed, Dinning moved to Indiana, for he realized that law officers in Simpson County would make no attempt to protect him and his family from the mob.[23]

For most Kentucky blacks, not being lynched or enduring a prison term would have been all that they could hope for after such an ordeal. Dinning, however, wanted justice. He hired Bennett H. Young, a former Confederate officer and one of Kentucky's most respected attorneys, to file suit in federal court against the men who had attacked him. Because they had testified at Dinning's trial, their identities were known. Fortunately for Dinning, his case was held in Louisville. After hearing the testimony, the judge instructed the jury to find in favor of Dinning. Going further, the judge remarked that the case was such that punitive damages could be imposed. The all-white jury heeded the judge's words, returning with a verdict of $50,000 in Dinning's favor against six of the twelve members of the mob. They even attached the estate of the deceased Jodie Conn to help settle the suit. As a reporter for the *Courier-Journal* explained, "Verdict is a vindication for Dinning even though he will probably not collect $1 since most of them own nothing or at best a homestead."[24]

Realizing the overwhelming odds against them, most blacks did not stand up to the mob. Those who simply left the state, or who anguished and stayed—their untold and often unknown stories are a further element of tragedy for those who bore the burden of being black in America at that time. Yet, as this study shows, while black Ken-

23. The various letters, from blacks and whites, can be found in the Bradley Papers. For an example of a letter from a white lawyer, see John H. Early of Chattanooga, Tennessee, to Bradley, July 7, 1897; see a letter from Danville blacks to Bradley, July 15, 1897; see the letter from John B. Grider, the attorney for Dinning, to Bradley, July 16, 1897. Also in the Bradley Papers, see the governor's handwritten, five-page untitled statement, dated July 17, 1897, announcing Dinning's pardon. W. C. P. Breckinridge, a prominent white who edited the Lexington *Morning Herald*, had praise for the pardoning. See the *Morning Herald*, July 7, 9, 1897.

24. Louisville *Courier-Journal*, May 6, 1899; Indianapolis *Freeman*, May 20, 1899. Immediately after Dinning had been found guilty in Simpson County, Young sent a telegram to Governor Bradley, July 8, 1897, urging him to pardon the black man: "Dinning violated neither human nor divine law[.] [Y]ou will honor Kentucky and yourself by his immediate pardon. Open the prison doors before the sun goes down." In Bradley Papers.

tuckians faced an intransigent form of racism that was irrational and unbending, they often were neither passive nor cowardly. That few changes occurred is not a reflection of a lack of effort by them or their few white allies but is a strong indictment of the racism that existed in Kentucky, the South, and America during that time. This book simply portrays the hardships Afro-Americans encountered in Kentucky and their efforts to end racial oppression. It is not a pleasant story, but it is one that must be told.

ONE

Reconstruction: Using Violence to
Preserve the Status Quo, 1865–1874

The end of the Civil War ushered in a prolonged period of racial violence in Kentucky. This violence would be just as severe and long-lasting as that found in the Deep South, but too often it escaped the immediate attention of federal officials. Because Kentucky had officially remained a loyal state, its citizens were allowed to rule their own affairs in a way not permitted in the former Confederate states, and that situation worked to the benefit of a large number of former Confederates who returned to their homes in Kentucky after the war. Also, many white Kentuckians who had supported the Union cause but had opposed emancipation and the elevation of Afro-Americans to equal citizenship were frustrated and tended to view the freed blacks with hostility. The first ten years of emancipation witnessed racial violence in many forms: numerous attacks on returning black soldiers who had fought for the Union cause, the forced removal of Afro-Americans from many rural communities, attacks by white mobs on black churches and especially on the freedmen schools, and the deaths of countless numbers of blacks at the hands of white mobs. In other words, many Kentucky whites were determined to preserve the racial subservience that had characterized the antebellum period, and others simply refused to acknowledge that slavery had ended and resorted to force to keep blacks enslaved.[1]

1. For general accounts of violence during Reconstruction, see George C. Rable, *But There Was No Peace: The Role of Violence in the Politics of Reconstruction* (Athens, 1984); Herbert Shapiro, *White Violence and Black Response: From Reconstruction to Montgomery* (Amherst, 1988), 5–29; Allen W. Trelease, *White Terror: The Ku Klux Klan Conspiracy and Southern Reconstruction* (New York, 1971); John A. Carpenter, "Atrocities in the Reconstruction Period," *Journal of Negro History,* XLVII (October, 1962), 234–47.

Violence often occurred when blacks attempted to free themselves from their former masters. The Emancipation Proclamation had freed the slaves in the rebelling states. During the war, some 28,000 black men in Kentucky joined the Union army, thereby gaining freedom for themselves and supposedly for their wives and children. But thousands of black women and children throughout the state remained in legal bondage until the passing of the Thirteenth Amendment in December, 1865. (Kentucky's legislators expressed their disdain for emancipation with their overwhelming negative vote against the measure.) Before the amendment was enacted, however, numerous black veterans opted for direct action and returned to the farms and plantations where they had been enslaved to free their family members. This led to violent confrontations and the deaths of some whites and of an even greater number of Afro-Americans. The Thirteenth Amendment and the determined effort of the black soldiers did not result in freedom for all blacks. John S. Graham, an agent for the Freedmen's Bureau who toured northern Kentucky in May, 1866, reported that a number of blacks remained in bondage in Boone County. It would take a military force of about thirty men to free the slaves, he estimated. Writing from Washington County, another agent said it had taken a writ of habeas corpus to obtain the release of two small black children being held by Robert Cray, a representative in the Kentucky legislature. The report of the bureau agent touring southwest Kentucky revealed that in Lyon and Trigg counties an undetermined number of blacks were still being held in slavery and were being treated "far worse than before the Government set them free." In December, 1868, three years after the ratification of the Thirteenth Amendment, the bureau agent assigned to northern Kentucky explained, "In the counties of Owen, Carroll, Trimble and several other Counties in my Sub-District negroes are kept in a state of vassalage tantamount to the old system of slavery. In these Counties Negroes are not permitted to live in homes or houses of their own; are not permitted to live apart from the white owners of the soil."[2]

Responding to a number of calls to assist Kentucky blacks in gaining their freedom and to protect them from white violence, the fed-

2. See Herbert Gutman, *The Black Family In Slavery and Freedom, 1750–1925* (New York, 1976), 363–431, for the confrontations between black soldiers and their former masters over the freeing of family members in Kentucky. John Graham to John

eral government agreed to the formation of the Freedmen's Bureau in the state in January, 1866. In justifying the need for the agency in a state that had not rebelled against the Union, Clinton Fisk, then the assistant commissioner of the bureau in Tennessee, said, "I am receiving a large number of complaints from Kentucky of the brutal treatment of returned colored soldiers and their families. . . . Many citizens write to Washington complaining of my delay in protecting the freedmen." Upon arriving in Kentucky, field agents wrote numerous reports detailing the violence. As one agent explained, "An examination of this sworn evidence . . . will reveal . . . sixty cases of outrage in a limited district and period, unparalleled in their atrocity and fiendishness; cruelties for which in no instance . . . is there the least shadow of excuse or palliation." This agent, like so many others, concluded that only the presence of troops would end the lawlessness in Kentucky. Assistant commissioner Jefferson C. Davis, described by one scholar as a conservative whose views on what steps the federal government should undertake in the state often clashed with those of his superiors, gave detailed information, including names and dates, on the deaths of 19 blacks and on outrages committed against another 233 people. Local and state officials, Davis explained, refused to apprehend the whites responsible for crimes against blacks.[3]

Blacks pleaded with federal officials to send troops to their communities as the only remedy for white violence. From Bowling Green, a group of Afro-Americans sent a letter to Washington Spradling, a Louisville black leader, informing him of conditions in this area and hoping that he would, in turn, enlighten bureau officials about the situation in that western Kentucky community. "We the Colored Citizens of Bowling Green, Kentucky, have assembled to night, for the purpose, of making an application for the Freed Men Beauro, here

Ely, May 27, 1866, James M. Fidler to Ely, June 30, 1866, John H. Donovan to Ely, June 1, 1866, John Peyton to J. C. Davis, September 24, 1866, J. S. Catlin to Benjamin P. Runkle, December 1, 1868, all in Freedmen's Bureau.

3. Clinton Fisk to Thomas E. Bramlette, January 24, 1866, in Freedmen's Bureau; *House Executive Documents*, 39th Cong., 1st Sess., No. 70, p. 201; Carpenter, "Atrocities in the Reconstruction Period," 243. A number of studies document the efforts of the bureau to protect Kentucky blacks. See Harry A. Volz, "The Administration of Justice By the Freedmen's Bureau in Kentucky, South Carolina, and Virginia" (M.A. thesis, University of Virginia, 1975); Claude L. Meals, "The Struggle of the Negro for Citizenship in Kentucky Since 1865" (M.A. thesis, Howard University, 1940).

as we are very much intruded, on here." In December, 1867, William
Sykes of Owensboro expressed his fears that the bureau might leave
the state: "The Bureau is our only protection in Kentucky. . . . Every
black man is threatened in the State by every rebel . . . upon the
removal of the Bureau." It would have been better for black people,
he explained, if the agency had never come to Kentucky if it was going to allow the rebels to control the state. "We trust that the party
who have stood by us and have done so much for us will still stand
by us until we are able to contend with an unrelenting foe," Sykes
concluded.[4]

Given the small number of agents assigned to the state and their
limited power, not to mention the determination of whites to dominate and repress blacks, the Freedmen's Bureau had, at best, mixed
results in Kentucky. Many of the agents, themselves believers in
white supremacy, were befriended by whites and readily agreed with
them on how to solve the "negro problem." It was not uncommon for
these agents to side with whites whenever disputes occurred. In a
long letter to a bureau official, Samuel McKee, a black from Mount
Sterling, stated bluntly that agents John Evans and Henry Clay Howard
swindled blacks and treated them with open contempt. "Your agents
here are in the bait of punishing colored men by beating them for alleged violations of their contracts. . . . It is no better than the old system of slavery. . . . Every rebel sympathizer here is delighted with the
workings of the Bureau and I have not met a solitary Radical Union
man who does not condemn its management."[5]

Despite some obvious shortcomings, the Freedmen's Bureau did
help Kentucky blacks. Nowhere is this more apparent than in the
legal arena. Kentucky blacks would be denied the right to testify in
court against whites until the early 1870s, a situation different from
that in the North and in the defeated South, where the Civil Rights
Act of 1866 had given blacks this right. Blacks in Kentucky would be
aided, however, by War Department Order No. 44, giving the Freedmen's Bureau the power to resolve conflicts between state and federal
laws. With Kentucky courts holding firm in denying black testimony,

4. Petition by Daniel W. Higdon and others, to Freedmen's Bureau, June 20, 1866,
William Sykes to T. D. Eliot, December 27, 1867, both in Freedmen's Bureau.
5. Samuel McKee to Ely, July 20, 1866, in Freedmen's Bureau.

the bureau consistently moved cases to the United States district court in Louisville under the jurisdiction of Judge Bland Ballard.[6]

Intervention by the bureau into legal proceedings prevented Louisville officials from sending Afro-Americans to jail on several occasions. In February, 1866, after a run-in with police officers, two black women were arrested and taken to city court on charges of drunkenness and disorderly conduct. Both were fined and sentenced to jail for three months. But immediately after the court decision, the captain of the bureau secured the release of the two women and carried them before the bureau court to allow them to testify against the police officers. Deciding that the policemen had been overzealous in arresting the women, officers of the bureau court decided that if the two women were compelled to serve time in jail, then the policemen would serve the same amount of time in the military prison. Not surprisingly, local officials complained about the meddling of the Freedmen's Bureau in civil affairs. The entire matter was allowed to drop after peace bonds were posted for the women and the officers. Clearly, however, local whites had received fair warning of the bureau's intention to work for equal treatment of blacks.[7]

Whites came to realize that having cases involving black testimony transferred to the United States district court in Louisville worked to their disadvantage. A number of whites received prison sentences from Judge Ballard for assaulting blacks or for being involved in terrorist acts committed by the Ku Klux Klan. In a court proceeding unheard of in Kentucky, William Bell was convicted, on the testimony of two black men, of murdering a Negro and was sentenced to death in 1868. That same year, two white men from Lewis County received the death penalty for the murder of four blacks. In all likelihood, these executions were never carried out. According to Victor Howard, white sentiment changed in favor of allowing black testimony in state courts by 1871. By then, the federal court docket was crowded with cases centering on black testimony. Whites involved in these cases found it time-consuming, as well as costly, to travel to

6. Victor Howard, *Black Liberation in Kentucky: Emancipation & Freedom, 1862–1884* (Lexington, 1983), 98, 105, 130–34; Ross A. Webb, *Kentucky in the Reconstruction Era* (Lexington, 1979), 48.

7. Louisville *Daily Democrat*, February 5, 17, 18, March 9, 1866; Louisville *Daily Journal*, February 16, 1866.

Louisville for court. Without question, Judge Ballard, by ruling "that as long as a right was denied to any freedman, no citizen of that class was really free, and all blacks were therefore entitled to transfer their cases to the federal court," had convinced Kentucky whites of the need to accept black testimony in the courts they controlled.[8]

Agents of the bureau worked, though often without success, to end a lingering vestige of slavery—the whipping of blacks. Numerous reports exist of whites beating their former slaves and of the refusal of local officials to take any steps to prevent this physical abuse. A girl, identified only by the name of Eliza, received a severe flogging from her employer in Covington in August, 1866. An agent of the Freedmen's Bureau examined the girl and found that her shoulders and back were "horribly lacerated." After obtaining affidavits from several blacks who had witnessed the incident, the agent ordered A. J. White, the man responsible for the flogging, to appear at the bureau office. White freely acknowledged beating the child, saying that any person he employed would be corrected when doing wrong. The court fined White fifty dollars and ordered him to cease whipping his workers. He refused to pay the fine, and no records exist showing that bureau agents had White arrested or punished in any manner for his defiance. White probably concluded that he could also ignore the court's edict on punishing black workers.[9]

Showing more determination than did their counterparts elsewhere in the state, Louisville's agents took steps to end the practice of whipping blacks. In June, 1867, they arrested five whites for beating blacks and lodged them in the military prison. Several months later, six additional white employers were arrested for the same offense. It is unknown how long these whites remained in jail; but according to a bureau report, conditions improved for the freedmen in Louisville as whites, realizing the risk for resorting to corporal punishment, found other ways to discipline black workers.[10]

Nevertheless, the beatings continued elsewhere. In September,

8. New York *Times*, March 9, 1868; Cincinnati *Commercial*, October 30, 1869; Louisville *Commercial*, August 9, 10, 24, September 25, 26, 27, 28, 1871; Howard, *Black Liberation in Kentucky*, 141–45; Webb, *Kentucky in the Reconstruction Era*, 76–77.

9. John Graham to R. E. Johnston, August 4, 1866, in Freedmen's Bureau.

10. Graham to Johnston, June 26, 1867, in Freemen's Bureau; New York *Times*, August 5, 1867.

1867, a bureau agent in a small community recounted for his superiors a conversation he had with a local white leader. "A man came to me, some weeks ago and said 'What am I to do with the woman I have hired, she wants to be a lady and I can do nothing with her without whipping her. Now, Sir, she must be whipped and I do not want the "Bureau" on my Back for doing so.'" The whipping of this particular black woman, he went on to explain, was "necessary for the well being of his plantation." That some bureau agents believed that blacks responded only to the whip further encouraged the practice among white employers. John Evans, identified by a fellow agent as prosouthern, allegedly whipped blacks for disobeying their employers. For several years after the Civil War, white mobs in Henderson continued whipping blacks who insulted whites. Agents of the bureau in Henderson failed to convince blacks that they would be protected if they came forward and identified the white ringleaders. The practice of whipping blacks still lived on eight years after the war. John Small, a Lexington black, was convicted of petty larceny, and the court handed down a sentence of thirty-nine lashes. This was administered in the jail, and according to the newspaper account, the other inmates—blacks as well as whites—watched and thoroughly enjoyed the beating. It reminded all of them of the good "ole days of slavery."[11]

In the years immediately after the Civil War, the Ku Klux Klan was responsible for much of the violence that the Freedmen's Bureau attempted to end. "For more than four years," writes Allen W. Trelease, the Klan "whipped, shot, hanged, robbed, raped, and otherwise outraged Negroes and Republicans across the South in the name of preserving white civilization." To be sure, in Kentucky and in the South a number of white organizations committed violent acts against blacks, but in the eyes of Afro-Americans and the general public, the name most associated with violence was the Klan. As scholars of southern history have noted, during these years the Klan and the Freedmen's Bureau were pitted against each other as both tried to determine the pace of life for Afro-Americans. For the most part, the Klan held sway in Kentucky, as the vast majority of whites, including elected offi-

11. A. W. Lawrill to Ely, September 30, 1867, A. B. Brown to Runkle, June 30, 1868, Samuel McKee to Ely, July 20, 1866, all in Freemen's Bureau; Louisville *Courier-Journal*, February 27, 1873. Rable, *The Role of Violence in the Politics of Reconstruction*, 21, notes that local courts in many southern communities allowed public whippings of ex-slaves for petty crimes.

cials, refused to denounce the mob. The violence perpetrated by the Klan in the Bluegrass State would equal in ferocity and frequency the attacks on Afro-Americans anywhere in the old Confederacy.[12]

Attacks by the Ku Klux Klan escalated in 1868, the very time that Kentucky blacks began holding conventions and organizing for political activities. In Lexington and in Fayette County, the Klan started harassing several black ministers and educators for appearing at political rallies and for calling upon state officials to extend the suffrage to Afro-Americans. That same year, the Klan suddenly appeared in Henderson and began physically attacking black Civil War veterans. Henderson's city fathers responded by passing an ordinance aimed at disbanding the "Kuklux," making it unlawful to wear masks and other disguises in public and to be involved in organized forms of intimidation. This was certainly a bold stand by Henderson leaders, considering the power of retribution exhibited by the Klan and the unwillingness of civic leaders and elected officials in other cities to express any displeasure over the group's formation. These outbreaks of Klan violence were by no means limited to Kentucky in 1868. "If enough potential Republican voters could be convinced that casting their ballots would be dangerous," George Rable explains, "the Democrats might well carry the southern states."[13]

During a three-year period beginning in late 1868, scores of whites identified as supporters of the Republican party received beatings and were run out of several counties in western Kentucky. Meanwhile, in the eastern Kentucky mountain counties of Magoffin, Perry, Breathitt, and Wolfe, nineteen white men, all Union veterans or supporters of the Grand Old Party, were murdered in a four-month period. Their deaths were attributed to the Klan. The New York *Times* strongly condemned the state's Democratic leaders for the violence, saying they refused to take any steps to end the Klan's lawlessness. In reaching this conclusion, the *Times* cited numerous editorials written by Henry Watterson of the Louisville *Courier-Journal*, one of the leading spokesmen for the

---

12. Trelease, *White Terror*, xi, 124–25; Rable, *The Role of Violence in the Politics of Reconstruction*, 92–98.

13. Lexington *Tri-Weekly Statesman*, September 5, 1868; Johnston to Runkle, August 31, 1868, A. B. Brown to Runkle, October 31, 1868, both in Freedmen's Bureau; Edmund L. Starling, *History of Henderson County, Kentucky* (Henderson, Kentucky, 1887), 238, 338–40; Trelease, *White Terror*, xlvii; Rable, *The Role of Violence in the Politics of Reconstruction*, 69.

Democratic party, calling upon his party to restore law and order in the state. As Watterson wrote in one editorial: "The Democratic party holds possession of every county in Kentucky. The military power of the State is at its call. It has the means to quell disturbances whenever it occurs. It must employ its resources vigorously."[14]

The Democratic-controlled legislature of 1871 refused to pass a law against mob violence. Many legislators openly endorsed the tactics used by the Klan, while others were afraid to support harsh measures for fear of incurring the Klan's wrath. An indication that the mob was operating without fear of the authorities was the bold assault on the Frankfort jail on February 24 by seventy-five masked men. They wanted to free Thomas Scroggins, who was charged with the brutal murder of a black man. Scroggins was awaiting trial in federal court, since blacks were prohibited from testifying in Kentucky's courts. The mob justified its actions on the grounds that no white man should be forced to defend himself in court against the word of a black man. By the end of the year, the violence of the Klan, having spread all over the state, even to the largest cities, could no longer be ignored. In his message to the general assembly, Governor Preston H. Leslie put the weight of his office behind legislation that made it a criminal offense to write or post threatening notices and to band together and wear disguises.[15]

Despite the governor's proclamation against mob violence, a large group of white renegades controlled fifteen counties in central Kentucky, usurping local government and becoming, for a time, more powerful than the law. Democratic and Republican newspapers published a series of stories detailing the lawless activities of the Klan. In November, 1872, for example, the New York *Times* ran a story, "Catalogue of Recent Outrages in Shelby County—A Fearful List of Murders, Arsons and Floggings Committed by a Band of Lawless Criminals." The anonymous writer gave details on scores of instances of blacks being whipped and their homes being robbed, and on the nu-

---

14. Louisville *Courier-Journal,* August 13, 1870; Louisville *Commercial,* December 28, 1870; New York *Times,* January 3, March 5, 25, April 21, August 25, 1871.

15. Hambleton Tapp and James Klotter, *Kentucky: Decades of Discord, 1865–1900* (Frankfort, 1977), 49–50, 381–82. Lewis Collins and Richard H. Collins, *Collins' Historical Sketches of Kentucky* (Rev. ed.; Covington, Kentucky, 1882), I, 213. See the Louisville *Commercial* for the entire month of July, 1871. This pro-Republican newspaper called upon state officials to enact a Ku Klux Klan Bill.

merous lynchings and murders attributed to the mob. After having rid their area of all whites who had openly supported the Republican party, the Klan turned to attacking those who employed blacks as sharecroppers and house servants. The writer for the *Times,* after giving specific dates and information on numerous criminal offenses committed by the Klan, concluded, "The above is but a part of their dark deeds. If a man should take the pains to collect together all the information necessary to write an impartial history of their crimes, and should write them in detail, they would make a large volume. And if traced by the pen of an able writer, the story, for its mingling of romance and horrors, would not be exceeded by any history of crimes."[16]

Because the New York *Times* was viewed as a newspaper whose primary purpose was to promote the Republican party, some readers undoubtedly dismissed its accounts of atrocities committed by the Klan. But in August, 1873, the *Courier-Journal* vividly described the violence occurring in Owen and Henry counties. According to the newspaper, at least eighty-eight raids had been conducted by the Klan in less than a year. Black landowners, described by the newspaper as "harmless negroes," were special targets. On numerous occasions, the Klan told those blacks to vacate the area; such warnings "answered the purpose of actual violence by breaking up happy homes and driving worthy citizens into exile." To counter any doubts about the validity of its stories, the *Courier-Journal* gave the names of people victimized by the Klan and the dates and places of these outrages. But not wanting the Democratic party linked with the violence, the *Courier-Journal* informed its readers that robbery, not politics, had been the chief motive. "Murders, whippings, warnings, are the pastime of the villains, or the means to facilitate their principal purpose." If politics had been the reason for the violence, the *Courier-Journal* stated with assurance, then it had obviously been the work of the "Radicals." This statement led to an immediate and sharp rebuke from the *Times:*

> But surely the *Courier-Journal* does not wish us to take seriously the hint that these masked assassins are acting in the interest of the "Radicals." Whatever else "Radicals" in the South may be, they are not such fools as to weaken themselves by driving out the negroes. If there is anything po-

16. New York *Times,* November 8, 1872.

litical in the crimes, it is plainly intended to be in the interest of the Democracy. That such is the fact is proved by the incident of a well-known citizen saying these outrages had made a "Grant man" of him. He was in the midst of them, and evidently did not believe they had been committed by "Radicals."

Although disputing the motives for the violence, both the *Courier-Journal* and the *Times* clearly identified the Klan as being responsible for the racial violence occurring throughout the state.[17]

Exactly one year later, in September, 1874, both newspapers contained long, highly detailed stories of a report by Willis Russell, a United States marshal who had worked undercover for four years as a clerk in a country store in Owen County. Entitled "Official Report of the Owen County Outrages," Russell's report explained that in 1870, "bands of armed men, disguised and masked, began committing depredations in Owen and Henry Counties." That year, four white men asked him to join the "Kuklux" for the purpose of driving "the negroes from the State." Russell declined, saying that their acts were neither lawful nor meritorious. These men later returned to the store where Russell was employed and purchased material for their gowns and masks. Once their costumes were ready, the men set out to destroy the homes and property of blacks in Stamping Ground, Scott County, because they had ignored a warning to leave the area. During the raid, one black died and several others sustained serious wounds. The blacks, however, chose to defend themselves and returned the gunfire and killed at least one Klansman. Although running the risk of revealing his true identity, Russell publicly applauded the actions of the Stamping Ground blacks, saying that "if the negroes had killed the entire party it would have been perfectly right." His statement, of course, drew the enmity of the outlaws.[18]

Despite several attempts on his life, Russell continued to gather evidence on the leaders of the Klan. On one occasion, a member of the Klan, tired of being involved in criminal activities but afraid to quit the lawless band, approached Russell and offered information in return for protection. Russell and the unidentified man held regular

17. Louisville *Courier-Journal*, August 25, September 9, 17, 1873; New York *Times*, August 27, 30, September 23, 1873.

18. The entire report by Russell was printed in the Louisville *Courier-Journal*, September 8, 1874, and in the New York *Times*, September 10, 1874. Another source, Collins, *Historical Sketches*, I, 208, also documents the raid on Stamping Ground.

meetings on the second Saturday of each month. He informed Russell of a planned attack on the black residents of Twin Creek in Owen County. Russell received arms from state officials and assisted the blacks in preparing for the attack, which was called off by the Klan. Taking the risk of being seen with Russell, the informant once made an unexpected visit on a Tuesday to warn Russell that on Thursday night the Klan planned to murder William Plasters and Russell, then travel to the small community of Brown's Bottom and kill the black residents. Once again, Russell's actions prevented these murderous plans from happening. In February, 1874, believing that he had a sufficient number of witnesses to testify against the Klan, Russell requested a squad of soldiers, which was supplied by both the state and the federal governments, and began arresting the leaders of the Ku Klux Klan in Owen and Henry counties. Taken into custody without a fight, all of the Klansmen posted bond, ensuring their appearances at the October Term of the United States district court in Louisville.

In his official report of the violence, Russell stated emphatically that "more than 100 men have been killed, wounded, or driven away from that portion of Owen and Henry Counties lying on the Kentucky River by the Kuklux in the last three years." Russell gave the names of some of the blacks who had been killed: Sam Crew and family, James Bourne and family, John Dickerson and family, Al Towles and family, Jordan Mosby and family, Wallace Dickerson, Levi Fishback, and Thornton Dunlap. In the small community of Sand Rippie, Henry County, he added, four blacks had been killed. Russell's report also listed the names of at least a dozen whites who had been forced to leave Henry County. Of the whites and blacks still residing in Owen and Henry counties, "the majority . . . are all good citizens, and are at heart opposed to those Kuklux, but they are under a reign of terror, and are really afraid to express their opinions, not knowing what moment they will have to pay the penalty," the United States marshal wrote. "Whenever the country is ridden of these pests, it will be as flourishing a community as it was before the Kuklux organization."[19]

On the heels of Russell's report, several local and state officials called for action. Issuing a charge to the grand jury to end the violence

19. See Jesse Fears, *Confession of Richard H. Shuck, A Member of the Owen and Henry County Marauders of the State of Kentucky* (Frankfort, 1877). This account further documents the lawlessness that was detailed in Russell's report.

in his area, Judge John McManama of Owen County said that blacks had suffered most from the Klan's lawlessness—"so great indeed that most of them have fled to other and safer localities." Because inefficient law officers had allowed the Klan to operate unchallenged, he said, "the people are too apprehensive of danger to condemn or applaud it." Although he had supported a law against mob activities in 1871, Governor Leslie had consistently ignored reports of violence within the state, proclaiming that the situation had been exaggerated by the Republicans for political reasons. Acknowledging the accuracy of Russell's report, however, Leslie agreed with Judge McManama and announced that troops would remain indefinitely in several counties and would be at the disposal of circuit court judges.[20]

It took, however, another tragic incident to fully capture the public's attention and to lead to a strong call to put down the Klan. The charges against the Klansmen were dismissed in United States district court in October, 1874, when the witnesses failed to appear. As Russell had feared, all of the men who had agreed to testify on behalf of the state had disappeared, probably having been murdered by the Klan. Raids by the Klan resumed almost immediately in several counties. Toward the end of the month, the mob invaded the eastern part of Shelby County, whipped three blacks, and threatened their employer, Thomas Ford, with violence if he persisted in hiring black workers. The mob then went to the home of a black farmer named Barringer. Tragically, Barringer's sixteen-year-old daughter responded to the knock on the door and was shot in the eye. She was killed instantly. This incident received widespread publicity. Henry Watterson, the prominent former Confederate editor of the *Courier-Journal*, condemned Shelby County officials for failing to form a posse to search for the outlaws. The governor offered a $9,000 reward for the killers of the girl and, in strong language, issued a proclamation denouncing the violence of the Klan in Shelby County. Governor Leslie also berated local officials for not stopping acts of lawlessness: "The local authority seem too often to forget that the whole power of the county is, by law, placed in their hands, and that on them, and not the State Executive, rests the first and chief responsibility for the repression and punishment of crimes committed within their jurisdiction." Despite the large reward offered and the anti-Klan sentiment expressed by the

20. New York *Times*, September 14, 28, 1874.

governor and other state leaders, the men responsible for the raid and for the murder of the Barringer girl avoided arrest and prosecution.[21]

Nevertheless, the governor's strong condemnation of the Klan had an effect: Law officers conducted raids on known Klan headquarters in Henry and Owen counties. During one such raid, they captured John W. Brothers, a member of the Klan, and forced him to identify other men who had been active in both counties. County sheriffs and a large group of citizens then "scoured the country, captured arms, implements, masks and disguises." Warrants were issued for the arrest of more than a dozen Klansmen but only four were captured; the others had already left the area. Whether the men who fled were eventually apprehended and made to stand trial is unknown.[22] But the mere fact they felt compelled to flee marked a significant change in Kentucky.

Several months later, in November, 1875, the four captured Klan members went on trial in Owen County. Three of them were found guilty of conspiring against the government by intimidating United States Marshal Willis Russell but not of the more serious crime of murder. When sentencing the men, the judge was apologetic, expressing a belief that even though they had been found guilty, they were honest, law-abiding citizens. The court sentenced one man to five years in prison and another to three years. In a peculiar show of leniency, the court postponed sending the third man to prison because of an injury he sustained while pursuing the marshal. The fourth defendant was acquitted.[23]

The New York *Times* explained that while the Klan was being hotly pursued by the authorities in Henry and Owen counties, another branch of this lawless group had become active in the southeast region of the state, making Todd County the "last rallying place of the outlaw band." On February 16, 1875, the Klan burned a black church to the ground. That was followed by the brutal whipping of a black leader by the name of Jessup. According to the newspaper account, members of the Klan, after flogging the man, administered salt and

21. Louisville *Courier-Journal*, October 27, 28, 29, 1874; New York *Times*, October 28, 30, November 2, 1874.

22. Louisville *Courier-Journal* and New York *Times*, April 1, 1875; Shapiro, *White Violence and Black Response*, 15, points out that throughout the South less than 10 percent of the members of the Klan stood trial for the crimes they committed.

23. New York *Times*, November 14, 15, December 25, 30, 1875.

pepper to his wounds. This violence was a warning for blacks to leave the area, but since they still refused to do so, the Klan started a full-scale assault on them in March. The Klan, having selected Edward Long as a target for their violence, set his cabin on fire and shot him to death when he came out of the burning structure. His wife was also wounded in the gunfire. After killing Long, the Klan proceeded to attack his neighbors. As the *Times* explained, "Negro people were taken out and whipped, cabins burned, and the old, long list of lawless acts were repeated."[24]

In a long editorial, the *Times* speculated on why Todd County whites had rallied around the banner of the Klan and had resorted to beating and murdering blacks. The reasons put forward are not only revealing about the raids in southeast Kentucky but also help explain Klan attacks elsewhere in the state. "The negroes of the region are thrifty, industrious, and prosperous. The 'poor whites' of old times are still poor and mean. Indolent and shiftless, they were fairly crowded out by the well-to-do and provident negroes. . . . One of the captured raiders was asked why they treated the negroes so cruelly. His sullen reply was 'We wanted to let the poor white man have a chance.'" The newspaper concluded that it was the "remnant of slave-holding thought" in whites that led to the formation of the organized terror of the Klan and the determination to drive blacks off their property. In short, the violence of the Klan was ultimately an attempt to keep Afro-Americans at the bottom politically and economically.

Using the same aggressive tactics that had brought most of the violence to a halt elsewhere, state officials were able to curtail Klan activities in southeast Kentucky by the end of 1875.[25] But the attempts in Todd County to force Afro-Americans to leave their homes and property would continue in other counties in that region of Kentucky until the 1930s. Later mobs would not always be labeled the Klan; nevertheless, their tactics were the same.

The murderous attacks of the Ku Klux Klan were only part of the violence perpetrated on Afro-Americans during the Reconstruction years. Other forms of violence existed and proved to be just as difficult to combat and bring to an end. Consistently, many ordinary white citizens rationalized their violence by saying they had responded with

24. *Ibid.*, March 18, 21, 28, 1875.
25. *Ibid.*, December 25, 30, 1875.

force to the criminal acts of blacks or to blacks' attempts to dominate whites by becoming involved in the political process. In other words, the violence of these whites was, in their own eyes, a spontaneous act of retribution against blacks and not the premeditated violence of the Klan. The destruction of black school buildings and churches, because they were often used as places for political meetings, became commonplace in the late 1860s. In Georgetown, a small town about fifteen miles from Lexington, a group of white men entered the black church during a religious service, not a political meeting, and "in a Shameful and Scandalous manner interrupted the minister during the services. Pistols were drawn by the whites and for a time general confusion ensued." Fortunately, only minor damage occurred, and the white men involved were arrested by the local authorities. On another occasion, however, a white mob entered a black church in Midway, a community located between Lexington and Frankfort, and proceeded to wreck the church, destroying the pews and shooting out the windows. Several people were injured by the many rounds of ammunition fired by the irate whites. The very next year in Frankfort, a band of white men attacked a group of blacks who had assembled to hear a preacher. One person was shot and a number of others "were shockingly beaten." According to the reporter of a pro-Republican newspaper, the only reason given by whites for their disruption of the church service was that "they intended to put a stop to any meeting or assemblage of negroes."[26]

That Afro-Americans desired an education offended many whites who viewed this as a step toward equality between the races. This prompted whites to destroy the schools for blacks in Kentucky and across the South as well. In 1867, when the Freedmen's Bureau and several white northern missionary societies conducted a major drive throughout Kentucky to establish schools, dozens of buildings were blown up. A report from Allen County correctly assessed the situation: "The opposition to the education of the freedmen is so great and universal that a school could not exist unless . . . protected by an armed force." This proved to be the case in the state's largest city: Louisville mobs resorted to arson to prevent several white businessmen from leasing their buildings for black schools. As late as 1873,

Louisville whites still protested the establishment of black schools. After learning that a school would be located at the corner of Sixth and York, the whites living in the area wrote angry letters to the newspaper and held several meetings.[27]

Clearly, many white Kentuckians, galled by the mere existence of schools for Afro-Americans, found it especially distasteful that white northerners had come to teach the former slaves. The abuse these teachers received in 1868 proved to be typical of what they experienced during the first five years after slavery. A young white woman from Cincinnati volunteered to teach in the school operated by the bureau in Bowling Green. After several weeks of being refused housing accommodations, even with "twenty seven loyal families in the city," she was allowed to stay at a boarding house owned by a former Confederate but found herself "severely left alone." Several months later, another teacher in Bowling Green, A. D. Jones, received a warning from the Ku Klux Klan to leave town within ten days. Then a third white teacher in Bowling Green, Mrs. L. A. Baldwin, received the following note:

KU KLUX KLANS!

BLOOD! POISON! POWDER! TORCH!
Leave in five days or hell's your portion!

Rally, rally, watch your chance,
First blood, first premium K. K. K.
If ball, or torch, or poison fails,
The house beneath you shall be blow to hell, or move you.

K. K. K.[28]

"During your absence in Washington, D.C. the Teacher whom you directed me to teach the Freedmen's school at New Castle, Kentucky was mobbed and driven out of Town shortly after reaching his desti-

27. For information on the educational activities of the bureau, see Educational Division of the Bureau of Refugees, Freedmen, and Abandoned Lands, Records, 1865–1871, Monthly Reports from Kentucky, National Archives (hereinafter cited as Kentucky School Reports); Wells S. Bailey to Ely, December 22, 1866, Noble to Eliot, December 31, 1867, C. F. Johnson to Ely, January 17, 1867, A. W. Lawrill to Runkle, December 28, 1867, all in Freedmen's Bureau; Louisville Courier-Journal, April 9, 11, 1873; Shapiro, White Violence and Black Response, 9.

28. House Executive Documents, 40th Cong., 2nd Sess., No. 329; Runkle to Burbank, "Freedmen's Affairs in Kentucky and Tennessee," Serial 1346, U.S., July, 1868, 19.

nation, and I believe before beginning to teach," was one report submitted to Thomas K. Noble, head of the Freedmen's Bureau education program in the state, in February, 1868. Several months later, the teacher at the school in Crab Orchard barely escaped a beating from a white mob. "Ever since he has been there, white children have habitually cursed and stoned him in the street as he poked to & fro his duty." The same situation existed in Danville, where a mob drove off the teacher in April, 1868, and "it is not deem safe to reopen the school at present." In early January, 1869, Noble wrote a long letter to John W. Alvord, the general superintendent in Washington, citing additional examples of teachers being abused. His letter also mentioned the destruction of several black schools that had occurred toward the end of 1868:

> In Hickman, Fulton County, Miss Jennie Mead (from Ohio) has been insulted many times in the streets and had been threatened with death. One of her pupils has been murdered.
> At Corydon, the teacher was driven from the town. Schoolhouses burned at Rock Springs. At Cadiz Mr. P. S. Reeves (white) was beaten while trying to organize a school. School burned in Germantown. The Noble schoolhouse in Shepardsville burned October 1, 1868. Two churches used as schools in Bullitt County were burned. Schoolhouse at Thompkinsville burned. The teacher in Mayfield was driven from the town. Now in other portions of the United States it is not uncommon for houses to be burned, but the motive is usually gain. The remarkable thing about Kentucky arson is the crime is committed from principle, here education is not believed in and schoolhouses are therefore burned . . . because instruction is given to ignorant freedmen.[29]

Berea College, which admitted white and black students, came under attack for several years after the war. Located in Madison County on the foothills of the mountains, Berea seemed an unlikely setting for school integration. Led by abolitionist John G. Fee on land donated by Cassius Clay, the school opened in the late 1850s but closed under pressure from proslavery forces on the eve of the Civil

29. A. B. Brown to Runkle, February 29, 1868, J. S. Catlin to Noble, February 27, 1868, H. D. Thomas to Runkle, April 13, 1868, all in Freedmen's Bureau; Noble to Alvord, in Roll 20, M–803, Kentucky School Reports; Noble to Alvord, January 13, 1869, Mary Fielding to Runkle, March 5, 1869, both in Freedmen's Bureau.

War. It reopened in 1866. That same year, Fee admitted several black soldiers to the school. As the daughter of John A. R. Rogers, one of the founders of the school, recalled,

> For four years (1867–71) the lives of Mr. Fee and my father were in more or less danger. On several occassions [*sic*] to prevent the school buildings being fired armed pickets patrolled around them all night. For years when my father was away at night my mother had us all sleep on the first floor on cots rather than in our bedrooms upstairs so that if the house were fired in the night we could be gotten out quickly. The anxiety was more intense at times than at others, but it was there for years. I have heard the bullets sing into our yard to strike the trees several times fired by drunken men at the house.

In 1871, Willard W. Wheeler, an employee of Berea College, traveled to Lexington and met with blacks interested in attending the school. After leaving the city, he was ambushed by a mob and almost killed. That same evening, a group of masked men took Wheeler from a hotel and gave him a severe whipping.[30]

Consistently, mobs that destroyed schools and assaulted teachers avoided prosecution. Viewing the northern missionaries as trouble-makers, local and state officials refused to apprehend their assailants even when they had been identified by bureau agents or other whites. Blacks who witnessed the destruction of schools were prohibited from testifying in Kentucky courts. To be sure, they could give evidence in the bureau's courts, but many of them refused to do so, fearing that instead of the criminals being punished, they themselves would be persecuted for having testified. On one occasion, bureau agent R. E. Johnston, determined to punish the whites responsible for the destruction of the black school in Midway, had them arrested and brought before the bureau's court. The county attorney chose not to participate in the case against the white defendants, so Johnston assumed the role of prosecutor: "I examined a large number of witnesses, both white and black, and I regret to say that I was unable to prove anything against them for the reason that the night was very dark and the witnesses were unable to identify any of the above named

---

30. William E. Ellis, H. E. Everman, and Richard D. Sears, *Madison County: 200 Years in Retrospect* (Richmond, Kentucky, 1985), 220–21.

party as having committed any such act, and I was unable to prove anything against them, I moved that the prisoners be discharged, and it was accordingly so ordered."[31]

White mobs not only forced teachers to leave their communities but also at times ran off landowning blacks or others they viewed as competitors for jobs. A black community in Lebanon was raided by a gang of forty men on the evening of October 19, 1866. After destroying the homes and the crops, the mob forced all of the residents to leave the area. On January 31, 1867, a mob posted signs in one area of Daviess County warning all blacks to leave by the next day. They also informed white farmers that all property rented or leased to the freedmen would be burned. In Franklin County several years later, a group of fifteen whites went to a farm occupied by several blacks, administered a beating to all of them, and ordered them to vacate their farm. As reported in the New York *Times*, "The next day the colored men packed up their things and went to Frankfort for safety." On another occasion in the same county, a white man who employed black sharecroppers received a visit from a mob, which broke all of the doors to the "negro cabins" and gave the workers several days to leave the area. Despite warnings from unknown whites, Lawson Johnson and Gabe Flood refused to leave their homes, which were in the eastern part of Shelby County. On the night of October 16, 1872, the mob carried out its threat against the two men. After driving Johnson from his home, the mob torched his barn. Next, they killed Flood to warn other Afro-Americans to get out of the area and to pay him back for firing at them when they had intruded upon his property to tell him to leave.[32]

In 1871, a number of black skilled workers moved to Estill County after securing employment with the Red River Iron Works Company. White residents of the county became incensed at the increase in black migrants, many of whom brought along their wives and children. The Ku Klux Klan began a series of raids that halted the mining operations. The blacks, whose numbers had reached four hundred, received notices to leave the area. Unwilling to take any measures that

31. Noble to Alvord, in Roll 20, M–803, Kentucky School Reports; R. E. Johnston to J. P. Collins, August 4, 1868, in Freedmen's Bureau.

32. Information on the raid in Lebanon can be found in Tapp and Klotter, *Decades of Discord*, 378–79; J. W. Finnie to John Ely, October 1, 1866, Lawrill to Ely, February 12, 1867, Runkle to Burbank, March 13, 1868, all in Freedmen's Bureau; New York *Times*, April 26, 1872, February 11, 1873; Collins, *Historical Sketches*, I, 233.

might result in further discord with the Klan and fearing the continued shutdown of the mines, company officials allowed the blacks to be driven off.[33]

Whites in northern Kentucky were determined to force blacks to move elsewhere, even though the number of Afro-Americans living there was relatively small in comparison with the black population in the rest of the state. About a year after the close of the Civil War, a large band of whites in Warsaw began whipping blacks, stealing their property, and ordering them to leave the area. Bureau agent J. J. Landrum, unable to prevent the violence, reported, "Some 200 negroes I'm informed crossed the Ohio above this place today others are preparing to leave for fear of . . . other abuses." In a second letter describing the situation in Warsaw, Landrum concluded that only by using the "bluecoats"—Union soldiers—would the outrages end. The report from another bureau agent in August, 1867, confirmed that blacks were still being ousted in northern Kentucky: "In a recent tour made by Captain Graham through Kenton, Boone and Grant counties he found the blacks very much excited, and in many instances they have left their homes in the Country, and come to Covington. They allege that since the election they have been told that they are all going to be re-enslaved again. They . . . complain bitterly . . . that they are living in a regular reign of terror." Attempts to force blacks to leave this area of the state would continue well into the next decade.[34]

In western Kentucky, the story was the same. Logan County and, in particular, Russellville, the largest town in the county, proved to be very inhospitable to Afro-Americans. A large number of former Confederate soldiers had returned to the area and remained openly defiant of the Union, proudly displaying the rebel flag at all public gatherings within the county. A number of former slaves who had served in the United States Army also returned to the county and were greeted with anger and told to leave the state. Ignoring these threats, a dozen or more blacks found employment at the Shaker settlement in South Union, Logan County, working in the woolen and flour mills. The Shakers allowed the blacks to build cabins, and for more than two

33. Louisville *Commercial*, July 9, 1871; Collins, *Historical Sketches*, I, 215; Trelease, *White Terror*, 316.

34. Landrum to Freedmen's Bureau office in Covington, August 3, 1866, Landrum to Ely, August 13, 1866, R. E. Johnston to Ely, August 31, 1867, all in Freedmen's Bureau; Collins, *Historical Sketches*, I, 246p.

years they worked peacefully in the area. Their mere presence, however, raised the ire of whites. Warnings were issued to the Shakers to fire the Afro-Americans and to force them to leave South Union. But just as they had remained noncombatants during the war, the Shakers assumed that by being neutral and treating all people with dignity they would be left alone. In late August, 1868, however, a mob of whites came into the settlement and burned some of the cabins occupied by blacks. The Shakers responded by offering a reward of five hundred dollars for the apprehension of the mob members. This led to the destruction of the Shakers' mills during the early morning hours of September 2. Their property was uninsured, and losses totaled about seventy thousand dollars. In a letter to a New York friend, one of the South Union Shakers wrote,

> All in the world we can tell you is that night prowlers and disguised men have been driving off the negroes we have hired, and endeavoring to make them return to their old masters, and telling the negroes they intend to drive our community from the country or reduce our town to ashes[.] I presume our offenses, we hire the negroes and pay them for their work, and nearly all around here want to work for us, because we treat them like men and pay them as such. We do not vote or take part in politics, but rejoice that the bonds are stricken from the limbs of the negro and that now we can pay him, and not be compelled, as heretofore, to work the dark skin and pay the white skin.[35]

The black men who had fought in the Civil War, perhaps more than any other group of Afro-Americans, found themselves unwelcome in their home communities. Upon returning to Union County in 1866, a group of black soldiers received abuse from former Confederates. The whites eventually seized the weapons owned by the blacks and told the veterans to leave the county. This mistreatment of black soldiers, which occurred all over the state, was similar to what was happening further south. As George Rable explains, "Negroes' weapons were seized, including hunting pieces and useless old guns." Afro-Americans in Paducah complained to agents of the Freedmen's Bureau about the ruling of a local judge that allowed former Confederate

---

35. For an account of the raid on the Shakers and a copy of the letter written to the New York Shaker, see the New York *Times*, September 24, 1868; see also the Louisville *Daily Courier*, September 3, 1868. Additional information on blacks and the Shakers in South Union can be found in Julia Neal, *By Their Fruits: The Story of Shakerism in South Union, Kentucky* (Chapel Hill, 1947).

soldiers to keep their guns, while any white man could disarm a black and keep his gun. This decision, of course, encouraged Paducah whites to disarm the blacks and harass them in many ways; some went so far as to tell blacks to quit looking for jobs. With any act on their part being viewed as militancy, black war veterans ran the risk of offending whites by just holding a meeting. Not surprisingly, a group of Louisville blacks greatly upset a number of whites when they started holding military drills (during which they displayed firearms) on Saturday evenings at a church. According to the Cincinnati *Commercial*, "Steps are being taken to ascertain whether their meetings are of a peaceful character, or warlike character. If the latter, they will be dispersed." In the late 1860s, a congressional report described the plight of black soldiers living in the remote and mountainous area of eastern Kentucky. Most of the veterans, for a variety of reasons, had not received their bounties: "Having served in the Union army, they have been the special objects of persecution, and in hundreds of instances have been driven from their homes." The outrages against the black veterans, the report concluded, had caused a great exodus from Kentucky into other states.[36]

Given the widespread mistreatment of Afro-Americans during Reconstruction, it is not surprising that many of them died at the hands of whites in a cold-blooded fashion. Most scholars have said very little about the lynchings that occurred during Reconstruction, concentrating instead on the period beginning in the late 1880s. One notable exception is Richard Maxwell Brown's work on violence, in which he notes that the Ku Klux Klan "initiated the wholesale lynching of blacks, and from 1868 to 1871, there were over 400 Klan lynchings." Brown's figure, astonishing as it is, greatly undercounts the lynchings that took place. More than one-third of the total number of lynchings that occurred in Kentucky (117 of 353) happened between 1865 and 1874. Without question, however, 117 is much too low (as is 400 for the entire nation or even the South alone), but it represents the number of lynchings that can be documented totally or in part with the names and the race of the victims, the dates and the places of the lynchings, and the reasons given by the mob for the murders. For

36. Starling, *History of Henderson County*, 238; Donovan to Ely, May 4, 1866, in Freedmen's Bureau; Rable, *The Role of Violence in the Politics of Reconstruction*, 27; Cincinnati *Commercial*, June 8, 1869; *House Executive Documents*, Report of Secretary of War, 40th Cong., 3rd Sess., No. 1, Vol. I, 1868–69, 1056.

instance, several accounts noted that from 1867 to 1871, as many as 25 lynchings per year occurred in central Kentucky, primarily in the rural areas around Danville, Harrodsburg, and Richmond. Unfortunately, the vast majority of the lynchings cited for this area, indeed, for the entire state, for these years are lacking in solid historical documentation (usually the only known details are newspaper accounts of someone's recollection that a lynching happened in a particular county some years ago) and therefore have not been counted among the 117. Nevertheless, even by being cautious and excluding most accounts of lynchings, I came up with 93 lynchings for Kentucky during that five-year period, with two years alone, 1868 (with 21) and 1870 (with 36), accounting for the extremely high number of 57. By contrast, the greatest number of lynchings in a five-year period after Reconstruction occurred between 1891 and 1895, the years often referred to by scholars as the heyday of lynchings, when 64 people died at the hands of lynch mobs.[37]

Using the nom de plume "Plato," a reporter for the Cincinnati *Commercial* wrote a long and, in some respects, thorough account of lynchings in Kentucky. That the *Commercial* was a Republican paper and that the writer refused to reveal his true identity can raise doubts about the validity of his article, but these facts do not, in the final analysis, discredit the story. "Plato" informed his readers that lynchings, which had been largely unknown in antebellum Kentucky, were occurring because white men were angry that slavery had been abolished and "were panting for a victim to glut the fury of their rage."

> The people . . . are becoming accustomed to these summary executions by unauthorized bodies of men. The hanging of Bolling comes hard on the heels of others, and the list runs back until name after name of those who have been hurried into eternity, on short warning, and often without a charge surviving the tragedy to tell that they were other than the victims of personal or party vengeance. Penny, Laws, Ryan, Cummins, Williams, Montford, Baker, Fields, Pierce, Davis, Hicks, Sutherland, Lawson, Divine, Gabeheart, Corrier, Jennings, Trowbridge, McRoberts, Stephens, Crowdus, Goode, Taylor, and others, whose names do not now occur to us, have successively died without the intervention of a regular trial, or the permission of testimony in their behalf.

37. Richard M. Brown, *Strain of Violence: Historical Studies of American Violence and Vigilantism* (New York, 1975), 214; Trelease, *White Terror,* 124–25; New York *Times,* August 4, 1869.

The lynchings of Al McRoberts (in Danville in December, 1866), of Trowbridge (whose first name is unknown but who died in Danville in February, 1867), and of George Bolling (in Harrodsburg in July, 1869, shortly before "Plato" wrote his story) can be documented from other sources. The deaths of the other twenty-one people listed by "Plato" could not be documented further and thus have not been included in the 117 lynchings for the Reconstruction years.[38]

If complete details existed on the many deaths at the hands of mobs that are cited in the Freedmen's Bureau papers, the congressional reports, and newspapers accounts, then the number of recorded lynchings in Kentucky would probably exceed three hundred for the first ten years of emancipation. As a bureau agent wrote to his superior about the high number of lynchings occurring in several counties, "Judge Lynch has on occasion been here, in Marion, Washington, Boyle, Casey, & Taylor Counties, absolutely superceding civil courts." The blacks living in isolated parts of the counties, great distances from the main cities, "are afraid to report outrages to me. They prefer to suffer known evils, to the unknown." Other reports show that whites lynched Afro-Americans at will during these years. As a Freedmen's Bureau Monthly Report noted on one occasion, "It cannot be denied, that if a Negroe commits a wrong, there is a strong disposition on the part of the whites to take the law into their own hands and inflict summary punishment."[39]

Rape or attempted rape was the cause of 16.2 percent of the lynchings during this time; of the nineteen men lynched after being accused of this crime, seventeen were Afro-Americans. In early May, 1866, a black described only as a sixteen-year-old named Charles was hired by A. J. Harrington to work in his home in Frankfort. Harrington had a six-year-old daughter, and he said Charles attempted to rape her. The black youth was arrested and taken to jail, where he remained for only a short time until a mob hanged him. The jailer had refused to fire on the mob or to resist it in any manner. When writing about the lynching, the Frankfort correspondent for the Louisville *Daily Courier* explained that the mob had been justified in resorting to a lynching. "We want you readers to distinctly understand that this was no mob, . . . no confusion and noise, and everything was done de-

38. Cincinnati *Commercial*, July 24, 1869.

39. James M. Fidler to Ely, July 1, 1867, Thomas Cheaney to [?] Henderson, Consolidated Monthly Reports for May, 1866, both in Freedmen's Bureau.

cently and in order. . . . It was a quiet uprising of the citizens, who are determined to put a stop to such outrages, the Freedmen's Bureau, Civil Rights bill, etc., etc., to the contrary notwithstanding." Writing in 1912, a historian of Franklin County also applauded the mob's lynching the black youth. "A merited punishment was sternly and speedily administered, an example was set which has been closely followed for half a century, and which ought to be a sufficient warning to the negro race, and the white too, as for that matter, that the women or girls of Franklin County must be protected."[40]

Two blacks were lynched after being accused of rape in May, 1868. The New York *Times* reported that "a negro living near Louisville, having committed rape on a little girl, was seized by citizens and preparations made to hang him. While these were in progress the father of the child came running up, revolver in hand . . . and attempted to shoot the negro, but in the confusion the black ran. But the mob ran after him, opening fire from a dozen revolvers and he was soon shot dead." No other details exist on this lynching even though it occurred in Louisville, the state's largest city and a place with several competing newspapers. Details are likewise sketchy on the death of a young black man named Tom who was hanged at the courthouse square in Owensboro toward the end of the same month. In both instances, the mobs encountered no problems in getting their victims from the police.[41]

In Frankfort, a fifteen-year-old white girl said she was seized by a black man, raped, and thrown over a cliff. She somehow survived this violent attack on her life. After being informed about the assault, the police quickly rounded up a number of black men, and the young woman eventually identified Jim Macklin as her attacker. Well aware of the lynching in Frankfort two years earlier, the sheriff posted additional guards at the jail. Nevertheless, a mob battered down the door, seized Macklin, and hanged him from a tree in the general area of the alleged crime. With Afro-Americans not allowed to testify in Kentucky courts, the United States district court assumed jurisdiction of the case and issued warrants against a number of Frankfort's influential citizens for being in the lynch mob. Tried in court, all of the de-

40. Louisville *Daily Courier*, May 9, 1866; L. F. Johnson, *History of Franklin County, Kentucky* (Frankfort, 1912), 164.

41. New York *Times*, May 9, 1866; *History of Daviess County . . .* (Chicago, 1883), 419–20.

fendants had the charges dismissed because no one would testify against them. Officials of the court had been particularly incensed over the lack of cooperation by Father Lambert Young, a Catholic priest who knew the details of the lynching because one of the men charged with the crime had confessed to him. Father Young refused to testify against members of the mob, even though he was held in contempt of court, fined fifty dollars, and forced to spend a month in jail.[42]

Members of the Frankfort mob had not concealed their identities. This proved to be the case elsewhere in the state during Reconstruction when mobs lynched blacks accused of rape. A band of three hundred men, none of them wearing a disguise, entered the Morganfield jail in August, 1871, and took two men, one black and the other white, and lynched them. Several years later, a black was lynched for rape in Nicholasville. The father of the "outraged girl" led the mob. Although he had assistants, the sheriff willingly turned over the accused man. Since the people involved could easily be identified, Governor Leslie wrote to the county judge and prosecuting attorney of Jessamine County, urging them to bring the members of the mob to justice. The governor promised that he would provide them with any assistance necessary to apprehend the lynchers. Nothing, however, came of his request.[43]

In April, 1874, Ed Shields was lynched in Taylorsville for the rape of Mrs. Morse Washington. On the surface, this mob murder seems no different from many others occurring during Reconstruction. What makes the Shields lynching especially significant is that he had been tried in court, found guilty of rape, and sentenced to twenty years in prison instead of being given a death sentence. No records of this case exist, but it does raise the question of whether he had actually raped the white woman. In justifying the lynching of Shields, local authorities said that he had been implicated in five other rapes, three burglaries, and one case of arson. But given the harshness with which Kentucky whites responded to blacks accused of serious offenses,

42. Several sources discuss the lynching in Frankfort and the controversy over the priest: Frankfort *Kentucky Daily Yeoman*, February 1, 1868; Johnson, *History of Franklin County*, 164–65; Collins, *Historical Sketches*, I, 191; Henry Deeds, *Sketches of the South and West: or Ten Months' Residence in the United States* (Edinburgh and London, 1869), 55–57. According to Deeds, Macklin had a solid alibi and was innocent of the crime for which he was lynched.

43. New York *Times*, August 30, 1871, September 7, 1874.

Shields probably would have been lynched, or at the very least convicted and sentenced to a long prison term, for merely being a suspect
in those cases. Undoubtedly, his "light sentence" for a conviction of
rape was used by whites to justify lynchings to protect white womanhood. In other words, the Shields conviction reinforced the lynch
mob's brutal deeds.[44]

Just as it is extremely difficult to determine if an accused black
had actually attempted to rape a white woman, it is equally difficult
to fully understand what had happened when a black was lynched for
the murder of a white person. Although blacks were lynched for murder and attempted murder, were these, in fact, cases of self-defense
where blacks could easily have been the victims? During slavery,
whites demanded that blacks be passive. And though slavery had
ended, Afro-Americans fully understood the consequences of having a
disagreement, no matter how petty, with a white man, much less of
having a full-blown, violent fight. Nevertheless, during the Reconstruction years eight blacks died at the hands of lynch mobs after
being accused of the murder or attempted murder of whites. The total
number of men put to death for murder was nineteen, the same number who died for alleged sexual assaults. More whites (eleven, compared with eight blacks) died after having been accused of murder or
attempted murder. If additional data could be found on the lynchings
whose causes are unknown, the number attributed to blacks killing
whites would most likely increase substantially.

On Christmas Eve in 1866, an altercation occurred between Al
McRoberts, a former slave, and W. A. Harris, a police officer in Danville. McRoberts had taken to carrying a gun after Harris had threatened to kill him. They met on the street, and the white policeman
demanded that the black man turn over his weapon. Angry words
passed between the two men. Then, according to the version of a
Freedmen's Bureau agent, McRoberts shot at Harris three times, but
all of the bullets missed. "McRoberts was arrested and taken toward
the jail followed by an excited crowd, who advised Harris to kill him.
On the way to jail Harris beat him severely with a large cane. . . .
On arriving at the jail, Harris took a pistol and deliberately shot
him, inflicting a serious . . . injury." Later that evening, a mob took
McRoberts from the jail, carried him to the outskirts of town, and

44. Louisville *Courier-Journal*, April 24, 1874.

hanged him. An inquest was held to determine how McRoberts had died and who was responsible. It ended within minutes with the verdict that "McRoberts came to his death by hanging by some parties unknown."[45]

In Nicholasville in April, 1867, Adam Smith, a teenager, shot and killed a white youth during an argument over an attack by Smith's dogs on some hogs owned by the white youth's family. Smith was taken to jail. That evening, five men entered the jail and demanded that the jailer hand Smith over to them. The jailer refused to do so, and the men shot the black youth while he remained in the cell. Smith identified his assailants before he died. After leaving the jail, the five men went to the farm of Price Penniston, took another black youth, and hanged him for being Smith's accomplice. A young black boy witnessed the second lynching, and agents for the bureau hoped that he could give evidence that would lead to the conviction of the five men. But as one agent wrote, "I entertain serious doubts as to sufficient legal evidence being obtained to convict them." He proved to be correct. An additional letter in the bureau records explains, "Received letter acknowledging that you have without success attempted to arrest the people who . . . killed the blacks in Nicholasville." Bureau agents remained determined to prosecute the lynchers. A special agent was hired (at a rate of three dollars a day) to locate the members of the lynch mob and bring them by force to the bureau court. After spending several weeks on the case, the agent concluded that the men had fled the state.[46]

In addition to rape and murder, personal property offenses and arson often led to lynchings. In October, 1872, Sam Bascom was arrested and charged with arson in Owingsville. Breaking into the jail, a group of men seized the prisoner and lynched him at the edge of town. They pinned a note to Bascom's dangling body: "Look Out. Penalty of house burners and horse thieves. He who moves the body before 10:00 will meet the same fate." The *Courier-Journal* and the New York *Times* denounced the lynching, saying that Bascom had a solid alibi and that all of the evidence against him was circumstantial "and rather flimsy at that, barely sufficient to have authority of a jury in

---

45. W. R. Roume to R. E. Johnston, January 5, 1867, in Freedmen's Bureau.

46. James K. Rice to R. E. Johnston, May 25, 1867, Ely to Johnson, May 31, June 12, 1867, all in Freedmen's Bureau. Details on this lynching can also be found in the Louisville *Daily Courier*, April 30, 1867.

finding a verdict of guilty." Furthermore, editor Henry Watterson explained that even if the black man had been guilty of arson, his crime was not a capital offense.[47]

During Reconstruction, more than any other time, whites lynched Afro-Americans because of their involvement in political affairs. Many of the lynchings where the exact causes are unknown were undoubtedly cases of black leaders being killed because of their political activities. These political assassinations served the dual purpose of removing the offending blacks and of warning others to stay out of politics. Like their counterparts elsewhere in the state, blacks in Versailles and in Woodford County formed political clubs in 1870 after the passage of the Fifteenth Amendment. Viewing the black vote as a threat to their domination of the county, a group of whites formed a militia company. Several weeks before the August elections, this company received a supply of guns from the Democratic-controlled government of Frankfort. One evening around midnight, the militia, numbering about thirty men, went to the home of Levi Parker and ordered him to tell the whereabouts of two influential black Republicans, James Parker and William Turpin. They then went to Parker's house and ordered him to open the door. He refused to do so, until the mob threatened to shoot him and his family. "As soon as he complied with the demand three shots were fired at him, one striking him on the breast killed him almost instantly." The militia next visited Turpin. Although unaware of Parker's lynching, he refused to open the door and attempted to escape by climbing out a back window. The mob, however, had the house surrounded and fired upon him, and with "three balls striking him, he fell dead." County officials held inquests and ruled that the men died at the hands of unknown parties. Members of the militia sent threatening messages to several other black leaders, warning that unless their political activities ceased immediately, they would receive the same treatment as Turpin and Parker. Although his party had supplied the mob with weapons, Governor John W. Stevenson denounced the lynchings, called upon Woodford County officals to arrest the guilty, and offered five hundred dol-

---

47. New York *Times*, October 30, 1872; Tapp and Klotter, *Decades of Discord*, 384–85. See also J. A. Richards, *An Illustrated History of Bath County, Kentucky, With Historical and Biographical Sketches and Notes and Anecdotes of Many Years* (Yuma, Arizona, 1961), 235–36.

lars for the arrest and conviction of each mob member. Local officials, however, refused to apprehend the lynchers. Meanwhile, white Republican leaders, after realizing no steps would be taken to protect them or the blacks, fled Versailles.[48]

Two blacks were lynched in Frankfort on August 7, 1871, in what would become the most publicized lynchings in Kentucky during Reconstruction. Blacks had been organized into a political group and were determined to vote in large numbers on election day. On that day, the police were out in force and attempted without much success to keep a safe distance between blacks and whites of competing parties. There are two different accounts of who sparked the violence, which came to be called the "Frankfort Riot." Viewing black political leaders as troublemakers, the pro-Democrat Louisville *Courier-Journal* said they were responsible. The paper went so far as to tie the black demand for political changes with the raping of several white women in the Frankfort area. On election day, Watterson's paper reported, whites had to take insult after insult from blacks. Then, without any provocation, a number of blacks opened fire, "killing two innocent whites" and injuring several others. On the other hand, the New York *Times* and the Louisville *Commercial*, both pro-Republican papers, blamed the police officers for the riot, saying that they had fired at blacks for no apparent reason, touching off the shooting from both sides. It is unclear whether any blacks were killed during the riot. The Democratic press said that none had been killed, while one Republican newspaper said that as many as six blacks might have died. As explained by the *Commercial*, "A considerable number of colored persons were wounded, but concealed their injuries for fear of being hung by the excited mob, that seemed to take the fact of a wound as proof of complicity in the riot."[49]

Henry Washington, a black political leader and the person identified by whites as having fired the first shot, was seriously wounded during the exchange of gunfire. Ignoring his injury, the police carried him to jail. Late that evening a large mob of more than 250 men went to the jail and demanded Washington and another black, Harry Johnson, who had been arrested for the recent alleged rapes. The jailer

48. Louisville *Commercial*, August 12, 1870; Collins, *Historical Sketches*, I, 206.
49. Louisville *Courier-Journal*, August 9, 1871; New York *Times*, August 9, 1871; Louisville *Commercial*, August 9, 24, September 25, 26, 27, 28, October 2, 1871.

willingly turned over the men, who were then carried across the Kentucky River to the edge of town and hanged from a tree. In denouncing the lynchings, the New York *Times* charged complicity on the part of officials, saying that the violence earlier in the day should have prompted officials to request state troops to guard the city and especially the jailhouse.

A number of whites from both political parties came forward to condemn the lynchings and to urge that steps be promptly taken to ensure that the mob did not resort to additional violence against Frankfort's black citizens. J. Stoddard Johnston, a former Confederate, historian, and local newspaper editor, said that the lynchings could not be justified for any reason: "We have no apology to make for the act, and no defense for the actors. We are of the number who believe that mob law and violence are wrong and not to be justified by any enlightened view, either in the light of punishment or revenge. . . . We care not what the grievance; it offers no remedy, . . . but tends only to aggravate instead of removing the cause." Normally, the coroner's report saying that the victims died at the hands of unknown parties closed the investigation of a lynching. The Frankfort case, however, would not end so easily. A number of state leaders called for the arrests of the leaders of the lynch mob. Advocating what many Kentuckians thought to be an extreme view, several Republicans called for federal rule over Kentucky as the only effective way to end lynchings and other lawless acts against Afro-Americans.[50]

To end the criticism that they were unconcerned about finding the whites involved in the lynchings, state leaders prevailed upon Franklin County officials to launch an investigation. For several days, testimony was heard from dozens of blacks and whites about what happened on election day. Nevertheless, the grand jury failed to reveal the causes for the riot or to identify anyone other than Henry Washington as having taken part in the disturbance. Highly critical of the investigation, the *Commercial* said with obvious sarcasm, "In all the long and scrutinizing examination of witnesses heretofore, none were found who possessed the slightest knowledge of, or interest, or curiosity in the exciting events of the night of the 7th of August. It was

50. Frankfort *Tri-Weekly Yeoman,* August 10, 1871; Carl E. Kramer, *Capital on the Kentucky: A Two Hundred Year History of Frankfort and Franklin County* (Frankfort, 1986), 174–75.

gratifying to know that there was one gentleman in Frankfort who proved an exception to this rule, and we are proud, for the sake of ordinary old-fashioned human nature, to hand his name down to posterity; his name is Silas Kersey."[51]

In a separate development, Deputy United States Marshal John Wyatt arrested Howard Smith, Richard Crittenden, and James Alley, all members of prominent families, and had them indicted in United States district court for taking part in the lynchings of Washington and Johnson. Judge Ballard agreed to hear the case, since the Kentucky courts still prohibited black testimony. In a surprise move, John Marshall Harlan, the leading Republican in the state, agreed to defend Howard Smith. Having urged the federal government to take whatever steps necessary to end the violence, Harlan now found himself in a paradoxical situation. In a letter to Benjamin H. Bristow, another Republican leader in the state, he justified defending Smith on economic grounds: "I once thought that I would have nothing to do with cases of this kind, but, upon reflection, I find that I must play lawyer in those as in other cases, [or] abandon good fees which I am not able to do." Harlan succeeded in having the case delayed. During the interlude, the state legislature extended to Afro-Americans the right to testify against whites in court. The case was transferred to the Franklin County Circuit Court, where the three men were easily acquitted. Content with his role in the case, Harlan said his client was innocent "for he clearly established an alibi and nobody believes him to have been guilty."[52]

Samuel Hawkins, a black political organizer in Fayette and Jessamine counties, received several warnings from the Ku Klux Klan to quit attempting to register blacks to vote. In early November, 1872, members of the Klan visited his home. While most white mobs usually directed their violence only at the black man they held responsible for causing trouble, this lawless band ordered Hawkins' wife and oldest daughter outside as well. The next morning their bodies were found hanging from a tree, suspended over a cliff. The Klan boldly stated that the lynchings were a warning to other blacks involved in

51. Louisville *Commercial*, September 28, 1871.

52. John Marshall Harlan to Benjamin H. Bristow, September 27, 1871, Bristow Papers, Manuscript Division, Library of Congress; Howard, *Black Liberation in Kentucky*, 141–45.

political affairs. The Lexington *Kentucky Statesman,* a pro-Republican newspaper, in perhaps the strongest attack against violence made by a white newspaper during Reconstruction, called the lynchings the most horrible and assassinlike outrage perpetrated by the Klan on Afro-Americans. "What human heart can be but shocked that such atrocity occurs in a Christianized and civilized country! . . . Let the county officers spare neither time, nor labor, nor trouble in hunting down these fiends as they would some mad animal that was loose in the community, destroying as it went." Two days later, the paper published a second editorial on the lynchings. Labeling the murders "The Midnight Crime," "a crime with a cruelty and fiendishness unparalleled," the newspaper called on the decent people of Kentucky to end the violence: "There must be an end to these things. . . . Civilization must end and barbarism begin, or law must reassert its majesty, and power. . . . Which shall it be, men of Kentucky: you who are responsible for the right conduct of human events in your reach—you who boast of superior civilization and talk of Bibles, and religion, and laws, and innocence, and personal rights,—you who claim a better nature than the relentless savage? The problem is before you—a more serious one than any Presidential contest, or the supremacy of any mere political organization. It must be solved."[53]

Just like members of the Hawkins family, a number of whites died at the hands of lynch mobs because of their political activities on behalf of the Republican party. When looking at the total number of lynchings that occurred during Reconstruction, it is clear that though Afro-Americans accounted for the greatest number of victims—eighty-seven blacks, compared with twenty-four whites, and six people unidentified by race—the heinous practice was not reserved solely for them. But of the causes that can be clearly documented, murder was cited most often for the lynchings of whites. Often the person lynched had been charged with killing relatives or friends. John Nevil of Metcalf County, for example, accused of killing his mother-in-law, was lynched in 1871. In 1872, a Richmond mob lynched Leonard Stough upon learning of the brutal manner in which

<hr />

53. New York *Times,* November 5, 1872; Lexington *Kentucky Statesman,* November 6, 8, 1872. No account of the lynchings of the Hawkins family could be found in the pro-Democratic Lexington *Kentucky Gazette,* and copies of the city's other Democratic paper, the *Observer and Reporter,* are not complete for November, 1872.

he had killed his wife: "Her throat had been cut from ear to ear, her windpipe severed, a fearful gash in the face, and a more terrible wound in the breast and bowels, and thirteen other wounds in different parts of the body, and one of her fingers completely cut off." Although he had been charged with murder in Harrison County in 1873, Robert Beckett remained free on bail a year later, to the disgust of the friends of the man he had allegedly killed. A mob of masked men grabbed Beckett at the home of his employer, carried him outside the house, and riddled his body with bullets. Further intent on showing their hatred for their victim, the men soaked Beckett's clothes with coal oil and set the corpse on fire.[54]

Whether pursued by lynch mobs, or forced to vacate their lands, or bedeviled by other forms of violence, Afro-Americans stood little chance of receiving justice in Kentucky's courts. As Leon Litwack notes, southern courts took steps to protect white supremacy. Describing the workings of the Kentucky courts, one bureau agent proclaimed, "I have yet to see a white man punished in a state court for maltreating a negro, and a negro acquitted of any crime however small!" Consistently, whites avoided prosecution after committing crimes against blacks. "This is a good time for white scoundrels of all descriptions in the country around Lexington," noted the sympathetic Louisville *Commercial* in 1871. "All they have to do to escape detection for any crimes . . . is to charge it to the negroes. As the mass of the negroes . . . are poor and ignorant, it is natural that they should commit a fair proportion of the crimes." A few rare cases exist in which a black filed a complaint against a white person and that person was actually arrested and convicted. In Louisville in April, 1875, policeman W. E. Buchanan was fined fifty dollars for beating a black woman with his cane, knocking her insensible. According to the paper, the policeman's conviction "was a just judgment and teaches a valuable lesson that some of the members of the police force should improve by." Unfortunately, however, as most blacks could attest, the conviction of any white, especially a police officer, occurred very rarely and usually only in Louisville.[55]

---

54. Louisville *Courier-Journal*, August 29, 1871; Louisville *Commercial*, October 18, 1871, February 5, 1872; New York *Times*, June 12, 1874.

55. Litwack, *Been in the Storm So Long*, 282–85; Louisville *Commercial*, October 5, 1871, April 9, 1875.

An incident from Anderson County provides additional proof that blacks had virtually no chance before the legal system. In April, 1874, Mark Rucker, a white man "addicted to drink," went to purchase some liquor at the home jointly occupied by Levi Thompson and Botts Hagerman. Finding no one there, Rucker decided to go inside and take a nap. Meanwhile, the wives of Thompson and Hagerman, opening the door to the house and seeing a strange man, began shouting and ran off. Several men came to their rescue. Even though it was dark and they could barely make out Rucker's figure, they fired anyway, killing him. In court, instead of saying that Rucker's death had been an accident, the men rested their defense on a belief that they had been shooting at a Negro. Finding this reasoning justified, the court dismissed the charges against the men. Perhaps the court assumed that if Rucker had been a black man he deserved to die without being allowed to give an explanation for his actions. The Louisville *Commercial* took the occasion to express its disgust at the court's lack of concern for the lives of blacks. "A stranger who happened to hear a part of the examining trial said, if ever he had occasion to kill a man he would try to decoy him to Anderson county and then kill him. He would certainly be in little if any danger if he will only plead he thought he was killing a negro."[56]

In Garrard County during the February, 1868, term of the circuit court, John Spilman was found guilty of the rape of Elizabeth Preston, a white woman, and sentenced to twenty years in prison. That a black man had a trial instead of being summarily executed may have been surprising given the anger whites expressed upon hearing the charge. That Spilman received a fixed prison sentence instead of death or life without parole stands in sharp contrast to what occurred in later decades whenever Afro-Americans were on trial for rape. An appeal for a pardon was made on his behalf after he had been confined for more than eleven years. (Spilman had been held in the local jail since July 1, 1866, when the rape charge had been made; his term in the state prison began in February, 1868). A number of Garrard County's leading citizens, including nine of the twelve jurors who had found him guilty (two of the jurors had died and the view of the twelfth one is unknown) sent a letter to the governor requesting a pardon. W. D. Hopper, for-

---

56. Louisville *Commercial*, April 22, 1874. See the Cincinnati *Commercial*, September 11, 1869, for another case of a white killing a black by "accident."

mer clerk of the Garrard circuit court, wrote a revealing letter on Spilman's behalf. He expressed a sincere belief that "the action of the jury was to a large extent influenced by popular clamor." The testimony presented against the black man, Hopper stated bluntly, did not warrant a guilty verdict. "At the time of the conviction of the said Spilman, the so called KuKlux were at the height of their power, and the court-room was filled by persons generally said to belong to that order, and when the verdict was rendered, one was heard to say, 'We are satisfied.'" Perhaps the most crucial and shocking letter was sent by Judge M. H. Owsley, who as commonwealth attorney had argued the case for the state. The judge wrote: "I have always had a doubt, and I think a reasonable one, that Spilman was not guilty of rape, and he has now been in confinement a long time." Governor James B. McCreary received these letters between October and December, 1877. Spilman was finally pardoned by Governor Luke P. Blackburn in 1879, after having been incarcerated for almost thirteen years.[57]

Fred Magowan, a black from Montgomery County, was sentenced to nine years in prison for the accidental death of a white woman "with whom he had been living for several years." No evidence was presented in court to dispute Magowan's claim that the death was purely an accident, that he had not intended to harm his common-law wife. Letters submitted by the leading white citizens of Mount Sterling and Montgomery County on behalf of Magowan spoke in glowing terms about his character. At the same time, however, they said the white woman was "very depraved." Nevertheless, it is clear that Magowan, who did receive a pardon after serving all but one month of his sentence, had been convicted because whites were offended that he lived openly with a white woman. In the early 1900s, state legislators passed a law against interracial marriage, but as Magowan's prison sentence reveals, prior to that time prosecutors and jurors obviously expressed their disdain for interracial relationships, especially when it involved a black man and white woman.[58]

In a practice that would become far more common later on, five blacks and one white were legally executed (all for murder) during Reconstruction. The law prohibiting blacks from serving as jurymen

57. Legislative Document No. 26, *List of Pardons, Etc., Granted by Governor Luke P. Blackburn* (Frankfort, 1882), 106–11.

58. *Ibid.*, 407–409; *The Kentucky Statutes, 1903* (Louisville, 1903), 842–45.

was changed in January, 1872, but none were chosen for the juries that sentenced these men to death or for any other juries considering capital punishment until well into the twentieth century. In August, 1872, a Lexington black, Will Carter, was sent to the gallows for the murder of a white sergeant, David M. Pugh. Shots had been exchanged between the two men, but neither had been injured. Pugh then warned Carter that if he remained in town beyond Friday night, "he would have to take the consequences." According to the newspaper account, on Friday evening Carter entered a room and shot Pugh twice, killing him instantly.[59]

On another occasion, George Miller died on the gallows for the murder of the white doctor who had been Miller's slaveowner. The newspaper said the motive may have been that the black man was on "too intimate terms" with the doctor's wife. For a while, the police held Mrs. Lucy Alfred as an accomplice, but they never brought formal charges against her. Shortly before his execution, George Miller wrote "a most affectionate letter" to Mrs. Alfred, asking her to visit him before he died. After reading the confiscated letter, one white man expressed a belief that "it was a singular letter for a negro to write to a white woman, and to the wife of the man whose life he had taken." Before Miller died, law officers unsuccessfully pressed him to confess the murder and to admit that Mrs. Alfred had assisted in the crime. It can be speculated that in the eyes of the all-white jury, the mere hint that Miller might have been intimately involved with a white woman could have been enough to bring about the guilty verdict.[60]

Despite the law that seemed to operate against them and the constant threats from white mobs, Kentucky's black citizens attempted to defend themselves not only by protesting unjust legal decisions but also by taking up their weapons to forcefully challenge the mob violence. In other words, at no time during Reconstruction did Afro-Americans willingly accept the many forms of racial violence they encountered. As scholars of slavery have shown, Afro-Americans adopted a wide range of ways to respond to treatment they despised. Some defense tactics were overt, while others were much more subtle. The same proved to be true from the very beginning of freedom as Afro-Americans adopted forms of protest to which other Americans

59. Louisville *Courier-Journal*, August 20, 1872.
60. *Ibid.*, May 1, 1874; Louisville *Commercial*, May 3, 1874.

could relate: sending petitions and holding conventions. Within weeks after the official end of slavery, a group of Louisville blacks sent a petition to the legislature calling for the repeal of the unjust laws prohibiting blacks from entering or leaving the state. Protection against violence was a major concern addressed in the petition. Only by having the rights of self-defense and of testifying in court against whites, these Louisville blacks argued, would they be protected from violent attacks by whites. Their petition ended with a call for the start of public-supported schools, for as they explained at length, no free people could live and hope to prosper without being educated. Louisville blacks would eventually join ranks with other black Kentuckians and hold a number of statewide conventions that expanded upon the points outlined in the first petition.[61]

In March, 1871, when the Ku Klux Klan had virtually usurped the local governments in several counties, a group of Frankfort blacks petitioned the United States Congress "to enact some laws that will protect us, and that will enable us to exercise the rights of citizens." They were compelled to turn to Washington, they wrote, because the Kentucky legislature had adjourned without passing any laws to suppress the Klan. "We regard them as now being licensed to continue their dark and bloody deeds under cover of the dark night." Fully aware of the attempts of Kentucky's elected officials to downplay the violence in the state, the Frankfort blacks explained: "We see that the Senator from this state denies there being organized bands of desperadoes in the State; for information, we lay before you a number of violent acts, occurred during his Administration. Although he, Stevenson, says half a dozen instances of violence did occur, these are not more than one-half the acts that have occurred. Where many of these acts have been committed, it has been proven that they were . . . done with arms from the State arsenal." They gave information in the form of names, dates, and places of 135 crimes committed by the Klan.[62]

61. New York *Times*, January 22, 1866, October 26, 1871; *Proceedings of the State Convention of Colored Men, held at Lexington, Kentucky, in the AME Church, November 26, 27, 28, 1867* (N.p., n.d.); *Kentucky State Colored Education Convention Held at Benson's Theatre, Louisville, Kentucky, July 14, 1869* (N.p., n.d.).

62. "Memorial of A Committee Appointed At A Meeting of Colored Citizens of Frankfort, Kentucky, and Vicinity," March 25, 1871, 42nd Cong., 1st Sess., Miscellaneous Document No. 49.

Holding conventions and sending petitions demonstrated a belief among Afro-Americans that the system would work on their behalf. On many occasions, however, blacks knew that they could not rely on state or federal officials for protection. They, therefore, defended themselves. Scholars must always be careful to explain fully, without glamorizing, how powerless people have fought back against a much more powerful foe. Kentucky blacks were not trying to be heroic when defending themselves against the Klan and other whites; they had no choice but to fight or be killed.

A common episode comes from Camp Nelson, in Jessamine County, where a large number of blacks had settled after emancipation because they believed that the presence of the United States Army headquarters assured their safety. For some unknown reason, a group of whites surrounded the house of a black man and began shooting. Two men were in the house, and one of them attempted to leave and was immediately shot to death. "The other stood his ground and made fight, returning their fire with his revolver, killing one of the party and badly wounding another." The mob finally gained admission into the house and overpowered John Burnside, the black man who had fought back. He was badly beaten by the mob and left for dead. Somehow, Burnside recovered from the attack.[63]

Any number of examples can be cited of Afro-Americans taking steps to defend themselves against the violence of the Klan. After being discharged from the Union army, Elijah P. Marrs, a former slave, moved to Henry County to teach in the school established for the freedmen. Members of the Klan openly expressed their contempt for the school and especially for the presence of black war veterans as teachers. Anticipating trouble, Marrs helped organize the Loyal League to protect blacks from the Klan. On several occasions, he succeeded in driving off the Klan by firing upon them. In his autobiography, Marrs claims that for three years he "slept with a pistol under my head, an Enfield rifle at my side, and a corn knife at the door." In 1871, the black residents of Watkinsville, learning that the Klan had killed a black in nearby Stamping Ground and were headed their way, armed themselves and fired at the first sight of the hooded outlaws. They successfully drove off the Klan, though three blacks died in the battle. In August and September of that same year, the Louisville

63. J. G. Nain to James H. Rice, November 23, 1866, in Freedmen's Bureau.

Commercial had stories about blacks killing Klan members who had attacked their homes. Arrested by local authorities, these blacks were usually ordered released by military officials. The *Courier-Journal*, though stating its opposition to the violence of the Klan, complained that the military authorities were "Kukluxing the Law" by placing blacks in the custody of military, not civilian, officials. In late December, 1871, the Klan went to the home of George Duncan in Brooksville to force him off of his property. The moment they broke down his door, Duncan fired, killing one member of the Klan. He was arrested and taken to jail. That evening, he was lynched, thereby becoming yet another victim of Klan violence. Duncan had, however, attempted to defend himself, first at his home and then before being hung, when he made a run for it but was stopped by a rock to his head. Finally, the various reports on violence in Henry, Owen, and Franklin counties and elsewhere contain stories of blacks killing members of the Klan. It is impossible to determine how many whites were killed when attacking blacks, for both sides had reasons for refusing to come forward.[64]

The presence of armed blacks prevented lynchings on at least two occasions. In August, 1871, the Klan attempted to raid the Danville jail and seize two black men. A group of blacks, however, had surrounded the jail and fired at the approaching Klansmen, driving them off. Three years later, a black man, Lewis Franklin, was arrested in Versailles and charged with a rape that had happened in Nicholasville. By that time, several lynchings had occurred in Nicholasville, and local blacks, fearful of yet another, armed themselves and stood guard over the jail after Franklin had been returned to the city. Early the next morning, a mob of about fifty white men came toward the jail. The account is unclear as to who shot first, but one member of the mob was killed, and the entire group disappeared. Given the white sense of justice, it is surprising that no charges were brought against any of the Nicholasville blacks.[65]

The first decade after slavery is significant for a complete under-

---

64. Elijah P. Marrs, *Life of Reverend Elijah P. Marrs* (Louisville, 1885), 57, 74–90; Tapp and Klotter, *Decades of Discord*, 383; Louisville *Courier-Journal*, August 14, 1871; Louisville *Commercial*, January 14, August 22, September 5, December 30, 1871; Collins, *Historical Sketches*, I, 208.

65. Louisville *Commercial*, August 29, 1871; Louisville *Courier-Journal*, September 5, 1874.

standing of racial violence in the Bluegrass State. Lynchings did not start all at once in the late 1880s but had been a part of white oppression of Afro-Americans since the beginning of emancipation. Also, seizing black property and forcing blacks out of certain occupations were violent acts that started immediately after slavery. Although it might be too harsh to label Reconstruction as the time of a new form of slavery, it was a time when whites were determined to keep blacks at the bottom of society. Clearly, during Reconstruction racial violence became a fact of life for Afro-Americans, with lynchings, "legal lynchings," and mob rule becoming common occurrences; they would be so for many years. The response of Afro-Americans also foreshadowed later activities. In later decades, just as they had in the first ten years of freedom, they would continue forming organizations, writing petitions, and adopting militant stances to combat racial violence.

"Lynchings Are Necessary," 1875–1899

Hallie Erminie Rives published a novel, *Smoking Flax*, to justify the lynchings that were occurring during the 1890s.[1] Dedicated to "My Mother and the South," the novel is set in Georgetown, Kentucky, and centers on Elliott Harding, a young white man from New England with radical ideas who moves to Kentucky—the South—to take control of the family property. From the start, Harding is unsparing in his criticism of local whites for condoning the lynching of Afro-Americans: "Think of it! More than one thousand human lives forfeited to Judge Lynch for the South's record for the past ten years. What a horrible record! It seems almost incredible that such lawlessness can exist in communities supposed to be civilized. Would to God it were but an evil dream and that I could to-day assure the world that this terrible condition is but the unfounded imagining of a nightmared mind." At some point, Harding meets and falls in love with a beautiful young woman. Shortly before their wedding, however, she is brutally raped and murdered by Ephriam Cooley, an educated Negro. The local sheriff, intent on justice being done, takes steps to prevent a lynching. Despite the horrible crime and the desire of whites to have the violent episode ended, the trial is delayed to locate several witnesses for Cooley. The trial is not quick; it takes all day to seat a jury. At last, Cooley is found guilty and sentenced to death. The entire ordeal, from the death of his future bride through the long trial, leads Harding to reassess his views on lynching: "Holmes, I have been thinking of my old views. God knows I have had time to think and

1. Biographical information on Hallie E. Rives can be found in Lucian L. Knight (ed.), *Library of Southern Literature* (15 vols.; Atlanta, 1907), XV, 371. Rives was a native of Christian County, an area where blacks made up about 40 percent of the population.

cause to think! I am appreciating now the problem you of the South
could not solve." Then two shocking surprises occur: Cooley's execution is delayed, and the governor commutes the death sentence to a
term of life in prison. The novel comes to a climax as the sheriff and
his men hurry to get Cooley safely on the train to be transported to
state prison. "There was a sudden rush and speeding through the
darkness; an unkempt figure, running staggeringly as though in ex-
haustion, leaped to the platform and pursued the moving train. A sudden flash, a sharp report, and Ephriam Cooley fell back dead, shot
through the heart. By the time the train had drawn back to the station, the platform was deserted; only the shrouding mists of blue
smoke remained." The identity of Cooley's killer is unknown. Obviously, however, it is Harding. The former radical from New England
now clearly understands and sympathizes with the view that lynching blacks is sometimes a necessity in the South.[2]

Several years after the publication of *Smoking Flax*, Rives wrote a
letter denouncing the death sentence given a white woman in Vermont. How could Vermont consider itself an enlightened "New England commonwealth" if it allowed this poor woman to be executed,
she asked. Regardless of the crime, women must be given mercy and
the chance to repent. "No Governor can evade that question when in
his hands lies the issue of life and death. It can give him small comfort
to decide to 'let the law take its course,' because the course of that
law is through his final executive hands. His own pen must sign the
sheriff's death warrant. If I do not stretch my hand to save the drown-
ing man I drown him." After denouncing the legal hanging of a woman,
Rives reaffirms the necessity of lynching blacks: "In the South men
are hanged with the formality of a trial, and without the formality of a
trial when Judge Lynch holds court. When the latter is the case it is a
deed performed under strong pressure of racial feelings, inspired generally by atrocities of which the North as a section can have no con-
ception, and by the necessity of furnishing example to a race which
is still (as a race) brutalized and subject." Rives concludes that the
horrible crimes committed by blacks justified their deaths at the
hands of the mob: "Lynch law is swift and sure—directed always to
example. It is the lurid object lesson necessary to impress the igno-
rance and passion which give it cause. It is thus a measure of self-

2. Hallie Erminie Rives, *Smoking Flax* (2nd ed.; New York, 1897), 232.

defense and prevention—which can be the only logical reason for the existence of capital punishment anywhere."[3]

Whether Rives's book and letter were widely read and had any impact on public attitudes about lynchings is unclear. Even without Rives's defense of lynchings, most southern whites found ample justifications for taking the law into their own hands. Like her, most of them believed that the primary cause of lynchings was the rape of white females by black "brutes." The law, they argued, was ineffectual and time-consuming, and most often it hindered justice. As the chapters on "legal lynchings" will show, Kentucky's governors, regardless of party affiliation, would not have commuted the death sentence of a black man found guilty of both rape and murder. Indeed, the governors applauded their fellow citizens for allowing the law to take its course and permitting a black to be legally hanged. Nevertheless, Rives uses the state's unwillingness to fully punish the black rapist/murderer as the cause of the lynching. Her novel, in short, agreeing with the view held by most whites of that day, depicted lynchers as sincere people forced to take the law into their own hands to ensure that their civilization was not destroyed by blacks. As the sheriff said to Harding when trying to console him for the loss of his beloved bride-to-be:

> "It is useless to attempt to convey in words what the South has long endured, but I believe she is on the point of struggling from beneath the crushing burden that weighs her down. A time will come when our southern governors will order a special term of Superior Court to try speedily a criminal and invariably fix the death penalty for the offense which is largely responsible for lynching. How much graver, deeper, more human now, must seem to you our tragedies and our defense. We would indeed welcome a worthier mode or the day when there will be no such tragedies."[4]

Like the novelist Hallie Rives, many observers in Kentucky, especially newspaper editors and local historians, stated that lynchings were necessary to punish murderers and rapists who might otherwise go unpunished and to show others what awaited them for engaging in outrageous criminal activities. Many editors claimed to be opposed to lynchings and would consistently denounce all acts of mob violence and lynchings that occurred outside their immediate areas. Whenever

3. Lexington *Herald*, December 19, 1904.
4. Rives, *Smoking Flax*, 229.

a lynching happened close to home, however, the editors first expressed their disapproval of the violent act but then explained that given the awful nature of the crime committed and the excitement it generated, a quick lynching had been the best way to bring the unrest to a close. In December, 1892, a black youth, Bob Harper, was arrested in Bowling Green on a charge of rape. Many whites expressed doubts about his guilt, but a white mob lynched him nevertheless. Writing about the lynching, a reporter expressed his approval of the killing of Harper: "There can be no question as to Harper's guilt, and though his punishment was not brought about according to the forms of the law, all will admit that it was a righteous one." Four years later, a black man was lynched in Mayfield for the rape of a white woman. Once again a local reporter explained why the lynching was justified: "While the *Monitor* deplores the necessity of mob violence, it realizes the fact that, owing to the delays and uncertainties of the courts, this is the only way to deal with men who are guilty of the crime which is recognized in all sections of the civilized world as a sufficient cause for summary punishment." Local accounts of lynchings explained how the members of the mob, usually described as some of the best people in the community, were serious and orderly during a lynching, as if to have been drunk and rowdy would have somehow made the act more of a criminal offense. Resorting to "Judge Lynch," white newspapers noted regularly, would be unnecessary in their communities if Afro-Americans lived upright lives.[5]

Three black men were hanged in Lexington in January, 1878. All were suspected of knowing the person responsible for the recent murder of a white man. The local newspaper, the *Kentucky Gazette*, published an editorial exonerating whites for the lynchings: "Every illegal act is wrong and should be reprobated; but so is midnight murder, and if midnight murder cannot be punished and repressed by legal process, are men to sit quietly down and see their neighbors murdered in cold blood?" Contradicting the *Kentucky Gazette*, the New York *Times* concluded that the men were innocent of any wrongdoings. This led to an angry response from the *Kentucky Gazette*: Blacks were responsible for at least twenty-five incendiary fires and the loss of countless horses and livestock. Lynchings were necessary, the

5. Louisville *Courier-Journal*, December 28, 29, 1892; Mayfield *Monitor*, December 23, 1896.

paper noted, because since the end of slavery "the negroes have been turned over to the officers of the law, and these are not numerous enough to control them as their masters did. The result is they harry over the county . . . and render the lives of our farmers and their families one of perpetual anxiety and apprehension. . . . If caught and convicted of stealing, or any crime less than murder, the only punishment is the pen for a year or two, and then they come back, burning with revenge, to repeat their former offense in an aggravated form."[6]

Henry Watterson, editor of the Louisville *Courier-Journal* for almost fifty years, took various stands on lynching. In a June, 1894, editorial he chastised Ida Wells-Barnett and the British press for criticizing the South over the continuation of lynchings: "The negro woman from Memphis is still stirring up the British over the barbarism of the Southern people in lynching negroes. The British ought to have no indignation for export. They need it all for home consumption. A people which have robbed and murdered more blacks than any other nation on the globe should have nothing to say because the Southern whites protect their women by killing their ravishers." Several years later, however, he wrote editorials calling for the punishment of those responsible for several lynchings in Mayfield and in Graves County. Good men had to take control of the situation, he declared, because an open defiance of the law existed. Surely the identities of the lynchers were known to hundreds of witnesses, and "if these are brought before the Grand Jury, they can be made to testify and the outlaws can be brought to justice, restoring the good name of Mayfield as a community determined to protect the legal rights of even its meanest citizens. If public sentiment approves the substitution of Judge Lynch for Judge Robbins, nothing will be done and very soon we may be regaled with another story of a victim hung or tortured." Three weeks later, after the grand jury had indicted eight men, Watterson lauded the actions of the "good citizens of Graves County [who] mean to wipe out the stain cast upon the . . . community by a lawless element in its population." Then, in a real shift from his editorial of 1894, Watterson expressed sympathy for Afro-Americans, the primary victims of lynchers: "What is worse, this has been done in the case of poor and friendless negroes. It does not appear that well-to-

6. Lexington *Kentucky Gazette*, January 19, 23, 1878; New York *Times*, January 18, 28, 1878.

do criminals have suffered at the hands of regulators. The lynchings have been shocking acts not only of lawlessness but of liability and injustice to the class whose rights above all should be shielded by the community, since they cannot protect themselves." It is difficult to determine which was the real Watterson, the one endorsing or the one protesting the acts of lynchers.[7]

Unlike Watterson, local historians have been consistent in justifying the lynchings of blacks in their communities. "One of the most atrocious murders that ever disgraced Union County, was the killing of Mr. Christopher Columbus Smith . . . by a negro named Jack Williams," wrote the local historian. After stabbing Smith to death, Williams fled, only to be captured and placed in jail. A week later, a mob took him from the jail and hanged him from the same tree that was used to hang at least four other people in Union County. "It would have been better for the county if Williams had been brought to justice and executed according to law, but the legal processes are so slow and sometimes so uncertain, that the mob thought it best to prevent any chances of failure in his execution." Rufus Browder, a black sharecropper, shot and killed a white farmer in self-defense. Four blacks, all friends of Browder, were arrested for allegedly approving of Browder's actions. They were taken from jail and lynched. Relying completely on the perceived white version of the lynchings, the historian of Logan County wrote more than fifty years after the incident that "the Negroes were thought to be organizing against the whites. It was thought they were marking certain people for death and naming certain of their color for the task. It was a time of hysteria and wild rumors." No contemporary accounts of the lynchings speak of Afro-Americans marking whites for death. The story of a black uprising was a rationale developed to help explain the killing of four innocent men.[8]

Even if lynching was too severe a punishment for the crime committed, local historians have depicted the black as being so totally worthless that the loss of his life was of no great concern. The person might be innocent of rape or murder, but surely he had been involved

7. Louisville *Courier-Journal*, June 8, 1894, March 9, 29, 1898.

8. *History of Union County, Kentucky* (Evansville, 1886), 380–83; Edward Coffman, *The Story of Logan County* (Nashville, 1962), 229–30.

in petty crimes and was thus a burden to the community. A typical comment comes from the book on Bath County by John A. Richards. In describing the lynching of Sam Bascom, who had been accused of arson, Richards explains that the mob failed to give Bascom a chance to prove his innocence. Nevertheless, Bascom "was a well known but indolent colored citizen who loafed in and around town." Alfred Holt was lynched in Owensboro on Christmas Day, 1896, for the murder of a police officer. Writing more than forty years later, William F. Hayes expressed no regret over the lynching: "As I remember him after all these years, Alf Holt was a typical 'darky' in appearance, chocolate colored and thick lipped. In character, like many of his race, but a larger portion then I think than now, he was ignorant, shiftless and given to drink, but he had not been considered dangerous."[9]

In his book *Southern Outrages: A Statistical Record of Lawless Doings*, Robert C. O. Benjamin, a black lawyer and newspaper editor who settled in Lexington in 1897, detailed some of the lynchings that occurred in the 1890s and challenged whites over the causes for these violent acts. Writing in a style that would be adopted by the NAACP when reporting on lynchings, Benjamin pointed out that rape was a smoke screen for the real issue—the determination of southerners to keep blacks at the bottom of society. "It is only since the Negro has become a citizen and a voter that this charge has been made. It has come along with the pretended and baseless fear of Negro supremacy. It is an effort to divest the Negro of his friends by giving him a revolting and hateful reputation." Benjamin dedicated his book to the "Widows and Orphans of the Murdered Black Men of the SOUTH."[10]

Writing in the early 1900s, Mary Church Terrell, an Afro-American woman who worked unceasingly throughout her long life to end racial injustices, agreed with Benjamin that rape was not the real cause for lynchings in the South. Race hatred, she forcefully argued, "the hatred of a stronger people toward a weaker who were once held as slaves," led to lynchings, as did a spirit of lawlessness that prevailed throughout the South. Terrell concluded that rape was simply the

---

9. Richards, *An Illustrated History of Bath County*, 235–36; William Foster Hayes, *Sixty Years of Owensboro, 1883–1943* (Owensboro, 1943), 374–77.

10. Robert C. O. Benjamin, *Southern Outrages: A Statistical Record of Lawless Doings* (N.p., 1894).

pretext for lynchings but ultimately not the cause of mob violence against Afro-Americans.[11]

The reason whites and blacks debated lynchings is obvious: Throughout the nation more than three thousand people were executed by "Judge Lynch" in the last quarter of the nineteenth century. As stated before, it is important to remember that while many lynchings were held in public and carried out in a dramatic fashion, some might have been conducted in secret. This was probably more true during the 1930s and 1940s, but no one can say for certain when this furtiveness actually started. Because of this possibility and, often, the absence of newspaper accounts and investigations by coroners, the exact number of lynchings is unknown.

Furthermore, in some of the cases of violent deaths, it is extremely difficult to determine whether the victims had been lynched or killed when attempting to defend themselves. The NAACP's study of lynchings between 1889 and 1918 lists the death of Robert Shaw, a black sharecropper in Hancock County, as a lynching. By my definition, this tragic death was not a lynching. After spending more than an hour in prayer on Sunday, May 21, 1905, Shaw threatened to kill several fellow sharecroppers. Convinced that her husband was insane, Shaw's wife notified the sheriff, who came to arrest him. By that time, Shaw, armed with a double-barreled shotgun and a huge amount of ammunition, had barricaded himself in a cabin. He fired upon the sheriff and his deputies. Over the next two days, Shaw kept at bay some three hundred men who had surrounded his cabin. Described as an expert marksman, he killed a deputy sheriff and wounded seven other men. Eventually someone crawled close enough to set the cabin on fire, and Shaw, unable to stop the spreading flames, emerged from the burning building with a gun in his hand. He was immediately cut down by a hail of gunfire. As he lay dying, a group of men attempted to hang him anyway but were prevented from doing so by the sheriff.[12]

In September, 1910, John O'Bryan, a black man, allegedly assaulted John Ashby, a deputy sheriff. A white newspaper reported that when O'Bryan was eventually cornered by a posse, he pointed a gun at Ashby, who shot first, killing the black man instantly. Ashby was ex-

11. Mary Church Terrell, "Lynching From A Negro's Point of View," *North American Review*, CLXXVII (1904), 853–68.

12. Louisville *Courier-Journal*, May 23, 1905.

onerated by reason of self-defense. It is possible that O'Bryan surrendered but that Ashby shot and killed him anyway. In other words, though Ashby's death is not listed as a lynching, it could very well have been one.[13] In both the Shaw and the Ashby cases, much doubt exists about what actually happened because the only source of information is white newspapers, which were often very biased against Afro-Americans.

Because Afro-Americans were frequently lynched in a dramatic fashion to warn others, it is possible that much more is known about their deaths than about those of the whites who died at the hands of lynch mobs. Unquestionably, the number of whites lynched in the remote mountain regions of the state, where the people had long believed in taking justice into their own hands, is unknown. The New York *Times* contained several articles in 1877 on outlaw gangs operating at will in Wayne and Carter counties in eastern Kentucky. Conditions were such that the governor sent the state militia to end the violence. In Breathitt County, several white gangs vied for supremacy. Among the many men hanged was a black man who had been recruited by the Strong family to take part in the mountain warfare. Arrested for harboring a fugitive, the black man was lynched along with a member of the Strong gang.[14]

Much of the white-on-white violence that resulted in lynchings started during Reconstruction and continued for decades. For years, the Simmons gang had operated in Owen and Henry counties, and its members were the prime suspects in many robberies, horse and cattle thefts, and cold-blooded murders. Jim Simmons and four members of his band were arrested at last in September, 1877. Several nights later, a mob seized the Simmons gang from the Henry County jail and lynched them. When investigating the many murders that had occurred in Henry and Owen counties, Judge John McManama proclaimed: "The blood of the slain cries for justice. Human life in Kentucky is not worth the snappings of a man's finger. . . . Acres of grass grow on graves of murdered men in my district." Two years later, the *Times* did a story entitled "Life Held Cheap in Kentucky: The Record of Murders and Murderous Assaults in Five Years." Based on a report

13. Owensboro *Messenger*, September 9, 1910.

14. New York *Times*, July 9, 10, November 24, 1877; Work Projects Administration, *In the Land of Breathitt* (Northport, N.Y., n.d.), 64–71.

of homicide within 20 counties in Kentucky, the report listed 717 homicides, an average of 36 for each county. "These statistics do not by any means cover all crimes of murder and malicious shooting and stabbing in the twenty counties, as they are confined to court records, and very many criminals have never been brought before courts." On several occasions in the 1880s, the *Times* ran stories about people forming vigilante committees to rid their communities of thieves and murderers. In 1883, for example, the paper noted, "A graphic picture of life in the remote neighborhoods of Kentucky have been unveiled recently in the accounts of the execution, without the formality of jury trial, of the leaders of a band of outlaws who have kept Caldwell, Hopkins, and Webster Counties in a state of excitement for years." Clearly, Kentucky's reputation as a violent place was well deserved.[15]

Despite the impossibility of knowing the exact number of whites and blacks who died at the hands of mobs, much can still be learned about lynchings from the figures gathered by the NAACP, the Tuskegee Institute, and the Chicago *Tribune,* and from stories in state and local newspapers. According to these and other sources, Kentucky had at least 353 people (258 blacks, 89 whites, and 6 unknowns) who were summarily executed.[16] The figures reveal that Afro-Americans accounted for 73 percent of the people lynched in Kentucky. At first glance, the figures seem to show that Ayers, Williamson, and others are correct—that the greatest number of lynchings occurred during

15. Mariam Sidebottom Houchens, *History of Owen County, Kentucky* (Owenton, Ky., n.d.), 89; New York *Times,* September 5, 6, October 16, November 11, 1877, September 24, November 18, 1879, March 5, 1883, July 24, 1885. For detailed accounts of white-on-white violence in Kentucky, see James Klotter, "Feuds in Appalachia: An Overview," *Filson Club History Quarterly,* LVI (July, 1982), 290–317, and William L. Montell, *Killings: Folk Justice in the Upper South* (Lexington, 1986).

16. I investigated every lynching cited by the NAACP, the Tuskegee Institute, and the Chicago *Tribune.* I then took a very conservative approach, deciding not to count many of the murders these sources concluded were lynchings. Incidents in which blacks apparently had weapons and were thus in a position to defend themselves, even if they were greatly outnumbered, have not been counted as lynchings. Also, several murders in the early 1900s that were attributed to the Night Riders of western Kentucky have not been included. For example, the NAACP lists the lynching of a white man in Goff, on April 1, 1910. In 1914, according to the NAACP, the Night Riders lynched twelve blacks, one of whom was Henry Alley in Hillside, as well as ten people in Rochester, Butler County, on November 13. No other sources could be found to substantiate these killings, and I have therefore not included them in my count of 353 lynchings in Kentucky.

TABLE 2   Lynchings by Decade

Decade	Blacks	Whites	Unknown	Total
1860–69	40	12	4	56
1870–79	58	22	2	82
1880–89	33	20		53
1890–99	66	26		92
1900–1909	41	3		44
1910–19	13	4		17
1920–29	6	1		7
1930–39	1	1		2

TABLE 3   Lynchings During Three Different Periods

Period	Blacks	Whites	Unknown	Total	% of Total Lynchings
1865–1874	87	24	6	117	33.1
1875–1899	110	56		166	47.0
1900–1934	61	9		70	19.9

the second period, which includes the late 1880s through the early 1890s (see Table 3). But when looking closer at the figures (and especially when viewing them in Appendix A, which lists each lynching individually), clearly the greatest number of lynchings occurred during the period immediately after the Civil War, from 1865 to 1874, when 117 people were the victims of lynch mobs. Without question, this ten-year period, along with the remainder of the 1870s, was the heyday of lynching in Kentucky. In 1870, an extremely violent year, 36 people died at the hands of lynch mobs. Furthermore, there is clearly an undercount of the number of lynchings for the 1870s, since none were found for 1875. Considering that there were five lynchings in 1874 and in 1876, in all likelihood there were several in 1875 as well.

Although lynchings occurred throughout the state, blacks were far more likely to be lynched in western and central Kentucky, the areas of the greatest concentration of blacks. That the number of blacks lynched in eastern Kentucky was small is not surprising, since only a handful of blacks lived in that area at the turn of the century. In 1900, some of the mountain counties had fewer than twenty black residents each. The vast majority of Kentucky's black population lived in Louisville and in Jefferson County, in the central Kentucky area around Lexington, and in an area in southwest Kentucky. Louisville had the largest number of blacks, about 44,000. An even greater concentration of Afro-Americans, however, lived in the twenty counties around Lexington and Fayette County. In 1900, Fayette County had 15,409 blacks; Boyle, Clark, and Franklin counties each had about 5,000 and Madison County had 6,690. In several of these counties, blacks made up as much as a third of the population. Region 2, especially Christian, Henderson, Daviess, and Hopkins counties, had a large concentration of blacks (see Map 1). In Christian County, for example, blacks composed 43.7 percent of the population.[17]

Regions 1, 2, and 4 accounted for 255 of the state's lynchings (Table 4). Jackson Purchase, comprising only seven counties, had 49 lynchings, most of which occurred in Fulton County (20 lynchings), and Graves County (13)—two of the counties with the most lynchings in the entire state. That western and central Kentucky had the most lynchings was consistent with the trend throughout the South, where the areas of the greatest concentration of blacks usually witnessed the most lynchings. That the Louisville metropolitan region had the fewest lynchings also follows the general pattern in the South, for lynchings were not common in the largest urban areas.

Why did so many of the state's lynchings occur in Fulton and Graves counties of Region 1 and in several counties in Region 2? Although many outsiders refer to Kentucky as a border state, the state's white citizens have always taken pride in their southern culture. Even more specifically, the white residents of Regions 1 and 2 have long prided themselves as southerners, pointing to their Confederate ties (though, of course, no area in Kentucky officially withdrew from the Union). Scholars have speculated that the people who settled in Region 1 came from North Carolina and Tennessee, bringing with them southern attitudes and culture. During the antebellum period, Kentucky for the most part was not a place of large plantations, though a few did (and still do) exist in the southwestern part of the state. That

17. U.S. Census Bureau, *Negroes in the United States, 1920–1932* (Washington, D.C., 1935), 15.

TABLE 4   Lynchings by Region

Region	Blacks	Whites	Unknown	Total
1. Jackson Purchase	44	5		49
2. Western Kentucky	81	18	1	100
3. Louisville Metro	3	2		5
4. Central Kentucky	83	20	3	106
5. Northern Kentucky	21	14		35
6. Eastern Kentucky	12	26	1	39
7. S. Central Kentucky	14	4	1	19

region was also the only section where cotton, itself a major symbol of plantation life in the Old South, was grown. Indeed, in Region 1, which borders the Mississippi River, many of the plantations are very much like those found along the Mississippi Delta. While other parts of the state, especially the region around Louisville and the suburbs of Cincinnati, found markets in the North, the southwestern part looked south, to Nashville, to sell its goods. This encouraged all the more the southern attitude on race of Regions 1 and 2. A final factor has to be the violent legacy of both regions, making them rivals with the eastern Kentucky mountain area for the claim as the most violent part of the Bluegrass State.[18]

An examination of when and where lynchings took place within Kentucky reveals that mob violence often occurred in cycles. Logan County experienced its first lynching in October, 1883, and from that point through 1895, thirteen lynchings took place. In the small Logan County community of Auburn, five blacks were lynched in 1886 alone: the first one, on March 10, for attempted rape; exactly two weeks later, three blacks, for attempted rape; five weeks later, yet another person, for attempted rape. Four lynchings occurred in or near Cadiz, Trigg County, in the early 1900s. In January, 1906, a black man was lynched for attempted rape. Two years later, another black man, Tom Weaver, was killed by Night Riders. The next year, in April, 1909,

18. Hughie G. Lawson, "Geographical Origins of White Migrants to Trigg and Calloway Counties in the Ante-bellum Period," *Filson Club History Quarterly*, LVII (July, 1983), 286–305; Daniel J. Singal, *The War Within* (Chapel Hill, 1982), 345–46.

Bennie Brame, a young black, was lynched in Hopkinsville, in nearby Christian County, for attempted rape. Several months later, Wallace Miller, also black, was lynched in Cadiz for attempting to rape a white woman. Three lynchings occurred in Shelby County in three decades. In July, 1891, a black man, Sam Pulliam, was killed for rape. On the night of October 2, 1901, Jimbo Fields and Clarence Garnett, both young blacks who had been accused of murder, were lynched. Then in 1911, two more black men, Wade Patterson and Eugene Marshall, died at the hands of lynchers.

In western Kentucky, seven men died at the hands of mobs from December 18 to 26, 1896. The first lynching occurred in Logan County when three whites, Arch, Dink, and Bill Proctor, were killed. On November 24, 1895, Arch had killed two men in the small community of Adairville. His father, Dink, and brother Bill were charged with being accessories to the crime. The Proctors had three separate trials; no verdict was reached in any of them. On the night of December 18, about one hundred men took Dink and Arch from the jail and hanged them from a cedar tree. Bill, described by the New York *Times* as "powerful and courageous," had sworn that no mob would ever take him out of a jail cell alive. He was shot an estimated thirty times. As the *Times* stated, "Though numbering over 100, the mob were afraid to risk their skin and shot him, in a cowardly fashion, through the door of his cell." The lynching of Bill Proctor was probably viewed as justice by the citizens of Logan County: He was one of four men who had been charged with the July 19, 1894, hanging of Edwin Traughber, a "white bad man" from Adairville. Reputedly, Bill had killed several other men and had been tried on four different occasions for his life but had always escaped, "and this fact caused the mob to take the law into its own hands in the present case."[19]

In Owensboro, on Christmas Day, a mob spirited Alfred Holt, a black man, from jail and hanged him from a tree in the courthouse yard. Holt had been charged with the murder of a police officer and was to go on trial the next day. The county judge and prosecuting attorney, both confident that the law would have punished Holt, harshly condemned the actions of the mob. Several days after the inci-

19. Chicago *Tribune*, December 19, 1896; New York *Times*, December 19, 20, 1896.

dent, the Owensboro Ministerial Association, a white organization, met and unanimously adopted a resolution calling Holt's lynching "a flagrant violation of decency and order; a clearly defined murder and a most unprovoked interference with the civil court."[20]

During the same week that the Proctors and Holt were lynched, three blacks died at the hands of a mob in Mayfield, leading to the threat of a race war in the city. Will Haley, white, and Henry Finley, black, sustained minor injuries during an argument. Late that evening, a white mob shot Finley to death. Commenting on the murder, the local newspaper explained, "The citizens in the section in which the negro lived, while deploring the necessity of violence, are glad to be rid of him, as he appears to have been a bad man and one whom the community can well afford to spare."[21] The very next day, Jim Stone, in jail on a charge of rape, was carried to the courthouse yard and hanged. The mob pinned a note to his body listing the names of several blacks who were to leave town or suffer the same fate. Tom Chambers, a black alleged to be involved in shady activities, armed himself in anticipation of the mob. Chambers opened fire on his attackers when they came to destroy his establishment, repulsing them. In response to Chambers' act of meeting violence with violence, practically every white man and boy in Mayfield and the surrounding countryside armed himself. By daylight, several hundred whites had assembled at the courthouse, poised for an attack from blacks. Every road into town was watched. That afternoon, a local black, Will Suett, arrived by train from St. Louis. Unaware of the recent lynchings but afraid of the armed men, Suett started running away as soon as the mob approached him. Refusing to halt on command, he was killed in a hail of gunfire. The death of this innocent man seemed to take much of the fight from the angry whites. They now realized that no group of blacks was making plans to attack the town. City officials ordered everyone (white as well as black) off the streets by 10 P.M. and declared that Suett's death was unprovoked.

20. Hayes, *Owensboro*, 374–77; Chicago *Tribune*, December 27, 1896; Louisville *Courier-Journal*, December 27, 29, 1896.

21. See the extensive coverage in the New York *Times*, December 22–26, 1896, of events in Mayfield; Chicago *Tribune*, December 24, 1896; Louisville *Courier-Journal*, December 25, 1896.

Some white citizens immediately announced their intention to raise funds to help support his aged mother.

The *Courier-Journal* reprinted comments from fourteen newspapers about the "lynching wave" in the state during the last week of December, 1896. In general, white editors in areas removed from the lynchings called upon state officials to end the violence. A number of harsh, sarcastic comments were made by out-of-state journals. "It was a Merry Christmas week in Kentucky—six lynchings within six days. But while this may be a joyous way of celebrating in Kentucky, we can not regard it with unmixed feelings of satisfaction from the standpoint of the country at large. If this thing continues there may be a joint Turkish and Spanish intervention in our domestic affairs in behalf of humanity." Although three of the people lynched were not black, another paper added, "In Kentucky this Christmas the favorite decoration of trees is strangled negroes."[22]

The causes for most of Kentucky's lynchings can be determined. To be sure, one must use caution when accepting the word of lynchers on why they took the law into their own hands and on whether the person was actually guilty of any offense. As Frederick Douglass noted, "When the will of the mob is accomplished, when its thirst for blood has been quenched, when its victim is speechless, silent and dead, his mobocratic accusers and murderers of course have the ear of the world all to themselves, and the world, hearing only the testimony of the mob, generally approves its verdict."[23] Given that no trial was held and few if any records exist, it is virtually impossible to determine guilt or innocence. Throughout this study, in the cases where a man was lynched for the alleged rape and murder of a woman, his lynching has been listed under rape, since this is the category that whites most often proclaimed as the cause of lynchings. Undoubtedly there were instances where rape was alleged as a way of securing tacit approval for the lynching. Therefore, we can assume that the figures for rape as a cause for lynching are inflated and that more people were actually lynched for murder and other reasons. Indeed, murder and attempted murder constitute the largest cause for lynchings, fol-

22. Louisville *Courier-Journal*, December 30, 1896.
23. Philip S. Foner (ed.), *The Life and Writings of Frederick Douglass* (New York, 1955), IV, 493.

TABLE 5   Causes of Lynchings

Causes	Blacks	Whites	Un-known	Total	% of Total Lynch-ings
Rape and attempted rape	85	16		101	28.6
Murder and attempted murder	62	41		103	29.1
Other	111	32	6	149	42.2

lowed by rape and attempted rape, and a wide variety of causes including theft, arson, known criminal status, robbery, and horse stealing (Table 5).

Twenty-eight percent of the people, white and black, lynched in Kentucky were killed for charges of rape or attempted rape; this figure is slightly higher than the percentage cited for the South and for the nation overall. Significantly, however, when considering blacks only, the figures show that rape was the number one cause for lynchings: 85 were lynched for rape or attempted rape, 62 for murder or attempted murder. That more blacks were lynched for rape than for murder reinforced what the majority of whites believed about lynchings. Actually, those 85 lynchings for rape or attempted rape accounted for only 33 percent of all lynchings of blacks (258). In no state in the South did rape as a cause for lynching approach 50 percent, even though the rape of white women was cited so often as the cause for lynchings that it became the gospel among practically all white Americans. President Theodore Roosevelt, who had a blind spot when it came to racial matters, said that "the greatest existing cause of lynching is the perpetration, especially by black men of the heinous crime of rape—the most abominable in all the category of crimes, even worse than murder." Although denouncing lynchings as acts of lawlessness, the president clearly believed that rapists should be dealt with quickly and firmly: "Moreover, in my judgment, the crime of rape should always be punished with death, as is the case with murder; assault with intent to commit rape should be made a capital crime, at least in the discretion of the court; and provision should be made by which the punishment may follow immediately upon the heels of the offense; while the trial should be so conducted that the victim need not be wantonly shamed while giving testimony, and that the least possible publicity shall be given to the details."[24]

When investigating lynchings in the early 1900s, Ray Stannard Baker, an "enlightened progressive," clearly blamed Afro-Americans for the lynchings resorted to by whites. In both the North and the South, he said, "I found that this floating, worthless negro caused most of the trouble." Their crimes were marked by an almost "animal-like ferocity." After thoroughly evaluating Baker's comments, one of his biographers has concluded, "Given the enormity of the crime of lynching, Baker's objectivity and his clear sympathy for lynchers as well as lynched seem now a cruel distortion." By contrast, another white writing in the early 1900s, W. D. Sheldon, strongly denounced lynchings under any circumstances and refused to accept the contention that the brutal criminal acts committed by Afro-Americans justified whites violating their own laws.[25]

Willis D. Weatherford, a southerner who considered himself to be working to end lynchings, explained in an address before the Southern Sociological Congress that the main cause of lynchings was the assaults on white women, committed primarily by black men. "I think there can be no doubt that a considerable amount of crime on the part of colored men against white men and women is due to a spirit of getting even. Not getting even with any particular individual, but just an indefinite getting even with the white race." Weatherford told his large, white audience that the argument being advanced by southerners—that lynchings would prevent other rapes from occurring—was erroneous: "Negroes have been known to assault white women on the way home from a most horrible and revolting lynching scene." Education, respect for the legal system and for the virtue of all women,

24. *A Compilation of the Messages and Papers of the Presidents* (20 vols.; New York, 1917), XVI, 7029–33; Thomas G. Dyer, *Theodore Roosevelt and the Idea of Race* (Baton Rouge, 1980), 114–15; Shapiro, *White Violence and Black Response*, 107.

25. Ray Stannard Baker, "What Is A Lynching? A Study of Mob Justice, South and North," *McClure's Magazine*, XXIV (January, 1905), 299–314 (February, 1905), 422–30; Robert C. Bannister, *Ray Stannard Baker: The Mind and Thought of A Progressive* (New Haven, 1966), 128; W. D. Sheldon, "Shall Lynching Be Suppressed, and How?" XXXVI (September, 1906), 225–33.

black as well as white, he concluded, were the only ways to end lynchings.[26]

Weatherford's comments are remarkable, but they may be representative of a person who was considered an enlightened white in the early twentieth century. His strong assertions that Afro-Americans were less advanced intellectually than whites and that blacks did in fact rape white women helped to justify lynchings. If Weatherford is at all typical of the southern whites who denounced lynchings, it is certainly debatable what impact they had on the practice coming to an end.

Not surprisingly, a number of Afro-American leaders sharply disputed this claim that the rape of white women was the actual reason for many lynchings. Francis J. Grimké, a prominent minister in Washington, D.C., explained that so often when the charge of rape was made, the black man and white woman involved had previously had a romantic relationship. Because the affair had become public or because the woman felt spurned, the claim of rape was convenient to end the matter and save the purity of the woman. Grimké discounted the claims of white lynchers that black men usually confessed their crimes of rape before being put to death. There is no reason for the Negro to confess, he reasoned, for to be guilty of such an offense meant certain death anyway. The purpose of these alleged confessions, just like the purpose of charging rape in the first place, was to provide an excuse for the lynching. "And so, the temptation always is to say, he confessed. Of course, if he confessed, that puts his guilt beyond all doubt, and his execution, though in an unlawful way, doesn't seem quite so bad as lynching an innocent man, or one about whose guilt there is some doubt." Newspaper editors Ida Wells-Barnett and Robert C. O. Benjamin published statistics showing that in no more than a third of the cases of lynchings was rape or attempted rape cited as the cause. Impartial court trials, both forcefully argued, would have reduced the number even further.[27]

26. Willis D. Weatherford, "Lynching: Removing Its Causes," address delivered before the Southern Sociological Congress, New Orleans, La., April 14, 1916.

27. Francis J. Grimké, *The Lynching of Negroes in the South: Its Causes and Remedy* (Washington, D.C., June, 1899), 14–15, 36–37, 43–44; Ida Wells-Barnett, *A Red Record: Lynchings in the United States, 1892–1893–1894* (Chicago, 1895); Benjamin, *Southern Outrages*.

Although one may argue with Grimké about romantic relationships between black men and white women, he was correct in saying that the cry of rape helped justify the practice of lynching. As Joel Williamson explains, to say that blacks were lynched for attacking white women was a way for whites to gain widespread acceptance for their lawless acts. He argues that the real reason for lynchings was to keep blacks in their place. The generation of Afro-Americans reaching maturity in the decades after the Civil War were viewed as aggressive and lacking in the qualities their parents and grandparents had acquired while under the control of slaveowners. A lynching was a just punishment for a black deemed guilty of some transgression, but just as important, it was a warning to others as well. Agreeing with Williamson, Suzanne Lebsock explains: "It was after the war that the mythology of rape became a prominent feature of white southern thinking. What more efficient way to reestablish the dominance of white men? The belief that black men were bent on raping white women justified the suppression of any form of black male assertiveness."[28]

White newspapers in Kentucky described the Afro-Americans accused of rape in derogatory terms. Such labels as "black fiend," "ape-like," "Darwin's missing link," and "beast" were used repeatedly. The expression "negro brute" seems to have been especially popular. The *Courier-Journal*, perhaps the state's most enlightened white newspaper, ran some headlines in bold letters, announcing, "A Black Ravisher Receives Proper Attention at the Hands of Judge Lynch" and "A Black Devil Hanged to a Tree Near Campbellsville: His Crime the Attempted Outrage of a Helpless Young Woman." On one occasion, an editor for the paper attempted to resort to wit when describing the lynch victim: "Blackbird on a Cherry Tree."[29]

White newspapers gave details on the method used to kill the victim and the manner in which he faced death; and because they viewed the black as deserving the punishment, the reporters often wrote about the lynching in what they thought to be a humorous manner. Regarding the lynching of Jim Mitchell in Mount Sterling for rape, the

28. Williamson, *The Crucible of Race,* 111–39; Ayers, *Vengeance and Justice,* 223–65; Suzanne Lebsock, *The Free Women of Petersburg: Status and Culture in a Southern Town, 1784–1860* (New York, 1984), 248.

29. Louisville *Courier-Journal,* June 16, 1882, March 15, 1888, June 1, 1892.

Courier-Journal correspondent said: "His captors took him to a railroad trestle, about half a mile from town, strung him up for safekeeping and left him. The lifeless body was cut down by the coroner this morning and planted. The general impression is that Judge Lynch did a very good job, considering the brief time the court had in which to make up its mind." Several years later, when discussing the lynching of Sam Scales in northern Kentucky, the same newspaper found humor in the fact that the black man acted cowardly when taken by the mob. The paper quoted at length an anonymous member of the mob who talked about the fun they had at Scales's expense: "Oh but that nigger did plead for mercy and go on like a baby. He didn't have no nerve at all. They pulled him out, though, threw him into a wagon and started down the pike with him to the woods, he a hollerin' and all the gang a yelling and firing their guns. . . . Scales begged awful hard to get off and said he wasn't guilty, but it was no go."[30]

Sympathy was always reserved for the woman who had been the victim of the black rapist. These women were described as being frail, yet brave; they had done everything possible to prevent the attack. That the woman was beautiful, the flower of the community, was always cited. One could logically assume from the newspaper accounts that every woman attacked was a member of one of the very best families in the community: "Miss Ella Dice . . . belongs to one of the best families in Adair County"; "Mrs. Glenn belongs to one of the best families in the county. She was a Miss Hettie Ballow, and about two years ago was married to Thomas J. Glenn, a prosperous and highly respected young farmer." It is ironic that one of the main justifications for lynchings—sparing white women the humiliation of court trials where all of the facts would be aired—was consistently ignored by the press. In account after account of lynchings, the white newspapers gave the woman's name, specific information about the attack, and how she somehow escaped to safety.[31] In speeches and articles during the 1890s, Frederick Douglass challenged whites about the necessity of resorting to lynchings to protect the modesty of white women, pointedly noting that their justifications were "contemptible and hypocritical." He wrote:

30. *Ibid.*, June 16, 1882, September 12, 1885.
31. *Ibid.*, July 21, 1891, June 1, 1892.

It is not only mock modesty, but mob modesty. Men who can collect hundreds and thousands of their kind . . . thirsting for vengeance, and can spread before them in the tempest and whirlwind of vulgar passion, the most disgusting details of crime, connecting the names of women with the same, should not be allowed to shelter themselves under any pretence of modesty. Such a pretence is absurd and shameless upon the face of it. Who does not know that the modesty of womanhood is always and in every such case an object for special protection in a court of law? On the other hand, who does not know that a lawless mob, composed in part of the basest men, can have no such respect for the modesty of women, as has a court of law? No woman need be ashamed to confront one who has insulted or assaulted her in any court of law. Besides, innocence does not hesitate to come to the rescue of justice, and need not even in this case.[32]

An important part of the entire rape ritual was for the white woman to identify the rapist. This too was ironic, since lynchers claimed that their actions were calculated to avoid the possibility of the woman ever again coming face to face with her attacker. Nannie Berry of Nicholas County was dragged into the woods and raped in July, 1879. After the man left, Berry proceeded to town and informed officials. A light-skinned Afro-American, John Breckinridge, was caught and taken before Berry, even though she was at home confined to bed. She quickly identified him as the "mulatto" who attacked her. At first, the mob turned Breckinridge over to the authorities but then quickly returned to the jail and lynched him. On another occasion in the same county, William Tyler was accused of the rape of Anna Campbell. The girl's father led a mob in breaking down the jail door with sledge hammers and seizing Tyler. Words were exchanged between the alleged rapist and the father of the victim. Tyler said: "Gentlemen, I am innocent of this. I did not do it. I am not guilty." Campbell responded: "Yes you are. My little girl said you did." That, of course, was enough. As the paper reported in its usual way of justifying the hanging, "The mob, which throughout the entire proceeding had conducted itself in a most orderly manner, consistent with its never-lost-sight-of object, formed a perfect cordon around the prisoner and took its stand upon the bridge." Mrs. Peter Crow was raped in July, 1889. After the attack, Mrs. Crow,

32. Foner (ed.), *The Writings of Douglass,* IV, 500.

who was described as a "small, delicate lady" (compared with the heavyset rapist, who weighed more than two hundred pounds), was confined to bed. Suspicion centered on Jim Kelly, who had been seen in the vicinity of where the rape had supposedly taken place. The mob spirited Kelly out of the Paris jail, intent on taking him to the home of Mrs. Crow to go over the details of the rape one last time. Her rapist, she had already told the leader of the mob, would be known by the scratch marks she had made on his face. Kelly did, in fact, have several scratch marks, though he said he had been in a fight with a tramp. After Mrs. Crow made a positive identification of Kelly, the mob carried out the lynching.[33]

In the majority of cases, no one challenged the word of a white woman when she identified her attacker. But assuming that a rape or even an attempted rape had occurred, it would have been understandable for the woman to be so upset that she might have been unable to identify the rapist; even worse, she might have identified the wrong person as the attacker. A few newspaper accounts, which were overwhelmingly unsympathetic toward blacks accused of crimes, suggest that the woman's memory of the attack left something to be desired. On December 14, 1892, Katie Anderson of Bowling Green claimed that she had been raped by an unidentified black man. After an investigation lasting several days, the police arrested Bob Harper. Because of the efforts of police, Harper was protected from the mob and came to trial two weeks after the alleged rape had taken place. The newspaper reported that Anderson "was very slow to make a statement implicating the negro, and it was only by dint of the most persistent questioning that she finally said that according to her best knowledge and belief Harper was the man who assaulted her." When summarizing the events of the first day of the examining trial (that this phase of the trial for a black man accused of rape lasted for more than one day was remarkable), the reporter concluded: "Miss Anderson's identification is not positive enough to warrant the more conservative thinking people in taking the law into their own hands, and this is all that saved Harper's life. It is now thought the trial will be permitted to

33. New York *Times*, July 14, 15, 1879; Louisville *Courier-Journal*, July 27, 1889, July 26, 1894. For another example of a woman identifying an alleged rapist, see the Louisville *Courier-Journal*, June 10, 1892.

come to a close. Public opinion is still divided as to the negro's guilt, and only a thorough investigation will determine it one way or the other."[34]

The newspaper's statement that Anderson identified Harper under persistent questioning is totally misleading in light of the exact words that were said at the examining trial. The official stenographer of Warren County Circuit Court, R. J. Jarboe, wrote down the young woman's testimony. Anderson was interviewed at great length by the prosecuting attorney, James C. Sims, and by William L. Dulaney, a prominent judge serving as one of Harper's attorney's. It was clearly established that the man had worn a mask and a bonnet when he first attacked Anderson, but he had willingly removed those items during the assault. This is important because Anderson had known Harper for years and had seen him recently. Some of the testimony follows.

> Q. HAVE YOU EVER SEEN THE MAN WHO COMMITTED THAT ASSAULT UPON YOU SINCE HE DID COMMIT IT?
> A. I DON'T KNOW.
> Q. Please tell the court whether either of the prisoners you have examined this evening, and sitting in this room, whether either one of them is the man that assaulted you and inflicted those wounds upon your person?
> A. (Witness looks at her father and says: "Papa, I don't know what to say.")
> Question by Judge H. B. Hines: It is necessary, in order that I can try the case, that you make some answer.
> A. (Witness does not answer.)
> Miss Cora Anderson [Katie Anderson's sister]: "You have thought now enough to answer it."
> Judge H. B. Hines: Miss Katie, can't you answer that question for us? If you can't answer, say so; and if you can answer, tell us. That is all we want to know. If you don't know, say so; and if you do, tell it.
> A. (Witness does not answer.)
> Q. Miss Katie, can you answer it?
> A. I don't know. To the best of my knowledge the last one that stood up (Harper) looks more like him than anyone I have seen yet.
> Q. Do you know Bob Harper?
> A. Yes, sir.
> Judge W. L. Dulaney on cross-examination:
> Q. Bob Harper was brought up to your house several times, was he not?

---

34. Louisville *Courier-Journal,* December 28, 1892.

A. Yes, sir.

Q. On that occasion didn't you look at Bob Harper and say he was not the man.

A. YES, SIR.

Q. And didn't you ask why they brought that man Harper there, and said there was no use in bringing him?

A. Yes, sir.[35]

The next morning as the examining trial continued, a mob of one thousand surrounded the courthouse while fifty armed men marched into the courtroom and took Harper. Although it was broad daylight, no one concealed his identity. In fact, the paper reported that the leaders were all well-known citizens. In his own defense, Harper made a statement as he was being carried away: "I have tried to do everything in the world to prove my innocence. I am not guilty, and die with this on my lips. I have never done anybody any harm. I am innocent." When informed of Harper's death, Anderson said quietly that "it was a comfort to her to know that he was beyond any question the guilty man." A few days later, however, Anderson stated emphatically to the public that Harper had been the rapist: "Only the fear that he would be instantly hanged before my eyes kept me from saying so positively all the time, and I could not rid myself of this fear, and I was so nervous and frightened when I was before the court that at times I could not command my voice to talk." She had no sympathy for the murdered black man: "It was a horrible death for any human being, but I would never have been without fear as long as he was alive." The local correspondent of the *Courier-Journal* applauded the manner in which the good citizens of Bowling Green had done an unpleasant but necessary chore: "No such work was ever done before in so orderly and quiet a manner. There was no loud talking, not a shot fired and no unusual demonstration. The men who composed the crowd were a resolute and determined set, and showed that they merely meant to protect the virtue of their homes and their families, and they proceeded about the work in a business-like way. There can be no question as to Harper's guilt, and though his punishment was not brought

35. Will Hobson, *About The Hanging of Robert Harper, By A Mob, Wednesday, December 28, 1892, at Bowling Green, Ky.* (N.p., n.d.), 4–14. A copy of this important pamphlet can be found in the Department of Special Collections, Kentucky Library, Western Kentucky University, Bowling Green.

about according to the forms of law, all will admit that it was a righteous one."[36]

Several days after the lynching, Harper's other attorney, Judge Will Hobson, began interviewing a wide range of people about whether or not his client had actually raped Katie Anderson. The testimony of many different whites, including law officers, and blacks placed Harper elsewhere in town when the alleged incident occurred. In contrast with the usual statements by whites that the lynched black was a "bad negro" and a menace in the community, all the people interviewed said that Harper was an ideal citizen. Several former employers remembered the black youth as honest and considerate (one woman said he always returned the correct change after purchasing her groceries) and, if anything, extremely shy, especially around white people.[37] More than fifty years after the lynching, attorney John B. Rogers, who had attended the examining trial, wrote that Harper was innocent of the rape of Katie Anderson. He accurately recalled the name of the man who led the mob and the details of the lynching:

> The mob is a beast and should always be so described. I have seen instances of it in my lifetime. When I was studying law in Bowling Green, over half a century ago, an unforgivable crime was committed against a Miss Anderson, who lived at the outskirts of Bowling Green, at the foot of the cedar now on the Nashville Road. . . . Great excitement prevailed. A negro, Bob Harper, was arrested. An examining trial was begun at the Court House and Mr. James C. Sims (who subsequently became my law partner) was prosecuting, representing the Commonwealth. A mob marched in with guns and took the prisoner from the Judge and carried him out to the old Fairgrounds, where Laurel Avenue now is, and there hung him. I saw it all. It made me sick. There were many members of the local militia company in the group, with guns taken from the armory. It was led by a prominent man, Crit Alexander, who was a leader in the Christian Church in Bowling Green. I saw them drag the poor fellow along and at the Fairgrounds he was placed in a wagon and a noose put around his neck. I saw the man who tied the noose. The wagon was driven from beneath Harper, who I saw dangling and kicking. Then I turned away with loathing. Nothing was ever done about it. No indictment was ever returned, although the mob was unmasked. Mr. Sims was outspoken in his criticism, although he was the prosecuting attorney. He laid some blame

---

36. Louisville *Courier-Journal,* December 29, 31, 1892.
37. Hobson, *The Hanging of Robert Harper,* 16–29.

on Dr. McCormack as encouraging the mob. Your cousin, Col. Will Hobson published a pamphlet to show that Harper was innocent, but Harper was under ground and the people lost interest.[38]

Why, after it had been clearly established that Harper was innocent of the attack on Katie Anderson, did the authorities and citizens fail to reopen the case? For one thing, it meant disputing the word of the white woman, since she had publicly stated that Harper had attacked her. Furthermore, it is obvious that Bowling Green officials were unwilling to admit their mistake in allowing the wrong person to be lynched, even though it meant that the real rapist (if Katie Anderson had been assaulted) avoided prosecution. Although it would have been a relatively easy matter to investigate and arrest the lynchers, the officials refused to do this as well.

For the most part, doubt was not a factor when blacks were lynched for raping white women. Indeed, to suspect that a black was contemplating an attack on a white woman would have been enough to justify his lynching. Proof of this comes from the many instances of blacks lynched for attempted rape. The newspapers called these justified lynchings, yet their own comments suggest that the intent of the "rapist" was not always known. The lynching of a black under these circumstances had to be viewed as a warning for other potential rapists, because usually the black had done little more than scare a woman or come up suddenly on her. Cabel Gadley of Bowling Green was lynched because "he crept up behind his employer's wife and contemplated an assault." One can imagine the impossibility of Gadley trying to prove his innocence. It was his word against that of a white woman. There is no way Gadley or any other black man could win that argument during the late nineteenth century.[39]

In February, 1897, Robert Morton of Rockford, a small community near Bowling Green, was lynched not for rape or attempted rape but for writing a letter to Tommie Johnson, a white woman. The relationship, if any, between Morton and Johnson is unknown, as are the exact contents of the letter. Somehow the letter, which whites de-

38. Letter from John B. Rogers to Mary R. Rodes Helm, July 29, 1944, in the John B. Rodes Manuscript, Kentucky Library, Western Kentucky University, Bowling Green (hereinafter cited as Rodes Manuscript).

39. For examples of blacks being lynched for attempted rape, see the Louisville *Courier-Journal*, March 7, 1882, June 13, 1883, June 27, 1894.

scribed as "insulting and insinuating," became known, and Morton was arrested. A group of men overpowered the jailer and took Morton to the edge of town, where they hanged him. As usual, the white newspaper justified the lynching by stating that the twenty-one-year-old Morton "did not bear a good reputation."[40]

Five blacks were lynched for attempted rape in Logan County in 1886. The first lynching occurred in March, when twenty-five masked men broke into the Russellville jail and took Handy Woodward, the man accused of attempting to rape a twelve-year-old white girl. The lynching of Woodward "met the approbation of the community." Two weeks later, three blacks were lynched for attempting to outrage a white woman. Most of the details about that case are obscure: "Her cries brought assistance, and the alarm being given, a posse followed and captured the fiends. A mob took the prisoners from the posse and strung them to a tree, where they are still hanging."[41]

On the night of April 28, someone tried to break into the room where Daisy, Ida, and Ella Freeman were sleeping. The intended rapist had a drug that would make his victims "insensible." Screams from one of his daughters awakened L. A. Freeman. Heavily armed, he and his son began an immediate search for the suspect. Below the window they found shoe tracks that measured twelve and one-half inches. A reporter explained, "This fact directed suspicion toward the negro Meredith Jones, who was known to have the largest foot in the village." The tracks led directly to Jones's cabin, a circumstance that, to whites, was sufficient evidence to implicate Jones. The sheriff issued an arrest warrant, and Jones was detained in an adjoining community. Even though four blacks had been lynched in the small community, also for attempted rape, Jones was returned to Auburn. Predictably, a mob stormed the jail, but to their surprise the officials refused to release Jones. The mob had to settle for shooting him in his cell. As usual, the lynching was more than justified by the black victim's alleged unsavory reputation: "Meredith Jones . . . was the most disreputable character in Logan County. He was a burly negro, six feet two inches in height, and weighed about 200. His career had been a succession of crimes of more or less magnitude, and a large portion of

40. Chicago *Tribune*, February 5, 1897; Louisville *Courier-Journal*, February 5, 1897.

41. Louisville *Courier-Journal*, March 11, 24, 1886.

his life was spent in prison at different times and places. There can be no doubt that it was his purpose to outrage the persons of the young girls after he had put them all under the influence of the drug."[42]

When removing a black rapist from jail, members of the mob shunned disguises in an overt demonstration that their actions not only were right but also had the approval of the community. They were determined to punish the rapist and let other blacks know they meant business. In September, 1897, sixteen-year-old Maggie Roberts was brutally beaten and left for dead. She somehow made it home and told her father about the incident. Within an hour, Raymond Bushrod was caught and taken before Roberts, who identified him as the rapist. Bushrod was then placed in jail. Two days later, on a Sunday afternoon in the middle of a religious revival, a crowd of some eight hundred "infuriated people" took Bushrod from the jail. The leader asked Bushrod to confess his sin, and he did so in a "long and fervent prayer." He was then hanged at the courthouse. The leader of the mob made an address: "Here's the protection we offer our wives and daughters." Apparently, the women appreciated the lynching. As the reporter explained, "During the entire time of the lynching not less than 200 women were on the hill overlooking the public square, and when the negro's dangling form went up their cheers rent the air."[43]

Even in cases such as this, in which the people involved wore no masks and conducted the lynching in public, officals still refused to identify members of the mob. Indeed, the coroner of Hancock County witnessed Bushrod's hanging and cut the body down four minutes after the black man was declared dead. Nevertheless, he rendered this verdict: "Bushrod came to his death at the hands of unknown parties." Governor William O. Bradley was outraged by the lynching and the refusal of the coroner and other officials to bring the guilty parties to justice. Commenting on the Bushrod murder some three months later in his annual message to the state legislature, the governor noted: "In Hancock County, in open day and without masks or even the pretense of secrecy, a Negro was forcibly taken from the jail and hung on the public streets of Hawesville."[44]

42. *Ibid.*, April 29, 1886.

43. Chicago *Tribune*, September 26, 27, 1897; New York *Times*, September 27, 1897.

44. New York *Times*, September 27, 1897; Lexington *Daily Leader*, January 4,

The final step in the drama of lynching an Afro-American accused of rape consisted of the victim or a member of her family choosing the form of death for the rapist. Most selected a symbolic location, such as the courthouse or a tree where a lynching had occurred. Many lynchings were carefully planned; the materials for a burning were obtained even before the black person was in police custody. In cases of death by torture, it was customary to allow the aggrieved family members to inflict the first pain. In one case, a lynch mob in Fulton was led by J. M. Morris, whose wife allegedly had been assaulted by a black man. Before the man accused of attempted rape could be carried away, Morris, in a fit of anger, shot and killed him on the spot, in the custody of the authorities. Morris thereby cheated the community of a public lynching. It also meant that everyone knew who had carried out the execution. An inquest was held and the jury returned a verdict of justifiable homicide.[45]

Two highly publicized lynchings occurred during the 1890s. In both cases, whites had openly predicted that the men, accused of rape and murder, would be lynched upon their return to the communities where the crimes had taken place. Without question, all lynchings were violent and brutal deaths, but these two proved to be especially so.

The bodies of Mary and Ruby Ray of Bardwell were found on July 5, 1893. A medical investigation revealed that both girls had been raped before they were killed. The only clue was a blue coat left by the murderer/rapist. A search party was quickly formed. Out in the woods, two men fired at a distant, fleeing figure but missed him. They agreed that the man was either a white or a mulatto. Bloodhounds tracked the fugitive to the Mississippi River, where the search party learned that a fisherman had rowed a "burly yellow negro" across in his skiff.[46]

A major breakthrough in the case occurred the next morning when

---

1898. For a similar case, see the Louisville *Courier-Journal*, October 16, 1894. Willis Griffey of Princeton, Caldwell County, was hanged for the rape of a white woman. The lynchers did not conceal their identities. The story concludes, "The coroner viewed the remains . . . and returned the customary verdict."

45. Louisville *Courier-Journal*, February 22, 1895.

46. My account of the incident, in this and following paragraphs, is based largely on Wells-Barnett, *A Red Record*, 36–42, Mayfield *Monitor*, July 12, 1893, and Louisville *Courier-Journal*, July 7, 8, 1893.

a brakeman on a freight train in nearby Missouri encountered a black illegally on board the train. The black was arrested. Having received a wire to look out for a suspicious light-skinned Negro, the authorities in Sikeston, Missouri, concluded that this was the man: "They telegraphed to Bardwell that their prisoner had no coat, but wore a blue vest and pants which would perhaps correspond with the coat found at the scene of the murder, and that the names of the murdered girls were in the rings found in his possession." The black man also had a pocket knife and a razor, both of which showed traces of blood.

Upon learning of the capture of a black man, whites in the communities of Bardwell and Wickliffe openly stated that the man would be lynched as soon as he arrived in the area. A special train was taken by the victims' father, the local sheriff, and a group of indignant whites to help return the suspect from Sikeston. Although they had no warrant for the prisoner's arrest, he was turned over to them. When he saw the man, the sheriff realized that he was dark-skinned instead of "high yellow." The two men who had shot at the fleeing target disagreed whether he was the man. "The gold rings found in his possession had no names in them, as had been asserted, and John Ray said they did not belong to his daughters." Ray, who had believed up to this point that a white man had killed his daughters, did agree, however, that Miller should be taken to Bardwell. Meanwhile, back in Bardwell, arrangements were being made to "burn the negro fiend."

Before being carried to Kentucky, the suspected black murderer/rapist gave a long statement trying to prove his innocence: "My name is C. J. Miller. I am from Springfield, Ill.; my wife lives at 716 N. 2d street. I am here among you today, looked upon as one of the most brutal men before the people. I stand here surrounded by men who are excited, men who are not willing to let the law take its course, and as far as the crime is concerned, I have committed no crime, and certainly no crime gross enough to deprive me of my life and liberty to walk upon the green earth." Leaders of the mob sent a telegram to the police chief of Springfield to verify Miller's statement. Several hours later, a message returned saying that Miller did not live in Springfield. That, of course, did not prove that Miller was guilty of rape and murder. Miller was put in jail when he arrived in Bardwell. He urged the mob to compare the blood found on his knife and his hand with that of the dead girls, but that report was never made public. By this time, a mob estimated at more than five thousand, many of them having come by special trains, had gathered outside the jail, waiting for Ray to choose the style of execution. Ray, still unconvinced of Miller's guilt, said that a burning should not take place. A hanging, he said, would be acceptable. Ida Wells-Barnett gave this report:

> There was a loud yell, and a rush was made for the prisoner. He was stripped naked, his clothing literally torn from his body, and his shirt was tied around his loins. Some one declared the rope was a "white man's death," and a log-chain, nearly a hundred feet in length, weighing over one hundred pounds, was placed around Miller's neck and body, and he was led and dragged through the streets of the village in that condition followed by thousands of people. He fainted from exhaustion several times, but was supported to the platform where they first intended burning him.
>
> The chain was hooked around his neck, a man climbed the telegraph pole and the other end of the chain was passed up to him and made fast to the cross-arm. Others brought a long fork stick which Miller was made to straddle. By this means he was raised several feet from the ground and then let fall. The first fall broke his neck, but he was raised in this way and let fall a second time. Numberless shots were fired into the dangling body, for most of that crowd were heavily armed, and had been drinking all day.
>
> Miller's body hung thus exposed from three to five o'clock, during which time, several photographs of him as he hung dangling at the end of the chain were taken, and his toes and fingers were cut off. His body was taken down, and placed on the platform, the torch applied, and in a few moments there was nothing left of C. J. Miller save a few bones and ashes.

In commenting on the lynching, the Mayfield *Monitor* described Miller as "a notorious character who lived by crime." This statement proved to be completely unfounded. After his death, it was verified that he lived in Springfield, Illinois, where he was a law-abiding citizen with no criminal record. Four years later, John Ray called for reopening the case. Although he had consented to Miller's hanging, he had believed that a white man had been involved. Ray had facts that would "incriminate a white man now living in Missouri. He is the son of a prostitute who lived in Mayfield about twenty-five years ago." The local police chief agreed with these recent findings, saying that he too had believed all along that Miller was one of two men who had committed the crime. It would have been impossible for Miller alone to overcome, rape, and then kill both victims, the sheriff explained. No records exist to show whether this white man was ever apprehended. Also, it is clear that no evidence existed that placed C. J. Miller in Bardwell on the day the two girls were raped and murdered.[47]

Described by contemporary observers as the most horrifying lynching in the state's history, the murder of eighteen-year-old Richard Coleman in Maysville on December 6, 1899, brought together a number of the different aspects of lynching Afro-Americans for rape: a family member of the victim selected the form of punishment, no one wore a mask, the lynching occurred in broad daylight, local citizens knew well in advance that a lynching would occur, and officials took no steps to prevent the lynching.[48]

James Lashbrook's wife, a "beautiful, innocent woman," was raped and murdered in October, 1899. After being questioned by the police, Coleman, who worked as a farm hand for Lashbrook, was arrested and charged with the crime. Fearing for Coleman's life in light of the highly emotional nature of the crime and the numerous lynchings that had occurred in Kentucky in the 1890s, the local sheriff took Coleman to Covington for safekeeping. Eventually, the Maysville grand jury indicted Coleman for rape and murder and ordered his return for trial. Relatives of the deceased woman had traveled to Covington to maintain a vigil at the jail where Coleman was being held. Upon being told that his case would be heard in Maysville, Coleman confessed to the crime, begging to be executed in Covington without benefit of a trial. Coleman's fears proved well-founded when members of the Lashbrook family boarded the same train compartment with him and the sheriff for the ride back to Maysville.

A telegraph telling of Coleman's return had been sent ahead to Maysville. By the time the train arrived, thousands of people, led by James Lashbrook, were on hand to meet the train. The crowd had been warned by Lashbrook's family and friends not to shoot Coleman, that he would be given a slow, painful death. Even though he and his men were heavily armed, the sheriff saw his role as merely returning

47. Mayfield *Monitor*, May 12, 1897.

48. A number of sources were consulted to compile, in this and following paragraphs, the account of Coleman's lynching: New York *World*, December 7, 1899; New York *Times*, December 8, 1899; Chicago *Tribune*, December 8, 1899; Louisville *Courier-Journal*, December 8, 1899. The most vivid, gruesome account, giving a step-by-step version of the incident, can be found in the Cincinnati *Enquirer*, December 7, 8, 1899.

Coleman to the town for the mob to do with him as they wished. When he got off the train, the sheriff released Coleman to the mob when requested to do so. Lashbrook, at the sight of Coleman, told a friend that no power on earth could restrain him. A quick "trial" was held, with Coleman confessing to Lashbrook that he had killed Lashbrook's wife. The Cincinnati *Enquirer* contained the final proceedings of the "trial":

"Mr. Lashbrook, we are willing to give you the choice of three things."
"What are they?" asked the excited husband.
"First, we will turn him over to the law."
"No."
"Second, we will hang him."
"No."
"Last, we will burn him."
"Yes."
"Men," shouted the spokesman, "are you satisfied with Lashbrook's decision?"
"What is it?"
"Burn him."
"Yes," shrieked the mob, and the victim began to whine and pray for mercy.

The mob then took Coleman to the pyre, which had been selected as the execution site several weeks earlier. Lashbrook set Coleman on fire, to the roar of the crowd. Hundreds of people, from little children, who placed weeds around Coleman, to the elderly, contributed to the fire. The newspaper spoke with approval of the heroic effort of an elderly woman confined to a wheelchair who slowly and painfully made her way through the crowd to add one little piece of wood to the fire. The corpse was eventually dragged through the streets, and people cut off fingers and toes from it for souvenirs.

Several newspapers wrote editorials about the Coleman lynching. Headlined "Burned At Stake, Richard Coleman Meets Death At Hands of a Frenzied Mob," the story in the *Courier-Journal* said the lynching would hurt the citizens of Maysville, especially the youth: "It was a scene the like of which probably was never witnessed in Kentucky; certainly not since the days of Indian warfare has there been a parallel to the three hours' horrible work of the frenzied mob which tortured and burned the young negro murderer, while thousands of people looked on with mingled exclamations of horror and approbation and others turned away sickened by the awful sight." With its eye-catching headline "Negro Boy Roasted Alive in Kentucky," the New York *World* detailed the lurid events and condemned the citizens of Maysville for not stopping the mob. "Instead, when some new torture was inflicted upon the shrieking, burning boy the crowd cheered and cheered, the shrill voices of women and the piping tones of children sounding high above the roar of men."

Long an outspoken foe of lynchings, the New York *Times* suggested that a mass sickness existed among whites when punishing blacks for certain crimes real or alleged: "The murder by burning of the negro Coleman at Maysville is an outrage so terrible and so shameful that it can only be explained as an outbreak of popular delirium." There is no question that Coleman would have been executed by the law, the paper noted. But "it was due in part to the feelings that the penalty fixed by law was inadequate to the offense, and in part to a wild and uncontrollable thirst for vengeance aroused by the most infuriating of crimes." The *Times* concludes with a most telling point: "Underlying these motives and rendering them more savage was the mysterious and subtle and venomous race hatred instilled in the days of slavery. These motives in combination produced what must be called temporary insanity."

No one involved in the Coleman lynching attempted to conceal his identity. The prosecuting attorney refused to file charges against Lashbrook and the other leaders. The county judge went a step further: "I am a police Judge but for once perhaps I forgot the duties of the office. Lashbrook has my sympathy." Although not fearful of arrest, Lashbrook announced plans to leave the state immediately after the sale of his farm, his livestock, and his farming implements. Governor Bradley sent a telegraph to a leading lawyer in Maysville, asking for advice on how the state should proceed in the matter. He was told that the lynching had not been planned in advance, that the "good people had acted naturally." Moreover, the lawyer replied, the good people of Maysville would not take kindly to any attempts to punish the guilty.[49]

49. "Inability Of The Governor Of Kentucky To Bring Lynchers To Justice," *American Law Review*, XXXIV (1900), 238–39; John Edward Bruce, *The Blood Red Record: A Review of the Horrible Lynchings and Burnings of Negroes by Civilized White Men in the United States* (Albany, 1901), 3.

Although the public execution of blacks for rape received the greatest attention and most surely aroused the frenzy of the white public, more lynchings resulted from murder and attempted murder. Of the 353 lynchings in Kentucky, 103, or 29.1 percent, were for murder and attempted murder. An obvious question regarding the lynching of Afro-Americans for murder is whether or not they had actually murdered whites or had merely defended themselves. Had trials been held, some reasons might have been presented as evidence to explain why a black had killed a white. Most criminologists seem to agree that murder, to a degree not found in other criminal offenses, often involves people who are equally at fault. From the end of the Civil War forward, blacks surely knew what penalty awaited them for murdering a white. Does this mean, therefore, that a significant number of the homicides of whites by blacks were really cases of self-defense? Admittedly, this is difficult to prove, since the accounts of blacks being lynched for murder contain no court records but come from local white sources. Not surprisingly, white newspapers and local historians have repeatedly stated that for unexplained reasons, blacks killed inoffensive whites.[50]

Members of the mob usually wore disguises when lynching a black for murder. Why? Perhaps there were questions about the innocence of the murder victim. These lynchings usually occurred in the middle of the night, thereby avoiding the large public displays that seemed to characterize lynchings for rape. In January, 1886, Calvin Simpson broke into the home of Mrs. Graves in Henderson County. Awakened by the loud noise, Mrs. Graves and her two daughters fled the house. Simpson caught the older woman and beat her to death with a blunt instrument. He then broke into another house but was captured by the authorities before injuring anyone else. He informed the police that God had told him to kill Mrs. Graves because of her refusal to pray. As a reporter explained, "He feigns craziness, is desperate in speech and behavior, claims to have captured the devil and set the world free." Around two o'clock the next morning, a mob took Simpson from the jail. He reminded the mob that he had merely done

50. See the following: New York *Times,* June 24, 1876; Louisville *Commercial,* June 25, 1876, July 25, 1895; *History of Union County, Kentucky,* 380–82; Richards, *An Illustrated History of Bath County,* 235–36; Louisville *Courier-Journal,* March 15, 1888, December 10, 1889; Chicago *Tribune,* April 17, 1891.

the Lord's bidding. Before Simpson was riddled with bullets, a member of the mob said, "Up you go to the Lord."[51] Clearly, the mob knew that Simpson was insane. Yet to allow any black to kill a white was to set a bad precedent. Members of the mob also knew that public approval of their actions might not be forthcoming, so they wore masks to conceal their identities.

In Lexington around the first of January, 1878, a black named Stiver killed a white man for some unknown reason and was immediately lynched. Several weeks later, a white mob, sure that three other blacks had assisted Stiver in the murder, decided to lynch them. The mob first went to the home of Tom Turner and shot him to death in the presence of his wife. Next, Edward Claxton and John Davis were taken from their homes and hanged in the woods near Brucetown, a small community on the outskirts of town. The New York Times reported the lynchings as part of its crusade to end the practice in Kentucky. In response to the Times's story, a Lexington newspaper proclaimed that the murder of the white man and the ongoing involvement of blacks in criminal affairs had led to the lynchings. But the account of the Kentucky Gazette, like practically all others detailing the lynching of blacks for murder, failed to explain why the white man had been killed in the first place.[52]

It is possible, for example, that the murder of a white barber by a black barber in Owensboro was motivated by a problem between the two men. On the evening of December 19, 1889, Dock Jones, the black barber, entered the establishment of John Westerfield. After a few words were exchanged, Westerfield shouted: "Dock, you are drunk. I don't want to have anything to do with you. Go away." Jones responded by cursing Westerfield, who then drew his pistol and slapped the black in the face. Jones withdrew but returned about twenty minutes later and shot Westerfield dead. He was immediately arrested, but later that night a masked mob took Jones from the jail and lynched him from the same tree that had been used to hang another black, Richard May, several years earlier.[53]

Some black men were lynched after killing whites over arguments

51. Louisville Courier-Journal, January 25, 26, 1886.

52. New York Times, January 18, 28, 1878; Lexington Kentucky Gazette, January 19, 1878.

53. Louisville Courier-Journal, December 20, 1889.

concerning black women. In August, 1890, John Henderson killed Gilbert H. Satterwhite, a white farmer he had worked for in Midway. Shortly before the murder, Henderson's wife had been hired as a cook for the Satterwhites. Henderson came to Satterwhite's farm, and an argument broke out between the two men. Although the sequence of events is uncertain, Henderson was shot in the breast, though not fatally, and Satterwhite was, as described by the white newspaper, "butchered with a razor," his head almost severed from his body. If this account is correct, it is obvious that Satterwhite attacked Henderson first. After being arrested, Henderson was taken from jail to the edge of town and hanged.[54]

The very next year in Georgetown, James Dudley caught Frank Hughes, his former employer, having an affair with his wife. According to Dudley, a fight ensued in which he was severely clubbed in the head, but he somehow managed to shoot Hughes. Several whites came forward with a different version: Dudley, in a fit of anger, had threatened to kill his wife and child, and she had fled to Hughes's apartment, which was in the same boardinghouse. (Given the rigid segregation of the time, it is surprising that they lived in the same boardinghouse.) Dudley followed his wife to Hughes's room and shot him dead. A mob of 125 masked men took Dudley from jail. Before hanging him, the leader of the mob said: "Nigger your last day on earth has come. I'll give you a few minutes to say your prayers, and to make a confession." Dudley then was lynched.[55]

There were cases of blacks being lynched by whites for the murder of blacks. In the small community of Warsaw, located on the Ohio River midway between Louisville and Cincinnati, the murder, in 1876, of Lake Jones shocked the community. Ben and Mollie French, whom Jones had befriended, were arrested and charged with the crime. They had attempted to rob Jones of his money. After several days in jail, the Frenches were visited by Judge Lynch. The reason for summarily carrying out the execution on the couple is obvious: Whites thought fondly of "old" Lake Jones, who had served faithfully, before and after emancipation, a prominent white man. He was, in the estimation of

54. New York *Times*, August 22, 1890; Louisville *Courier-Journal*, August 20, 22, 1890.

55. Georgetown *Times*, August 26, September 2, 1891; Louisville *Courier-Journal*, August 28, 1891.

Warsaw whites, "the best nigger in the country." As usual in the white version of the lynching, the blacks put to death were known throughout the neighborhood for their bad reputations. The Frenches were thoroughly disliked in the community, the paper noted, and Ben was a well-known chicken thief. Two lynchings, those of Ernest Humphries in Princeton in October, 1890, and Tom Holmes in Mayfield in February, 1898, were for the murders of their mistresses or wives. In both cases, whites justified the lynchings on the grounds that they were men of bad character.[56]

Taken as a whole, more lynchings occurred not for murder or for rape but for "other causes." Including a range of alleged offenses from arson to robbery, this category of lynchings is often more difficult to define than is murder. What did whites mean when saying that a black was "troublesome" or a "bad character"? When looking at lynchings throughout the nation, some scholars have speculated that "other causes" could mean standing up for themselves against whites or "being uppity," behaviors which, if applied to whites, would have been acceptable. One black, Eph Brinkley, was hanged in Madisonville in 1897 for "general principles." Several weeks earlier, a prominent citizen had been assassinated, and though no evidence linked Brinkley to the crime, his "evil reputation" made him a suspect. Given how whites often thought of blacks as comical and childlike, the labeling of a lynching as "general principle" seems to suggest a trivial offense. But to link a black man with an assassination and to then lynch him to avoid other assassinations shows that the person was far from being thought of as a comical character. It is possible that much more about the relationship between Brinkley and the murdered well-to-do white was known by the mob.[57]

At the risk of making Afro-Americans accused of certain crimes seem heroic, it is possible that some offenses alleged to have been committed by them might have been their way of "standing up to the man," of fighting back. Scholars of slavery have long pointed out that among the oppressed there are many different methods, besides overt violence, used to express discontent. This may have been the case

56. Louisville *Commercial*, May 5, 9, 1876; Louisville *Courier-Journal*, October 3, 1890; Chicago *Tribune*, February 24, 1898.

57. New York *Times*, July 23, 1897; Chicago *Tribune*, July 23, 1897.

among Afro-Americans in the decades after slavery as well. Eli Nary, who had been arrested for barn burning, was lynched in Fulton County in March, 1888. His motive for destroying the barn is unknown, but arson was often a tool used by the oppressed. That same year, Thomas Reney was hanged in the Bowling Green area for poisoning twenty horses owned by Marion Sloss. After a dispute over working conditions, Sloss had fired Reney, who had then vowed to get even. Although Reney ultimately paid with his life, the black man had indeed found a way to resolve the argument in his favor.[58]

At least 166 people were executed without the benefit of trials during the last twenty-five years of the nineteenth century in the Bluegrass State. Instead of finding this inexcusable, most white Kentuckians hailed lynch law as a necessity because of an inept legal system that allowed reoccurring criminal activities. Moreover, to the protest that lynching was another form of discrimination, reserved for blacks, they could cite examples of white "bad men"—rapists, and murderers—being lynched.

A few instances exist of whites, accused of rape, dying at the hands of lynch mobs. In July, 1877, the body of Miss Burton, who had been missing for more than a month, was found in Point Oliver, Allen County, near the home of her brother-in-law, George Stark. The victim had been raped and shot twice in the head. Stark, believed to be on intimate terms with Burton, was arrested and placed in jail. He was taken out and lynched. The mob murder of Peter Klien was similar to that of many black men accused of rape. Arrested and charged with the rape and robbery of a farmer's wife in Newport, Klien was carried from jail by several hundred men. They took Klien to the home of the farmer for a positive identification. Then he was hanged. The lynching of Klien in a blinding snowstorm, the newspaper concluded, was a picturesque event.[59]

Yet it is revealing of the racial prejudice of that day that, as far as can be determined, no whites were lynched for attempted rape. The case against them had to be solid and even then they might avoid the hangman's noose. In September, 1887, two whites and one black were in jail in Flemingsburg on charges of attempted rape against

58. Louisville *Courier-Journal*, March 16, May 11, 1888.

59. New York *Times*, July 12, 1877, March 17, 1879. The reporter's comment on the lynching was surely not in keeping with the New York *Times*'s strong denouncements of such events.

white women. A mob broke into the jail and took the black, Charles Coleman. He was hanged from a railroad trestle. The two white men remained unharmed in jail. After the Coleman lynching, officials took steps to further safeguard the two whites, but in reality the mob had already had its chance.[60]

Whites were far more likely to be lynched for murder than for rape. Most often it was the kin and a few close friends who sought revenge for the death of a white murder victim. Several men were lynched after killing someone during domestic disputes. In Vanceburg during the 1870s, Washington Lee shot and killed Robert Ellis because an intimate relationship existed between Ellis and Lee's wife. Usually this would be grounds for a justifiable homicide, but the very evening of his arrest, Lee was taken from jail and hanged. In Paris, John Winn killed William Mooreland during an argument over Winn's relations with Mooreland's mother. When the mob came to lynch him, Winn refused to leave peacefully and was shot in his cell. Austin Porter killed his wife during an argument in Grayson, Carter County, in June, 1892. After a meeting with the county attorney, friends of Porter's wife agreed to allow justice to take its course if the trial moved speedily and was held in the same county. But upon learning that Porter's attorney would seek a change of venue and his removal to another county for safekeeping, the mob swung into action. Around 150 armed men came to the jail after midnight and demanded Porter. Despite his pleas for mercy, he was hanged from the railroad bridge.[61]

Whites were quick to lynch members of their own race for killing law enforcement officers. Allowing the death of policemen to go unpunished, they argued, would weaken respect for the law. This position, of course, was highly hypocritical since the very act of lynching reeked with disdain for the law. "Judge Lynch came into town at 1:00 this morning and took the bench. His jury and officers consisted of 300 or more well-armed men." This account describes the lynching of Harvey and Joe Gilland on September 15, 1891, for the murder of the sheriff in Somerset. A similar story could be recounted for the lynching of O. A. Smith for the murder of the marshal in Elkton in 1889, or

60. Louisville *Commercial*, September 4, 1887.

61. New York *Times*, July 20, 1876, April 29, 1881; Louisville *Courier-Journal*, June 7, 1892; Hickman *Courier*, June 17, 1892; Boone County *Recorder*, July 18, 1894. For an account of four white men hanged for murder in London in the 1870s, see the London *Sentinel-Echo*, August 12, 1954.

for the death of Oscar Morton in Beattyville in 1894 for the murder of the sheriff.[62]

Although it was more by accident than design, a white woman was lynched in Kentucky. Appalled by the open, illicit love affair between William Dever and Mrs. T. J. West, a group of Marion County citizens went to the house where the couple was and ordered them to come outside. They refused to do so. The mob then set the house on fire. Dever came out and was shot to death. The mob shouted for West to come out of the burning house, that no harm would be done to her, but she chose to perish in the house. The New York *Times* denounced the deaths of West and Dever as the latest "example of the murderous lawlessness which goes unpunished in Kentucky." Going further, it added that "the stolidity with which these avengers of the 'honor' of a community withstood the pleadings of a child whom they were making an orphan does not belong to civilized life." Just as he had when other act of lawlessness occurred during his administration, Governor Bradley condemned this incident, calling the lynching of Dever and the "creamation" of West an outrageous and barbarous crime.[63]

On a few occasions, whites proclaimed that black law-abiding citizens applauded lynchings and took part in some of the mobs that meted out justice to rapists and murderers. In July, 1882, Helen Brewster, a fourteen-year-old black girl, disappeared from Bellefield. She was last seen in the company of William Ritter. Her body was eventually discovered, and the medical report revealed that Brewster had been raped prior to being killed. Ritter was arrested and taken to jail in Henderson. About fifty masked men overpowered the jailer, took Ritter, and lynched him. "Most of the lynchers were negroes," the paper noted, "but the number of whites among them was sufficient to show that others than the murdered girl's race were determined to see her cruel murder avenged." At the turn of the century, three blacks were arrested in Wickliffe and charged with the murder of an-

62. New York *Times*, September 16, 1891; Louisville *Courier-Journal*, November 25, 1889, October 4, 1894. The Kentucky *Explorer* of February, 1988, reprinted a long, detailed account from the Beattyville *Three Forks Enterprise*, October 19, 1894, of Morton's lynching. See the Louisville *Courier-Journal*, February 29, 1888, for the lynching of two men in Clinton: Samuel Price, white, who had killed a sheriff, and Bill Reams, black, who had shot a white farmer.

63. New York *Times*, December 30, 31, 1895.

other black. The white newspaper stated that "several negroes were among the leaders of the mob" that took the three men from jail and lynched them. According to one account, black residents of Maysville viewed the lynching of Richard Coleman and voiced their approval.[64] Although it is possible that these white accounts of Afro-Americans taking part in lynching other blacks are accurate, they should be viewed with extreme skepticism. Numerous examples exist of whites attacking the black community after a lynching (usually for rape), warning the residents that others would die unless they mended their ways. Not surprisingly, fearing that the wrath of the mob might quickly shift to them, blacks remained away from the site of a lynching, coming to recover the body only after whites had left.

Furthermore, as we have seen, most white reporters found comfort in portraying members of the mob as upstanding citizens intent on punishing criminals and maintaining respect for law and order. With such a romanticized view of lynchers firmly etched in their minds, many whites—far more than the ones saying that blacks took part in lynching—were led to believe that Afro-Americans could not have been involved in lynchings. On one occasion, the racist view of a white reporter led him to conclude that blacks lacked the capacity to conduct a proper lynching. When speculating on who might have been in the mob that lynched the Frenches for the murder of Lake Jones, the reporter at first said that all of the lynchers must have been Afro-Americans. But upon reflection, he concluded: "The latter theory is hardly plausible if taken into consideration how promptly and in what business-like style the lynchers acted. The thing worked like a clock."[65]

Afro-Americans, and especially their leaders, of the nineteenth century realized that it would seriously hurt the race if they condoned the acts of black criminals. Yet despite the assertions by some whites that blacks often applauded mob justice, in reality they seldom, if ever, took part in lynchings. Instead, blacks consistently

64. Louisville *Courier-Journal*, July 13, 1882, September 12, 1902; Tuskegee Clippings, Reel 221, Frame 72; see also the Hopkinsville *Daily Kentucky New Era*, January 25, 1904. John B. Rodes, in his highly informative letter to Mary Helm, July 29, 1944, mentioned that on one occasion in Bowling Green, a group of blacks formed a lynch mob to revenge the murder of a black by the superintendent of the waterworks company. A group of armed white men stopped the blacks. In Rodes Manuscript.

65. Louisville *Commercial*, May 5, 9, 1876.

called upon whites to abide by their own laws and to give all of the accused—black as well as white—the right to defend themselves in court. Furthermore, all Afro-Americans, regardless of station, knew that they could very easily be accused of attacking white women or be viewed as "uppity" for merely defending themselves against whites, thereby becoming the target of lynch mobs.

THREE

"To Hang in an Orderly Fashion,"

1900–1940

From 1900 to 1940, 70 people—61 blacks and 9 whites—were lynched in Kentucky, a considerable decline from 166 during the previous twenty-five years and 117 in the first decade of emancipation. And of the lynchings in Kentucky that have occurred in this century, 44 of them (63 percent) occurred in the first decade of the century. Even so, 44 signaled a significant decline from 92 in the 1890s, and the decline would continue with 18 lynchings from 1911 to 1920, 7 in the 1920s, and 2 in the 1930s.

Although the number of lynchings steadily declined in Kentucky, it is difficult to see why some years had 1 or no lynchings while other years experienced several. In 1900, only 1 lynching occurred. During the next two years, however, there were 16 lynchings. Yet after climbing to 9 in 1902, the number dropped to 2 in 1903 and remained at no more than 3 in any year until 1908, when 14 people (13 Afro-Americans and a single white) were killed. The Night Riders were largely responsible for much of the violence in 1908. By 1910, state officials had taken steps to end the lawless acts of the Night Riders, and Kentucky experienced its first year without a recorded lynching since 1875. Interestingly, however, the next five years, 1911 to 1915, witnessed 12 lynchings in Kentucky. During the First World War, a time when lynchings increased again throughout the nation, no rise occurred in the Bluegrass State. Indeed, from 1917 to 1920, there were only 4 lynchings in the state.

That whites covered up many lynchings is an important reason for their apparent decline in the twentieth century. To be sure, the exact number of lynchings for any time period is difficult to determine. Yet many lynchings from the 1880s and 1890s can be documented because they were held in public. But by the 1920s, after Kentucky had passed legislation calling for stiff penalties for members of lynch mobs and had elected officials willing to press for arrests and convictions, it is clear that several lynchings were covered up with claims that heavily armed blacks had fired on whites. In July, 1929, details were released about two black men shooting and killing John O. Silvey, a railroad foreman in Greenup. Silvey had supposedly ordered the men to leave the property of the Chesapeake and Ohio Railroad, and they returned and ambushed him. A posse was formed, comprising the sheriff and white railroad workers. According to the members of the posse, they had no choice but to kill the two blacks because they would not surrender. Walter White, of the national office of the NAACP, wrote to Edward E. Underwood, a black physician who served as president of the Frankfort branch, urging him to investigate the matter. "It has been our experience that within recent years due to publicity against lynchings, there is a marked tendency to cover up lynchings by calling them murders or killings 'by posses,'" White explained.[1]

Of the seventy lynchings, eighteen—26 percent—were for rape or attempted rape, which is comparable to the nineteenth century, when 28 percent of the total lynchings had been attributed to this offense. In many cases of lynchings as a result of rape, the problem remains one of fully understanding the relationship between the alleged black rapist and the white victim. On several occasions it was rumored, at least among Afro-Americans, that an intimate relationship had existed. In the lynching of Silas Esters in Hodgenville, the sources are vague on details of the incident, leading one to speculate that a homosexual act, either a rape or a mutually agreed relationship, had occurred. Esters was arrested in October, 1901, charged with forcing Granville Ward, a fifteen-year-old white boy, to commit an "unnameable act." A mob of seventy-five men, led by Thomas Ward, the boy's father, demanded the keys to the jail, which were freely given to

1. New York *World,* July 20, 1929; Walter White to E. E. Underwood, July, 1929, Underwood to White, July 22, 1929, both in the National Association for the Advancement of Colored People Papers, Manuscript Division, Library of Congress (hereinafter cited as NAACP Papers). The NAACP listed the deaths of the two anonymous blacks as a lynching. However, as mentioned previously, I have decided not to count as a lynching any incidents where Afro-Americans had weapons and were in a position to defend themselves, even if they were greatly outnumbered.

them. The mob then took Esters to the courthouse yard to hang him. But before he could be hanged, the mob riddled his body with bullets.[2]

Continuity existed from the old century to the new in the lynchings of Afro-Americans accused of raping white women. Whites justified the lynchings of black rapists as the best way to end the assaults and as a warning to other blacks not to commit such an offense. Before lynching a black for rape, the mob maintained the tradition of having the woman identify her attacker. In February, 1902, Della Powell, "one of Jessamine's most estimable young ladies," was assaulted on her way home from school. Although dazed, she somehow made it to her brother's house and told of the incident, saying her attacker was a "heavy set, yellow negro." Shortly thereafter, Thomas Brown was arrested. Police officials took him to Miss Powell, who quickly identified Brown as her attacker. That evening, a mob, led by Powell's relatives, requested that officials take Brown once again to be identified because "some of Nicholasville's best and most law-abiding citizens wanted to be sure that Brown was the guilty party." After this was done and before Brown was returned to jail, the "good citizens" of Nicholasville hanged him in the courthouse yard. In its editorial, the local newspaper proclaimed its outrage at any act of lawlessness, even lynching a "negro fiend" like Thomas Brown who "met the death that all such villains deserve." Yet, after condemning local whites for the lynching, the editor concluded with a warning that was reminiscent of many written in the nineteenth century: "May this serve as an object lesson to all who harbor these fiendish thoughts in their minds, that our daughters, wives, sisters and mothers may have protection from such red-handed scoundrels."[3]

That the Nicholasville mob felt compelled to take Tom Brown before Powell for a second look suggests that she might have been unsure about the identity of the rapist. Just as in times past, however, blacks were lynched even if the white woman had doubts about the man in custody. Ernest Baker was arrested in Cadiz after an attempted rape had been made on Mary Gentry. For whatever reasons—from a state of shock, or because it was dark and the man had sneaked up

2. Louisville *Courier-Journal*, October 31, 1901; New York *Times*, November 1, 1901; Tuskegee Clippings, Reel 221, Frame 72.

3. Jessamine *Journal*, February 7, 1902; Lexington *Morning Herald*, February 7, 1902; Louisville *Commercial*, February 7, 1902.

on her—Gentry could not positively identify Baker as the attacker. Nevertheless, a mob spirited Baker from jail and lynched him.[4]

Sometimes the husbands and fathers of rape victims still refused to conceal their identities and exacted their revenge on blacks, unafraid of being prosecuted for taking part in a lynching. A 1905 lynching in Normandy resembled in some respects the fictional account from Hallie Rives's book, *Smoking Flax*. Lon Beard was arrested and charged with the attempted rape of Mrs. Chester Crawford in Spencer County. Fearing for the black man's safety, the sheriff decided to take Beard by train to Shelbyville for safekeeping until the trial. When the train stopped in Normandy, twenty-five men, including Chester Crawford, went on board. Even though Beard was handcuffed between the sheriff and a deputy, Chester Crawford, whom the white newspaper described as a "mild mannered . . . young farmer," shot Beard seven times. Crawford was immediately arrested. But "without leaving the room, and with the negro's body still on the floor, the bond was signed (fixed at $1,000) by fifteen of the best men in the county, and accompanied by a few friends, Crawford went to his home." The outcome of the case is unknown, but the paper speculated (probably correctly) that Crawford would not be prosecuted. "It is the general impression that no action whatever will be taken in the case by the grand jury. The negro bore a bad reputation in the neighborhood, and his tragic death was no surprise, as it had been predicted that he would sooner or later be shot to death."[5]

On one occasion, the mob restrained a father from killing a black accused of attempting to rape the man's daughter so that they could hang him in an "orderly fashion." In April, 1909, Ruth Gee was allegedly raped in Flat Lick, near the Christian-Trigg county border. After an all-night search, the mob apprehended Bennie "Booker" Brame. They took him before the girl, who made a positive identification. The girl's father wanted to shoot Brame on the spot, but the mob refused his request, carried Brame back to Flat Lick and hanged him from a tree. The coroner of Christian County was James L. Allensworth, a black man, who had held that elective post since 1897. Two of the seven men empaneled by Allensworth to rule on Brame's death

4. Paducah *News-Democrat*, January 25, 1906.
5. Louisville *Courier-Journal*, July 8, 1905; Lexington *Herald*, July 8, 1905; New York *Times*, July 8, 1905.

were also blacks. Despite three Afro-Americans taking part in the investigation, no one was charged with the lynching. Allensworth explained that Brame had been dead at least forty-four hours when he viewed the body; therefore, he had no clues to the identity of the mob members. The other men agreed, ruling that "Brame was hanged to a tree by parties unknown to this jury."[6]

Just as the lynching of one black for attempted rape in Auburn in 1886 ushered in a period during which four more were lynched, such seems to have been the case in the new century, though the numbers were not as dramatic. The small community of Elkton, Todd County, had the state's lone lynching in 1900. Fraten Warfield was jailed on the charge of attempted rape. From the moment of his arrest, threats were made on his life, but the jailer refused to take any steps to prevent a lynching. When the mob came, the jailer turned over the keys without a struggle, and Warfield was lynched "quietly and quickly." Almost five years later to the day, another lynching occurred in Elkton. Frank Leavell, a black man whose left leg had been cut off at the knee, was suspected of attempted rape on a white woman. He eluded the police for a while. At a train stop, three white men captured Leavell but decided not to turn him over to the authorities, hoping to get a reward. But upon learning that the reward offered by Todd County officials was only fifteen dollars, they reluctantly released Leavell to the Elkton sheriff. That evening a group of masked men took him from the jail and hanged him from a tree about a mile from town.[7]

Several alleged rapes occurred near the Trigg-Christian county border in 1909, leading to an uproar among whites and the deaths of at least two blacks. In January, Arthur Wilson was convicted and sentenced to death for the rape of a white woman. No record exists of his execution, and in all likelihood he was not put to death. Taking no chances with the court, the mob in Christian County lynched Bennie Brame in April. About four months later, it was reported that an attempted rape had occurred in the Caledonia area of Trigg County. A mob, led by the brothers of the intended victim, captured the ac-

6. Hopkinsville *Kentuckian*, April 10, 13, 1909; Louisville *Courier-Journal*, April 10, 1909; New York *Times*, April 10, 1909; Boston *Guardian*, April 17, 1909. For the story of Allensworth's election to office, see the Hopkinsville *Kentuckian*, November 5, 1897.

7. Lexington *Morning Herald*, October 19, 1900, October 13, 1905; Louisville *Courier-Journal*, October 18, 19, 1900, October 13, 1905.

cused black, Wallace Miller. They decided to take him to the police in Cadiz, but they failed to arrive in town. It was several days before Miller's body was discovered. The details concerning his lynching are so scarce that the exact manner of his death is not known. Miller's lynching is an example of a black being killed quietly, out of the limelight. As we will see in another chapter, the hanging or shooting of blacks in isolated places occurred a number of times in the new century.[8]

Three highly publicized lynchings involving charges of rape or attempted rape occurred between 1911 and 1920. These incidents would lead many influential citizens, white as well as black, to denounce "mob justice." Around two o'clock on January 15, 1911, at least fifty masked men entered Shelbyville. They turned off the electric power, cut the telephone wires, and proceeded to batter down the door to the jail. They had come for Jim West and Wade Patterson, both accused of detaining a fourteen-year-old white girl. The jailer offered no resistance. Meanwhile, one of the deputies seized all the keys to the cells and hid in a closet at the rear of the building, proclaiming that he would die before turning over the keys. The mob simply ignored the deputy and broke the lock to the cell holding the blacks. There were eight blacks in the cell, and in addition to taking West and Patterson, the mob decided to hang Eugene Marshall, who had been convicted of killing an elderly black woman. As the lynch mob left the jail with the three black men (it had taken almost an hour to break the lock), the two whites on duty did not intervene, explaining later that it would have been futile to draw their guns. The mob carried the three black men to the Chesapeake and Ohio Railroad Bridge—the site of the lynching of Jimbo Fields and Clarence Garnett a decade earlier—and hanged them.[9]

8. Louisville *Courier-Journal*, August 10, 1909.

9. In a long story that was otherwise sympathetic to the black men who were lynched, Louisville *Courier-Journal* reporter Denny B. Goode found humor in the response of the five other prisoners when the mob came for the three men. They were so badly frightened, Goode informed his readers, that their teeth were still chattering twelve hours after the incident. "White folks, hones' befor' Gawd, we wuz jus as white as you is when them lynchers come," he quoted one black inmate as saying. They had sat "passively in their cells or covered their heads under their bunks." See the Louisville *Courier-Journal*, January 16, 1911. Several sources discuss the lynchings in detail: Louisville *Courier-Journal*, January 16, 17, 18, 1911; New York *Times*, January 16, 17, 1911; Shelby *News*, February 2, 1911; Hopkinsville *Kentuckian*, January 17, 18, 1911.

Or so they thought. The men were thrown over the bridge at the same time, but the rope holding Patterson broke, and he fell into the water and attempted to escape. Members of the mob jumped into the water and started chasing him. Patterson's body would be found at the Seventh Street Bridge, some three hundred yards from the Chesapeake and Ohio Bridge, riddled with bullets. Meanwhile, Marshall strangled to death, but West, who was left dangling, somehow untied his hands, removed his head from the noose, fell into the creek, and escaped. The *Courier-Journal* reported, "An all day search failed to reveal the body of the third negro, but that he met a violent death no one here doubts." But in the days after the incident, members of the mob grew worried that West might reappear and identify them. Law enforcement officers staked out his home and urged his family to turn him in. About a week after West's near-lynching, his relatives announced to the press that he had made a successful escape.

White law officers mounted a search for West, and the Shelby County judge offered a $200 reward for his return. The state's Republican governor, Augustus E. Willson, an outspoken foe of lynchings, refused to offer a reward for West but put up $500 for the arrest and conviction of each member of the lynch mob, a step which led the white citizens of Shelby County to denounce the governor. Ultimately, no one collected on either reward. Several months after the lynchings, the Shelby County grand jury investigated the crimes, but not surprisingly, no indictments against members of the mob came out of the hearings. West's exact whereabouts remained unknown for years. He would enlist in the United States Army and fight in the First World War. West, who almost died at the end of a rope on a railroad bridge in 1911, lived another eleven years, though the cause of his death, like much of his life, remains a mystery. What is known, however, is that when his body was returned to Shelbyville for burial, he was treated as a hero by Afro-Americans.[10]

Shelby County officials were condemned for the lynchings and for their failure to prosecute members of the mob. Rumors that West and Patterson would be lynched had circulated for several days, yet nothing had been done to protect the men. Governor Willson ex-

10. Tuskegee Clippings, Reel 223, Frame 252; Louisville *Courier-Journal*, January 30, 1911, May 12, 1911; Earlington *Bee*, January 15, 1911; Shelby *News*, February 2, 1911.

pressed his feelings about lynching when he offered the rewards for members of the mob. An editorial in the New York *Times* criticized the jailer for not protecting the prisoners, saying that no harm would have come to him and his family. The *Courier-Journal*, in an editorial entitled "Shelbyville's Peace Conservators," expressed contempt for the law officers: "The jailer's plan of defending the jail from mob attack and protecting his prisoners was to squat in a dark corner with the keys in his pocket. . . . Apparently it did not occur to the jailer that his presence as guardian of the keys was not strictly necessary, while his presence at the jail door, if he had been willing to shoot, might have dispersed the mob. Whether it was mere cowardice or mere stupidity . . . is not apparent. It is a matter into which the grand jury might profitably inquire." Law officers in Shelbyville might have been criminally negligent in the case, the *Courier-Journal* concluded.[11]

Such actions were not confined to the central part of the state. In western Kentucky, two blacks were lynched in Paducah in October, 1916, in broad daylight before a white crowd estimated from 5,000 to 10,000. This lynching was significant for several reasons. First, while most of the lynchings during the twentieth century took place in small rural areas, this episode occurred in the largest city in western Kentucky, with a population of more than 25,000. The mob's intentions were well known, yet nothing was done; by this time, the mid-1910s, lynchings in many places in the state had been prevented by removing the accused black to Lexington or Louisville. Also, it took the mob several hours to break down the jail cell, surely enough time for the police to mobilize in defense of the prisoner. Indeed, immediately after the lynchings, when it was rumored that blacks were arming themselves for revenge, the police quickly deputized dozens of men, proving that it was a relatively simple matter to round up manpower to put down a threatened riot.

The cause of the lynching was the alleged assault and robbery of Mrs. George D. Ross by an unidentified black man in her home on October 13. As soon as they were notified, the police put bloodhounds on the trail of the rapist. All of western Kentucky, the local paper said, was involved in the massive manhunt. When the man was not found by the end of the first day, a reward was offered. Two days later, Brock

11. New York *Times*, January 17, 1911; Louisville *Courier-Journal*, January 17, 1911.

Henley was arrested and charged with the crime. The evidence against him was never fully explained, remaining something of a mystery. Nevertheless, that he would be lynched was a foregone conclusion. Within hours of Henley's arrest, the men involved in the manhunt stormed the jail. Leading the way was the husband of the victim. As a precaution, Henley had been locked in a steel cell, and though the jailer refused to turn over the key, he took no other steps to stop the mob. Members of the lynch mob decided to summon a foundryman to cut the steel bars. This took time. The newspapers differ in how long: one said it took more than an hour; a second paper, at least three hours; a third newspaper, five hours. Regardless, it is obvious that the police were not interested in preventing the lynching.[12]

After taking Henley from the jail, the mob made him walk three miles to the home of the victim for a positive identification. Along the way, circuit judge William M. Reed confronted Ross and the other members of the mob and tried to talk them out of the lynching, to no avail. Then an unusual event occurred. It is not clear whether a black man, Luther Durrett, had merely been observing the event, whether he attempted to confront the mob, or whether he was identified as a friend of Henley, but the mob decided to lynch him as well. The two men were taken to a site that had been selected for the lynching. Durrett and Henley were hanged, their bodies riddled with bullets and then burned beyond recognition. The huge white throng expressed its approval of the lynchings. Mrs. Ross thanked the mob for its actions, saying, "I did not know I had so many friends."[13] After an examination by a physician, Mrs. Ross declared the lynching of Henley had led to an improvement in her condition.

Even though George Ross and the others involved in the lynching made no attempt to conceal their identities, the coroner's report concluded with the usual verdict: Henley and Durrett had died at the "hands of a mob composed of unknown persons." This was even more of a farce than usual, since the circuit judge, government officials, and civic leaders of Paducah had witnessed the lynchings. Reed refused to call a special term of the grand jury to investigate the lynchings and to

12. See the following sources for the details of the lynchings: Paducah *News-Democrat*, October 14–20, 1916; New York *Times*, October 17, 1916; Chicago *Tribune*, October 17, 1916; New York *Evening Globe*, October 16, 1916; Tuskegee Clippings, Reel 221, Frame 375.

13. Paducah *News-Democrat*, October 17, 1916.

indict leaders of the mob. It would be impossible to secure evidence, he explained. Several days later, after protests were registered from outside the area, the grand jury did look into the matter. Nothing came of their deliberations. Interestingly, the Ross family left Paducah, citing a fear of revenge by blacks as their reason for leaving.

Of all the newspapers covering the lynching, the *Courier-Journal* responded with the sharpest attack: "The lynching at Paducah was an exhibition of bestiality too disgusting to be described adequately. . . . Everyone knew the possibility of it happening in Paducah was great, yet no effort was made to take the prisoner out of danger or to offer real protection. Those features make the degradation of Paducah complete." Meanwhile, the Paducah newspaper refused editorial comment on the lynching, apparently concluding that enough was being said by papers elsewhere.[14]

The third highly publicized lynching occurred at the end of March, 1920. Grant Smith, who worked as a laborer on the Anderson farm in Maysville, was accused of raping fourteen-year-old Ruby Anderson. Smith eluded the authorities for more than two months before being captured in Pontiac, Michigan. Instead of returning him to Maysville, the authorities held Smith in Covington until his trial. Twenty-one years earlier, the lynch mob from Maysville had been informed of Richard Coleman's every move in the Covington jail, and so too were the men who vowed to lynch Smith upon his return to Maysville. After receiving a tip about the train on which Smith was to return, they made plans to burn him alive, just as the mob had done to Coleman. The lynchers, numbering about forty, stopped the train at the Maysville-Lexington Turnpike and removed Smith. Fearful of the authorities, however, they decided not to burn Smith but settled for hanging him from a telephone pole. Several weeks later, the *Courier-Journal* published a story by two women reporters from a small weekly newspaper who had been allowed to witness the lynching. They boasted about their "scoop," of being the only reporters to witness the Smith lynching. Both women approved of the lynching and referred to Smith in derogatory terms. One noted, "There hung the blackest Negro you ever saw." Not to be outdone, the second one said, "The moonlight shone full on the darkey."[15]

14. Louisville *Courier-Journal*, October 17, 1916; Tuskegee Clippings, Reel 221, Frame 287; *Crisis*, XI (January, 1916), 117.

15. *Crisis*, XXI (February, 1921), 160–61; Maysville *Bulletin*, April 1, 1920; New

By the time of Smith's death, the national office of the NAACP had adopted a policy of investigating every lynching in the nation. Contact was made with a black physician in Maysville to look into the matter. After several weeks of snooping around, Dr. W. C. Patton wrote to the national office about the case. His primary contacts were several black women who had worked as domestics over the years in the Anderson home. Patton noted that the white girl—Ruby Anderson—was considerably older than fourteen, as had been mentioned repeatedly in the newspapers. Even more significant, however, was his conclusion that Grant Smith and Ruby Anderson had been involved sexually "and the agreement was mutual." Smith's widow knew about the relationship, but she, like the black domestics, was afraid to talk about the matter publicly. Patton ended his letter by denouncing Maysville whites for being hypocritical regarding interracial sex: "At the same time almost that this man was being lynched, a younger colored girl was giving birth to one by the member of a family in whose employ she was. And the mother of the girl has to take it. I wish you only knew just half" of what happens to black people in Maysville, Patton concluded.[16]

Although alleged rapes by Afro-Americans may have aroused the most fury among whites and received far more coverage in state and national newspapers than any other crimes, in actuality more Kentucky blacks died at the hands of lynch mobs for murder or attempted murder than for any other offense in the twentieth century. Of the seventy lynchings, twenty-eight (40 percent) resulted from murder or attempted murder. Clearly, whites remained determined to punish with a vengeance any black accused of committing a violent crime or who had simply defended himself.

Shelbyville was the site of the mob deaths of Jimbo Fields and Clarence Garnett in October, 1901. According to the newspapers, these two teenagers (Fields was sixteen and Garnett was eighteen) murdered Will C. Hart, a white man who was romantically involved with Fields's mother, Annie. On the night of the murder, the two youths had supposedly argued with Hart at the Fields home. After

York *Journal*, March 30, 1920; New York *Times*, March 30, 31, 1920; Tuskegee Clippings, Reel 222, Frame 49; Louisville *Courier-Journal*, April 8–10, 1920.

16. W. C. Patton to Robert Shillady, April 18, 1920, in NAACP Papers. This collection also contains newsclippings from the New York *Times*, the New York *World*, and the New York *Call* regarding the Smith lynching.

Hart's body was discovered near the residence, the teenagers were arrested. When rumors of a lynching surfaced, the jailer took steps to guard the young men but opted not to transport them to Louisville for safekeeping. The jailer, Ben Perkins, repelled the first attempt by the mob to storm the building. But several nights later the mob returned. Perkins refused to open the door. "Without further parley one of the mob produced the key to the lower door, which had been taken when the other attempt to lynch them was made." Using a sledge hammer, mob members then broke down the cell door. Meanwhile, the jailer's wife, who was already ill, became so overcome with shock and fear that she suffered a fatal heart attack. The two youths were removed to the Chesapeake and Ohio Railroad trestle, only five hundred yards from the county jail, and hanged. Although the lynchings had occurred at night, the bodies were not cut down until late the next day after having been viewed by hundreds of people, including schoolchildren and the delegates of the Kentucky Conference of the Methodist Episcopal Church who were attending a convention in Shelbyville.[17]

Three years later, a lynch mob killed a black woman in Lebanon Junction for the murder of a white farmer. Marie Thompson, referred to by one reporter as a "negro Amazon," had attempted to break up an argument between John Irvin and her son over a missing pair of pliers. Thompson claimed that she cut Irvin with a razor in self-defense, a statement that undoubtedly would have saved her life if she had been a white woman. Thompson, however, was arrested and charged with murder. A group of black men guarded the jail and prevented the mob's first attempt to spring Thompson. But at two o'clock in the morning, the mob, meeting no opposition from the authorities, took the woman and tried to lynch her from a tree in the jail yard. Thompson refused to die without a fight: "The woman was struggling and fighting like a tiger all the time, but the mob was too much for her, and a minute later she was swinging in the air, with her feet several inches from the ground. All of a sudden she twisted around and grabbed a man by the collar, jerked a knife from his hands and cut the rope that was choking the life out of her." Dropping to the ground, Thompson started swinging at the men. She eventually broke away but was shot down in a hail of gunfire.[18]

17. Tuskegee Clippings, Reel 221, Frame 72; New York *Times*, September 26, 1901; Louisville *Courier-Journal*, October 2, 1901; Shelby *News*, October 3, 1901.

18. New York *Times*, June 16, 1904; Louisville *Courier-Journal*, July 15, 16, 1904.

Several lynchings resulted after whites expressed disapproval over the sentences given blacks for murdering whites. In Elizabethtown in 1902, Harlan Buckles was sentenced to life imprisonment for the murder of deputy marshal Robert Reid. The cause of the murder is unknown, but for Buckles to be given life in prison instead of death for the murder of a law officer suggests that some aspects of self-defense might have been involved. Nevertheless, the day after his sentencing but before he had been removed to the state prison, Buckles was taken from jail by seventy-five men and hanged. In London several years later, Virgil Bowers was taken from jail and lynched after he had been sentenced to life for the murder of a white man. Circuit judge H. C. Faulkner of Laurel County was outraged by the mob's act and called for a thorough investigation of the incident. In a very moving speech to the grand jury, the judge said the law had been served in the case by sentencing Bowers to prison:

> You can imagine my horror, when upon being awakened at midnight I found that citizens . . . had taken this man from the jail . . . and hung him almost under the shadow of your Courthouse. . . . Already there are those in your midst who are apologists for the members of this mob. . . . No sophistry can whitewash their character. They will live and die as common murderers, and fill a murderer's grave. They are infinitely worse than Virgil Bowers. . . . They took an unarmed man from his cell in the jail, and from the officers of the law and killed him—murdered him in cold blood and sneaked away to their homes.[19]

In 1921, Richard James was convicted of the murder of two white men in Midway. Although it found James guilty, the all-white jury failed to agree on a penalty. After the jury had been hopelessly deadlocked for some hours, the foreman told the judge that no verdict could be reached. A mob then decided to administer its own punishment: James was taken from the jail and hanged. The grand jury hastily investigated the lynching before making the usual conclusion, and the county judge refused to offer a reward for the killers, saying it would be a waste of time.[20]

The lynchings of Miller in 1893 and of Coleman at the end of that decade, both for rape and murder, had received more publicity than

19. Louisville *Courier-Journal*, November 17, 1902, October 20, 21, 1905; New York *Times*, November 17, 1902, October 18, 1905; H. A. Sommers, *History of Elizabethtown, 1869–1921* (Owensboro, Ky., 1981), 81–82.
20. Tuskegee Clippings, Reel 22, Frame 311; *Crisis*, XXII (May, 1921), 31.

any other lynchings in the nineteenth century. But in the new century, one case involving attempted murder received national and international attention because of the manner in which the mob chose to lynch its black victim. Undoubtedly, were it not for the April, 1911, lynching in Livermore, that small western Kentucky community would have been just as unknown to the American public as were the hundreds of other small towns and villages scattered throughout the state. Will Porter, a black man, shot Frank Mitchell during a barroom brawl. Porter was arrested. At this point, the versions of what happened differ. The account from the New York *Times* says that the sheriff, fearing a lynching, took Porter to the local opera house for safekeeping. All the doors were bolted and the prisoner hidden in the basement under the stage. But the mob easily found Porter and quickly decided to kill him right there in the opera house.

> The shooting of the negro was done in a weird scene. Against the wall props, long unused, were bare windows, and startled from the night's rest, rats scurried across the floor. Against such a background the negro was bound hand and foot and placed in the centre of the stage. Many of the lights when the current was turned on refused to burn, and in the semidarkness the mob silhouetted against the theatre walls, awaited the signal of their leader. When it was given fifty guns fired in unison, one piercing scream was heard, and their work was over. The lights were extinguished, the curtain lowered, and the mob then filed out.

An editorial followed the story, explaining that Livermore whites had found a new way to lynch Afro-Americans: "Whatever else may be said about the inhabitants of Livermore, Kentucky, it cannot be denied that in them the dramatic sense is strongly developed." The editorial ended with a tone of sarcasm: "It [the lynching] may even be called reformative, the highest praise that can be given to any punishment, since it is quite certain that the negro who made in the Livermore 'opera house' his first and last appearance on any stage will never again offend the delicate and tender sensibilities of his fellow-townsmen."[21]

A second version, the one popularized by several Kentucky newspapers and given a national audience by the NAACP, says that a mob took Porter from the jail to the opera house and charged admission to see the lynching. "Those who bought orchestra seats had the privilege

21. New York *Times*, April 21, 22, 1911.

of emptying their six shooters at the swaying form above them, but the gallery occupants were limited to one shot, and the money taken in at the door went to the family of the white man the Negro had killed."[22]

The dramatic details of the lynching of Will Porter were used by the NAACP in its campaign to pass a national antilynching bill and further fueled the fires in Kentucky for similar legislation. At its May 2, 1911, board meeting, the executive committee of the NAACP adopted a resolution condemning Porter's lynching. They sent a memorial to the president and the members of Congress urging them to denounce publicly the practice of lynching. A letter was written to Governor Willson. He responded positively, saying that he wanted the lynchers brought to justice. White citizens in various parts of Kentucky called for the arrest of the lynchers. That same month, the McLean County grand jury returned indictments and issued arrest warrants for eighteen men for their involvement in the lynching. "Practically all of the men indicted are well known in Livermore and McLean County, and the news of the action of the grand jury came like a thunderbolt from a clear sky." Of the eighteen, Lawrence Mitchell, the brother of the man Porter shot, and two others were cited as the leaders and were indicted separately on a charge of murder. The bonds for the men ranged from five hundred dollars to one thousand dollars. The county attorney promised to prosecute the men fully "to erase the blot on the fair name of McLean County." Despite his promise to press for convictions of the men on a charge of murder, all of the defendants won quick acquittal. Nevertheless, they had been identified, arrested, and tried, something unheard-of in Kentucky.[23]

At least seven blacks accused of murder or attempted murder were lynched in Kentucky in the two decades following Porter's lynching. Several of the cases involved Afro-Americans who were described by white newspapers as "bad men" involved in many criminal violations. Charlie Lewis, a war veteran, was lynched in Hickman after he

22. Minutes of the executive committee of the NAACP, May 2, 1911, in NAACP Papers.

23. *Ibid.*, May 2, June 6, 1911; Louisville *Courier-Journal*, May 13, 1911; New York *Times*, May 13, 1911; *Crisis*, II (June, 1911), 53, 61; Charles Flint Kellogg, *A History of the National Association for the Advancement of Colored People, 1909–1920* (Baltimore, 1967), 210.

allegedly assaulted the sheriff while resisting arrest. The lynchers justified their action in part by saying that several years earlier Lewis
had killed a white man. In 1926, when Primus Kirby was lynched in
Guthrie for the murders of his wife and a law officer, the newspaper
made much of the fact that he had recently been released from prison.[24]
Yet, in contrast to Lewis and Kirby, most of the other blacks lynched
during the 1920s and 1930s were not habitual criminals but had the
misfortune of becoming involved in disputes with whites. At least
two lynchings resulted from love triangles. Leonard Woods argued
with two white men who had been "joyriding" with two black women.
Woods killed one of the men in a fight. Along with Woods, the two
black women were arrested. According to an anonymous source, "the
High Sheriff, M. T. Reynolds, two deputies and all other peace officers
were there and watched the mob at work in breaking into the jail."
Woods and the two women were taken to a wooded area to be lynched.
The white man involved in the incident pleaded that the women's
lives be spared, and the mob relented, allowing them to return to jail.
Woods was shot and his body burned. The lynching of Woods was
the last one of a black man in Kentucky for seven years, but during
that time, two white men were lynched: Chester Fugate in Breathitt
County on December 25, 1929, and Walter Merrick in Princeton on
June 1, 1932.[25]

The last recorded lynching in Kentucky occurred in Hazard in
January, 1934. Rex Scott, a black coal miner who had served time

24. See an anonymous letter to the editor of the *Crisis*, XVII (December, 1918), urging the NAACP to investigate the Lewis lynching. The national office sent a telegram
to the governor about this lynching. A copy of the telegram can be found in Box C-356,
NAACP Papers. See also the Louisville *Courier-Journal*, December 16, 1918, the New
York *Evening Sun*, December 23, 1918, the New York *Call*, December 19, 1918, and
Crisis, XVII (February, 1919), 180–81. For information on the Kirby lynching, see the
Owensboro *Messenger*, June 15, 1926, Tuskegee Clippings, Reel 224, Frame 653, the
Louisville *Courier-Journal*, June 16, 1926, and the Louisa *Big Sandy News*, June 18,
July 2, 1926. According to the *Messenger*, Kirby was hanged from the "lucky tree." He
was the fourth black to be lynched there.

25. Anonymous letter, mailed from Whitesburg, to Carl Murphy, editor of the Baltimore *Afro-American*, December 13, 1927; see also a letter from Lawrence D. Kellis, of
Whitesburg, to James Weldon Johnson of the NAACP, December 14, 1927. Both letters
can be found in the NAACP Papers. For information on the lynching of Fugate, see
Tuskegee Clippings, Reel 226, Frame 419; on Merrick, see Tuskegee Clippings, Reel
227, Frame 142, and the Louisville *Courier-Journal*, May 14, 1933.

in prison, was standing outside a restaurant near an area frequented by white prostitutes, when Alex B. Johnson, a white man who also worked in the mines, approached him and made an insulting remark. According to the report of the NAACP, "Johnson had been drinking liquor and was in a quarrelsome frame of mind." A fight quickly broke out between the two men. At some point, Scott struck Johnson in the face, knocking him to the pavement. While Johnson was on the ground, Scott struck him again, this time on the right side of his head. While Johnson was being carried to the local hospital, Scott was being arrested for attempted murder. Johnson died without ever regaining consciousness.[26]

Scott was charged with the murder of a white man in Perry County, an area where tensions had remained high since the hotly contested sheriff's election the previous November. The loser, who had challenged the vote on grounds of fraud, had been attacked and killed one morning as he left his home. After the death of his opponent, the sheriff repeatedly failed to take any measures to end crime and vice in Hazard. Rumors circulated that Scott would be lynched by Johnson's friends, yet the sheriff refused to increase security at the jail. On Sunday night, miners from the small communities of Defiance and Vicco, where Johnson had lived and worked, came to Hazard. Although fully aware that the miners, some of whom were wearing masks, were congregating in the building next door, both the jailer and the turnkey decided not to sound an alarm. When the mob came inside the jail, the turnkey at first attempted to lock himself and the keys in a cell but quickly changed his mind and simply handed over the keys to the leader. Scott was placed in a truck and driven toward Vicco. Unconcerned about law officers pursuing them, the miners casually stopped at a country store and purchased a rope for the hanging. An investigator of the lynching wrote to the NAACP of how Scott met his end: "Rex was hanged upon a small sassafras tree, the girth of which was not larger than that of my coat sleeve, and the limb from which they suspended the body was not larger in circumference than a man's

26. A thorough investigation of the death of Johnson and the lynching of Scott was conducted for the NAACP by J. Wesley Hatcher, professor of sociology at Berea College: "Report on Lynching Occurring at Hazard, Perry County, Kentucky, Jan. 24, 1934," in NAACP Papers. See also Tuskegee Clippings, Reel 228, Frame 733, and the Louisville *Courier-Journal*, January 25, 1934.

thumb. They drew him up until his feet cleared the ground, fastened the rope to the tree, and then shot his body full of bullets."

In addition to being lynched for murder—like the one Scott was charged with committing—and rape, Kentucky blacks in the twentieth century were summarily executed by white mobs for several other reasons. In the nineteenth century, "other causes" had actually been the single largest category of lynchings, and many of these were rather vague and difficult to determine. By contrast, in the 1900s, some lynchings for "other causes" were specific: Four blacks were killed for stealing and robbery; five, for supposedly approving of the murders or rapes of whites; seven, at the hands of Night Riders. In several additional cases, however, it proved to be impossible to determine the reasons whites gave, if indeed they had given any at all, for the lynching of blacks. Of the whites lynched in the twentieth century for "other causes," one died for setting dynamite to a store and the other two were put to death for unknown reasons.

Several factors probably account for the decline in lynchings for causes other than murder or rape. Because some of the lynchings in the new century received little or no press coverage, many of the details, including what led to the incident, are lost. More important, however, law officers might have taken steps to prevent lynchings for criminal offenses that did not involve bodily harm to whites. Indeed, on a number of occasions between 1900 and 1930, sheriffs attempted to defend their prisoners in a manner that they had previously refused to do when a white mob threatened to lynch an Afro-American for something other than the rape or the murder of a white person. For scholars of racial violence, a continuing problem is the difficulty in determining whether some deaths of blacks at the hands of whites were murders or lynchings. In 1945, for example, in the small mountain community of Neon, in Letcher County, a group of drunken whites murdered two blacks for refusing to dance when ordered to do so. The national office of the NAACP urged their branches within the state to investigate the incident, calling it a lynching. Except for one letter briefly describing the event, no facts are known about the case.[27] Moreover, under the definition of lynching used in this study,

27. A copy of the letter from Donald Jones, of the NAACP, to the Reverend Louis W. Faulkner, of the Boyle County NAACP, November 23, 1845, can be found in the NAACP Papers.

the death of the "two Negro boys" was not a lynching but a vicious and senseless murder.

Twelve of the people lynched for causes other than murder or rape died in 1908, all in the western part of the state. Many area farmers had banded together to withhold their tobacco in an attempt to extract a higher price from a tobacco trust. These farmers became outraged when a few of their neighbors refused to join the association. In response, a group that came to be called the Night Riders started destroying crops, burning tobacco barns, whipping reluctant farmers, and, ultimately, murdering several outspoken foes. The number of whites killed by the Night Riders is unknown but probably reached a dozen or more. These deaths have not been counted as lynchings in this study since few details exist. Black farmers initially cooperated with the association. Nevertheless, the Night Riders soon targeted Afro-Americans for abuse. This form of violence peaked in the spring and summer of 1908. On the evening of March 23, some twenty-five to thirty Night Riders invaded Golden Pond, Trigg County, took Tom Weaver from his bed, and ordered him to run. When he refused, the mob shot him to death. Weaver's "crime" was migrating to the area to pack tobacco for several large companies, and the mob lynched him as a warning to other blacks to steer clear.[28]

The lynching of David Walker and his family is an example of how the Night Riders appointed themselves to keep "uppity" blacks in their place. The precipitating cause is not clearly known. It seems that Walker, a farmer in Hickman, had been involved in a dispute with a white woman, which of course was more than enough of a transgression for whites to take action against a black man. On the night of October 3, about fifty Night Riders surrounded Walker's home and ordered him to come out. When he would not do so, several members of the mob poured coal oil on the house and set it on fire. Walker, pleading for mercy for himself and his family, finally opened the door. He was met with gunfire. Walker's wife then appeared at the door. "She held in her arms their infant child and begged the Night Riders for mercy. Disregarding her pleadings the infuriated mob opened fire and a bullet pierced the body of the infant in its mother's arms. A second shot struck the mother in the abdomen and she fell, still holding the dead body of her infant." Next, three children came out to more

28. Louisville *Courier-Journal*, March 27, 1908.

gunfire. Walker's oldest son, however, refused to leave the burning cabin. As the *Courier-Journal* noted, "There is hardly a doubt but the oldest son of Walker preferred death by burning rather than to placing himself at the mercy of the mob, and it is probable that his charred body will be found among the debris."[29]

Nothing was done to bring the lynchers of the seven Walkers to justice. Fulton County whites justified the lynchings by explaining that David Walker had a bad reputation and was a "surly negro." Relying totally on the view of these whites, the *Courier-Journal* noted that Walker had not only cursed a white woman but had also threatened to shoot the white man who came to her defense. Was Walker guilty of these offenses? Given all of the lynchings that had occurred in Fulton County over the years, Walker surely must have known that hostile actions toward whites, especially a white woman, would result in death for himself and possibly for members of his family as well. Clearly, the paper blamed the black man for the incident: "The mob, it is believed, visited the home of Walker with the original intention of horse-whipping him, but when he fired into their midst he so aroused their indignation that their thirst for blood was not satiated until the last member of the Walker family had been shot." The paper fails to explain why the Night Riders brought along coal oil if all they intended to do was to whip Walker. Also, the *Courier-Journal* claims that Walker fired the first shot. This, of course, may have been the case. But again, surely he must have known the consequences for doing so when his house was surrounded by fifty armed men.

Logan County, which like Fulton County witnessed a series of mob murders of Afro-Americans over the years, had its final lynchings in 1908, when four black youths were killed. In July, Rufus Browder, a black sharecropper, argued with James Cunningham, the white farmer for whom he worked. As Browder attempted to walk away, Cunningham cursed him and struck him with a whip. Then he drew his pistol and shot Browder in the chest, whereupon Browder drew his pistol and killed Cunningham. After having his wound treated by a doctor, Browder was arrested and sent to Louisville for safekeeping. Several days later, the police raided a lodge meeting being conducted by four black sharecroppers, all friends and lodge brothers of Browder.

29. *Ibid.*, October 5, 1908; New York *Times*, October 5, 1908; Chicago *Tribune*, October 5, 1908; Paducah *News-Democrat*, October 8, 1908; Eugene P. Lyle, "Night Riding: A Reign of Fear," *Hampton's Magazine*, XXII (April, 1909), 472.

Supposedly, Virgil, Robert, and Thomas Jones, and Joseph Riley had expressed approval of the killing of Cunningham. A rumor was also circulating that the members of the Negro lodge were targeting several prominent whites for assassination. Even though they were meeting in a private home, the four blacks were arrested for disturbing the peace. On the night of August 1, one hundred men entered the Russellville jail and demanded that the four men be turned over to them. The jailer did so. They were hanged from the same cedar tree used to lynch Arch and Dink Proctor on December 18, 1896. A note was pinned to one of the bodies: "Let this be a warning to you niggers to let white people alone or you will go the same way." It is highly possible that the four men were lynched because they, like Browder, were farm laborers who were unhappy with their working conditions. The white farmers of Logan County well knew what could happen if all of their poorly paid, overworked black sharecroppers quit the area. A point made by Richard Maxwell Brown might be appropriate to the lynchings in Russellville: Mass lynchings were often done to stop black opposition to white oppression in a given area.[30]

As far as can be determined from existing data, fewer Afro-Americans died at the hands of lynch mobs in Kentucky during the first three decades of the twentieth century than during the last third of the nineteenth century. Significantly, however, several years in the new century—1902, 1903, and 1908—witnessed as many lynchings as some of the worst years of the post–Civil War period. The mob deaths of those years and the others that occurred during this century are a strong indication that many Kentucky whites still did not hesitate to take the law into their own hands, to turn to the rope or the rifle to keep blacks in their place, and to stamp out any acts that suggested militancy on the part of Afro-Americans.

30. Louisville *Courier-Journal*, August 2, 1908; New York *Times*, August 2, 1908; Paducah *News-Democrat*, August 6, 1908; Boston *Guardian*, August 8, 1908; Richard M. Brown, *Strain of Violence: Historical Studies of American Violence and Vigilantism* (New York, 1975), 216. In Stephensport in July, 1904, a black was shot and killed by a group of whites for the murder of a white man. Intent on making sure that other Afro-Americans knew the consequences of having disputes with whites, members of the lynch mob ventured into the Afro-American community and chased other blacks through the streets. Hundreds of shots were fired, though no one was killed. Blacks had been duly warned, however, of the penalty for killing a white man. See the Louisville *Courier-Journal*, July 18, 1904.

FOUR

Ousting "Troublemakers"

Mob rule, like lynchings, was another tactic used by Kentucky whites to get rid of offending blacks and to warn others of what could happen to them for overstepping their bounds. Yet, in one respect, mob rule differed from lynchings: It was done first and foremost for economic gain. Of course, the ramifications of a lynching might mean that blacks would stay "in their place" and not complain about working conditions. But it is obvious that in Kentucky and elsewhere, whites terrorized blacks because they resented Afro-Americans as successful independent farmers, skilled workers, and businessmen, all of whom by their very presence challenged the doctrine of white supremacy.

Whites as well were often the targets of Night Riders and other criminal bands. During outbreaks of lawlessness, white undesirables—vagrants, prostitutes, and petty thieves—received whippings and notices to leave town immediately.[1] On a few occasions, outspoken judges and prosecutors, calling for the end of mob law and the fair treatment of Afro-Americans, received whippings at the hands of mobs. Unquestionably, however, the cases of whites as targets are far exceeded by the numerous attempts of white mobs to force Afro-Americans to leave an area or by the random beatings of blacks that occurred in certain parts of the state.

Throughout Kentucky, there were counties that had only a few Afro-Americans, even though adjacent counties might have had sizable black populations. Whites in some of the former counties had resorted to violence to get rid of Afro-Americans and to let it be known

---

1. See the New York *Times,* March 12, 1890, for the details of a raid by "White-cappers" in the Covington area.

that black migrants were not welcome. Several counties in Regions 5, 6, and 7 that had no reported lynchings of blacks also had at the most only a handful of black residents. Afro-Americans in these areas worked as domestic servants, farmhands, or common laborers—jobs considered appropriate for them by whites. Blacks encountered hostility whenever they attempted to settle in Elliott County, located in Region 6. If the figures obtained by census takers are even close to being accurate, the number of blacks living there was minuscule: In 1880 there were 43, declining to 27 in 1890, and then plunging to 2 at the start of the new century. During these same years, the white population increased from 8,000 to more than 10,000. Richard Watson, one of two Afro-Americans living in this eastern Kentucky county in the early 1900s, owned land. The target of whites who resented his success, Watson was killed in January, 1909, for no reason other than his being an Afro-American. The census from the year after Watson's murder recorded 1 black still living in Elliott County. Clearly, Afro-Americans in many parts of the state had to stay "in their place." To be outspoken meant oppression, to acquire land and other possessions could lead to being condemned as a "troublemaker" and result in death.[2]

In August, 1877, a group of Afro-Americans was forced to leave Henry County, an area that had only a few blacks to begin with, after one of them was accused of slandering the virtue of a white woman. The incident centered on Smith Reed, a former slave, and Alice Campbell, the daughter of Reed's former master. Reed and Campbell had been friends all of their lives: "As children the white girl and the mulatto boy were very affectionate playfellows, and after both had grown up and were married they continued to be on rather friendly terms, considering differences of color and station." Rumors began circulating that a "criminal intimacy" had occurred "between the wife of a wealthy and respectable white farmer and a young mulatto farmer." The mob that confronted Reed with this accusation was led by a young farmer, named Asher, who was not Campbell's husband but who also seems to have been involved in a relationship with her. (According to the *Courier-Journal*, the last time Reed went to the

---

2. U.S. Census Bureau, *Negro Population in the United States, 1790–1915* (Washington, D.C., 1918), 811. The Elliott County *News*, January 1, 1988, contains a story on the life of Richard Watson.

Campbell farm he had been prevented from seeing his lifelong friend because she and Asher had locked themselves in one of the rooms in the house.) A member of the mob shot Reed, though not fatally, and they debated whether or not to hang him. It was decided that Reed and all of his kin had to leave Henry County. Led by Asher, the mob took some thirty blacks to the Louisville Short Line Depot at Newburg and purchased tickets for them on the train bound for Cincinnati, even though some of the Reed clan had expressed a desire to go to Louisville. "[All of the] men, women, and children were banished in this way, and had to leave behind their household goods, furniture, farming implements, horses, and other stock, and their standing crops." According to the New York *Times*, all of the blacks either owned or rented good farms and were doing quite well. "James Garnett, we believe, had forty-five acres of corn and six acres of tobacco in prime condition."[3]

In an article headlined "The Facts: Base Slander of an Innocent Woman," the *Courier-Journal* proclaimed its intention of setting the record straight on the forced removal of the Reed family. A local correspondent for the paper interviewed a number of Henry County whites, and all of them "deny in toto the accusations of misdoings by Mrs. Campbell, and defend the unceremonious ousting of the black community of which Reed was a member on the ground that it was composed of suspect characters." As the reporter explained, though Campbell had always been friendly to her father's former slave, nothing had ever happened between them until June 29, when Reed made an "awful proposal" to Campbell, who rebuked him and said that she would tell her husband. Reed then choked her, threatening to kill Campbell and her husband. When he learned about Reed's attempt to seduce his wife and the assault on her, Campbell's husband had to be restrained by friends from killing Reed. He then agreed to the forced removal of Reed and his kin from the county as the best way to avoid bloodshed. In blunt words, the *Courier-Journal* said that Reed lied about having an intimate relationship with Mrs. Campbell: "Is there a sane married man on the face of the earth that believes his wife could have criminal intimacy with any person, much less a negro, and

3. There are several accounts of the incident: New York *Times*, August 12, 1877; Louisville *Courier-Journal*, August 9, 10, 1877; Cincinnati *Commercial*, August 8, 1877.

he never suspected her fidelity? It is too absurd to be believed." The newspaper applauded Henry County whites for taking action against anyone who would demean the character of their women: "This community has shown by her actions that she is always ready to defend virtue, and no man, be he white or black, can remain in this community and seduce or attempt to the ruin of an innocent virtuous woman." The correspondent next discussed the character of Reed and the other blacks: "As to the other parties who were sent with Reed, they have long been suspect as dangerous, bad men. Some of them have been suspected of knowing too much about the burning of certain property, thieving, and other crimes. Reed stated that he owned 50 acres of land, which is false. He never owned a foot in his life, nor did any of the rest of them."[4]

It is difficult to assess all of the facts of the case. As we have seen, if a black had been accused of making a lewd proposal to a white woman, then choking and threatening to kill her and her husband, he would have been lynched. Yet Reed was not lynched. Surely at the very least Reed would have been arrested, tried, and sent to prison for assault. Forcing Reed to leave Henry County meant that no trial would be held where the white woman might have been asked about her involvement in the criminal act of having sex with a Negro. It was typical of the white community and newspaper to cast the victimized blacks as criminals. Afro-Americans who were strongly suspected of

4. A search of "Tax Books of Kentucky Counties (Henry County)," in the Kentucky Department for Libraries and Archives in Frankfort, for the entire decade of the 1870s failed to find information about Smith Reed, James Garrett, or the other blacks ousted from Henry County as landowners. (Both Reed and Garrett are also absent from the 1870 Manuscript Census of Henry County.) Their absence from the tax rolls, though giving some validity to the charge that these blacks were not landowners, does not prove conclusively that the whites were correct when making this assertion. Thomas D. Clark, a leading scholar of Kentucky history for more than four decades and the author of numerous books, explains that the absence of someone from the property and deed rolls does not automatically mean that he did not own land. On occasion, he notes, deeds were not recorded. Also, to avoid paying taxes, people living in remote parts of counties were often successful in hiding their income. James Klotter, the general editor of the Kentucky Historical Society and the author of numerous books and articles on the state's history, speculates that since Kentucky maintained separate tax rolls for black and white public schools until 1882, it is very likely that a separate book containing a list of black property owners and taxpayers existed but has probably not been preserved. Dr. Thomas D. Clark, interview with author, March 18, 1988, Frankfort; Dr. James Klotter, telephone interview with author, March 25, 1988.

theft or arson would have been lynched or forcefully removed from most counties in Kentucky long before the alleged incident of June 29. In short, given the nature of race relations in Kentucky during that time, it is extremely doubtful that the version of the expulsion of the Reed family from Henry County as reported by the *Courier-Journal* is an accurate one.

The practice of forcing blacks to leave an area occurred on many different occasions between the 1880s and the 1930s. In many of these cases, like the one involving Reed and his clan, whites justified the ousting of Afro-Americans by claiming they were criminals or vagrants. Whites rarely acknowledged publicly the two leading reasons for forcing blacks out of their communities: They resented black involvement in politics, especially in the Republican party, and they felt threatened by the presence of blacks as successful farmers or as skilled, competitive workers. A few of these incidents received as much media attention as some of the highly sensational lynchings. More often, however, except for coverage in a small town weekly newspaper, no other records exist of blacks being compelled to leave an area. The New York *Times* and the Louisville *Commercial*, both Republican newspapers, were far more likely to carry stories of blacks being run out of a region during an election year. During the late nineteenth century, the *Courier-Journal*, a Democratic paper, rarely ran stories of blacks being forced out, except to explain why whites had resorted to such drastic tactics.

Several black leaders living in the westernmost region in the state were the targets of whites a number of times during the early 1880s. Political differences lay at the root of the problem. Whites in the Democratic party felt challenged by several blacks attempting to rally support for Republican candidates. In contrast to the Deep South, where blacks were eventually eliminated from the political arena, black Kentuckians maintained the franchise and, by voting solidly Republican, often played a significant role in close elections in Paducah, Hopkinsville, and other western Kentucky cities. In August, 1880, Henry Seay of Hickman County was beaten by whites and told to leave the county. The local police promised to arrest the guilty parties, but nothing came of the matter and Seay was forced to flee. Two years later, a white guerrilla band began whipping black political leaders in the city of Hickman, in Fulton County. After the beatings failed to stop black political activity, the heavily armed whites started shooting the blacks, though none were fatally wounded. Having no legal recourse or protection from the authorities, the beleaguered blacks left the area, to the delight of the Democrats.[5]

Black politicians were not the only "undesirables" forced to leave town. In the late 1880s, about fifteen men visited the farm of Milt Barclay in Pulaski County to punish a black tenant they accused of stealing a horse and farm equipment. According to the newspaper account, "The 'cappers' gave the negro a sound whipping and ordered him to leave the state, which he did without further ceremony." Holding the white farmer responsible for the transgression of his tenant, the mob then gave Barclay a "sound thrashing." The mob threatened to hang Barclay if he hired such an unworthy Negro again. Once word circulated about the incident, local white citizens were upset about the beating given Barclay but said nothing about the punishment and banishment of the unnamed Afro-American.[6]

Sometimes, a lynching sparked a movement by whites to rid their area of blacks viewed as troublemakers or as criminals. White newspapers often stated that since a lynching had at last occurred—and it could have happened to any number of black criminals found in the community—steps should be taken to compel others to abide by the law or leave town. After lynching Dick Allen, the Mayfield mob pinned a note to his body warning seven blacks to leave town by noon on Thursday. "Nearly all of them took the advice." Their departure did not satisfy the mob; within days another list surfaced naming ten additional blacks who were to leave Mayfield. Noah McReynolds, accused of spying on a bathing white woman, balked at leaving. On Saturday night, a mob took him from his home and administered twenty lashes to his back. The following morning, McReynolds left town on the train. "In all perhaps thirty or forty negroes have left since the hanging." In Russellville, after the hanging of four black youths in 1908, the mob issued a general warning to Logan County blacks to shape up or expect similar treatment.[7]

It can be reasonably assumed that the greatest number of Afro-Americans were forced to leave communities all over the commonwealth not because they were warned out of town after lynchings nor

5. New York *Times,* August 28, 1880, October 14, 1882.
6. Louisville *Courier-Journal,* July 27, 1889.
7. Mayfield *Monitor,* March 2, 1898; New York *Times,* August 2, 1908.

because they were involved in political activities, but because whites were determined to eliminate them from the workplace. The irony, of course, is that during labor shortages on farms or in expanding industries, whites had urged blacks to move into an area. In the early 1900s, white farmers in several western Kentucky counties complained about the shortage of black tenant farmers and sharecroppers. According to one account, twenty-five blacks left one community in March, 1904. In urban areas, whites also needed additional black workers but only for the lowest paying, least prestigious jobs. Although his statement should be viewed with caution, a manager of a brick-making plant in Paducah claimed in 1906 that it was impossible to hire black workers: "I will venture to say that I have asked 300 colored men if they wanted work, . . . and all but three of them with grins on their faces answered in the negative." Also in the early 1900s, coal companies in both eastern and western Kentucky sent agents into the South to lure thousands of blacks to work in the mines. Their reasons for wanting to hire Afro-American workers was obvious: They viewed blacks as strikebreakers who would depress wages for all coal miners. Once hired in the coalfields, the blacks were assigned the worst, most dangerous jobs and received the lowest pay.[8]

But when employment was difficult to find, whites tried to undermine the presence of blacks in the work force. In Louisville, one of the few places in Kentucky where European immigrants settled, the Irish complained about the large number of successful black barbers, self-righteously proclaiming that they lacked a sense of pride for refusing to cut the hair of fellow blacks for fear of losing their white customers. Although the rhetoric was harsh, it rarely turned to violence. The coalfields and several other industries presented a different case entirely, as clashes occurred between black and white workers

8. Christopher Waldrep, "Planters and the Planters' Protective Association in Kentucky and Tennessee," *Journal of Southern History*, LII (November, 1986), 580–81; Paducah *Weekly News Democrat*, October 25, 1906. On blacks in the mines, see Sterling D. Spero and Abram L. Harris, *The Black Worker* (New York, 1931), 206–45, Ronald D Eller, *Miners, Millhands, and Mountaineers: Industrialization of the Appalachian South, 1880–1930* (Knoxville, 1982), 165–75, *Crisis*, XII (June, 1916), 63, and two works by Ronald L. Lewis: "Job Control and Race Relations in Coal Fields, 1870–1920," *Journal of Ethnic Studies*, XII (Winter, 1985), 36–64, and *Black Coal Miners In America: Race, Class, and Community Conflict, 1780–1980* (Lexington, 1987).

on several occasions from the early 1900s to the Great Depression. Signs were posted at the Chess Weymond Stave Mill Company in McFarland, Monroe County, in November, 1908, warning the fifteen black workers to quit and leave at once. White workers proclaimed that the presence of the "negroes had become obnoxious." In response, several residents of McFarland, sympathetic to the black workers, said that the signs and the threatened violence were the "work of persons who had expected to be employed at the mills, and were deprived of the employment by the negroes." This group urged blacks to ignore the threats. Nevertheless, the black workers took seriously the warnings, quickly gathered their belongings, and left the area.[9]

The Night Riders were largely responsible for the ousting of blacks from parts of western Kentucky in the first two decades of the twentieth century. An agreement by the American Tobacco Company and several European tobacco concerns to control prices paid to farmers led to the violence of the Night Riders. This tobacco trust divided up the territory, fixed prices, and refused to engage in competitive bidding. Tobacco farmers realized that steps needed to be taken to combat the monopoly created by the trust, and at a crucial meeting in Guthrie on September 24, 1904, they formed the Dark Tobacco Association, later changing the name to the Planters' Protective Association of Kentucky. Their purpose was clear: to regulate the price they received by pooling and holding their tobacco crop until the trust met their price. After the crop was stored in warehouses, the association would arrange for the grading, financing, and selling of the tobacco. In the first year of the plan, the association sold 70 percent of the tobacco grown in Kentucky. The trust grudgingly increased its price, and all farmers, even those who had remained aloof from the organization, received higher prices for their crops. Despite repeated warnings from the association that anything short of total unity would destroy the trust, many independent farmers refused to join, saying that the association's charges for selling their tobacco were too high.[10]

9. George C. Wright, *Life Behind A Veil: Blacks in Louisville, Kentucky, 1865–1930* (Baton Rouge, 1985), 77–101; Louisville *Courier-Journal*, November 9, 1908.

10. Many sources discuss the activities of the Night Riders. For contemporary accounts, see Eugene P. Lyle's three articles in *Hampton's Magazine*, XXII: "They That Ride By Night" (February, 1909), 175–87, "Night Riding in the Black Patch" (March, 1909), 339–52, "Night Riding: A Reign of Fear" (April, 1909), 465–73; as well as "The

Deciding that only militant action would persuade the "hillbillies" to join, an inner circle of association members formed the Night Riders. Adopting the tactics and the regalia of the Ku Klux Klan, the Night Riders began destroying crops and burning tobacco barns. On several occasions, they invaded towns, destroying warehouses that stored the tobacco purchased by the trust. Damage ran into the millions of dollars. From the start, the Night Riders whipped and occasionally murdered their outspoken foes. Members of the outlaw band traveled to the small community of Goff in late March, 1910, to whip all of the males in the Carroll family. As his older brother was being severely lashed, Charles Carroll attempted to run off. Even though he was only twelve years old and most surely not responsible for his family's unwillingness to cooperate with the Night Riders, he was killed by gunfire. Many law officers and elected officials joined the Night Riders or at least gave tacit approval to their violence, thereby undermining the law's obligation to apprehend them. On the rare occasions when Night Riders were arrested and taken to court, they were provided with strong alibis from leading citizens. As one contemporary source explained: "There is war in Kentucky. In a score of towns what is virtually a state of martial law exists. In the farming districts cellars have been fortified and loaded arms stacked within easy reach."[11]

The Night Riders eventually harassed people who had no connection with the tobacco controversy. Initially, blacks, who seem to have joined the association in the same proportion as whites, were not viewed as a special target by the Night Riders. Nevertheless, at some point they began attacking blacks in various parts of western Kentucky. In January, 1907, Night Riders destroyed the barn owned by David McGraw and Frank Coleman of Christian County. "It is not clear why the barn was burned, unless it was the beginning of a move

Night Riders," *Outlook,* LXXXVIII (February 29, 1908), 482–84, Charles V. Tevis, "A Ku Klux Klan of Today: The Record of Kentucky's 'Night Riders,'" *Harper's Weekly,* LII (February 8, 1908), 14–16, Edward A. Jonas, "The Night Riders: A Trust of Farmers," *World's Work,* XVII (February, 1909), 11213–18, and John G. Miller, *The Black Patch War* (Chapel Hill, 1936). See also Marie Taylor, "Night Riders in the Black Patch" (M.A. thesis, University of Kentucky, 1934), Bill Cunningham, *On Bended Knees: The Night Riders Story* (Nashville, 1983) and Waldrep, "Planters and Planters' Protective Association."

11. Louisville *Courier-Journal,* April 2, 1910; Tevis, "The Record of Kentucky's 'Night Riders,'" 14–16, 32; Jonas, "The Night Riders," 11216.

against Negroes," speculated a white newspaper. This proved to be the case: Farmers were warned to not employ black workers. The tobacco fields of several black sharecroppers were destroyed, even though these farmers had not expressed any opposition to the association. Night Riders next attacked blacks in Lyon County. For no apparent reason, members of this outlaw band went to the home of Arthur Blue, firing shots and ordering him to leave the county. When denouncing the episode, a white newspaper said: "Blue has lived in Lyon county for thirty-five years and is one of the most industrious and respectable negroes in the county. No possible excuse for the outrage is known." The very next evening, the home of a white farmer, John Manning, was riddled with bullets because of his refusal to dismiss his black workers. At least six other black families received notices to leave Lyon County but were able to remain because, in part, of the timely intervention of Sheriff Sam G. Cash, who refused to be intimidated by the mob. On yet another occasion, the Night Riders traveled to Eddyville, the largest city in Lyon County, and whipped ten men, six of whom were Afro-Americans. The men had publicly denounced the raids. Black workers in other western Kentucky communities came under attack as well. In Caledonia, a Mr. Howell was warned to get rid of his black workers or expect a midnight visit from the Night Riders. Black coal miners in Hopkins County, whose employment was far removed from the concern of tobacco farmers, were attacked. As a contemporary source explained, "Negro laborers are an offense to the coal miners' union in Hopkins County and Night Riding is invoked." Rural blacks in several southern states were also victimized by white bands during the early 1900s. In three counties in Mississippi, lawless bands calling themselves "Whitecappers" posted signs ordering blacks to leave, whipped and murdered a number of them, and attacked whites who expressed sympathy for the Afro-Americans. Commenting on the violence in Mississippi, a scholar observes, "Probably no group espoused this anti-Negro sentiment more strongly than the small farmers who for so long had experienced hard times."[12]

12. An important source of information on the violence of the Night Riders is the Augustus E. Willson Papers and Scrapbooks at the Filson Club in Louisville (hereinafter cited as Willson Collection). Information on the destruction of property of Christian County blacks can be found in his Scrapbook of Newspaper Clippings for January, 1907. Letter from Sam G. Cash to A. E. Willson, February 19, 1908, in Willson Collection;

Night Riders succeeded in forcing almost all of the black residents to leave several small communities in southwest Kentucky. Although blacks living in many different areas of Regions 1 and 2 experienced the violence of the lawless band, the two main targets, suffering repeated assaults, were the blacks in the small communities of Golden Pond in Trigg County and Birmingham in Marshall County. Economic motives lay behind the attacks: The blacks owned good farm lands or were employed by the tobacco trust. Since the end of the Civil War, Afro-Americans had lived in Birmingham, a port town on the Tennessee River. Commenting on this predominantly black area, the *Courier-Journal* (which covered in far greater detail than did the local newspapers the violence against western Kentucky blacks in the early 1900s) explained, "Birmingham [has] . . . some of the best farming land in the Purchase, and around there is to be found practically the entire Negro population of Marshall County."[13]

Attacks on Birmingham blacks began in February, 1908. Toward the end of the month, after having suffered through several raids, community leaders finally went to the authorities, pleading in vain for protection. The blacks had been told to leave Birmingham but had refused to do so, and the mob now resorted to murder, apparently concluding that it would take more than a few warning signs and small brush fires to oust the entrenched Afro-Americans. In addition to being landowners, some of the Birmingham blacks worked at the tobacco factory in the county, which further incensed the Night Riders. Officials of the tobacco company were warned to fire all Negro hands but had likewise failed to act. As a reporter for the *Courier-Journal* accurately predicted, the unwillingness of law officers to intervene sealed the fate of the Birmingham blacks: "Apparently encouraged by the failure of Marshall County officials to prosecute whitecaps who have warned and whipped blacks, 100 men rode into Birmingham on March 8, and shot seven men and whipped five others." John Scruggs and his granddaughter died from wounds sustained during the raid. All of the blacks in the area were given another warning to sell their

Lyle, "Night Riding: A Reign of Fear," 472; Louisville *Courier-Journal*, March 27, 1908; Paducah *Weekly News Democrat*, February 20, 1908; William F. Holmes, "Whitecapping: Agrarian Violence in Mississippi, 1902–1906," *Journal of Southern History*, XXXV (May, 1969), 165–85.

13. Louisville *Courier-Journal*, March 11, 1908.

lands, resolve all of their personal and financial matters, and leave Birmingham within ten days. Most of the blacks soon left for Paducah or Nashville, and in their rush for safety they left behind household goods and farm equipment. A final story concerning the Birmingham blacks appeared in the *Courier-Journal* toward the end of March: "Only six blacks remain since the notices to leave town were posted. A steamer from Marshall County brought in seventeen black families and their household goods. In all about 100 blacks got off the steamer when it arrived in Tennessee."[14]

Shortly after their successful removal of the Birmingham blacks, the Night Riders adopted the practice that seems to have been widespread in Kentucky during the first two decades of the twentieth century and posted a sign near the railroad station in Marshall County telling anyone who somehow remained uninformed about the ousting of blacks that their community was for whites only. The words "Niggers Don't Let the Sun Set on You" were clear in their meaning; and against the backdrop of the destruction of property, whippings, and murders, these words must have invoked fear in Afro-Americans venturing in the county. Since the raid, Marshall County has had a reputation as a place where no blacks live, though this has actually become the case only in the last few decades. The United States census for 1900 lists 348 black residents in Marshall County. By 1910—after the Birmingham raid—the number within the county had declined to 135. According to the 1930 census, only 62 blacks lived in the county; thirty years later, it had no blacks. It is obvious that the few blacks living in the area after March, 1908, were not viewed as a threat to whites. They were, unlike the ones removed, employed as house servants and farm laborers, occupations whites found necessary for their own well-being and appropriate for Afro-Americans.[15]

What happened to the land, farm equipment, and livestock left behind by the Birmingham blacks in their rush to vacate Marshall

14. *Ibid.*, March 11, 17, 24, 28, 1908; Madisonville *Hustler*, March 17, 1908; Taylor, "Night Riders," 57; Cunningham, *On Bended Knees*, 145–46. Upon hearing the details of the bloody March 8 raid, Judge Crumbaugh of Lyon County, who like Sheriff Cash was outspoken in his defense of blacks having the right to reside in the communities, said, "The scoundrels ought to be in the devils belly." See his letter to Governor Willson, March 12, 1908, in Willson Collection.

15. U.S. Census Bureau, *Negro Population, 1790–1915*, 484, and *Fifteenth Census of the United States, 1930* (Washington, D.C., 1932), III, 957.

County? Given the scanty records (and the same problems that exist when trying to discover how many Afro-Americans had owned land in Henry County in the 1870s), it is difficult to determine the number of Birmingham blacks who were landowners. It is known, however, that Nat L. Frizzell of Birmingham had, on December 17, 1896, purchased land from D. L. Nelson. The land, valued at $300, was to be paid off in $100 installments plus interest beginning March 1, 1897. No one is sure what became of Frizzell's land and that owned by other ousted blacks. A prominent lawyer living in Marshall County today speculates that once the blacks had settled in surrounding areas, someone from Marshall County went to them and got them to sign away their land for little or nothing.[16]

About two weeks after the raid on Birmingham, a group of Night Riders terrorized the black residents of Golden Pond and several other communities. At Golden Pond, the mob shot into the homes of Afro-Americans, then went to the servant quarters of the Golden Pond Hotel and forced Tom Weaver, an employee of a tobacco company, out of bed. As noted earlier, they shot him. His death was more of a warning to other black workers to leave the area than a result of any offense he had committed. Because of this raid, some, but not all, of the blacks left the area. During the same time period, Night Riders also warned some blacks to leave the small community of Murray. Several Afro-Americans had purchased homes in white neighborhoods, an obvious sign that they were getting out of their place. No figures exist showing how many blacks fled western Kentucky in the wake of raids by the Night Riders. Clearly, Afro-Americans quit Birmingham entirely, and some left other areas. As the *Courier-Journal* noted when discussing the overall attempts by Night Riders to rid numerous areas in western Kentucky of blacks: "The same policy has been pursued in Lyon County in the vicinity of Kuttawa and along the Cumberland River. At Calvert the negroes were long ago driven out."[17]

Although it can only be speculated, blacks apparently defended their families and homes from attacks by the Night Riders to a degree not found when they were threatened with lynching. To be sure,

16. At the Kentucky Department of Libraries and Archives, see Marshall County Deed Book, XXIV, 226–27 (Microfilm No. 999838); Tip Reed, attorney, interview with the author, April 1, 1987, Mayfield.
17. Louisville *Courier-Journal*, March 11, 17, 25, 1908.

blacks deplored the practice of lynching and saw it as a threat to their own well-being, but some blacks probably felt that the people lynched had brought troubles on themselves by being involved with white women or by challenging whites too aggressively. In other words, while there may have been some doubt about the guilt of a few of the blacks who were lynched, none existed about the blacks who were run off their property in Birmingham, Golden Pond, and other places in western Kentucky. After the first raid on their community, Birmingham blacks prepared for other attacks. According to the *Courier-Journal*, three Night Riders were killed by blacks during the raid on March 8. A letter to Governor Willson from Judge W. L. Crumbaugh of nearby Lyon County substantiates the point that though blacks were eventually forced out of Birmingham they had defended their homes:

> I have learned that a man in this county saw the gang on its march to Birmingham counted them, saw them as they returned, . . . [and] one man was lying on his horse, head hanging on one side, feet on the other, another was held in the saddle by a man riding behind. . . . I had also heard through my Kuttawa friend that one man lives at home both eyes out, four others are visited by a doctor from Kuttawa after night, the doctor crosses the river after all persons have retired, is gone about three hours and returns to river ferries himself over, thinking himself unseen. . . . [T]here were three secret burials in this county and one in Marshall.

Yet a week later, Crumbaugh wrote a second letter to the governor, explaining there was some doubt over how many Night Riders, if any at all, had been killed during the raid. Whether or not men were secretly buried is all but impossible to determine, since no one is sure exactly where the Night Riders lived. Undoubtedly, some of them resided in areas close to the black communities in Golden Pond and Birmingham, but is also likely that some had come from further away to take part in the raids. In short, given the clandestine nature of the Night Riders, it is virtually impossible to know if members of this white mob were killed or severely wounded in the March 8 raid on Birmingham and if these were the only fatalities suffered during raids on black communities.[18]

18. Louisville *Courier-Journal*, March 24, 1908; Crumbaugh to Willson, March 19, 25, 1908, in Willson Collection.

Within days after the last raid on Birmingham, a group of black leaders filed criminal charges in Benton against three Night Riders. Additional charges were brought against Rob Wood for sending the threatening letter that had warned blacks to leave their homes. With justice extremely color-conscious in Kentucky's courts, it did not surprise blacks (or the Night Riders) when the whites won acquittals. But, nevertheless, blacks had forced the issue. Contemporary and scholarly accounts reveal that whenever charges were made in court against Night Riders, there was a strong possibility that some of their cohorts served on the juries. For instance, after the Lyon County grand jury was convened in December, 1908, to investigate a series of charges against the lawless band, the county attorney informed the governor that at least six men chosen as jurymen had participated in raids: "Three fellows according to good proof which I have were in the Eddyville raid. One that was in the Marshall County raid on Birmingham, . . . [and] two that were in the Crittenden County raids."[19]

After settling in Illinois, Lee Baker, Nat Frizzell, and the Scruggs family, all former residents of Birmingham, hired prominent white lawyers to recover damages for the beatings they had sustained and the property that had been stolen from them. The blacks identified more than thirty men who had taken part in the raid. Their case was held in federal court in Paducah, since the blacks and their attorneys knew that it would have been unrealistic to expect a ruling from a state court dominated by Night Riders. A year after the raid, Baker and Frizzell recalled with vivid details how they were tied and were beaten with a whip until it cut into the muscles of their legs. In a surprise move, several whites came forward to testify in behalf of the ousted blacks. Otis Black, a confessed Night Rider, told of the raid and identified all of the defendants as Night Riders. Arthur Griffin confirmed the validity of Black's testimony, saying that Dr. E. Champion, the leader of the mob, made him accompany the Night Riders and hold their horses while the Negroes were being whipped. A third white, Dr. Robert Overby, warned out of Birmingham for dressing the wounds of several blacks, also testified in Baker's and

19. Louisville *Courier-Journal,* March 25, 28, 1908; Paducah *Weekly News Democrat,* April 2, 1908; Walter L. Krone to A. E. Willson, December 7, 1908, in Willson Collection.

Frizzell's behalf. After hearing the evidence and being told that the defendants refused to offer a defense for their actions, the federal judge told the jurors to perform their duty and render a verdict not only sufficient to cover the actual damages suffered by the Birmingham blacks but vindictive damages to any amount not exceeding $25,000. He would be surprised and disappointed, the judge warned the jury, if verdicts were returned for inconsequential sums of money. The jury heeded the words of the judge, awarding $25,000 each to Baker and Frizzell, the full amount requested. It is likely that the blacks did not receive these huge amounts, however. "It is said the defendants against whom judgments were accurred have no property." Also involved in the suit was the Scruggs family, whose grandfather and infant daughter had died during the raid. However, the family members had been prevented from taking part in the deliberations because they were quarantined with smallpox in Illinois. Their case was to be continued. The exact outcome is unknown, but in all probability it was resolved in favor of the Scruggs family.[20]

Within the Kentucky courts, only a handful of men were indicted and prosecuted for the many crimes committed during the Night Riders' five-year reign of terror in western Kentucky. The same scenario was played out in practically every county: The grand jury refused to return indictments against Night Riders, or on the few occasions when a member of the band was brought to trial, the jury was packed with his former associates. Dr. David Amoss, the person largely responsible for the start of the secret brigade, was tried and found not guilty in Hopkinsville in 1911. All told, three men were convicted and sent to prison, each for only one year. It is doubtful that any blacks, including Baker, Frizzell, and the Scruggs family, recovered their property and goods. By contrast, in Mississippi hundreds of men suspected of being involved in attacks on blacks were fined $25 and given suspended jail sentences of thirty days; significantly, a number of men were found guilty of murder and received terms in prison ranging from ten years to life.[21]

20. Madisonville *Hustler*, July 14, 1908; Paducah *News-Democrat*, April 20, 21, 1909; New York *Times*, April 21, 1909; Louisville *Courier-Journal*, April 21, 1909; Taylor, "Night Riders," 57; Lyle, "Night Riding: A Reign of Fear," 470. Unfortunately, the ruling of the federal court in the Scruggs case was not recorded in the *Federal Digest* or in the *Federal Reporter*.

21. Augustus E. Willson, "The People and Their Law," a speech delivered before the

That only a few Night Riders were prosecuted and then found not guilty or at most handed extremely light sentences tended to encourage the return of the lawless band. As explained by a reporter for the New York *Times*, by 1915, the Night Riders had resolved "to regulate the conduct of the community through intimidation, displace negro labor with white and fix prices which merchants should charge for merchandise." In outlying areas of Christian and Crittenden counties, farms, houses, and buildings owned by Afro-Americans were riddled with bullets. Placards were posted on these farms, instructing the blacks to leave the area or suffer the consequences of remaining. Eighteen men were eventually arrested and arraigned on charges of being Night Riders and terrorizing blacks. All of the men were acquitted. After the verdict, a score or more black farmers, realizing that the law would not protect them, moved from the area. Several months later, the Night Riders attacked blacks living in Ohio County. One black, Peter Hart, was killed. Hart had received a death threat telling him to leave the area and had ignored the warning. Dozens of blacks, including Reuben Howard and his wife, were flogged. They received a small measure of justice when the Ohio County Circuit Court indicted sixty men for being Night Riders. Two Night Riders pleaded guilty, throwing themselves on the mercy of the court, and were sentenced to three years in prison. They agreed to testify against the others, but the outcome of those trials is unknown. Regardless, as late as 1920 the Night Riders remained active. Upset over the steady decline in tobacco prices and lacking an effective means of protesting to the large tobacco companies, a small band of farmers in Mayfield and Graves County resorted to destroying crops and setting warehouses on fire. And as had happened previously, some of the violence carried over into renewed attacks on Afro-Americans.[22]

The running off of blacks and the destruction or seizure of their property was not limited to the western part of the commonwealth.

American Bar Association at Detroit, August 25, 1909, pp. 14, 19 (copy in Division of Special Collections and Archives, University of Kentucky). For the trial of Amoss, see the Hopkinsville *Kentuckian*, March 11–18, 1911; Holmes, "Agrarian Violence in Mississippi," 180–84.

22. See the Louisville *Courier-Journal* during January and February, 1915, for a number of stories detailing the actions of white mobs in Christian and Crittenden counties; Tuskegee Clippings, Reel 221, Frame 277; New York *Times*, August 26, 1915, March 28, 1920; Paducah *Evening Sun*, August 25, 26, 28, 1915, March 24, 27, 1920.

Thousands of blacks, primarily from Alabama and Georgia, migrated to the eastern Kentucky mountains during the coal-mining boom of the early 1900s. Although they accounted for only a small percentage of the population, these newly arrived blacks found racial segregation just as severe as in the Deep South. As explained by Ronald D Eller: "Coal operators usually segregated the black population into 'Colored Towns' consisting of the least desirable houses in the camp. Schools and churches, where provided, were segregated, as were recreational facilities, restaurants, and saloons." In the coal-mining community of Wheelwright, company officials made sure that no contact occurred between blacks and whites once they left the mines. The town had a black police deputy to control "Hall Hollow," the Negro section of town. Wheelwright had three boardinghouses: one for whites, one for foreigners, and one for blacks.[23]

After the First World War, hundreds of southern black men found good-paying jobs at the Louisville and Nashville Railroad Company (L&N) in Corbin. Many of these Afro-Americans were employed as skilled laborers for the construction of a new railroad terminal in the southern part of the city. A major cause of the riot that occurred in October, 1919, was white resentment of blacks coming to Corbin to work these relatively high-paying jobs. Local legend has it that Corbin was free of crime and vice—until the arrival of the southern blacks, when the city experienced numerous assaults and robberies. Whites also blamed the black immigrants for the presence of prostitution and bootlegging, vices already in operation in Corbin long before blacks came to that mountain community.

About 9:00 in the evening of October 30, 1919, a rumor began spreading in the white saloons that A. F. Thompson, a night watchman, had been robbed and stabbed by two unidentified Afro-Americans. Within an hour, a mob of at least 150 white men, all of whom were heavily armed with rifles, pistols, stones, and large pieces of lumber, took to the streets, and the rioting began. The men first went into the restaurants and office buildings, seizing the black employees and taking them to the train station. They then ventured into the black community and forced all of the black railroad workers to the depot. Any number of other blacks, seeing the approaching mob, fled Corbin on

23. Eller, *Miners, Millhands, and Mountaineers,* 170–71; Lewis, *Black Coal Miners in America,* 145–48; Spero and Harris, *The Black Worker,* 236–38.

foot. When the L & N train arrived at 2:15 in the morning, an extra car was added and all of the blacks who had been detained were loaded on; mob leaders ordered the conductor to keep the blacks on the train until it arrived in Knoxville, ninety miles away from Corbin.[24]

The mob, however, was far from satisfied. Realizing that a number of black workers had escaped, some of the mob members spent the night searching for the blacks; most were captured at the outskirts of the city. Other whites returned to the now vacant area where the blacks had been living and destroyed the tents, shacks, and boarding cars that had been home for the railroad workers. Having used the pretext that the criminal act of two black railroad employees justified the removal of all of their fellow workers, the mob turned its attention to the Afro-Americans still remaining in Corbin, even though no one suggested that they were responsible for the assault on the night watchman or the "crime wave" in the city. The entire crew of forty black employees of a Louisville contractor, who had been constructing Center and Main streets for the past six months, was rounded up and taken to the train depot. The decision to remove the "grade negroes," as local whites contemptuously called them, meant that the only blacks left untouched were those who had been living in Corbin before the black railroad workers arrived. As reported in the newspaper: "The negro families who have been residents of the city for years are those of John Barry, Alex Tye, John Turner and Emma Woods. Some members of the mob advocated allowing the family of John Barry, who has been a resident of Corbin 33 years to remain, saying he was a 'good nigger.' Others favored ridding the place of all negroes." Ultimately, all of the black "old-timers" were allowed to remain. Meanwhile, the authorities had at last heard of the violence and arrived at the depot where the blacks were being held. Instead of freeing them and disbanding the mob, the police agreed that the blacks should be compelled to leave, though the police did inform the mob that further violence would not be tolerated. With the police now maintaining "order" (they had searched the Afro-Americans to make sure that none of them had weapons but made no attempt to

24. For newspaper accounts of the Corbin riot, see the following: New York *Times*, November 1, 1919; Corbin *Times*, October 31, November 7, 1919. Most of the comments made in the following paragraph have been drawn from the account of the Louisville *Courier-Journal*, November 1, 1919.

search and disarm the whites), local officials, who had, of course, remained silent throughout the night, said that no state troops would be called since everything was under control. "The work of deporting the negroes progressed today without serious trouble," the newspaper noted. All told, as many as 250 blacks, and maybe at least another hundred more, were forced out of Corbin by the white mob.

Although they had agreed with the blanket indictment that the black railroad workers were responsible for numerous criminal acts, most local whites seemed to be appalled by the ouster, saying that the riot would hurt the growth of Corbin. Letters were written to the local newspaper calling for the arrest and prosecution of the men involved in the incident. Labeling the riot "deplorable," the editor of the Corbin *Times* was nevertheless relieved to note that the riot was led by lower-class whites. Right from the start, there was speculation about the "two unidentified Negroes" whose alleged robbery had sparked the riot. Writing in 1981, a Corbin historian noted, "Later it was thought that the blacks were not involved in the lawless act that triggered the incident, but that it was committed by two white men whose names were not publicized."[25]

Corbin's white leadership may have been troubled by the forced removal of hundreds of innocent Afro-Americans, but they failed to adopt any measures to allow the safe return of the black railroad workers.[26] In reality, of course, whether or not two blacks had committed the robbery and stabbing was secondary to the mob's aim of removing all blacks as job competitors. During the riot, a few whites had been sympathetic toward black domestics—blacks, in the view of whites, who "knew their place." Lillian Butner, a young girl at the time of the riot, recalls: "My father was tipped off by a white man. He hid us across the street with a white family. . . . The Negroes they found were herded into pens like cattle and shipped off on trains."

25. See John Leland Crawford, *A Tale of One City: Some Highlights in the History of Corbin* (Chicago, 1981), 58–60. The part of the book discussing the 1919 riot is entitled "An Unsavory Incident."

26. The L & N Railroad Company made no public statements denouncing the violent attacks on its workers. It is also obvious, though no records exist to verify this position, that the company relented to the demands of local whites and did not return black workers to the Corbin area. No mention of the Corbin riot is contained in the voluminous L & N Papers, housed at the Archives and Records, University of Louisville.

Long after all hostility over the incident had ended, no blacks moved into the city. Corbin had room only for those Afro-Americans performing service jobs. For instance, Mrs. Butner's husband worked at the Wilbur Hotel for more than forty years, and, as she explains, he encountered no racial problems. However, the Butner family and most of the other blacks employed in Corbin lived in London, twelve miles away, and commuted to work. From the end of the riot to the present, the only blacks living in Corbin have been a handful of servants, and in 1988 only one of these families still remained in Corbin. As a way of making sure that other blacks knew that they were not welcome in Corbin, local whites adopted the practice that seems to have been used in an undetermined number of Kentucky cities: They put up a sign saying "Niggers Don't Be Here When The Sun Goes Down." The sign was displayed in Corbin until the 1960s.[27]

What happened in Corbin was not an isolated incident; whites in at least two other areas of eastern Kentucky forced blacks to leave in the 1920s. Unfortunately, the paucity of historical data coupled with the unwillingness of white residents to discuss these incidents have resulted in very little coming to light about these violent incidents beyond the obvious fact that blacks feared to remain in a given area. In the ousting of blacks from Ravenna, a small community in Estill County, one can only speculate about why whites compelled blacks to leave the area. Historically, few blacks have lived in Estill County. The 1890 census lists 581 blacks, composing 5 percent of the total population, and 10,255 whites. At the start of the century, the number of blacks had declined by more than 60 percent, to 223, while the number of whites had increased to 11,446. Blacks in 1900 made up less than 2 percent of the population. Ten years later, the number of blacks had decreased by another 50 percent, to 106, while whites had increased to 12,167. At that point, blacks were 0.9 percent of Estill's total population. Interestingly, however, the number of blacks increased by the time of the 1920 census to 204, or 1.3 percent of the population. Whether the increase in the number of blacks had anything to do with the incident that occurred in the county is unknown. In many instances, an increase in the black population, even one as insignificant as that in Estill County, led to trouble as whites felt that

27. Lillian Butner, interview with author, January 30, 1987, London. Clark said that he saw the sign in Corbin warning blacks to avoid the area. Interview with author.

blacks were "invading" their communities, taking their jobs and lowering the value of their homes. Also, considering that the 1920 census data were probably not collected until sometime toward the fall of the year—that is, after the Ravenna incident—it is likely that the number of blacks had increased at an even greater rate in the county, leading directly to problems in the small community. When discussing the ousting of blacks from Ravenna, the Maysville newspaper said: "All negroes have been ordered out of this place because of sentiment against them, following an attack of a negro man on a white boy. The facts have not been fully disclosed, but the negroes are leaving town without delay." By the time of the next census, in 1930, the number of blacks had decreased to 145 while the number of whites had risen to 16,934. Blacks were once again less than 1 percent of Estill County's citizens.[28]

The brief newspaper account of the ousting of blacks from Ravenna does not reveal a significant fact about this small community: Like Corbin, the area had been selected by the L&N as the site for the construction of a large railroad terminal. This undoubtedly meant that black railroad workers had come into the area. Again, because of an absence of sources, the exact cause of the incident at Ravenna can only be speculated. But it is revealing that the newspaper mentioned that a black man had assaulted a white youth, an incident similar to that rumored to have happened in Corbin. Surely the whites responsible for the forced removal of Afro-Americans from Ravenna must have known that once the blacks had been ousted in Corbin, their employer, the L&N Railroad, had acquiesced in the matter.

Only oral accounts remain about the removal of blacks from Cary, a small community in Bell County. Practically everyone living in that part of Kentucky labored in the coal mines; blacks and whites worked on the same jobs for the same pay. Away from work, however, segregation was rigidly enforced in schools, churches, and public accommodations.[29] As told by Jim Garland, a longtime resident of the area, whose narrative was recorded and eventually published, the 1923

28. U.S. Census Bureau, *Twelfth Census of the United States, 1900* (Washington, D.C., 1901), I, 540, *Fourteenth Census of the United States, 1920* (Washington, D.C., 1921), III, 372, *Fifteenth Census of the United States, 953*; Maysville *Bulletin*, April 8, 1920.

29. For detailed descriptions of racial segregation in Bell County, see Joseph Williams, secretary of Bell County NAACP, to William Pickens of the national office,

Cary riot centered on a dispute between two men, one white and the other black, for the affections of a black woman. A shoot-out occurred, and the white youth, Girt Roark, was killed. When informed of his son's death, the elder Roark "went berserk and began shooting at every black person he saw." Other whites quickly joined Roark, and they decided to drive out all the black residents. As usual, the blacks' appeal to the authorities for protection was a waste of time, even though they had lived in Cary for many years and had not been accused of criminal acts. "My own feelings and those of my family were all in sympathy with the Negroes, but we were definitely in the minority. All we could do was help secretly." Going further, Garland says: "This was a sad day. I had known many of these people all my life. I had had them as customers when I sold newspapers, I had sold them blackberries, I had worked with them, I had gone with my mother to see their babies. Given only two days to get out of Cary, these people had to leave everything they had." One black, for example, was forced to abandon his three cows and nine hogs. After being forced out of Cary, blacks continued to work in the mines in the area and live in the other nearby towns, but none moved back into Cary.[30]

Were Corbin, Ravenna, and Cary isolated incidents or part of a pattern of racial violence in eastern Kentucky? Blacks were part of the out-migration from the mountains that started in the late 1920s, when the coal boom had become a bust. Like whites, Kentucky blacks moved to Detroit, Cleveland, Indianapolis, and other northern cities in hopes of finding jobs in industry. The desire to educate their children also led blacks and whites to move from isolated parts of the Kentucky mountains. There is no way of knowing, however, the number of blacks who left during these years under duress. It is not difficult to imagine that once layoffs started in the coal industry, any blacks still working came in for abuse from frustrated, unemployed whites.

An incident similar in some respects to the Corbin riot occurred in

January 15, 1940, and J. Johnson Williams of Bell County NAACP to the national association, July 17, 1942, both in NAACP Papers.

30. Julia S. Ardery (ed.), *Welcome the Traveler Home: Jim Garland's Story of the Kentucky Mountains* (Lexington, 1983), 113–15; Walter Hurst, interview with the author, November 15, 1984, Lexington. Hurst, a retired coal miner, lived and worked in Straight Creek, Bell County, which is near Cary. He knew accounts of the Cary incident.

1924 at Dix River, in Mercer County, the site of a dam construction. About eight hundred black men had been brought into the area to work on the huge project. Away from work, both white and black men spent their time gambling, drinking, and fighting, though usually on a segregated basis. On November 9, 1924, Edward Winkler was killed by two blacks who were convinced that he had cheated them at cards. However, white construction workers were told not that the men had been gambling and drinking but that a group of unidentified blacks had killed Winkler during a robbery attempt. As a white newspaper explained, "Incensed by the murder, a group of residents of the Dix River area and white construction workers invaded the camp site of blacks with clubs, sticks, pistols and shotguns and forced all of the 800 black workers to leave the camp." Just like at Corbin, where whites had invaded restaurants and office buildings to seize peaceful blacks, at Dix River the huge white mob attacked dozens of blacks at the barber shop and movie house, forcing them to leave as well. The whites decided to march all of them to the railroad depot in Burgin, several miles away, and they were ordered to remain in the depot until a freight train could be flagged down. Many Afro-Americans had sustained severe beatings: One man had his knee shattered, and several needed immediate medical attention for gunshot wounds. Indeed, after the police ended the riot by talking the white mob out of the idea of putting the blacks on the train, dozens of black men were treated at the hospitals. James Bond, investigating the incident for the Commission on Interracial Cooperation, reported that the black workers had been robbed of their clothing and other valuables and had been physically assaulted during the riot. "Many of these colored people were found the next day in different sections of the country wandering about dazed without sufficient clothing and in a highly excited state of mind." One white newspaper, the Lexington *Leader*, went to great lengths to explain that the vast majority of black workers were innocent of any wrongdoings. "It was," the newspaper added, "purely a massacre of that element of hard working Negroes by that class of whites who carry a grudge and foment trouble when coming in contact with Negroes."[31]

31. Accounts of the Dix River riot can be found in the following sources: James Bond, "Report of the Director" (January, 1925), in Commission on Interracial Coopera-

As we have seen, the authorities usually failed to intervene when whites forced blacks out of an area. After the Dix River riot, however, state officials and the construction company, L. E. Meyers Company, moved quickly to end the disturbance and return things to normal. Within twenty-four hours of the outbreak of the riot, members of Troop A, 54th Machine Gun Squadron of the Kentucky National Guard, arrived in Mercer County. With the state troops protecting their living areas, practically all of the black workers returned to the construction site. Mercer County authorities arrested two blacks, Walter Chance and John Williams (known as Big Jelly Roll and Little Jelly Roll) for the murder of Edward Winkler. They charged a third black, Jack Johnson, with complicity in the crime. Denied bail, the men were held until the February term of the Mercer County grand jury. Eventually three other blacks were arrested for their alleged knowledge of the murder. In a surprise move, the police arrested and charged with assault and other offenses more than a dozen white men who were identified as leaders of the riot. These whites were also held in jail until February. The grand jury released all of the whites, citing a lack of evidence. Charges against most of the blacks were also dropped. Indicted for murder, Chance and Williams were convicted and received prison sentences. Given the reality of black life in Kentucky and the "legal lynchings" that often occurred, going to prison, instead of to the electric chair, was a rather light punishment.[32]

That the black workers went back to the construction project at Dix River suggests a different attitude compared with earlier disturbances; in those incidents, whites let it be known that they would not welcome a return of the ousted blacks. By the mid-1920s, white leaders throughout the state agreed that steps had to be taken to eliminate mob rule. The beating of black farmers in isolated areas could be ignored or covered up, but an incident as blatant as the forced removal of eight hundred men could no longer be tolerated. Most important,

tion Papers, Special Collections and Archives, Woodruff Library, Atlanta University (hereinafter cited as CIC Papers), the Lexington *Herald*, November 10, 11, 15, 18, 1924, the Lexington *Leader*, November 22, 1924, and the Harrodsburg *Herald*, November 14, 21, 1924.

32. Lexington *Herald*, November 11, 18, 1924, February 13, 1925; Harrodsburg *Herald*, February 27, 1925.

however, the labor of the men at Dix River was necessary for the successful completion of the project. Obviously some of the whites resented blacks working on the project and wanted them fired, but this disdain for Afro-Americans failed to secure their removal. The company needed the workers and had, therefore, assisted the state in providing police protection to ensure that the blacks could perform without the overt threat of violence.

The November, 1924, riot at Dix River might have been the last attempt by a white mob to force an entire black population to leave an area. This does not mean, however, that many other actions by whites to keep blacks "in their place" ceased. Individual blacks were still beaten and given warnings to leave their homes, just as other Afro-Americans had experienced in Kentucky since emancipation. One of these incidents occurred in Hopkinsville in the spring of 1932 when Jim Hill, a black worker for the Moore Construction Company, had three teeth knocked out by L. J. Swift, the road boss. Hill immediately left the job and went to the county prosecutor to obtain an arrest warrant against Swift on a charge of assault and battery. The prosecutor refused to issue one, saying that Hill should work out a peaceable settlement with his attacker. Ignoring this advice, Hill brought a civil suit against Swift. An all-white jury heard the case in court. Swift acknowledged striking Hill in the face, saying that the Negro had talked back and made threats against him. Swift's brother and several friends testified in his behalf, corroborating the testimony that the black man had made threatening statements. Hill's suit was thrown out of court.[33]

One week later, Hill was awakened by a rap on the door. After being informed that it was the sheriff of Christian County, he opened the door, whereupon pistols were stuck in his face. Hill was nervous, but he recognized almost all of the men in the mob before a sack was placed over his head. As Hill was being carried off, his wife appeared at the door with a lamp and a gun. The light was shot out of her hands. Hill was then tied down in a car. Worried that Hill's wife could recognize them, several men returned to the house, only to find that

33. The details of the incident involving Hill and Swift can be found in a long letter from Edward M. Bacoyn, a white attorney in Hopkinsville, to Walter White, of the NAACP, May 19, 1932, in NAACP Papers.

Mrs. Hill had made a successful escape. The men then drove into Tennessee, finally stopping in a deserted area. There the mob beat Hill with tobacco sticks "till blood oozed forth from his body and his heavy underclothing blood-soaked, stuck to his back." Although no bones were broken, his hands, arms, and back were "beaten almost to a jell." The mob left Hill along the highway, warning him not to return to Kentucky.

As he had indicated earlier when attempting to file charges against Swift, Hill was not easily intimidated. Despite the mob's warning, he returned home. Hill told Edward M. Bacoyn, a white attorney, about his beating. Hill named T. J. Swift and Paul Street, a law officer, as the leaders of the mob. In the company of Bacoyn, Hill went to see the county judge, "who was so sorry [about the beating of Hill] he almost cried, but could not help." The local prosecutor once again proved to be unconcerned, refusing to hear the facts of the case. Hill decided to appear personally before the Christian County grand jury when it convened in May. Word quickly spread that Hill had talked to the authorities and was determined to press the matter further. Dave Oats, one of Hill's attackers, visited the black man to verify his intentions of testifying before the grand jury. Hill replied that when appearing before the grand jury he would name Oats as a member of the mob. After Oats left, however, Hill realized that no one would help him if the mob decided to return. He and his wife immediately left Christian County for parts unknown. Hill, a man who had served his nation in the Great War, who had lived all of his life in the area, was forced to leave his home because the law would not protect his right to live peacefully in the then unsuitably named Christian County.

In Middlesboro, one of the largest cities in eastern Kentucky, a black physician, Dr. I. H. Miller, was active in politics, to the dismay of local whites. Miller demanded that white politicians be accountable to blacks and that deserving Negro political leaders be rewarded with patronage positions. One evening, a mob kidnapped Miller and took him to a remote mountain area outside of Middlesboro. Word of his seizure spread, and the police began a search for the black physician. Miller was found several hours later, severely whipped and barely conscious. Telling Miller that he had been "too officious in politics," ten men—all of whom he could identify—had administered the beating. Miller was provided with police protection at his home and office. Nevertheless, as a newspaper speculated, Miller would be compelled to leave town once the guards were removed because little could be done to prevent another attack, and maybe his death.[34]

The plights of Hill and Miller show clearly what happened to those black Kentuckians whose actions were viewed as a threat to white supremacy. Neither man had committed rape, murder, or other offenses. Swift, of course, testified in court that Hill had threatened him. If that had been true, Hill would probably have been lynched instead of whipped. It is extremely difficult to know how long this harassment of individual blacks continued. Lynchings and murders often caught the attention of the public, but forcing a black to leave town could easily be kept from the newspaper. Compelling a black to leave a community could have occurred so often that the act might not have been deemed newsworthy at all. White mob rule proved to be very effective in the Bluegrass State, as perceived black troublemakers and competitors were eliminated. The Afro-Americans who remained knew that their farm lands, livestock, businesses—indeed, all they had accumulated—could be taken from them. Security was for white men.

34. Tuskegee Clippings, Reel 228, Frame 709; Louisville *Defender*, September 2, 1933.

FIVE

Holding Back A Rising Tide, 1875–1899

A fro-Americans consistently attempted to end the numerous lawless acts occurring in Kentucky. In strong terms, they denounced
lynchings and mob rule, often urging the state and federal governments to intervene to protect their lives and their property. On rare
occasions, county judges, prosecuting attorneys, and concerned civic
leaders called for the adoption of appropriate measures to prevent
lynchings, even when they believed that a black was guilty of an especially heinous crime. But clearly, the usual response of whites continued to be one of support, not condemnation, of lynch law (even
though they simultaneously spoke of their respect for the law). Nevertheless, by the 1890s, a number of white leaders, primarily Republicans, agreed with blacks that the state had to take a strong stand
against mob rule. Because of their efforts, Kentucky became one of a
handful of states to pass an antilynching law.

After a lynching, whites often feared some form of retaliation from
Afro-Americans. Although unconcerned about being prosecuted by
the law, the leaders of lynch mobs sometimes sold their property and
left the area after the incident out of fear that Afro-Americans would
seek a measure of revenge. Blacks, for example, were responsible for a
series of fires in Georgetown and other cities after lynchings had occurred. In short, despite the lynching epidemic in Kentucky in the
late 1800s, blacks were far from passive and attempted in a number of
ways to combat the problem.

On at least one ill-fated occasion, a white sheriff attempted to prevent a mob from taking his black prisoner. Richard May was arrested
on a charge of rape in Owensboro in July, 1884. Rumors circulated for
several days that May would be lynched. The sheriff, a former Confederate, boldly stated his determination to protect May's life: He would

die in the line of duty if necessary. On the night of July 14, a mob of heavily armed men stormed the jail. True to his word, sheriff William J. Lucas tried to repel them, firing thirteen shots into the mob and seriously wounding one of the men. The sheriff's opposition seemed to arouse the fury of the mob. They responded by shooting at Lucas; several bullets hit their mark. As Lucas lay dying, his wife picked up the fight, attempting to turn back the mob, but greatly outnumbered, she was quickly overpowered. The mob broke down the cell door with a sledgehammer, took May, and hanged him from a tree outside the courthouse. Instead of giving other sheriffs and deputies the courage to stand up to the mob, Lucas' decision to protect his prisoner might have convinced them even more that their lives were not worth risking for Afro-Americans accused of murdering and, especially, of raping white women.[1]

Throughout the late 1800s, law officers and state officials were far more likely to challenge a lynch mob if the intended victim was white. A white man named Roberts was on trial for murder in Vanceburg in July, 1877. Officials had forty armed guards protect him during his trial. Roberts was not lynched. Two white men sought in the brutal murder of Pearl Bryan were returned to Kentucky from Ohio in May, 1896. To protect them, state officials sent forty rounds of ammunition and wagonloads of overcoats and blankets to the area. These men, too, were not lynched.[2]

One of the most widely publicized efforts by state officials to prevent lynchings occurred in northeast Kentucky in the early 1880s. In Ashland on the night of December 23, 1881, three white men, later identified as George Ellis, William Neal, and Ellis Craft, entered the home of Mrs. J. W. Gibbons and raped and murdered her two daughters. Her son was also killed. After their arrest, the three men were taken to Lexington for safekeeping until the start of the trial, which was moved only a short distance from Ashland to Cattlesburg. Ellis, the first defendant to go on trial, was found guilty of murder and quickly agreed to testify against Neal and Craft in hopes of avoiding the gallows. But before the start of the next trial, several hundred men

---

1. Louisville *Courier-Journal,* July 15, 1884; New York *Times,* July 15, 17, 1884; Hayes, *Owensboro,* 370–72.

2. New York *Times,* July 6, 1877; Chicago *Tribune,* May 12, 1896. For another prevented lynching, see the New York *Times,* April 12, 16, 1890.

from Ashland arrived in the town, overpowered the jailer, and lynched Ellis from a sycamore tree.[3]

The authorities decided to postpone the trial of Neal and Craft for several months, but the delay had no effect on the mob's desire for revenge. Fully aware that a lynching might occur, local officials requested state troops to guard the two men when the trial began in Cattlesburg on November 1. Once the trial started, the defense lawyers requested a change of venue. In a concession rarely granted to black defendants, the judge agreed that Neal and Craft could not receive fair trials in the same environment where Ellis had been lynched and ordered their return to Lexington until the start of the trial in Carter County. However, leaders of the Ashland mob were determined that the men would not leave the area alive, even if it meant a fight with the state troops. Upon learning that the roads and the trains from the area were being closely watched by the mob, Major John Allen, commander of the state troops, took control of the steamboat *Granite State* to carry his group to Maysville or to Huntington, West Virginia. But when it left the shore, the steamboat came under gunfire from members of the mob who had seized a train that ran parallel with the river. On orders from Major Allen, the state troops returned the fire, killing two of the mob and wounding almost a dozen others before returning to shore at nightfall. The confrontation continued in the morning when the mob seized a ferry in a desperate attempt to intercept the steamboat. Again, the troops fired, killing three more men. (Estimates of the number of people killed in these incidents would vary from five to sixteen; some said that a number of innocent women and children died.) The state troops with their prisoners were then allowed to leave the area without further trouble. Governor Luke Blackburn issued an order commending the state troops. Using words that Afro-Americans accused of crimes would have appreciated, the governor proclaimed that the state needed to maintain the law and must not be ruled by lynchers, regulators, and others intent on taking the law into their own hands.[4]

3. Louisville *Courier-Journal*, June 3, 4, November 2, 1882; New York *Times*, November 2, 3, 12, 14, 1882.

4. A detailed account of the actions of the state troops and the decision to fire on the mob is in Legislative Document No. 29, *Report of the Adjutant General State of Kentucky to the Commander-in-Chief, for the Years 1882–83* (Frankfort, 1883); see

On several occasions after a white had been lynched, officials conducted extensive probes and attempted to bring the guilty to justice to demonstrate that the law could not be violated in their community. On the first day of the year in 1895, a mob seized Thomas Blair, a white man "reputed to be a desperate character," from the jail in Mount Sterling. Blair had recently been acquitted of murder but was back in jail on a charge of reckless shooting while drunk. Thirty masked men easily surprised the jailer. They carried Blair to the yard of the Kentucky and South Atlantic Railroad and hanged him from a wooden trestle. A note was pinned to his body: "We find Thomas Blair guilty of the murder of Capt. J. L. Bowman, and hang him this January 1, 1895, to avenge the rights of law-abiding citizens. Friends of Capt. J. L. Bowman."[5]

A number of civic leaders of Mount Sterling were determined that the lynchers be punished. At a mass meeting on the night of January 14, several hundred people approved the naming of a committee to assist the police in their investigation. They did so because of growing displeasure with the police department's lack of interest in the case and its report that the men responsible for the lynching were unknown. Funds were raised to secure the services of George W. Drake, a private detective, to help identify the lynchers. The investigation was given a boost when the county judge not only issued a charge to the grand jury to indict the men responsible for Blair's death but also extended the term of the grand jury into February in the hope of solving the matter. The lynching indicated that lawlessness existed in Mount Sterling, the judge explained. Drake and the committee produced immediate and startling results when they identified a number of prominent citizens as having been involved in the lynching. Drake had both the county jailer and the chief of police arrested as leaders of the mob. Over the next few days, more than a dozen men were arrested, including the county sheriff's son. One attempted suicide. The investigation created further controversy when the people under indictment charged that Drake was employed by their political oppo-

<hr/>

also Louisville *Courier-Journal,* October 13, November 2, 1882. Craft died on the gallows in Grayson on October 12, 1883. To the dismay of many citizens in the Ashland area, Neal would live for another year and a half, finally being put to death in Grayson on March 27, 1885.

5. Lousiville *Courier-Journal,* January 2, 1895.

nents, who were determined to take control of Mount Sterling. In an attempt to further discredit the investigation, the men charged with Blair's lynching had Drake arrested on a murder warrant for participating in the mob that hanged Oscar Morton of Powell County (a white man who had killed the sheriff of Beattyville in the fall of 1894). Ultimately, the entire controversy ended with no one standing trial for the lynching. Yet the outrage of the people did have an effect: Blair would be the last person lynched in Mount Sterling.[6]

As the Blair lynching shows, most white Kentuckians were opposed to lynchings in principle but approved of the mob murders that happened in their own area. Henry Watterson proved to be an exception: He moved from justifying lynchings and rebuking those who denounced the practice, to condemning lynchings regardless of the offense committed. In Louisville, there was another outspoken white foe of lynching who, in fact, denounced the practice much earlier than did Watterson. In 1886, John Albert Broadus, a minister and a professor at the Southern Baptist Theological Seminary, wrote a long letter to the *Courier-Journal* addressing what he called a question of "justice, of fundamental right, of essential civilization, of human welfare." The practice of lynching was growing worse all the time and would prove to be, Broadus predicted, destructive of civilization. Unlike most of his contemporaries, he believed that the threat of being lynched did not deter criminals: "The idea of having all the facts searched out and proved against him, having his guilt fully established, and then having to wait for weeks, with a knowledge that at last he will be hung, there is really something more terrible about this than attaches to the prospect of lynching." Compounding the problem in the South was the presence of "many ignorant and often degraded white people" and "this mighty mass of colored people." But significantly, Broadus quickly and forcefully explained that not all blacks were alike, that within the South there existed a group of Afro-Americans that whites must work with: "There is a goodly number of intelligent Negroes who really take sound and wholesome views of

6. Extensive coverage of the events in Mount Sterling can be found in the Louisville *Courier-Journal* and the Cincinnati *Enquirer* for much of January and February, 1895. Two Mount Sterling newspapers, the *Advocate* and the *Sentinel-Democrat*, also devoted considerable attention for almost two months to the lynching and the public outcry over mob violence.

the situation. If we continue to tolerate lynching, we lead these better Negroes to think that we are the enemies of all their race. We alienate the better class from the support of justice and government and civilization." Broadus concluded: "I appeal to thoughtful men wherever the 'Courier-Journal' is read, will you not come out and condemn this business of lynching? Will you not openly discourage and oppose and stop it? We can stop it. Is not this our duty? Is it not high time?"[7] Considering that this letter was written when the American public often applauded the "lynching bees," when views on blacks as inferior were widely voiced, the opinions of Broadus are enlightening. He, unlike the majority of whites of that day, saw the importance of not alienating this better class of Negroes. Broadus even went so far as to write the word "Negro" with a capital N, a polite—and correct—gesture that white newspapers and magazines refused to follow.

Like Broadus, a number of prominent blacks spoke out against lynchings, pleading with white America to take steps to end the practice. Frederick Douglass, the nation's most respected black, pointed out that lynching was destroying the moral fabric of the nation. Under no circumstances could a society excuse or defend lynch law because, as he forcefully argued, by its very nature lynching was a "crime more far-reaching, dangerous, and deadly than the crime it is intended to punish." In his view, northern whites were as guilty as southerners for the continuation of this brutal practice: "The sin against the negro is both sectional and national, and until the voice of the North shall be heard in emphatic condemnation and withering reproach against these continued ruthless mob-law murders, it will remain equally involved with the South in this common crime."[8]

According to newspaper editor Ida B. Wells, black people defending themselves provided the only sure remedy to the lynching epidemic. Citing an incident in Paducah in which blacks had armed themselves to prevent a lynching, she explained, "The lesson this teaches and which every Afro American should ponder well, is that a Winchester rifle should have a place of honor in every black home, and it should

7. A biographical account of Broadus can be found in Archibald Thomas Robertson, *Life and Letters of John Albert Broadus* (Philadelphia, 1910). The letter denouncing lynchings can be found on pp. 352–54.

8. Frederick Douglass, "Lynch Law in the South," *North American Review*, CLV (July, 1892), 17–24.

be used for that protection which the law refuses to give." Once whites realized they were likely to be killed for attacking a black, they would avoid lynching parties. But if blacks remained passive and depended on the white legal process, then more lynchings would occur. "The more the Afro American yields and cringes and begs, the more he has to do so, the more he is insulted, outraged and lynched."[9]

Picking up their weapons, as advised by Wells, was only one of several methods blacks used to challenge the numerous assaults and lynchings in Kentucky during the last thirty-five years of the nineteenth century. In the years immediately after slavery, they sent several long, detailed petitions to Congress, documenting racial violence and urging that body to intervene in their behalf. But it would be in the many conventions held in the late 1800s where black leaders best expressed their disappointment with the lack of positive action to end racial violence. In a large gathering in Lexington in November, 1867, they protested discrimination in public accommodations and the lawlessness rampant in the state. At a convention in Louisville almost two decades later, blacks were still demanding that state officials grant them equal rights and take measures to end lawlessness. "When charged with grave offenses the jail is mobbed and the accused is taken out and hanged; and out of the hundreds of such cases since the war not a single high-handed murderer has been even brought before a court to answer." The group urged the state legislature to appoint an investigative committee to find out why lynchings were occurring and what could be done to stop them. Growing out of the 1885 convention was a relatively short-lived organization, the State Protective Union, whose avowed purpose was to "defend ourselves against mobs, assassins, and other obstructions that impede our progress." Founders of the union said that only by collective action could blacks hope to end white violence: "Since freedom we have been the prey and game for prejudicial whites, and will continue so, as long as we are scattered like the dust in a whirlwind." At the end of the century, black leaders at another convention urged state officials to adopt measures to ensure that the rights of blacks were no longer violated at will. We ask not for special treatment, just equal treatment, the black leaders stated. The delegates at the 1898 convention concluded with a ringing

9. Ida B. Wells, *Southern Horrors: Lynch Law In All Its Phases* (New York, 1892), 22–23.

denouncement of lynch law: "Men of our race have been lynched in this State when they had only been accused of crime, ranging from simple petit larceny to murder and rape, and as some members of the bar are in favor [of lynchings], we are indeed amazed."[10]

As the appeals from the conventions show, black leaders of the late nineteenth century tried to work within the system and avoided urging members of their race to adopt a more militant stance. On at least one occasion, however, an anonymous writer urged Kentucky blacks to meet violence with violence. (It is not at all surprising that the writer chose to remain anonymous, for he surely must have known how whites would react to such a call.) His comments appeared in the New York *Freeman*, a newspaper that circulated widely in a number of Kentucky cities during the 1880s. Blacks, he declared, were not receiving justice in the state: "White men black their face to commit crimes and elude the law. . . . The whites concoct all kinds of devilish schemes in the South, and lay them on the colored man or woman, so they can slyly exterminate us by mobs or imprisonment." To prove his point, he then produced figures, from some unknown source, on the number of blacks who had been victimized in Kentucky: "There have been shot 250; assassinated 78; burnt 26; waylaid 62; mobbed 629. Total, 1,045 killed since 1869, and still Judge Lynch devours us every day. . . . We have seen our mothers, wives, sisters, and daughters beaten, shot, cut, seduced, deprived of the protection of the law. . . . We have appealed to the courts but in vain. . . . We are hung or sent to prison for merely nothing. The county . . . sheriff or jailer opens his prison doors to the mob." His figures are suspect, since he failed to provide any documentation. Clearly, however, this anonymous writer had lost patience with the system: "We cannot stand it any longer. We should kill as well as be killed."[11]

Despite the risk of having whites misconstrue their attempts at self-defense as threats of black domination, Afro-Americans did at times resort to arms to protect themselves and their families. That several blacks were indicted on charges of killing Klan members attests in part to their willingness to defend themselves. Afro-Americans

10. *Proceedings of the State Convention of Colored Men at Lexington;* New York *Times,* October 16, 1885; New York *Freeman,* November 7, 1885; Louisville *Courier-Journal,* October 7, 1898.

11. New York *Freeman,* July 25, 1885.

often stood watch over jails to prevent lynchings. In September, 1889, a black was arrested in Mount Sterling on a burglary charge. Fearing that he would be lynched, a group of blacks armed themselves and stood watch over the jail. Whites were upset, claiming that blacks intended to release the suspect from jail. Although the situation remained tense, no lynching occurred. More often, however, attempts by blacks to prevent a lynching failed, not for a lack of determination to face the lynch mob, but because local officials refused to allow armed blacks to remain in the vicinity of the jailhouse.[12]

Rumors of retaliation by Afro-Americans became commonplace after many lynchings. It is unclear, however, whether they had actually made threats or whether white insecurities resulting from the lynchings led to these wild rumors. In 1886, five blacks died at the hands of lynch mobs in the small community of Auburn, Logan County. The day after the last lynching, that of Meredith Jones, a newspaper correspondent noted that blacks had congregated on several street corners where they gestured toward "whites in an ominous manner." Rumors quickly spread that blacks were threatening to kill the constable, who had been guarding Jones, and several men identified as members of the lynch mob. "I passed a street corner where a number [of Negroes] were talking, and one said, 'there would be a heap of houses burned in Auburn this summer.'" Whether this account is accurate or the figment of a white reporter's mind is impossible to tell. Nevertheless, for a period of time after the lynching, Auburn whites, with the assistance of heavily armed men from nearby Russellville, guarded the streets at night. For whatever reason, no further lynchings occurred in the community.[13]

White fears about blacks seeking revenge for lynchings most surely continued during the 1890s. The lynching of John Henderson in Midway for the murder of Gilbert Satterwhite led to a period of unrest among whites. According to the Louisville Courier-Journal, groups of Afro-Americans visited the site of the lynching for several days after Henderson's death. Once again a white reporter heard blacks make threats against whites. Ultimately, no violence occurred; whites had remained armed and on guard for some time. The next year in nearby Georgetown, blacks did resort to arson after the lynching of James

12. Louisville Courier-Journal, September 8, 1889.
13. Ibid., April 29, 1886.

The Shelbyville lynchings, depicted in *Petit Parisien*, a Paris newspaper, on October 20, 1901. The newspaper's account of the incident was greatly distorted: "A few days ago, in Shelbyville, Kentucky, . . . 23 Negroes, charged with murdering a white female, were torn away from their cells by the crowd. Despite their protestations, their prayers, their tears, all of them were hanged."

The lynching of Will Porter, as depicted in *Le Petit Journal*, a Paris newspaper, on May 7, 1911. The newspaper's story of the lynching is accurate, but it did err in reporting that the shooting victim was murdered. He recovered. "Despite the efforts of American authorities, it is still very common for Negroes to be lynched in the United States. Here is one case, performed with unique taste. In Livermore, Kentucky, a Negro charged with murdering a white male, was dragged away by the crowd to the Opera, and there, tied to a post. Then, some people in the crowd fired shots at the Negro, and killed him."

The lynching of four black men in Logan County, Kentucky, August, 1908.
Photograph used by permission. The Kentucky Library, Western Kentucky University.

The public hanging of Rainey Bethea in Owensboro, Kentucky, on August 14, 1936. The circuslike atmosphere of this event hastened the end of public executions in Kentucky. *Acme News Photo, used by permission of The Filson Club, Louisville, Kentucky*

A hearse encounters difficulty making its way through the crowd of twenty thousand people who witnessed Bethea's execution in Owensboro, Kentucky. Schoolchildren and mothers with their babies were among the throng. The hearse was trying to get to the gallows to remove Bethea's body.

Dudley for murder. During the night following Dudley's brutal death, the property of several prominent citizens believed responsible for the lynching was set on fire. After additional fires occurred on successive nights, Georgetown officials requested one hundred rifles from the state capital. A group of men patrolled the streets and issued warnings to Afro-Americans not to venture out after dark. But after the show of force, white leaders thought it necessary to seek the assistance of black leaders in resolving the matter; "A conference was held yesterday with the more conservative colored men, and they pledged to keep the peace. They talked with the 'obstreperous element.'" Georgetown, like Auburn, would have no additional lynchings.[14]

On June 10, 1892, Charley Hill of Paducah was lynched for the attempted rape of a white woman. In July, the arrest of a black man for peeping through windows at white women sparked hostilities and an outcry from blacks that nothing had been done to apprehend the men responsible for Hill's death. A black leader, identified only as Parker, convinced several men to stand watch in front of the jailhouse to prevent another lynching. On the night of July 11, a group of whites approached the area. The blacks fired, fatally wounding a white soldier, Elmer Edwards. That blacks had dared shoot upon whites and kill one of them led to a panic in Paducah and wild rumors of black domination. It was widely believed in the white community that in the month since Hill's death, black leaders had secretly shipped weapons to Paducah. The headline of the Hickman *Courier*, the newspaper of a nearby city, proclaimed: "Race War at Paducah."[15]

Paducah authorities, who had been reluctant to act when the life of a black man had been threatened, quickly moved into action. At the urging of the mayor, the governor sent the state militia to Paducah. Police officers seized all of the weapons from the hardware stores and dispersed them among white citizens instead of locking up the weapons for safekeeping. The city council instituted a dusk-to-dawn curfew. According to rumors, blacks were making plans to attack the

14. *Ibid.*, April 29, 1886, August 20, 22, 1890, August 29, 30, 1891; Georgetown *Times*, August 26, September 2, 1891.

15. Unfortunately, no Paducah newspaper for the 1890s has been preserved. See the Hickman *Courier*, July 15, 22, 1892, and the Mayfield *Weekly Monitor*, June 15, 1892. The Louisville *Courier-Journal* gave extensive coverage to the incidents in Paducah. In its accounts the paper consistently took the stance that blacks were intent on murdering innocent whites. See the Louisville *Courier-Journal*, June 10, July 10–16, 1892.

city and lynch a white man who was in jail for the murder of a black man. The sheriff deputized seventy-five men to protect him from the anticipated mob. Another story circulated of a Negro's "bold deed": An unidentified black had attempted to kiss a white woman.

Two black men entered town after dark on the evening of July 13. The armed whites ordered the men to halt. Obviously afraid, one of the blacks panicked and ran and was shot down. Shortly thereafter the troops arrived from Frankfort. City officials decided that a search of the woods and the black community would be conducted in the morning to end the trouble. An untold number of Afro-Americans, all identified by whites as "leaders," were arrested, and more than two hundred firearms were seized. By July 16, with the trouble past and his men ready to leave town, the adjutant general of the state troops issued a parting statement. The whites of Paducah, he bluntly said, had blown the trouble in their town out of proportion.

In Mayfield, a community thirty miles from Paducah, Jim Stone and Henry Finley were lynched and another black was killed in December, 1896, a time when several other lynchings occurred in Kentucky. The accounts presented by white newspapers, even the New York *Times* and the Chicago *Tribune,* said that a conspiracy by Afro-Americans had precipitated Stone's lynching on December 22. According to the *Tribune:* "While the reports in many cases are somewhat vague, belief that they have some real foundation is shown by the fact that before Stone was killed he and other negroes were unusually insolent toward white people, that they were armed, and omitted no occasion to provoke quarrels with unarmed whites. It was Jim Stone's conspicuous leadership in this sort of behavior that caused his taking off by mob violence." This view, of course, did nothing more than provide a rationale for the lynchings. Indeed, after lynching Stone, the white mob left a note warning several other blacks to leave town, and these threats on their lives caused a number of blacks to arm themselves and prepare for an attack.[16]

Within hours of Stone's death, several "incendiary fires" lit up the sky. Blacks were blamed for the fires, even though no witnesses placed them at the scene. Details are equally vague on who shot Charles Bolin. He was wounded during an exchange of gunfire when he and

16. Chicago *Tribune,* December 24, 1896; New York *Times,* December 22–24, 1896.

other whites entered a bar in the Afro-American community to begin the forced removal of the "notorious blacks." The Bolin shooting, though he might have been accidentally wounded by a member of the white mob, led to wild rumors that blacks were attacking whites. When spreading these rumors, whites failed to note that blacks were merely protecting their property. Instead of calling upon the state for support, Mayfield whites proclaimed their determination to end the crisis themselves. More than a hundred men were deputized, given arms, and told to guard the streets. Whites also took steps to disarm all Afro-Americans. With the blessing of city fathers, the white deputies entered the black community and burned to the ground four homes owned by men identified as troublemakers. Shots were fired into scores of other homes. Fearing for their lives, the blacks who had been warned to leave fled Mayfield, probably never to return. Throwing up the white flag, more than one hundred blacks sent a petition to city hall asking for an end to the violence and promising that no Afro-Americans would seek revenge for the lynchings and the destruction of numerous black-owned properties. By Christmas Eve, "peace" had been restored in Mayfield.[17]

Several points must be emphasized about the alleged black uprisings in the 1890s. Local authorities consistently refused to take steps to prevent the lynching of a black. In Paducah, even after the arrest of a second black on a "sex crime," they still refused to adopt measures to deter the mob. Yet at the very suggestion that blacks might try to prevent a lynching, city officials responded as though blacks were seeking revenge and asked the governor to send men and weapons. By picking up arms to prevent lynchings or forced removal from their homes, blacks in Paducah, Mayfield, and other Kentucky communities asserted the right to defend themselves. Whites, however, viewed this as a militant threat to the status quo and took steps to disarm and punish the blacks they deemed responsible. If white authorities are to be believed, in the vast majority of lynchings it proved impossible to identify, much less arrest and prosecute, the whites involved in mob murders. Yet even without eyewitnesses, the Paducah authorities had no problem arresting the Afro-Americans believed responsible for the

17. New York *Times*, December 25, 1896; Louisville *Courier-Journal*, December 25, 1896.

riot and for the death of the white soldier. The same proved true in Mayfield; the homes of the alleged black instigators were put to the torch.

Without question, Afro-Americans, outraged by the lynchings, were determined to bring the practice to an end. The evidence suggests that Paducah blacks guarded the jailhouse only to prevent another lynching, not to have an excuse for hanging a white murder suspect or to seek revenge on white lynchers. Blacks were compelled to act because they understood that all of them were vulnerable to mob attacks. Their efforts to prevent further lynchings brought mixed results: In some areas, the "lynching bees" ended, while in Paducah, for example, another black was seized by a mob the very next year. Nevertheless, blacks had shown that they were far from passive and were willing to do more to protest racial violence than write letters to newspapers.

During the 1890s, Kentucky blacks had two important white allies in their efforts to end racial violence. In January, 1895, Judge M. L. Buchwalter of Cincinnati sparked a bitter controversy between Ohio and Kentucky officials when he refused an extradition request from Kentucky to return a black man wanted for shooting a white man. Buchwalter used the occasion to denounce "lynch law" in the Bluegrass State and to rebuke Kentucky officials for not protecting the lives of their citizens. According to accounts from white Kentucky newspapers, A. H. Hampton, a black school teacher in Whitewood, Green County, assaulted J. C. Durham in June, 1893. Hampton had owned money to Durham, a local merchant, but had refused to pay. Durham made one last effort to collect the payment, and Hampton, according to the white newspapers, was greatly enraged. After the white merchant left, Hampton, unobserved by Durham, "slipped close behind him and [placed] the muzzle of a pistol immediately under Durham's ear, but it misfired." Durham fell to the ground, and the black man struck him repeatedly with a stone. This brutal attack left Durham near death, and two years later he was still "far from being a well man." As usual, the white newspapers found the black to be undesirable in other respects as well. The *Courier-Journal*, quoting whites from Green County, said that Hampton's "reputation here is decidedly unsavory. . . . About five years ago he was charged by the trustees of the colored schools with having seduced one of his pupils, a girl under 12. A warrant of arrest was issued but the girl was spirited away and the charges dropped."[18]

After the incident with Durham, Hampton fled Green County and somehow made his way to Cincinnati. Under the name of Alex Jackson, he became the pastor of a small black church. A deputy sheriff from Green County, W. W. Penn, a relative of Durham, spent more than a year following leads before finding Hampton in Cincinnati. In late December, 1894, while Hampton was preaching, Penn and Cincinnati law officers placed him under arrest. (Penn would later say members of the congregation threatened his life when he removed the black preacher.) Penn then appeared before the local judge—Buchwalter—to have Hampton's extradition papers signed. At the hearing Hampton protested, saying that his return to Green County meant death, even though he was only accused of assault, not murder. Judge Buchwalter agreed, declaring that Hampton would remain in the custody of Cincinnati authorities until Governor John Y. Brown of Kentucky and the sheriff of Green County gave assurances that Hampton would be protected from a mob. Buchwalter then made a dramatic statement: He was greatly distressed by the many lynchings occurring in Kentucky, and especially that of Louis Lafordette in Burlington, Boone County, in July, 1894. Buchwalter had agreed to the request of Governor Brown to return Lafordette to Kentucky.[19]

Kentucky's governor wasted little time in replying to Buchwalter. Personally offended by the suggestion that he failed to enforce the law, Brown explained that the Constitution of the United States called for the return of fugitives to the place where their crimes had been committed. He had gone through the proper channels, sending a requisition to Ohio governor William McKinley for Hampton. Therefore, it was the duty of Buchwalter to abide by the law instead of indulging himself "in an unwarranted arraignment of Kentucky." Brown then made a revealing statement. "It is much to be regretted that we have occasionally had mob violence in this Commonwealth, but it has al-

18. Extensive coverage of the entire incident involving Buchwalter and Hampton can be found in the January, 1895, editions of the Louisville *Courier-Journal* and the Cincinnati *Enquirer.*

19. According to the New York *Times,* July 22, 1894: "Twenty masked men took Louis Lafordette from the jail at Burlington, Boone County and hanged him. He was a tramp who murdered William Whitlock a farmer."

ways been when the passions of the people have been inflamed by the commission of the most atrocious crimes." His statement was a frank admission that lynchings were necessary to avenge "the most atrocious crimes." During Brown's four years as governor, from 1892 to 1895, fifty-six lynchings occurred; but instead of denouncing this lawlessness, he justified it. Indeed, Brown went on to say: "I venture the suggestion that communities in Ohio have not escaped the manifestation under similar circumstances." Buchwalter's actions, Brown concluded, practically invited other fugitives from justice in "the South to make Ohio their asylum with the assurance that if their return shall be demanded it will be ignored." Showing that they, too, wanted to uphold the honor of the state, members of the rival Republican party of Kentucky strongly endorsed Brown's comments.[20]

On January 4, Buchwalter heard arguments on whether or not Hampton should be turned over to Green County officials. The papers requesting Hampton's return, his lawyer persuasively argued throughout the hearing, were vague and probably not valid. The attorney with deputy sheriff Penn did admit to having only duplicate copies of the requisition and the indictment issued for Hampton by the Green County grand jury. The next day, Buchwalter issued his ruling, freeing Hampton on "purely technical [grounds] of irregularity and informality in the requisition documents from Kentucky." Although resorting to a technicality to throw out the extradition request, Buchwalter had been compelled to act because of his belief that Hampton would be lynched. To make sure that Kentucky authorities clearly understood why he was allowing Hampton to go free, Buchwalter also issued a lengthy opinion. His statement, which was unsparing in its condemnation of lynch law in the Bluegrass State, also spelled out the responsibility of judges to ensure that all citizens receive the protection of the law:

> The proof before me not only raises a strong probability, but, is convincing that the prisoner would have been dealt with unlawfully had I re-

20. See the Louisville *Commercial*, January 1–6, 1895. Unlike its main rival, the pro-Democrat *Courier-Journal*, this newspaper devoted scant attention to the controversy. The Republicans were trying to maintain a low profile in hopes of winning the upcoming governor's race. The *Commercial* refused editorial comment on Buchwalter and on the many lynchings in Kentucky during the previous twelve months. On the other hand, editorials in the *Courier-Journal* were especially harsh in condemning the stance adopted by the Ohio judge.

manded him just preceding New Year's Day, and would be now without any outspoken assurance from those in authority that he will be protected. His own testimony was peculiarly impressive, giving corroborating facts and circumstances as to threats and the probabilities of violence in that vicinity, especially to one of his color charged with an offense against a white man. Some of these circumstances are tacitly admitted by the agent of Kentucky in his statement.

The statistics before me show that 19 people have been illegally executed in the Commonwealth of Kentucky within the past 12 months by lynching in the exercise of individual vengeance, twelve of them within the past six months, whose names and places are given in the statistics. One of those was Louis Lafordette, killed at midnight, July 18, 1894, just after I, as Judge of this Court, had remanded him upon requisition of the Governor of Kentucky and the warrant of the Governor of Ohio. The processes of law were in due form. His offense was shooting to wound the prosecuting witness, who soon after appeared in this Court with his wounded hand to identify the prisoner. So far as I can learn, there has been no effort by the executive officers of Kentucky to prosecute his murderers, nor in fact any of the 19 mobs who murdered citizens in that state. Nor have I learned of any regret expressed to those who love law and order for the bad faith in thus killing the prisoners remanded from this state upon the faith that he would be tried according to law upon the charge contained in the requisition.

I do not recite these horrible deeds to irritate or to be disrespectful to any one, but these are facts brought to my knowledge, and as to Lafordette painfully so, and are proper to be considered by me in connecting with the other proof as to any duty in remanding this prisoner.

Looking backward to the Lafordette case, is it not now quite certain that those desiring to lynch him went through the form of beginning criminal proceedings and based on them, they obtained the requisition of the Governor of Kentucky, and then the warrant of the Governor of Ohio, and finally the order of this Court? Is there any doubt but that the forms of the law were used for none other than the wicked and unlawful purposes of bringing the prisoner to a convenient place to kill him? Had we the information by foresight that we now have by hindsight is to be held to be the law that the Constitution of the United States would have made it the duty of either of the Governors or myself to aid in thus surrendering that prisoner to violence because it was asked in due form of law?

When I am now satisfied that a like purpose is intended in these proceedings as to Hampton, is it my duty because of the due form of law to send him to death unlawful? I answer no! It would be a perversion of the purposes of the constitutional provision. Most certainly I agree that when the proceedings are in due form of law good faith is to be imputed to them, and to the purposes for which they are instituted, but that presumption may be overcome by proof to the contrary.

I felt myself in duty bound to do this before I became a judicial agent to deliver a second prisoner most probably to violent hands. If the Governor had thus been forewarned in Lafordette's case I might not now have the recollection that I was unwittingly an agent in the name of law to his violent death. And had such assurance been given either directly to the Judge or indirectly through the Governor of Ohio, it would have been in the interest of humanity and have served in the execution of justice according to the forms of law.

Besides, it would have rallied the adherents of law and order who predominate in numbers in every community of that state, as elsewhere in this country.

If I have erred in an overzealous care in this regard (owing to my peculiar experience in like proceedings) it is to my mind with a higher sense of duty under my oath to support the Constitution of the United States than if I negligently aided in executing a process under constitutional form used for ulterior and illegal purposes.

I would hold the prisoner on this ground for the further consideration of the Governor of Ohio, but considering the defect heretofore found in the requisition papers after a second attempt to have them correct, I now discharge the prisoner.[21]

Afro-Americans in Kentucky and Ohio applauded the actions of Judge Buchwalter. After thanking the judge for saving his life, Hampton said that Cincinnati would be his permanent home. A group of Ohio blacks met and praised Buchwalter, saying that his name would rank with that of William L. Garrison and other abolitionists. (One enthusiastic black wrote a poem in honor of the judge.) They vowed to form a civil rights league to protect blacks and to challenge whites to abide by the law. In a parting shot at Kentucky officials, Ohio blacks urged them to uphold the law in their state. Yet they also reminded blacks who were prone to commit crimes to not assume that Ohio had become a haven for criminals.[22]

21. Buchwalter's opinion can be found in the Cincinnati *Enquirer,* January 6, 1895.

22. Indianapolis *Freeman,* January 12, February 2, 1895. The poem "Buchwalter" was composed by W. Noel Johnson, Lockland, Ohio. It can be found on the front page of the *Freeman* of January 12. Except for being mentioned in newspaper accounts in January and February, 1895, Judge M. L. Buchwalter seems to be a virtual unknown. For instance, it is not known if he made any statements whenever Ohio blacks died at the hands of lynch mobs. As far as can be determined, Buchwalter has not been mentioned

Governor Brown issued a few parting words of his own. Buchwalter had usurped powers that clearly rested with Ohio governor William McKinley. With his eye toward a run for the White House, McKinley had stayed clear of the controversy, saying that whether or not Hampton was returned to Kentucky was Buchwalter's decision to make. Brown added: "The statements of the Judge are grossly inaccurate. His argument is a mere subterfuge and quibble. . . . He has deliberately refused to execute the plain command of a law of the United States, and subordinated it to his own caprices. He has reproached Kentucky for crimes of which his own great State is not guiltless. He has accepted the statement of a fugitive from justice that he feared unlawful violence if removed, as a sufficient reason for his discharge."[23]

Green County officials made one last attempt to have the black minister returned. Word reached Cincinnati that extradition papers were being prepared again—this time, properly—now charging Hampton with grand larceny. Allegations were being made that in addition to shooting J. C. Durham, the black man had stolen his watch. This effort failed as well; the validity of the papers had never been the main issue that concerned Judge Buchwalter. Instead of adopting a position against lynch law that would convince the judge that Hampton would be protected, Governor Brown tried to show Ohio officials once again that he, not they, upheld the law. Upon receiving extradition papers from Dayton, Ohio, for the return of a woman, he was quick to comply. As the Cincinnati paper speculated, "It was the intention of Governor Brown to heap hot coals on the heads of Ohio officials by granting the request."[24]

Brown's successor as governor, Republican William O. Bradley, who had been elected with the solid backing of Afro-Americans, worked to end racial violence, consistently denouncing lynch mobs: "Those who congregate and conspire to take human life are legally greater criminals than those whose lives they seek to take, for no crime is so base and repulsive as that committed under cloak of pre-

---

in the various scholarly accounts of Ohio blacks or studies of race relations in the Buckeye State.

23. Not surprisingly, the editorials in the Kentucky white newspapers expressed outrage over Buchwalter's actions. For example, see the Boone County *Recorder*, January 9, 1895 (this is the area where Louis Lafordette was lynched), and the Newport *State Journal*, January 11, 1895.

24. Cincinnati *Enquirer*, January 18, February 3, 1895.

tended vindication of law."[25] Addressing the Anti-Mob and Lynch Law Association in Springfield, Ohio, in January, 1898, the governor declared that because mob violence was open contempt of the laws, the courts, and the administration of justice, it should be prevented at all cost and, when committed, should be quickly and severely punished. "The commission of crime to punish crime can find no apologist in Christian civilization." It is difficult to imagine most of the governors from the border or southern states appearing before an anti-lynching organization and making such comments. Bradley's Springfield presentation drew the applause of northern Republicans and blacks from all parts of the nation.[26]

Bradley made a number of critical comments about the lack of action by the county judge and other officials of Maysville after the lynching of Richard Coleman. He chastised Judge James P. Tarvin for refusing to request state troops to protect Coleman upon his return from Covington. Bradley was extremely disappointed that the judge failed to apprehend the leaders of the mob or to offer rewards for their arrest. Under Kentucky law, the governor could offer a reward for the arrest and conviction of members of a lynch mob, but the request to do so had to originate in the county where the lynching occurred. Tarvin responded by blasting the governor, saying that Bradley had sent troops to the Maysville area without a request when he thought their presence would benefit the Republican party during an election but wanted to shift his lack of action during the Coleman lynching to local authorities. Like everyone else, the governor knew what awaited Coleman's return to Maysville, the county judge harshly concluded.[27]

25. William O. Bradley, "Message to the General Assembly, March 13, 1897," in *Public Documents of Governor William O. Bradley* (Louisville, 1899), 55. For biographical data on Bradley, see Adalaide Abel Barker, "William O'Connell Bradley" (M.A. thesis, University of Kentucky, 1927). Information on Bradley's views of lynchings and his relationship with Afro-Americans can be found in the William O. Bradley Scrapbooks, Division of Special Collections and Archives, University of Kentucky (hereinafter cited as Bradley Scrapbooks). See also M. H. Thatcher, *Stories and Speeches of William O. Bradley* (Lexington, 1916).

26. In the Bradley Scrapbooks, see the newsclip of the Springfield (Ohio) *Republican*, January 18, 1898.

27. Newsclip, the Lexington *Standard*, December 26, 1899, in Bradley Scrapbooks; Cincinnati *Enquirer*, December 10, 1899. See an article on Bradley, "Inability of the Governor of Kentucky to Bring Lynchers to Justice," *American Law Review*, XXXIV (1900), 238–39.

Other Kentuckians joined Judge Tarvin in criticizing Governor Bradley for the Coleman lynching and the many other mob-caused deaths that occurred during his administration. The Democrats delighted in reminding the public of Bradley's campaign promise to end mob violence. In the last week in December, 1896, when a record number of lynchings (at least since the days of Reconstruction) occurred and violence was rampant in eastern Kentucky, Bradley was roundly condemned in the newspapers, including some that were pro-Republican. After detailing candidate Bradley's many boastful statements to end mob violence, the Bowling Green *Times* concluded that he seemed incapable of doing anything to end the spirit of mob law rampant in the state. "In fact, it must have dawned upon him by this time that the Democratic Administrations were not, after all, wantonly remiss in the matter of crushing out the mob spirit in the State, and that it is a much bigger undertaking than he imagined." Several newspapers throughout the nation found Bradley's attitudes toward the lynchings extremely puzzling. The Pittsburg *Post* expressed the sentiment of many others, observing that Governor Bradley had made "no effort to suppress the lawlessness" that had claimed seven lives in Kentucky within one week.[28]

Despite the criticism, Bradley did take steps in December, 1896, to stop the bloodshed. He helped prevent a lynching in Paris, where Johnson Howe, a black man, was being held for the murder of a Cynthiana policeman. Without waiting for a request from local authorities, Bradley had the 2nd Regiment on alert in a nearby community. He also wired several western Kentucky communities to learn if the rumored black attack on Mayfield was real or imagined.[29] And in spite of all the criticism, the number of lynchings declined significantly during Bradley's four years as governor, compared with the number of mob deaths during the Brown administration. A total of fifty-six lynchings occurred while Brown was governor: ten in 1892, fourteen in 1893, seventeen in 1894, and fifteen in 1895. During Bradley's term, twenty-five people died at the hands of lynch mobs: nine in 1896, seven in 1897, seven in 1898, and two in 1899.

28. These and other editorials were reprinted in the Louisville *Courier-Journal*, December 30, 1896.

29. Louisville *Courier-Journal*, December 27, 1896; Chicago *Tribune*, December 28, 1896.

Bradley kept his campaign promise and worked diligently for the passage of an antimob law. He called the legislature into special session in March, 1897, to enact laws protecting the citizens from mobs and turnpike raiders. He wanted a bill making each county liable for damages from lynchings in the county, hoping that since all of the citizens would suffer financially, they would take the necessary steps to halt mob violence. Bradley's proposed bill placed the burden for prevention of a lynching on those in charge of the intended victim. "When a prisoner is taken from the custody of a sheriff, jailer, or peace officer, the officer in charge knowing of the crime, and having reasonable opportunity to take charge fail to do so, shall forfeit his office." The governor's most radical proposal called for the arming of prisoners to protect themselves. "No mob would be able to stand before the prisoner fighting for his life and the jailer or sheriff fighting for his office," the governor reasoned.[30]

By early May, compromises had been reached, and the proposed antilynching bill was introduced into the Senate by a Republican ally of the governor. When considering the number of lynchings in the state and the adamant refusal of local authorities to apprehend members of mobs, it is surprising that there was very little debate among the legislators over the proposed law. One newspaper speculated that the bill might die anyway, not because of any controversial features, but because the members of the Senate wanted to adjourn so they could travel to Louisville for the Kentucky Derby. On May 11, however, the bill passed overwhelmingly in the Senate and went to the House. Finally, a negative voice was raised against the bill. The representative from Graves County, an area where several recent lynchings were still fresh in the minds of the people, explained that his objection to the proposed law was the feature allowing the "Sheriff [to] summon any citizen to assist in arresting a mob, and a refusal to go would subject any citizens to a fine of not less than $100, without making any provision for allowing him to give a good excuse." Despite his objection, and that of one other member, the House passed the bill by a vote of 55 to 2; it was immediately signed into law by the governor.[31]

30. Bradley, "Message to the General Assembly," 57.

31. Newspaper accounts of the entire debate on the antilynching law can be found in the Louisville *Courier-Journal*, May 11–22, 1897. A survey of newspapers through-

Entitled "An act to prevent lynching and injury to and destruction of real and personal property in this Commonwealth," the new law contained eleven sections. The first three sections defined what constituted an unlawful mob and prescribed the penalties for inflicting punishment or death on persons removed from the custody of the law. Section Four gave law officers the power to summon able-bodied men to help protect the prisoner and levied a fine against them for refusing to do so. This section also gave the sheriff discretion to arm his inmates to protect themselves. One of the key provisions of the new law, and perhaps the most controversial, was found in Section Six: If a county judge, circuit judge, sheriff or other peace officer failed to act, "he shall upon conviction be fined not less than $100 nor more than $500 and shall forfeit his office as a penalty, in addition to the payment of said fine." Section Eight authorized the governor and the county judges to offer rewards for the apprehension of members of lynch mobs. County judges would use local funds for rewards, while the governor would tap the state treasury for reward money. The governor could employ detectives to assist local officials in the investigations of lynchings. Section Nine levied a fine and a jail sentence against anyone circulating threatening letters or notices. The eleventh section called for the immediate implementation of the new law: "As mobs and riotous assemblages of persons in certain counties of this Commonwealth have for several months past been engaged, and are now engaged, in injuring and destroying real and personal property, and the good name of this Commonwealth demands that such unlawful conduct should be stopped as soon as possible, it is hereby declared that an emergency exists, and this act shall take effect when approved by the Governor."[32]

Kentucky's law against mob violence was similar in many respects to the antilynching laws enacted in three northern and five southern states during the 1890s. In most places, especially in the South, these

---

out the state reveals that the white editors chose to see the debate as not being newsworthy. See, for example, the Hickman *Courier*, May 21, 28, 1897, the Paducah *Daily News*, a racist paper, which had no coverage of the bill, and the Hopkinsville *Kentuckian*, May 26, 1897. The Louisville *Commercial*, the Republican paper, gave minor mention of the bill from May 12 to 21, 1897, though it did, in an editorial of May 14, support the bill's passage.

32. *Acts of the General Assembly, 1897* (Louisville, 1897), 29–33.

laws proved to be ineffectual because officials at every level of government refused to take the steps necessary to enforce them. For instance, nearly all of these laws called for removing sheriffs who allowed their prisoners to be lynched. When this was not done, however, the law had been effectively nullified. Like Kentucky, a number of states called for a special tax to be placed on a county where a lynching occurred. But as James Cutler, a professor who conducted research into the antilynching laws at the turn of the century, explained: "The possibility of an increase in the rate of taxation does not seem as yet to have had any restraining influence on the actions of people . . . when occasion has arisen for a lynching." Race prejudice, the professor concluded, was the primary reason why the antilynching laws were not enforced. "It is difficult to create a public sentiment against lynching because of the racial antipathy which aggravates the evil in certain sections of the United States."[33]

Although the antilynching law had been in effect for only a few years, several members of the Kentucky House and Senate called for changes at the turn of the century. Adopting the same attitude as that of the legislators of 1897, members of the general assembly chose not to publicly debate the proposed changes. On March 17, 1902, the lawmakers completed their task when they amended and reenacted the antilynching law; Sections Five, Six, and Seven had been eliminated. Section Five, calling upon the county judge and sheriff to form a posse of no more than ten men to prevent a tollgate house or bridge from being destroyed by a mob, and Section Seven, specifying the amount of pay each guard was to receive when summoned into service to prevent a lynching, were rather minor. But the deletion of Section Six, which had called for the fining and removing of officials who failed to prevent lynching, was a serious blow to the antilynching law. The motivation for weakening the law against mob violence is unclear. Perhaps members of the legislature were moved, for instance, by a concern that if lynchings continued in their counties, judges or sheriffs, who wielded considerable power and influence in local affairs, stood the risk of being forced from office if the law was ever fully enforced.[34]

33. James E. Cutler, "Proposed Remedies for Lynchings," *Yale Review*, XIII (August, 1904), 194–212. See also Cutler, *An Investigation into the History of Lynching in the United States.*

34. *Acts of Kentucky, 1902* (Louisville, 1902), 55–60.

It is extremely difficult to fully assess the impact of Kentucky's antilynching law. At least thirteen people died at the hands of mobs from July, 1897 (with Ephraim Brinkley, a Madisonville black, being the first) through the end of 1899. This period included the lynching of Richard Coleman in Maysville, where the antilynching law was openly flouted in a circuslike atmosphere. Also, seventy more people were killed by lynch mobs from 1900 to 1934. Do these lynchings mean that the law was ineffective? On the other hand, since the number of lynchings declined in the twentieth century, does that mean that the law prevented an even greater number of lynchings? Also, did the passing of a second antilynching law in 1920 indicate that the first law was lacking in several crucial respects? Or is it possible that the passing of antilynching laws in 1897 and again in 1920 reflected the public's growing uneasiness with lynchings—and that even without the laws the number of lynchings would have decreased anyway? As has often been asked on numerous issues concerning race relations, did the law set the tone or did it reflect public attitudes?

Within Kentucky, some of the credit for the decline in lynchings must be given to the new law. Several weeks after the law went into effect, a black man, Talbott Stone, was arrested and charged with the rape of a white woman in Glasgow. Rape, more than murder or any other charge, usually led to a lynching. The sheriff, realizing that Stone might be lynched if he remained in Glasgow and that the lynching of the black man could cost him his job, had the prisoner carried to Bowling Green for safety. In all likelihood, this was the first time a sheriff had removed a black alleged rapist to a safe location until the start of his trial. The final outcome of the case is unknown, but significantly, Stone did not die at the hands of a lynch mob. He also escaped the gallows, something that blacks had long argued would happen if accused rapists were protected from lynch mobs and given the chance to defend themselves in court.[35]

35. Lexington *Morning Herald*, June 2, 1897.

six

Meeting Mob Violence with Renewed
Determination, 1900–1940

The twentieth century would see the continuation of efforts to
eliminate mob violence in Kentucky. Just like William O. Bradley
before them, various governors adopted measures, some of which
were drastic and highly controversial, to end lynchings. White newspaper editors began denouncing all acts of violence, even when Afro-
Americans were guilty of rape or murder. A number of organizations
also joined in the quest to end violence. All along, Afro-Americans,
through a variety of ways, including armed resistance, remained determined to end racial violence.

Despite these efforts, racial violence remained a fact of life in Kentucky. At least seventy people died at the hands of lynch mobs between 1900 and 1934, including four innocent youths in Russellville,
David Walker and his family in Hickman, Will Porter at the Livermore Opera House, and two men in the largest town in western Kentucky in 1916. During the early decades of the new century, an unknown number of blacks were forced to flee their homes after being
attacked by Night Riders in several western Kentucky counties and
by hostile white railroad workers or coal miners in parts of eastern
Kentucky.

With the possibility of a lynching being a constant concern to
them, blacks—especially during the first fifteen years of the 1900s—
continued taking up arms to prevent mobs from removing black prisoners from jails. On several occasions, they even went so far as to shoot
as soon as whites approached the jailhouse. Obviously, a few Afro-
Americans had come to realize that only by adopting this tactic could
they hope to turn back a white mob. About sixty men rushed the jail in
Maysville on January 14, 1902, in an attempt to get Charles Gaskins,
on trial for the murder of a Flemingsburg police officer. Making no

attempt to protect their prisoner, the sheriff and his twelve deputies allowed the mob to break the windows and the door and then to batter down the cell door with a sledgehammer. Just as the mob was about to seize Gaskins, shotgun fire came from across the street. According to the newspaper account, "This had the effect of scattering the mob, which left as quickly as it came." The blacks responsible for the shooting were never identified, though they were believed to be Gaskins' relatives. After the incident, a report circulated that the sheriff and his men had been ordered not to fire their weapons. Without question, blacks had saved Gaskins' life.[1]

Around midnight on June 14, 1904, a group of whites went to the jail in Lebanon Junction intent on lynching Marie Thompson, who had been arrested for the murder of a white farmer. After the men had completely surrounded the jail, one of them secured a sledgehammer and began pounding at the large padlock that held a heavy iron bar in place across the door. Meanwhile, from the rear of the mob, a group of blacks approached and opened fire on the whites. Taken completely by surprise, the white men fled, getting off a few wild shots in their hurried escape from the scene. The gunfire brought most of the people of the village to the jail. The blacks then made a mistake that cost the black woman her life: They dispersed after the sheriff and his men promised to protect Thompson if the mob returned. Two hours later, however, nearly a hundred shots were fired, and the woman was dead. Angry over Thompson's death, blacks blamed the sheriff for refusing to move the woman from Lebanon Junction and for handing her over to the mob. Fearful that blacks would seek revenge, whites in Lebanon Junction armed themselves and waited several nights for an attack that never materialized.[2]

In 1908, a shootout occurred near the small western Kentucky community of Dixon when blacks attempted to prevent a lynching. Jacob McDowell, described as a "hardworking colored man of mature years," had an argument with Smith Childress, a deputy marshal in Providence, over the white man's intimate relationship with a young black girl. As McDowell started to walk away, Childress attempted to

---

1. Lexington *Morning Herald*, January 16, 1902; Tuskegee Clippings, Reel 221, Frame 112. The outcome of this case is unknown, though it is certain that Gaskins did not receive the death penalty.

2. Louisville *Courier-Journal*, June 16, 1904.

shoot him. The black man ran into a drugstore, with Childress close on his heels. Somehow McDowell got the pistol and shot Childress, though not fatally. McDowell went immediately to the police station and explained the incident to the authorities. Fearful that the black man would be lynched by the "notorious, disorderly and violent element in Providence," the police judge had McDowell sent to Dixon, the county seat of Webster County, for protection.[3]

Upon learning that a lynch mob was forming, Providence's sheriff telephoned Dixon officials to have McDowell moved to Henderson. Harve McDowell, knowing only that a mob was preparing to attack the jail at Dixon and lynch his father, rounded up eleven blacks, several of whom were relatives, and headed for that city, hoping to prevent the lynching. While on the road to Dixon the blacks heard the sound of horses and realized that the white mob was about to overtake them. At this point, their exact actions become unclear. Instead of confronting the mob, they decided to hide in the field. Did Harve McDowell and the others attempt to hide in the field, as the whites would later contend, to bushwhack them? The blacks would testify in court that they decided to get off the road and hide in a field to allow the whites to go on without a confrontation. This seems rather strange, since they were traveling as fast as possible to arrive at the jail in Dixon *before* the mob and protect Jake McDowell. Allowing the white mob to pass by would have meant in all likelihood that nothing would be done to stop the lynching. But in the words of Harve McDowell:

> When we got up the road further we were walking awful fast and we heard a noise behind like horses traveling in the road when someone of the boys spoke up and says boys there is a crowd of men behind us on horses and said if they were to be the mob we are in danger and lets get

3. Accounts of the episode can be found in the Louisville *Courier-Journal*, March 16, 19, July 21, 1908, and in the Paducah *Weekly News Democrat*, March 19, 1908. The Madisonville *Hustler*, March 17, 1908, in a story headlined "Negro Attempts to Kill Officer at Providence Saturday," reported that Childress was a good citizen, while McDowell had a bad disposition. An invaluable source, and one that most surely disputes the view of the characters of both men as portrayed by the *Hustler*, is a pamphlet published by a group of Providence white leaders, *The Jake McDowell Tragedy* (N.p., n.d.). A copy of this work can be found in the Augustus E. Willson Papers, Kentucky Department for Libraries and Archives, Frankfort (hereinafter cited as Governor Willson Papers).

over the fence and let them pass and in getting over the fence Haywood got hung on the fence in some way and his gun went off and one of the shots hit me in the leg and I said, "Oh, boy you have shot me," and by that time then they commenced shooting and we shot back at them and run right off down the hill; some of the boys were over the fence and some of them were right at the fence and one or two were running back down the hill and kept running.[4]

During the exchange of gunfire, one white was killed and another seriously wounded. Ironically, these two men were not from the area but were traveling salesmen who had come along for the adventure of being involved in a lynching. After notifying the authorities in Dixon that they had been attacked by blacks, the whites, according to one account of the incident, "roamed the county over all day Sunday, and on Monday they picked up 25 Negroes, and out of this number they learned the names of the 12 men that went to protect Jake McDowell's life." The police arrested the blacks but refused to arrest any of the whites. About a month after the shooting, McDowell was returned to the jail in Dixon. The protection afforded him proved to be lax, and his son and the other men were unable to provide protection, since they were still held in jail in another city. About two o'clock on the morning of May 30, the jailer awakened to find himself surrounded by a group of masked gunmen. They took McDowell to the Providence Road and riddled his body with bullets. In the pamphlet about McDowell's lynching, the author charged Smith Childress with leading the mob: "Had McDowell lived to go on the witness stand, he (Childress) would have been the man scandalized." Going further in his condemnation of the white "law officer," the writer noted that several days before the lynching, Childress made a threat on the life of the lawyer who had been hired to defend McDowell. Childress was, the writer concluded, afraid that the lawyer would not only uncover evidence to prove that McDowell was the victimized party but would then learn the details of Childress' illicit relationship with a young black female.[5]

In Stanford several years later, an argument between two young

---

4. *Commonwealth of Kentucky* v. *Tom Croe and Others,* Webster Circuit Court (1908). The entire transcript of the trial can be found in the Governor Willson Papers. The quote from Harve McDowell is on page 56.

5. *The Jake McDowell Tragedy,* 4; Louisville *Courier-Journal,* May 31, 1908.

blacks and three white farmers ended with the whites shot and the blacks under arrest. Believing that the men would be lynched, fifteen armed blacks from Macksville, a Negro settlement near Stanford, stood guard at the jail. "They built a bonfire in the street back of the courthouse and several shots were heard from the camp during the night." Prepared for violence, the men wore white handkerchiefs on their left sleeves to avoid shooting a fellow black by accident. Their show of force and determination to prevent a lynching spurred the jailer to action. He armed the black prisoners, undoubtedly a measure to which few, if any, other white jailers had resorted, and locked his son in the cell with them. The anticipated mob never materialized.[6]

The lynchings of Brock Henley and Luther Durrett led to a period of turmoil in Paducah. Rumors of black revenge began circulating immediately after the lynchings of the two black men. Giving fuel to the rumors was the unsuccessful attempt by an estimated fifty blacks to acquire pistols and rifles from the hardware stores. Acting on the advice of the police, the merchants refused to sell weapons to blacks. Just as the police had done in the 1890s, city commissioners, believing that blacks would riot, deputized dozens of men and provided them with arms. In another event that seemed to be a replay of 1892, a white in jail for the murder of a black person was moved to the state prison after city officials heard rumors that he had been targeted for death by Afro-Americans. Also, city fathers instructed police chief J. W. Eaker "to break up any meetings or gatherings of negroes and to prevent trouble if possible."[7]

Although running the risk of white backlash, blacks refused to let the matter rest. George Ross, who had led the lynching to avenge the alleged assault on his wife, decided to leave Paducah after receiving several death threats from Afro-Americans. Blacks also took out some of their frustrations on a white police officer, Ollie Childress, who attempted to break up a Halloween celebration in the black community by pulling masks off a number of people and by using profanity at them. Several men responded by beating Childress, who remained in a dangerous situation until other officers arrived in the black neighborhood. As a sign of unity and approval of the beating, no one came

6. Tuskegee Clippings, Reel 221, Frame 163; Louisville *Courier-Journal*, February 17, 1911.

7. Paducah *News-Democrat*, October 17–31, November 1, 1916.

forward to identify the men who had attacked Childress. The Paducah newspaper mentioned that dozens of blacks protested the lynchings of Henley and Durrett by leaving town and going to the North where they were confident of finding better jobs and an improvement in race relations.

As had been the case in the late nineteenth century, whites assumed that an attack was imminent whenever blacks became vocal in their protests of a lynching. After the lynching of Rex Scott in Hazard in January, 1934, whites feared the worse. In his long, detailed account of the incident, Berea College professor J. Wesley Hatcher concluded with a "postscript" explaining that the report of blacks planning an attack on the white coal miners was groundless: "They had no such intention, and did not discuss it. But the rumor greatly frightened the miners, and the operators armed them with dynamite to meet the attack, and they waited in vain through the night for their coming. The Negroes thought it a 'good joke.'"[8]

From the administration of Augustus E. Willson through that of Ruby Laffoon, the governors proved to be important allies of blacks in their attempts to end lynchings. Without question, these governors were far more committed to ending acts of lawlessness than their nineteenth-century predecessors had been, and this was true even of the men elected with little or no support from Afro-Americans. These early twentieth-century governors were concerned about Kentucky's reputation. They were tired of reading magazine accounts and editorials in the New York *Times* that described Kentucky as one of the most violent states in the Union. Willson, responding to the letter from the NAACP about the lynching of Will Porter at the Livermore Opera House, assured the interracial organization that he, too, was outraged over the incident and wanted the guilty brought to justice. He agreed that unless something was done to punish members of the mob and prevent such incidents from recurring, the Livermore lynching would be a blot on Kentucky's name. Several years later, Democratic governor Augustus O. Stanley, confronting the western Kentucky mob intent on lynching a black man, said that to allow a lynching to take place would bring disgrace to the state, and the rest of the nation would view Kentuckians as uncivilized. Furthermore,

8. J. Wesley Hatcher, "Report on Lynching Occurring At Hazard, Perry County, Kentucky, Jan. 24, 1934," 7, in NAACP Papers.

the governors agreed that mob rule was akin to an epidemic, that one lynching led to others, and that the violence of the Night Riders would spread like an infection until all law-abiding citizens were at risk. Just like government officials in the Deep South, Kentucky's chief executives realized that to attract industries, the state had to be presented as a place where law and order existed. In their attempts to prevent lynchings and mob violence, the governors also went to great lengths to reassure the "good citizens" (who often took the law into their own hands) that they, too, wanted criminals to pay for their transgressions, that they were not soft on crime, but, as the governors steadfastly maintained, that punishment must be meted out by local and state officials. In their quest to end violence, the governors acknowledged that blacks were the primary targets of mobs. Nevertheless, they did not seek to improve the overall conditions of Afro-Americans as a way of helping to end lawlessness. In short, most of the governors refused to make any comments that suggested any displeasure with Kentucky's Jim Crow society. Only two Republicans, Willson and Edwin P. Morrow, went that far, calling not only for an end to mob violence but also for an end to racial discrimination in most areas of society.

When he became governor in 1907, Willson took immediate steps to try to end the lawlessness in western Kentucky. He called for the prosecution of criminals and chastised several county attorneys and judges for saying that the Night Riders were well-meaning, but frustrated, citizens. In words rarely used by an elected official in Kentucky, Willson denounced the Night Riders for the lynching of David Walker and his family in Hickman: "If two or three men had gone to this poor cabin and murdered this family, the crime would have shocked humanity with its revelation of incredible weakness, brutality and dastardly cowardice. That a larger number—some fifty men—joined in such a crime, multiplies its cowardliness and wickedness fifty fold, and makes every member of the band guilty of murder in the first degree." The lynchings of the Walkers, he concluded, were "an outgrowth and the logical results of the toleration of night rider crimes in the state. It is only one step removed from civil war." The governor offered rewards up to five hundred dollars for the arrest and conviction of any Night Rider. He also urged law-abiding citizens to defend themselves, promising to pardon anyone who shot a Night Rider. This strong belief in self-defense was a view Willson had long expressed. Indeed, many years earlier, when applauding George Dinning for firing on the mob, Willson had written: "Every man who takes the law in his own hand and especially every man who is a member of a lawless band that goes with the double cowardice of those who enter upon lawlessness with the protection of night and of overwhelming numbers against one poor and helpless man, . . . takes his life in his hands, and if the victim in despair kills him, no one has any right to complain."[9]

At the cost of hundreds of thousands of dollars, Willson sent state troops to western Kentucky and kept them there for more than a year. Prominent citizens in a number of counties eventually came forward and cooperated with the governor in the formation of county law-and-order leagues that "helped patrol the roads and guarded their neighbors."[10] Guns and ammunition, shipped from Frankfort, were given to people who remained under constant threat of attack from the Night Riders. Hopkinsville, where a massive raid had occurred, received a Gatling gun. The show of force initiated by Willson succeeded in bringing the violence to a halt in 1910. The Night Riders remained dormant for the rest of his administration but started a second wave of attacks around 1915.

Willson strongly pushed for the prosecution of lynchers during his administration. He criticized Shelbyville officials after the lynchings of Eugene Marshall and Wade Patterson and the near lynching of Jim West. His willingness to press for the conviction of the people involved in the opera house slaying of Will Porter surprised and pleased the NAACP. Indeed, Willson's assertion that something had to be done led to the arrest and trial of a number of men, though, of course, none of them were found guilty by their fellow townsmen. Willson started the movement that ultimately led to the passage of a new antilynching law almost a decade after he left office.

Ironically, Augustus O. Stanley, a Democrat who lacked Willson's commitment to black progress, received praise throughout the nation as a southern governor who combatted lynching. On January 9, 1917,

9. Augustus O. Willson, "The People and Their Law," a speech delivered before the American Bar Association at Detroit, August 25, 1909 (copy in Division of Special Collections and Archives, University of Kentucky); Eugene P. Lyle, "They That Ride By Night," *Hampton's Magazine*, XXII (February, 1909), 178; New York *Times*, October 13, 1908; Willson to Governor William O. Bradley, July 8, 1897, in Bradley Papers.

10. Willson, "The People and Their Law," 11.

Lube Martin went on trial for the murder of Guthrie Diuguid, a police-man in Murray. Fully aware of the hostile environment and the strong possibility that a mob might try to lynch his client, Martin's attorney requested a continuance in the case. Judge Charles H. Bush agreed and ordered Martin sent to Hopkinsville for safekeeping. The next day, a mob surrounded the judge's office and threatened to lynch him unless he had Martin brought back and turned over to them. Incredibly, the judge gave in to the mob's demand and sent word for Martin's return. Fortunately for Martin, someone informed Governor Stanley of these developments, and he quickly countermanded Bush's order. Deter-mined to prevent another embarrassing lynching like those of Henley and Durrett several months earlier in Paducah, Stanley then wired a message to officials in Murray, saying that he was coming by express train to the city and that if the mob members desired, they could lynch him instead of Martin. Once in Murray, the governor, a native of western Kentucky, quickly won the admiration of the mob. Stanley told them of his oath to uphold the law and added that under no cir-cumstances would Martin be turned over to them.[11]

The national press wrote accounts of Stanley saving the black man's life. Yet as the governor wrote in a confidential letter to Bush, he had come to Murray "not so much to save the life of this negro, who was for the time being secure, but to save your own, which I had every reason to believe was in imminent peril." The national office of the NAACP contributed to the incident's widespread publicity by having an article published showcasing Stanley as a governor willing to put his own life on the line to uphold the law. Roy Nash of the na-tional office wrote to Arthur Krock, managing editor of the Louisville *Courier-Journal*, asking him to send a reporter to Murray to write a story about the incident. The NAACP agreed to cover the expenses of

11. There are numerous sources that discuss this incident. See the Augustus O. Stanley Papers, Division of Special Collections and Archives, University of Kentucky (hereinafter cited as Stanley Papers). Especially see a revealing letter from Stanley to Judge Bush, January 24, 1917. The NAACP Papers have information on both Stanley and Lube Martin. See, for example, "Minutes of the Executive Committee of the NAACP," February 13, 1917, March 12, 1917, and December 8, 1919. See also Thomas Randolph, "The Governor and the Mob," *Independent,* LXXXIX (February 26, 1917), 347–48, Thomas W. Ramage, "Augustus Owsley Stanley: Early Twentieth Century Democrat" (Ph.D. dissertation, University of Kentucky, 1968), 206–208, New York *Times,* January 12–14, 1917, Tuskegee Clippings, Reel 221, Frames 560, 678.

the writer. T. R. Moss of the editorial department accepted the assignment with one stipulation, that his name not be used on the story. Nash replied, "If the story is published, we will run it over the name of Thomas Randolph as you suggest and you can rest assured that your connection with the matter will be kept entirely confidential."[12] The article "The Governor and the Mob," with its laudatory account of the actions of Stanley, was published by the *Independent* in late February. The article also helped the NAACP: The organization was trying to convince the U.S. Congress to pass a federal antilynching bill and wanted to show how local officials were often at the mercy of lynch mobs.

A year after the incident, Stanley was still being praised for saving Martin's life. On one occasion, he appeared before a cheering crowd of blacks at a religious convention in Frankfort. Under his administration, all Kentuckians would receive fair hearings, and he would take whatever steps necessary to prevent lynchings, the governor informed the crowd. Clearly, the incident in Murray strengthened Stanley's determination to denounce mob rule. In August, 1917, he returned to western Kentucky to prevent the lynching of another black man.[13]

Republican Edwin P. Morrow, elected governor in 1919, made the ending of mob violence a high priority in his administration.[14] Like Stanley, he received national attention for preventing the lynching of a black man. In rural Fayette County on February 4, 1920, ten-year-old Geneva Hardman was murdered and perhaps sexually assaulted. A black army veteran, Will Lockett, quickly became the leading suspect. After being arrested and taken to police headquarters, he confessed to the murder. Fearing a mob might storm the jail, the authorities rushed the black man to the state penitentiary in Frankfort. The day after Lockett's arrest and confession, the grand jury, which had

12. Stanley to Bush, January 24, 1917, in Stanley Papers; in the NAACP Papers, see a letter from Roy Nash to Arthur Krock, January 22, 1917, and a telegram from Nash to Krock on the same day.

13. Louisville *Courier-Journal,* August 21, 1917; Tuskegee Clippings, Reel 221, Frames 569–73, 581, 596.

14. For biographical information on Morrow, see Willard Rouse Jillson, *Edwin P. Morrow—Kentuckian* (Louisville, n.d.); for Morrow's comments and actions against mob violence, see the following: Box 88, CIC Papers; Edwin P. Morrow Papers, Division of Special Collections and Archives, University of Kentucky; and "Biennial Message of Governor Edwin P. Morrow," January 3, 1922, also in Morrow Papers.

been called into session solely to investigate this one incident, indicted him for murder. The county judge announced that in Lockett's case there would be no delay or change of venue and that the trial would start in Lexington on Monday, only five days after the murder.[15]

Governor Morrow assured Lexington officials that troops would be sent to protect Lockett on his return to the city. When giving orders to the adjutant general of the state militia, the governor reportedly said: "Do as much as you have to do to keep that negro in the hands of the law. If he falls into the hands of the mob I do not expect to see you alive."[16] In an attempt to convince the public to allow the law to take its course, the city's two daily newspapers, the *Herald* and the *Leader,* said that Lockett's trial would be quick and the outcome certain. Under heavy guard, the black man was returned to Lexington early that Monday. All of the seats in the courtroom were quickly taken, and the majority of people had to remain outside. The trial started promptly at nine o'clock and ended in less than thirty minutes. Lockett simplified matters by pleading guilty, though he asked for a life sentence instead of death. In what had to have been an unusual move (but one done obviously to appeal to the hostile crowd), the judge agreed to a request by the prosecuting attorney that the jury reach a decision without leaving the courtroom. To no one's surprise, they sentenced Lockett to die in the electric chair. But then a riot occurred. As explained by historian John D. Wright, a movie cameraman urged some of the people in the crowd outside the courtroom to shake their fists and yell, for the benefit of the camera, as the trial was ending. The noise led some people to think that an attack was being made, and they rushed toward the courtroom door. The commander of the militia "struggled with several men before firing two shots from his pistol, a signal for the troops to fire. A deadly volley left bodies scattered all over the courthouse steps. Some of the crowd fired at the troops and police, injuring one policeman so badly he had to

---

15. A number of sources can be consulted regarding this incident: the NAACP Papers, Group 1, Series C; *Crisis,* XIX (April, 1920), 298; Joe Jordan, "Lynchers Don't Like Lead," *Atlantic* (February, 1946), 103–108; J. Winston Coleman, *Death at the Court House* (Lexington, 1952); John D. Wright, "Lexington's Suppression of the 1920 Will Lockett Lynch Mob," *Register of the Kentucky Historical Society,* LXXXIV (Summer, 1986), 263–79.

16. The quotation comes from the St. Louis *Post Dispatch,* February 15, 1920, which can be found in the Tuskegee Clippings, Reel 222, Frame 109.

have an arm amputated. Five of the mob were killed outright; another died a few days later. . . . It was estimated that as many as fifty received wounds of varying severity, twenty-one of them being treated at the city hospitals."[17]

Governor Morrow received praise throughout the nation for the repelling of the mob by the state militia. Trying to downplay his actions, he asked: "What else was I to do? Don't people expect Governors to do their duty?" Almost all the newspaper accounts were favorable, saying that the law must be upheld. Writing in the *Crisis*, W. E. B. Du Bois called the incident "The Second Battle of Lexington." After reminding his readers about the shots that had been fired in the name of freedom at Lexington and Concord in 1775, he said: "In Kentucky, . . . five men were killed in the second battle of Lexington. Was it worth while? Already lynch law has cost America 3,000 lives, and mob law has taken ten times as many. If further bloody toll can be saved by five deaths, we have gotten off far more cheaply than we deserve." Officials of the NAACP sent a glowing telegram to Morrow. They hoped his actions would be emulated by other southern governors. The NAACP also made much of the fact that even before ordering the troops to Lexington to protect Lockett, Morrow had spoken out for a national antilynching law.[18]

Six years later, a second trial involving a Lexington black made national news, and the state's governor was praised for upholding the law and preventing a lynching. On January 19, 1926, Clarence Bryant and his two children were murdered and Mrs. Bryant was raped. Guilt quickly centered on their farmhand, Ed Harris, alias John Henry Jones. He was captured on a freight train leaving town. Just like Lockett before him, Harris was taken to Frankfort for safekeeping. Democratic governor William J. Fields quickly took control of the situation, proclaiming that "no half way measures will be adopted should there be an attempt to lynch Harris." Working with Lexington and Fayette county officials, the governor announced a number of measures to discourage a mob from forming when Harris returned for trial in early February. For the duration of the trial, the city would be placed under martial law. A large contingent of guardsmen would keep the peace and protect the courthouse. The main roads leading into Lexington

17. Wright, "Suppression of the Lynch Mob," 270–71.
18. *Crisis*, XIX (April, 1920), 298; Tuskegee Clippings, Reel 222, Frame 109.

would be closed. Public transportation on an interurban train and on bus lines would be stopped. Most of the businesses located in the city, including the stockyards and tobacco houses, would be shut down. Everyone entering the courthouse would be searched. Several tanks would also be brought to the city to assist the already heavily armed guardsmen.[19]

On the morning of the trial, Harris was wrapped in a blanket, placed in the car of the adjutant general, and driven to Lexington. Meanwhile, a guard was carried out of the prison in a blanket, put in a tank, and also driven to Lexington. Given all of the strict measures instituted and the presence of more than a hundred troops, it would have been surprising—and suicidal—for a mob to attempt to seize Harris. Indeed, the citizens of Lexington surely knew that at the slightest sign of provocation the troops would be given the order to fire, just as they had at the trial of Lockett. With the jury already sworn in (and obviously having already made up their minds), Harris' entire trial lasted sixteen minutes. He was, of course, given the death sentence. Harris was on his way back to Frankfort before many of the spectators had arrived at the courthouse.

Just as before, nearly all observers said state and local officials had no choice but to adopt such drastic methods and to resort to a quick trial if a lynching was to be prevented. In an editorial entitled "Lexington's Guarded Court House," the New York *Times* explained that "law respecting citizens of Lexington cannot take exception to the elaborate preparations to prevent a lynching when they remember that since 1888 no less than 168 lynchings have occurred in Kentucky." The state's violent past more than justified the action of the governor in placing the city under martial law, the paper concluded.

Had Morrow and Fields gone too far in their attempts to prevent lynchings? When considering the racial violence in Kentucky and how lynch mobs often performed their grisly tasks at will, unafraid of law officers, it is difficult to criticize the governors for using the maximum amount of force. Fields probably felt pressured into taking a tough stance. Perhaps he thought that his actions were being measured against Morrow's, and he was afraid of being criticized for not

19. Coverage of the entire case can be followed in the Lexington and Louisville newspapers from January 20 to mid-March, 1926. But perhaps the best accounts can be found in the New York *Times* for those same dates.

doing everything within his power to prevent a lynching. In both cases, however, the governors and the Lexington officials trampled on the civil rights of the accused men, making fair trials impossible. That Lockett and Harris would be found guilty and dealt with quickly had been openly admitted by officials prior to their trials. The decisions to avoid long trials and to not grant changes of venue were in one sense giving into the spirit of the mob: The accused men were dealt with quickly and severely and were not given a chance to defend themselves.

As we have seen, several governors received praise from the national office of the NAACP for their efforts to end mob violence. From its inception in 1909, the NAACP staked much of its reputation on ending mob violence. As Robert L. Zangrando explains: "The antilynching drive had [for the NAACP] an urgency, a public visibility, and a dramatic quality that no other civil rights activity quite matched. It was through the antilynching struggles that the NAACP gained much of its stability and recognition." At the end of the First World War, the NAACP became committed to the passage of a federal antilynching law. Introduced by Leonidas C. Dyer, a Republican, the bill was designed to protect citizens of the United States against lynchings when their states refused to act. Like most of the antilynching laws passed by the states, the bill called for fines and imprisonment for officials who knowingly allowed lynchings to occur and refused to apprehend members of the mob. Counties in which lynchings occurred would be required to pay restitution to the family of the victim. Southern congressmen staunchly opposed the legislation, saying that the Dyer Bill infringed on the rights of the states. The bill passed the House on three occasions, but each time it was defeated in the Senate. In the early 1930s, the Southern Commission on the Study of Lynching did a survey of southern lawyers, judges and other officials, asking their opinions of whether or not federal legislation should be enacted to prevent lynchings. The response of the southerners was clear: "Out of 213 responses, 194 expressed emphatic disapproval; only 14, approved; and 7 were qualified."[20]

20. Robert L. Zangrando, *The NAACP Crusade Against Lynching, 1909–1950* (Philadelphia, 1980), 20, 43–50; Nancy J. Weiss, *Farewell to the Party of Lincoln: Black Politics in the Age of FDR* (Princeton, 1983), 99–119; James Harmon Chadbourn, *Lynching and the Law* (Chapel Hill, 1933), 117–19. See also Charles Flint Kellogg, *A*

Most of Kentucky's congressmen refused to support the Dyer Bill. In 1922, when the bill passed the House for the first time, only Ben Johnson, a Democrat, and John M. Robison, a Republican, supported the measure. Meanwhile, 2 other Republicans had tried to straddle the fence. John Langley voted "present"; C. F. Ogden, who had been elected in part on the strong black vote from Louisville, was absent. The Dyer Bill died in the Senate without coming to a vote. Nevertheless, Senator A. O. Stanley, the former governor who had been praised for saving Lube Martin's life and who knew firsthand the horrors of lynching in Kentucky, had not been in favor of the bill. In describing Stanley's lack of support for the Dyer Bill, the Louisville *Leader,* a black newspaper, said that "not withstanding his Kentucky Negro friends, and the votes they might cast in November, Senator Stanley is a Democrat, pledged to the Democratic caucus, and bound to vote with the Democratic South on all measures affecting the Negro." This view would apply to most of Kentucky's representatives. In 1937, the NAACP secured the signatures of 202 congressmen in support of the Gavagan petition to bring the antilynching bill to the floor. Walter White of the NAACP wrote to a black leader in Hopkinsville, saying that Kentucky's representatives had not signed the petition, which was sixteen votes short of going to the floor. Included among the 6 Kentuckians was Fred M. Vinson, who would eventually serve on the United States Supreme Court.[21]

Alben W. Barkley was one of Kentucky's most influential voices in Washington in the twentieth century. Barkley enjoyed a long and distinguished career in politics: He served in the United States House of Representatives from 1913 to 1927, in the United States Senate from 1927 to 1949 and from 1954 to 1956, as majority leader of the Senate from 1937 to 1949, and as vice-president of the United States from 1949 to 1953. As majority leader, Barkley was placed in the center of the controversy over the antilynching bill. In 1937, Walter White informed the Kentucky branches of the NAACP that the national office appreciated Barkley's efforts to bring the bill to a vote: "I know you

History of the National Association for the Advancement of Colored People, 1909–1920 (Baltimore, 1967).

21. Louisville *Courier-Journal,* January 27, December 3, 1922; Louisville *Leader,* February 11, May 13, 1922, October 4, 1924; Walter White, of the NAACP, to Walter Robinson, of the Hopkinsville NAACP branch, March 27, 1937, in NAACP Papers.

will be happy to hear how courageous and completely fair Senator Barkley has been with respect to the bill. . . . Throughout all this difficult parliamentary procedure, Senator Barkley has with rare courage stood firmly for complete adherence both to the letter and to the spirit of the special order voted by the Senate last August 12 to make the anti-lynching bill the first order of business after the farm bill."[22]

Three years later, however, a sharp exchange took place between the two men. White accused Barkley of stalling on the antilynching bill and of refusing to discuss the proposed legislation with members of the NAACP. White reminded Barkley of a statement he had made in the New York *Herald-Tribune* of April 1, 1940: "The sooner Congress adjourns the less the likelihood will be that the bill will have to be taken up by the Senate." In response, Barkley claimed that he had done everything to bring the bill to a vote: "When I labored through a six weeks filibuster in the last Congress, making every possible effort to bring the Anti-Lynching Bill to a vote, you were quite familiar with the situation and expressed your appreciation for the efforts which I had made." He did concede, however, that he was reluctant to bring the bill up until all other legislation had been disposed of, "for the reason that whenever this measure is taken up all other business, no matter how urgent, would come to a stop and the Senate would find itself in the midst of another filibuster." White concluded by saying that Barkley and the senators opposed to the filibuster of the southerners lacked "the moral courage to oppose the brazen tactics of the minority which is fighting this bill. With such weak opposition to filibustering, there is no wonder that the filibusterers are so cocksure and are so confident that they can once again prevent a majority of the Senate from voting one way or the other on this legislation. It is this situation which is resented by citizens, white as well as colored, and South as well as North."[23]

Although failing in its attempt to have a federal antilynching law enacted, the NAACP worked for the passage of a law against mob violence in Kentucky. The state had, of course, passed an antilynching

22. Walter White, to the Kentucky branches of the NAACP, November 26, 1937, in NAACP Papers.

23. Alben W. Barkley to Walter White, April 22, 1940, White to Barkley, April 23, 1940, both in the Association of Southern Women for the Prevention of Lynching Papers, Special Collections and Archives, Woodruff Library, Atlanta University (hereinafter cited as ASWPL Papers); Zangrando, *The NAACP Crusade*, 164.

law in 1897 and had modified it five years later. But because of the brazen way lynchers often carried out their tasks, many people assumed that the state had no antilynching law, not that the law was simply being ignored by mobs and officials alike. Surely the NAACP attorneys knew that Kentucky had passed an antilynching law. It is clear, therefore, that much of the impetus by the NAACP for antilynching legislation was simply an attempt to keep the issue in front of the public. Also, they hoped a new law would force officials to come out openly and forcefully against lynchings.

Actions by branches of the NAACP in Kentucky proved key to the efforts of the association to pass a new law. The first branch had been founded in Louisville in 1914, primarily to challenge the Louisville Residential Segregation Ordinance, which prohibited blacks from living in certain sections of the city. The United States Supreme Court overturned that ordinance in November, 1917. Members of the Louisville NAACP then turned their attention to other discriminatory laws and to lynchings and helped form branches in other cities. The Frankfort branch, founded during the First World War, quickly became the leading civil rights organization in central Kentucky, and because of its location in the capital city, members of the branch had contact with elected officials as well.

The Frankfort branch was led by Edward E. Underwood, a dynamic physician who had been active in the struggle for black equality in Kentucky since the early 1890s. The branch began what turned out to be a three-year struggle for the passage of an antilynching law immediately after Governor Stanley prevented the lynching of Lube Martin in Murray in 1917. Underwood called upon the governor, asking his assistance in securing the passage of a law to prevent mob violence. According to Underwood, Stanley readily assented. On another occasion the black physician showed the governor copies of the antilynching laws of Ohio, Illinois, and Indiana to convince him of the necessity of supporting within the bill a feature calling for the automatic removal of peace officers after a lynching had occurred. As Underwood explained, "Lynchings are made possible either by the cowardice of the peace officers, or their secret collusion with the mob." The NAACP, in other words, was pushing for one of the main features of the 1897 law that had been eliminated in 1902. Without such a feature, Underwood informed the governor, the law would not be enforced: "The Constitution at that time did not permit removal of officers except by impeachment or indictment, and we had little faith in courts or juries to secure our ends by either of these means." The antilynching law was not submitted to the Kentucky General Assembly, however, until Edwin Morrow became governor, partly because he, even more than Stanley, was committed to the passage of the bill.[24]

The proposed legislation placed the burden of preventing mob violence on the sheriff and the other officers in charge of a prisoner. Section Three of the new law clearly explained that if any prisoner was taken from the sheriff or peace officer and lynched or injured, that act "shall be prima facie evidence of neglect of duty on the part of such officer, and when such failure in, or neglect of duty" was made known to the governor, he would declare the office vacant. Section Four also proved controversial: It gave the county judge the task of selecting someone to fill the vacancy. On several occasions, county judges merely selected the wives of suspended jailers to serve out their terms. Section Five of the proposed law outlined the procedure to be followed by the suspended jailer when petitioning the governor for reinstatement to office. Morrow had argued that for the law to be effective it was important that the governor, not local officials, handle the appeal. As he explained, "We had to fight at the last legislature to prevent the anti-mob law being passed with a provision under which the peace officer removed by Governor might appeal to the courts for reinstatement, thus throwing his case back into local politics." The final section noted that any officer removed by the governor was disqualified from holding any office in Kentucky for four years. Introduced into the Senate on February 20, 1920, the bill passed without a dissenting vote and sailed through the House several weeks later, also without negative votes. The unanimous approval of the antilynching bill indicates that public support of mob law had become unacceptable, at least among Kentucky's elected officials. In the presence of Dr. Underwood and other members of the NAACP, Governor Morrow signed the bill on March 22, 1920. He then presented the gold pen to Underwood to acknowledge his crucial role in the passage of the antilynch law.[25]

24. Louisville *Courier-Journal*, November 5, 1919; Edward E. Underwood to John R. Shillady, national secretary of the NAACP, April 9, 1920, in NAACP Papers.

25. *Kentucky Acts of General Assembly for the Year 1920* (Frankfort, 1920), 186–87; Frankfort *State Journal*, March 23, 1920. Morrow was quoted in the Chicago *Whip*, March 26, 1921. According to Chadbourn, *Lynching and the Law*, 58, Kentucky

The automatic removal of a peace officer, the NAACP proclaimed, would ensure enforcement of the new law. Anything short of his death, the law said, meant neglect of duty. Commenting on this portion of the law, Governor Flem D. Sampson once noted: "I do not believe that a mob can ever take a prisoner from a jailer who is really in good faith and trying to prevent the taking [of the prisoner]. . . . The trouble has been the jailers have joined in the mobs or tacitly consented to the crime."[26] That the responsibility for reinstating the officer rested with the governor—who could not be reelected—and not with the courts or local jurymen, who could easily be intimidated, was viewed as significant. Also, the burden of proof was placed on the peace officer asking for reinstatement; the state did not have to prove neglect of duty.

Grant Smith died at the hands of a lynch mob ten days after the law had been approved. The new law, however, was not to go into effect for ninety days. Dr. Underwood informed NAACP officials that calling for the immediate implementation of the antilynching law would have greatly weakened its chances for passage. The national office wrote immediately to Governor Morrow, urging an investigation and the prosecution of Smith's lynchers. But beyond the usual protest, nothing was done.[27]

Governor Morrow called for a speedy investigation after Richard James was lynched for murder in March, 1921. He offered a $500 reward for the arrest and conviction of each mob member. Acting under the law, he removed Versailles jailer John H. Edgers from his post. The jailer applied for reinstatement, describing how he had attempted to prevent the mob from taking the black man. In denying the request, Morrow stated, "It is the duty of a jailer to resist a mob until he is beaten into insensibility or killed." Versailles officials refused to assist the governor in the investigation. In fact, they were unhappy only about the jailer being removed from his post and not about the death

was one of nine states that enacted provisions calling for the removal of peace officers who failed to prevent lynchings. By the early 1930s, forty states had passed laws against mob violence and lynchings. See Chadbourn, Appendix C, "Existing Legislation," 149–214.

26. Flem D. Sampson to George F. Milton, editor of the Chattanooga *News*, October 11, 1930, in CIC Papers.

27. National office of the NAACP to Governor Edwin Morrow, March 30, 1920, in NAACP Papers; Tuskegee Clippings, Reel 221, Frame 46.

of James. In a blatant attempt to skirt the new antilynching law, the county judge appointed the wife of the jailer to fill the vacancy. Governor Morrow denounced the grand jury for saying that nothing could be done to bring the lynchers to justice: "If a gang had gone into Versailles and robbed a bank they would have formed a posse and gone after them; and the grand jury would have remained in session until it had accomplished something. The grand jury convened at 9 and adjourned at 3 and whitewashed everybody, but had no word of condemnation for the mob. . . . It is absurd to think that a grand jury could make a real investigation of such an affair as that in six hours." The Frankfort branch of the NAACP closely monitored the situation, and though disappointed that the lynchers were not brought to justice, they had nothing but praise for the actions of the governor.[28]

Morrow was determined to remove from office any jailer who allowed a prisoner to fall into the hands of the mob. In late August, 1922, Jack Eaton, a traveling showman, was arrested in Georgetown and charged with assault on several young girls. In court, however, the parents of the girls refused to press formal charges. As soon as he was released from jail, Eaton, a white man, was seized by a mob, carried to the countryside, and severely beaten; turpentine was put in his cuts. After several anonymous sources contacted his office, the governor had the incident investigated by a private detective whose findings indicated that the sheriff, Sam Moss, had "knowingly and willfully delivered Jack Eaton into the hands of a mob." On September 11, the governor removed Sam Moss as jailer of Scott County. Afro-Americans were obviously elated over Morrow's stance. Often victims themselves of beatings by mobs, they hoped the governor's actions would convince other sheriffs and jailers to abide by the law.[29]

Kentucky's NAACP branches aggressively pushed for the enforce-

28. Morrow's statement to the jailer can be found in Chadbourn, *Lynching and the Law*, 73; his other quotation can be found in the Tuskegee Clippings, Reel 221, Frame 311. See also the Louisville *Leader*, March 19, 1921; P. W. L. Jones, of the Frankfort NAACP, to Walter White, March 26, 1921, White to Jones, March 30, 1921, Edward E. Underwood to White, March 29, 1921, White to Underwood, April 4, 1921, all in NAACP Papers. The Frankfort branch informed the national office that immediately after the lynching, the State Medical Society of Kentucky refused to meet as planned in Versailles. According to the president of the organization, members of the medical society changed to another site as a protest of the lynching.

29. Tuskegee Clippings, Reel 222, Frame 936.

ment of the law whenever a lynching occurred. In a few instances, their efforts led to arrests and indictments. In February, 1930, eight men were indicted in connection with the lynching of Chester Fugate in Breathitt County. The circuit judge ordered that seven of the men remain in jail until their trial started, the other, a sixteen-year-old, was permitted out on bail. Even though Fugate was white, all eight men charged with the lynching won acquittal.[30]

The refusal of local communities to convict their fellow citizens greatly disturbed the NAACP. They argued in vain for legislation moving trials of lynchers to other communities. And in the view of the NAACP, most of the governors failed to fully utilize the various measures of the antilynching law. A case in point was the mob murder of Leonard Woods in December, 1927. Lawrence D. Kellis, a black schoolteacher from Letcher County, wrote a poignant letter to James Weldon Johnson of the national office, pleading for help in bringing the guilty to justice: "Please post a reward and force Gov. Sampson to act. . . . Ky had a law on its statue [sic] book which says that any peace officer that permits a mob to take a prisoner the officer should be removed from his position immediately. The law is not being enforced in case with the Sheriff and jailer of this county." It would not be difficult, the black schoolteacher emphasized, to identify the members of the mob. "If you want the names conclusive and definite just send some person to me who can pass for white and I can show him where and who to see and get all the names and evidence you need." Kellis' letter clearly points out that the governor and Letcher County officials were reluctant to investigate the matter. No one was charged with the lynching, even though Kellis had explained that everyone in the community knew that "Deaton Father member of Mob and father fired the first shot in Wood body." In short, during the 1920s and 1930s the governors proved best at preventing lynchings, not in bringing the guilty to justice.[31]

The NAACP was not the only organization committed to ending the practice of lynching. Immediately after the Great War, a group composed of the "better element" of southern whites and moder-

30. For the attempt to convict the men for the lynching of Chester Fugate, see "Legal Punishment of Lynchers, 1899–1930," in Folder 155, Box 134, CIC Papers.

31. Lawrence D. Kellis to James Weldon Johnson, December 14, 1927; see also a letter from J. B. Howard to Johnson, December 22, 1927, both in NAACP Papers.

ate black leaders formed the Commission on Interracial Cooperation (CIC) to help ease racial tensions. The organization did not seek a revolution in southern race relations but merely called for improved schools and other facilities for blacks (still in a segregated setting) and, above all, for the end of racial violence.

At the first statewide meeting in Louisville, from July 23 to 24, 1920, the people affiliated with the Kentucky CIC agreed on a preamble to guide their actions:

> Not in passion or prejudice, but in the broad spirit of those seeking patiently and in faith to find a solution of the delicate inter-racial problems that menace the peace and divide in hurtful antagonism the energies of our people, we desire to mobilize the better sentiment of both races in the state for the removal of the causes of friction and strife, to the end that equal justice may be secured to all and the energies of the two races may be joined in the great common task of building a better world for our children and our children's children to live in.[32]

Governor Morrow, who had issued the call for the first meeting, served as honorary chairman of the organization. In his keynote address, he reminded whites of their obligations to uplift black Kentuckians. Leaders of the organization called for a common-sense approach to solving racial matters; treating everyone with dignity, for example, would improve conditions. Various white and black CIC workers wrote articles in newspapers throughout the state emphasizing black improvement and showing examples of blacks and whites working in unity and harmony. "The interracial committee for Breathitt county helped a group of whites and blacks work together to secure three acres of land and build a school for blacks" was a typical press release from the CIC. Believing that education would solve many of the problems faced by blacks, the organization devoted considerable time to helping Afro-Americans acquire high schools in many parts of the state for the first time.[33]

Led by its black director, James A. Bond, the CIC tried to ease racial tensions and called for the punishment of anyone, black or

---

32. See the pamphlet of the first meeting, *State Inter-Racial Conference for Kentucky, July 23d and 24th, 1920* (Louisville, 1920), in CIC Papers.

33. For a positive article on the accomplishments of the CIC in Kentucky, see George Madden Martin, "Race Cooperation," *McClure's Magazine*, LIV (October, 1922), 9–20.

white, who committed crimes that threatened peaceful race relations. A branch of the organization was formed in Whitley County shortly after the Corbin riot of October 30, 1919. Members of the branch agreed "to secure the conviction and punishment of the mob that drove the colored people out of town." Both the county judge and the prosecuting attorney, who joined the CIC, agreed. As a result, the man identified as the ringleader received a two-year sentence in the penitentiary and twenty-nine other white men were indicted for their role in the riot. (The ultimate outcome of these indictments is unknown.) The CIC sent workers to the site of the Dix River riot, and they worked, so their annual report proclaims, to ensure that whites as well as blacks were arrested for the racial outburst. CIC reports also claim that on several occasions leaders of the organization stood up to mobs and persuaded them to not lynch a black person. A Madisonville police officer was killed by Lee Ellison in 1920. The CIC reminded local whites that only one black, not the entire Afro-American community, had committed the crime and said that Ellison should receive a fair trial. After the incident was resolved, the CIC proudly informed the public that Madisonville blacks had helped apprehend Ellison, who was duly tried and executed. The same proved true in Hardinsburg, in Breckinridge County, where a black man was accused of killing one white and wounding another. The incident "aroused the evil passions of large numbers of white people in the county. The colored members of the committee . . . called a hurried meeting, drew up a statement declaring that the colored people had no sympathy for the black, Charles Miller, who had committed the horrible crime, and urged that the law be allowed to take its course. White members of the committee joined in." In the eyes of the CIC, Miller received a fair trial, and his death by electrocution was justified.[34]

With the cooperation of the governor, the CIC gave awards to sheriffs for preventing lynchings and publicized these events as examples for other lawmen to emulate. In April, 1927, a medal was given to

34. For an account of the investigation by members of the CIC in Corbin, see *Crisis*, XXI (April, 1921), 250. For a number of yearly reports of the Kentucky commission, especially the years 1923, 1925, and 1928, see Folder 157, Box 167, CIC Papers. See also "Minutes of Special Interracial Committee," January 12, 1921, in CIC Papers. For articles discussing the role of CIC members in preventing lynchings, see *Southern Workman*, LXV (March 1931), 126, and *World Outlook*, XXVI (May, 1936), 30.

Sheriff P. R. Brown of Graves County, a place long associated with violence. A year before, a mob had descended on the Mayfield jail to lynch Willie Busby, a black charged with the rape of a white girl. With the aid of his deputies, Brown drove seventy-five miles to carry Busby to safety. For performing this "noble deed"—which was certainly his responsibility—Brown was congratulated by Governor William J. Fields for the "splendid service he had rendered his state and nation." The governor gave the sheriff a bronze medal, which had a "heroic figure with drawn sword standing in front of a temple of justice." Inscribed in bold letters was "In Defense of Law and Civilization."[35]

The CIC, though never ending its involvement in the antilynching movement, allowed much of its efforts to be taken over by the Association of Southern Women for the Prevention of Lynching (ASWPL), an organization that CIC officials helped create. As explained by Jacquelyn D. Hall, the central argument of the southern women was their rejection of the long-established belief that lynchings protected southern white womanhood. They also argued that lynchings brought disgrace upon America as the only civilized nation where such violence occurred. Instead of upholding the law, the practice of lynching totally discredited the legal process and eroded respect for officers of the law, ASWPL spokeswomen consistently explained.[36]

The CIC planted the seeds of the Kentucky ASWPL in December, 1923, with the organization of a subcommittee of thirty women, all prominent citizens from communities throughout the state, to work vigorously in the interest of justice and good will between the races. In their first pronouncement, the women congratulated Kentucky on the absence of lynchings for over a year, called for the rejection of racial prejudice from political campaigns, and demanded the protection of life and property of white and black alike. Practically all of the women involved in this committee formed by the CIC would become members of the ASWPL.[37]

35. Press release from the CIC headquarters in Atlanta, April 19, 1927. For the entire file containing letters and newspaper clippings on the sheriff, see Folder 156, Box 135, CIC Papers.

36. Jacquelyn Dodd Hall, *Revolt Against Chivalry: Jessie Daniel Ames and the Women's Campaign Against Lynchings* (New York, 1979), 194–97. See also Julius Wayne Dudley, "A History of the Association of Southern Women for the Prevention of Lynching, 1930–1942" (Ph.D. dissertation, University of Cincinnati, 1979).

37. CIC press release, "Kentucky Women Seek Good Will, and Join Interracial Commission and Ask Justice for All," December 12, 1923, in CIC Papers.

Board members of the CIC worked with Jessie Daniel Ames, the central figure in the ASWPL throughout the South, to formally organize a branch in Kentucky. In a letter to J. Max Bond, who had become the director of the CIC upon the death of his father, Ames emphasized that the work of the ASWPL would be independent from the CIC, thereby "bringing into it many women who may not be sympathetic with the principles of the Commission, but certainly sympathetic with law enforcement." (To Bond, a black man, Ames mentioned specifically that only white women should be invited to join.) At the meeting, held on February 26, 1931, Ames gave a long address outlining the work of the organization and the need for a Kentucky branch. The women agreed to form a Kentucky branch and, as required of all new affiliates, passed a resolution. Like their southern sisters who had joined the ASWPL, the Kentucky women expressed their opposition to mob violence: "We repudiate the claim that lynching is in defense of the white women in the South, holding that the mob spirit is a greater menace than any other form of crime in the United States, brutalizing the community, men, women and children, where it occurs, discrediting American institutions, and confessing to a breakdown in government." They promised to do all in their power to "eradicate this crime in our State by helping to build up a profounder sense in young and old of law and order and the need therefor."[38]

Members of ASWPL wrote numerous letters to every sheriff in the state, keeping them informed of the threats of lynchings and urging them to make sure that none happened in their communities. "Last year, for the first time since 1929, Kentucky had a lynching," a letter of January, 1933, said. "We had thought, when the movement of Southern Women against lynching was started, that our State needed no such education. Our citizens were committed against this crime. Last year's record shows that we were mistaken." The organization told the sheriffs of their goal of a "Lynchless South in 1933." They also noted, however, that if a lynching should occur, it would be the responsibility of the sheriffs to pursue the mob members vigorously and

38. J. Max Bond to Jessie Daniel Ames, February 12, 1931, Ames to Bond, February 13, 1931, Ames to Mrs. Attwood Martin, February 13, 1931, especially see "Minutes of a Meeting Called for the Consideration of the Subject of Lynching in Kentucky and the South," Louisville, Kentucky, February 26, 1931, and "Pronouncement of the Kentucky Association of Women for the Prevention of Lynching," February 26, 1931, all in ASWPL Papers.

to prosecute them in court. The next year, the women urged the sheriffs to sign pledges to prevent lynchings. As the many letters from sheriffs clearly show, ASWPL succeeded in getting them to agree to the pledges. The ASWPL also issued yearly reports of where lynchings had been prevented in the state.[39]

Realizing that the support of all elected officials was essential to ending lynchings, the Kentucky affiliate invited the governor, the attorney general, and numerous local officials to their conferences. Before the governor's race of 1935, it sent a lengthy questionnaire to the leading candidates asking them to explain their positions on violence and the measures they would adopt to ensure that no additional lynchings disgraced the Commonwealth. All of the replies from the candidates were released to the public.[40]

Tension eventually surfaced between the officers of the Kentucky affiliate and Jessie Daniel Ames over a federal antilynching law. Although she devoted much of her life's work to ending lynchings, Ames opposed federal legislation, agreeing with most white southerners that any action by the government would infringe on the rights of the states. She also counseled the affiliates against working with members of the NAACP because, in her view, it was misguided in calling for a national antilynching law and was committed to breaking down the walls of racial segregation. By the late 1930s in Kentucky, however, nearly all the members of ASWPL, as well as leading citizens such as Mark Ethridge, the highly influential editor of the *Courier-Journal*, had come out in support of federal legislation against lynchings. And instead of viewing the NAACP as an adversary, members of the Kentucky ASWPL realized the value of cooperating with the organization and had even appeared on several programs sponsored by the Louisville branch. After stating her support for federal legislation, Mrs. G. W. Hummel, the president of the Kentucky affili-

39. Letter from G. W. Hummel, chairman of the ASWPL, to the sheriffs of Kentucky, January 23, 1933, in ASWPL Papers. For an example of the sheriffs signing the pledge, see, in the same collection, the letter from Hummel to Ames, December 27, 1934, and "Signatures, Officers of the Law," in Folder 84, Box 16, ASWPL Papers.

40. Louisville *Leader*, March 4, 1933; "Plans of Actions to Prevent Lynchings," in Folder 82, Box 15, ASWPL Papers; Report of the Kentucky Council, ASWPL, "The Candidates for Nomination of Governor of Kentucky and Lynching, 1935," in ASWPL Papers.

ate and one of its founders, offered her resignation to Ames, who declined to accept it, saying that agreement on all principles was not a requirement of membership in the ASWPL. Although they never resolved their differences with Ames, the Kentucky women continued their efforts to prevent lynchings until the organization was absorbed into the Southern Regional Council in 1942.[41]

The lynching of Rex Scott in January, 1934, proved to be the occasion for all of the groups active in preventing lynchings to work together. Immediately after the lynching, Patrick Henry Callahan, a Catholic lay leader representing the CIC, and Mrs. Hummel of the ASWPL called on Governor Ruby Laffoon to investigate the lynching. The governor responded by removing jailer Troy Combs for making no effort to prevent the lynching. The state legislature, without a dissenting vote, adopted a resolution condemning the lynching and promising to support the governor in whatever steps would be taken to identify members of the mob. Both the CIC and the ASWPL contacted members in the Perry County area and urged them to press for the arrests of the lynchers. A special grand jury convened in Hazard and eventually handed down indictments against four men. One of them, Lee Gibson, had openly bragged about the lynching, saying he had fired the first shot into Scott's body. The Louisville NAACP also played a role in the case. Their attorney, Charles W. Anderson, a recent graduate of Howard University Law School, went to Hazard to assist in the prosecution of the case. The Perry County prosecutor announced his delight in having a black lawyer assist him. Anderson quickly realized, however, that the prosecutor had little desire to convict the men and that "mountain kinship" would prevent justice from being done. All of the men were given alibis. Gibson, the first one brought to trial, won easy acquittal, as would the others. Anderson refused to be discouraged by the outcome of the trials. As he explained in a letter to Walter White of the national office, the men were arrested and indicted for a lynching, something rarely done in Kentucky or the South.[42]

41. Dudley, "A History of the Association of Southern Women," 257–59, 309–10, 353; John Shelton Reed, "An Evaluation of an Anti-lynching Organization," *Social Problems*, XVI (Fall, 1968), 172–82.

42. The ASWPL Papers contains numerous letters and newsclips regarding the case. See, for example, "Report on Action of Kentucky ASWPL on Lynching at Hazard,"

Although applauding the efforts of many individuals and organizations to end mob violence, a few observers questioned whether the
number of lynchings was actually declining or whether instances
of this brutal phenomenon were going unreported. Writing in 1928,
I. Willis Cole, the editor of the Louisville *Leader* and a member of the
NAACP, argued that lynching as a practice had not declined. "There
have been long intervals between lynchings during the year, which
goes out with a better record than the previous year, but this does not
mean that lynching is on the decline; but that somehow the Negro
has followed such a straight and narrow path that there has been no
grounds for a killing." In two well-documented articles, the ASWPL
carefully explained that by the end of the 1930s public opinion in the
South had turned against lynchings. But blacks were still—even in
the 1940s—being lynched for minor offenses. This suggested "the
rigid determination of white citizens to maintain and protect at any
cost their absolute social control over the Negro." In the second publication, the ASWPL acknowledged that in every state it was possible
that the number of lynchings had not declined but merely had gone
"underground." Lynchings, except on rare occasions, were no longer
dramatic public displays. Instead, countless blacks were lynched each
year, but "their disappearance is shrouded in mystery, for they are dis-
patched quietly, and without general knowledge. . . . This is the new
and dangerous method, devised by those who seek to rule by terror
and intimidation." Indeed, some students of mob violence speculated
that since lynchings had been used by whites primarily to control
Afro-Americans, whites had probably adopted new and equally effective ways to keep blacks in their place.[43]

As we will see, a leading cause for the decline in lynchings might

prepared by Miss Schmitt, February 9, 1934. Anderson kept Walter White informed
about the case. See four letters from Anderson to White: February 27, March 2, 12, 15,
1934, in NAACP Papers. In the same collection, see the press release of February 26,
1934, "Louisville NAACP to Aid Hazard Prosecution." The NAACP Papers also has a
letter from Scott's mother, Lydia, to the national office, December 10, 1934. Louisville
Courier-Journal, January 25, 26, 1934; Louisville *Times*, January 25, 1934; Louisville
Leader, June 2, 1934.

43. Louisville *Leader*, August 11, 1928; *Lynchings Go Underground* (Atlanta, n.d.,
but probably 1940); Jessie Daniel Ames, *The Changing Character of Lynching* (Atlanta,
1942).

have been that the state often took over the role of the mob and punished with impunity many Afro-Americans accused of crimes. On numerous occasions, the whites demanding "justice" for blacks relented to the appeals of CIC and ASWPL members to allow the law to run its course—and the law, spokesmen for these two groups promised lynchers, could be counted on to deal harshly with people convicted of heinous crimes.

SEVEN "A Sacrifice Upon the Altar of the Law," 1875–1899

When a rumor began circulating in Mayfield on January 12, 1898, that a young white girl named Tennie Bailey had been raped, attention centered on Robert Blanks, a black man in his mid-30s. Realizing that being accused of such a crime could lead to his lynching, Blanks quickly fled the state and successfully eluded the authorities for four months. Mayfield's police chief eventually tracked the accused rapist to Cairo, Illinois, where he was working in a strawberry field when arrested. After having Blanks placed in jail, the chief requested that the black man be returned to Mayfield to stand trial. The governor of Illinois agreed, but Governor William O. Bradley, who had pledged to end lynchings during his administration and who was extremely sensitive to the racial violence that had occurred in Mayfield in December, 1896, denied the request. In a dramatic statement, he said: "The wholesale slaughter of Negroes by mobs in Graves County and the failure to punish their murderers satisfies me that to have this man sent back there would be to have him sent to his death, and that he could not obtain even a semblance of a fair trial. If guilty he deserves death, but punishment should be inflicted by law and not by mob. I decline to issue the requisition." The governor's action had probably saved the black man's life. When first commenting on the rape and the capture of Blanks, the white newspaper wrote in a matter-of-fact manner that once Blanks returned to Mayfield, "the usual result will follow, as the crime was one of the most heinous ever perpetrated here."[1]

The Kentucky *Standard*, a black weekly published in Lexington,

1. Bradley was quoted in the Kentucky *Standard*, May 28, 1898; Louisville *Courier-Journal*, January 13, May 21, 1898.

wrote that the governor had once again demonstrated beyond any doubt his concern for the race. What went unreported, however, was Bradley's decision to have the black man sent to Louisville until he was assured that Blanks would be protected when he was returned to Mayfield for trial. The governor informed Graves County officials of this action and told them to proceed with plans for the trial. The governor also warned them against any violence occurring during the trial; to ensure the prisoner's safety, Bradley sent along state troops to protect the accused rapist. Bradley agreed that the trial could be held in Mayfield but insisted that the jury come from Hickman County. Protected by fifty guards, Blanks arrived in Mayfield on July 5 for his trial. As the local newspaper stated, "Several hundred people were at the depot to witness the strange spectacle of a company of soldiers coming to Mayfield to save the neck of a brutal negro from a mob." Blanks had three attorneys, including Augustus E. Willson, the future governor. Nevertheless, he was found guilty and sentenced to death.[2]

Six months after Blanks's conviction, attorney Willson argued before the Kentucky Court of Appeals that because of the sensational rumors published in the newspapers, it had been impossible for his client to receive a fair trial in Graves County. The same would have been true, Willson said, if the case had been moved to Ballard, Hickman, Fulton, or Carlisle counties. Whites living in these areas of western Kentucky, the attorney explained, almost universally agreed that Blanks was guilty of raping a young white female—a crime regarded with high emotions. And, said Willson, the death sentence should be overturned because the court had refused to grant a change of venue from Graves County. Willson informed the justices that when Blanks and the soldiers arrived in Mayfield, they were surrounded by "a great throng of hundreds of men and boys . . . shouting, 'Hang him!' 'Take him out!'" The court of appeals rejected the motions presented by Willson, dismissing his argument that prejudiced newspaper accounts played any part in inciting the public's indignation over Blanks's alleged offense. Concerning the second motion, the justices made a brief statement: "We are not prepared to say that the court erred in overruling the motion for a change of venue." It is not a mandate that a criminal case be transferred to another area

2. Mayfield *Monitor*, July 6, 13, August 24, 1898.

simply because such a move was sought by the defendant, the justices explained.[3]

Clearly, in their ruling in *Blanks* v. *Commonwealth*, the justices of Kentucky's highest court chose to ignore the obvious, that for decades the mere rumor that a black might have raped a white female created, as Blanks's attorney argued, an emotionally charged situation and had led to numerous lynchings—or at the very least to white mobs dominating court procedures, demanding quick "justice" for black rapists. In the opinion of the appeals court, the fact that a hostile mob had met Blanks and the soldiers at the train depot, followed them to the jail, surrounded the jail until Blanks was taken to court, and crammed into the courtroom throughout the trial, making known its opinion of Blanks's testimony by loud outbursts, had no effect on the outcome of the case.

Willson next turned to Governor Bradley in an attempt to save Blanks's life. He was defending Blanks, Willson informed the governor, "without fee or reward, or expectation of any fee or reward" because of a sincere belief that justice must be served in the case. The guilty verdict and death sentence handed the black man had convinced Willson that mob justice prevailed in Kentucky:

> This Bob Blanks case is a case in which Providence tests the soundness of our whole system with the wager of an utterly unimportant human cipher. Bob Blanks is the cipher, whose case tests the soundness and the justice of our institutions, as much as if he were the most precious life that ever was thrown in the scale. The lighter the weight that establishes the scale is not true, the easier it is to prove the system unsound, and Bob Blanks' case seems to establish by the lightest possible evidence that the scale of justice is not held evenly in our state.

Willson urged the governor to give Blanks a ten-year prison sentence since he had admitted under oath to having sex with the young white girl.[4]

Although swayed by Willson's compelling arguments, Bradley de-

---

3. *Blanks* v. *Commonwealth,* 48 Southwestern Reporter, 161–64 (1898).

4. Augustus E. Willson to William O. Bradley, November 2, December 8, 1898, in Bradley Papers; see also the undated letter from Blanks to Bradley, informing the governor of his innocence and stating that it had been impossible for him to receive a fair trial. Also within the Bradley Papers are numerous letters, both pro and con, over whether Blanks should be executed.

cided to hear from Graves County officials before making a final decision on the fate of Blanks. He wrote to J. E. Robbins, judge of the Graves County Circuit Court, who had presided over the case, and two days later received a lengthy reply. In Robbins' opinion, Blanks had committed rape and had received a fair trial and a just verdict. The judge then appealed to the governor to allow the death sentence to be upheld for the good of the state. Carrying out death sentences, he argued, was the most effective way Bradley could end lynchings in the state. Many "very reputable and good citizens," he explained to the governor, have applauded the outrages committed by the mob because of their belief "that the courts will not enforce the law, and that executive clemency constantly interferes to prevent the proper punishment of crime." Fully aware of Bradley's commitment to uplifting blacks, the judge next said that upholding the death sentence in the Blanks case would in the long run aid Kentucky's black citizens: "If Bob Blanks should not be executed but have his punishment commuted, or be pardoned, the effect on the colored race in this state would be dreadful. If such action be taken the life of any colored person who hereafter commits any kind of crime will be very little value to him, for no amount of vigilance on the part of judges and other officers of the law can further restrain the infuriated masses from acts of violence against the colored race."[5] The letter from the judge proved persuasive. Assured that his actions of having the accused taken to Louisville, having him escorted to Mayfield by fifty troops, and bringing in jurors from another county had led to a fair trial for Blanks, Governor Bradley refused to prevent the execution. Blanks died on the scaffold in Mayfield on April 18, 1899, before a white crowd numbering in the thousands.[6]

On December 9, 1916, deputy constable Guthrie Diuguid of Murray was shot and mortally wounded by Lube Martin. According to the version that several whites told in court, Diuguid, a peaceful man, had several run-ins with Martin, and the Negro had gone so far as to threaten to kill him. Diuguid, according to this account, was approaching the street when he was attacked by two relatives of Martin, making it easy for Martin to fire six shots into his body. Several whites testified that Diuguid's dying words were that Martin had, as

5. J. E. Robbins to William O. Bradley, December 15, 1898, in Bradley Papers.
6. Mayfield *Monitor*, April 12, 19, 1899.

vowed, killed him. In his own defense, Martin swore that Diuguid had, on several occasions, threatened to kill him. In March, after local authorities refused Martin's request to have Diuguid quit harassing him, Martin left Murray but returned four times for brief visits. While there in September, Martin ran into Diuguid, who drew a gun on him, saying: "I am going to kill you, you black son of bitch. I have been looking for you all this year and you have been gone." Martin was able to escape by hiding in a building, and he left town immediately thereafter. He remained in Tennessee for four months and returned to Murray in December to see a physician. Realizing that it would be impossible to avoid Diuguid indefinitely in the small town and that the police had refused to help, Martin carried a pistol for the inevitable confrontation. While walking to his father's house, Martin explained, he came upon Diuguid, who reached for his weapon. Martin, however, reached his gun first and shot Diuguid six times. The testimony of Ann and Sylvester Martin substantiated this view.[7]

After his dramatic, highly publicized trip to Murray, Governor Stanley vowed that Martin would be protected when he returned for trial. Five weeks after the incident, Martin arrived back in Murray accompanied by members of the Kentucky National Guard. Presiding over the trial was Charles H. Bush, the judge who had demonstrated such little concern for Martin's life that he had ordered the black man returned to Murray so that he could be handed over to the mob. State officials, however, were confident that Martin would now receive a fair trial. They brought in sixty men from Christian County, which they proudly said was not adjacent to Murray, so that twelve of them could be selected to hear the case. Everyone entering the courthouse was searched. After hearing evidence for more than two days, the jury deliberated for only an hour before deciding on the death penalty for Martin. Diuguid's death statement had been crucial to their decision, the jury foreman explained. Furthermore, the white witnesses had

7. *Martin* v. *Commonwealth*, 178 Kentucky Reports, 540–47 (1917); *Martin* v. *Commonwealth*, 199 Southwestern Reporter, 603–10 (1917); Paducah *News-Democrat*, for most of December, 1916, through February, 1917, especially December 10, 1916, January 10–12, February 20, 23, 1917; Murray *Ledger*, February 15, 22, 1917; board minutes of the executive committee of the NAACP, March 12, 1917, December 9, 1918, in NAACP Papers.

told the truth, and Martin's witnesses—his relatives—had not. Sufficient funds were raised by the NAACP to have the case appealed. The
death sentence was affirmed by Kentucky's highest court. Governor
Stanley, who received praise for preventing a lynching, now felt that
justice had been served. Lube Martin died in the electric chair July 25,
1919. Interestingly, while applauding Stanley for saving Martin from
the lynch mob, the *Crisis* had sounded a note of caution that turned
out to be prophetic: "Thus Lube Martin has been saved from the
mob—at least temporarily. As to justice for a man who killed his
assailant in self-defense, that, even in Kentucky, is quite another
story."[8]

Black Kentuckians should not have been surprised that governors
Bradley and Stanley believed that justice had been served with the
executions of Blanks and Martin. Although condemning mob violence
and lynchings, they had acknowledged that whites were often frustrated and tried to reassure them that the guilty would be punished to
the fullest extent of the law. During Bradley's term, fifteen men were
put to death by the state, eight of whom were Afro-Americans. After
denouncing the continuation of mob violence against blacks in his
message to state lawmakers, Bradley called attention to the subject of
rape. Juries have a right, he declared, to sentence not only convicted
rapists to death but also those convicted of attempted rape. "The
fiend who makes an assault on a defenseless woman, with such a
hellish purpose in view is equally guilty with who accomplishes
his purpose."[9] Six of the nine men executed during Stanley's term
were black. (He was governor for only three years and five months,
resigning to assume a seat in the United States Senate.) When staring
down the mob in Murray, Stanley said: "I'll see that the laws are
enforced and enforced with vigor. I'll protect that negro from mob
violence. And I believe in the death penalty, too. If cold-blooded murder is committed, then that murderer should pay with his life. But
he should die only after twelve men have weighed the evidence carefully, painstakingly and in fear of their God, and have declared him
guilty. He should be a sacrifice upon the altar of the law." Several
years after Martin's execution, Stanley debated the famous attor-

8. *Crisis*, XIII (March, 1917), 227.
9. Bradley, "Message to General Assembly of the Commonwealth of Kentucky,"
86–87, in Bradley Papers.

ney Clarence Darrow about the death penalty. Stanley took the pro-capital-punishment view, saying that it was a protection to society.[10]

Both governors, therefore, believed they had done the right thing in the cases. Clearly, Blanks was guilty of having sex with Tennie Bailey. In court, his attorneys argued that Tennie Bailey was considerably older than twelve years and, more important, that she was a prostitute, "an inmate or regular attendant at a house of ill fame, and that her reputation for virtue and chastity among those who knew her and among whom she lived was bad."[11] According to the white newspaper (which of course must be viewed with suspicion when it reported the rape of a white female by a black man), Blanks had said, before being put to death, that "the girl gave her consent to the commission of the deed, and that he paid her a dollar." On the other hand, the evidence against Martin strongly suggests that he was justified in thinking that his life was threatened by the white deputy sheriff. But even if both black men were guilty and the evidence against them overwhelming, how could the governors honestly think that returning them to the same area would result in fair trials? To be sure, the juries were composed of white men from other counties, but they came from western Kentucky communities that experienced lynchings and attempts to run blacks out of town. These whites' strong emotional feelings about a black raping a young girl or killing a law officer likely did not differ from the feelings of others in the area. Furthermore, given the racial hostility displayed during the trials, it is not difficult to imagine what would have happened to the white jurymen at either trial if they had voted for acquittal. Undoubtedly, the presence of the troops prevented lynchings, but their presence was also an indictment of the concept of a fair trial. When commenting on how the law should be allowed to carry out its duty, neither governor expressed any reservations about Afro-Americans being excluded from the jury process. Both Bob Blanks and Lube Martin were convicted by all-white juries during a time in Kentucky when no blacks were included in the pools of jurors. To be sure, Bradley and Stanley had pre-

10. Paducah *News-Democrat*, January 10, 1917. For details on the debate with Darrow, see the Stanley Papers and the Louisville *Herald-Post*, March 15, 1925.

11. *Blanks* v. *Commonwealth*, 163. In court, attorney Willson noted that the white men who had kept the "house of ill fame" had left Mayfield, and all efforts to locate them for the trial had proved futile.

vented lynchings from happening; but by allowing Blanks and Martin to be tried by all-white juries in environments where whites threatened to lynch the men if they were not quickly convicted and executed by the state, they had allowed "legal lynchings" to occur. They had indeed surrendered to the will of the mob.

Although claiming to be opposed to lynchings, many white Kentuckians were perfectly content to see blacks legally executed. They failed to question the procedures used in the cases or to ask why trials were not moved from areas where lynchings had been threatened. They must have thought that the absence of blacks from the jury box was as natural as the exclusion of Afro-Americans from most other areas of society. Furthermore, few if any whites seem to question the fact that virtually all of the blacks sentenced to death for rape were young, poor, and often illiterate. Whites, in fact, described many of these Afro-Americans as being "retarded," "mentally deficient," and lacking in intelligence. This was as true in the late 1930s as it had been in the 1880s. On occasion, white authorities and community leaders pleaded with the mob to allow justice to take its course, and when a black was accused of rape or murder, "justice" was swift and sure. Countless numbers of black men were tried in hostile environments; judges and juries were convinced of their guilt before hearing any evidence. To the satisfaction of many "law and order" Kentucky whites, the number of lynchings declined in the twentieth century, but this coincided with a rise in the number of legal lynchings in the state. Indeed, it must be emphasized that a crucial reason for the decline in lynchings was related to how white Kentuckians consistently manipulated the legal system, ensuring that any black accused of certain crimes received the same punishment as that meted out by the lynch mob.

On the other hand, of the nearly one hundred whites put to death by the state from 1870 to 1940, none of them lost their lives for transgressions against Afro-Americans. There would be a few occasions when whites were charged with the rapes or the murders of blacks, but all-white juries would not convict their white neighbors of such crimes. Typically, when charged with the murder of a black, a white defendant would say that the black had threatened his life or had somehow offended him or a female relative. In the eyes of the jury, therefore, the white was justified in his claim of self-defense. Cases of whites raping black women rarely were taken to court. According to the *Courier-Journal*, a sixteen-year-old black girl was raped by a white man in Dishman Mill, not far from Bowling Green, in 1888. Calling the incident a "diabolical outrage," the paper noted that during the struggle the young girl had her clothes torn off. The authorities had a complete description of the man, and it was predicted that he would be caught easily. No further stories exist, however, telling of the ultimate outcome of the incident.[12] At the most, a few whites were tried for detaining a black woman. In fact, as far as can be determined from available data, no man—white or black—was executed in Kentucky for the rape of a black woman. (During the 1870s, for example, at least three black men, Thomas Coleman of Bath County, James Brown of Gallatin County, and Joe Sharp of Taylor County, were found guilty of raping black women and sentenced to state prison. None of them, however, was given a life sentence, and all were eventually pardoned by Governor Luke P. Blackburn.)[13]

The research of several scholars agrees that the decline of lynchings throughout the nation was due in part to the states taking the role of the mob. Writing in the 1930s, James Harmon Chadbourn and Arthur Raper said that a pro-lynching sentiment was evident in the judicial process. After a careful examination of white justice meted out to blacks, Raper concluded that a legal lynching was little—if indeed any—improvement over an extralegal lynching. A more recent scholar, Jacquelyn Hall, is not impressed that the number of lynchings declined in the twentieth century as compared with the late 1800s. Many people put to death in the 1920s, she observes, were executed by the state in a manner that shows that they were just as much victims of lynching as others had been earlier: "The thwarted lynch mob frequently demanded that public officials impose the death sentence in a hasty mockery of a trial. If these 'legal lynchings' were included in the statistics, the death toll would be much higher."[14]

Roger Lane, in a study of blacks and violence in Philadelphia, argues that despite discrimination in Philadelphia society, the courts lived up to the ideal of equal justice. Lane rejects the conclusion of

12. Louisville *Courier-Journal*, March 17, 1888.

13. Legislative Document No. 26, *List of Pardons*, 395–99, 405–406, 409–11.

14. Chadbourn, *Lynching and the Law*, 23; Raper, *The Tragedy of Lynching*; Hall, *Jessie Daniel Ames and the Southern Women*, 133.

W. E. B. Du Bois that in Philadelphia the courts favored the rich over
the poor and whites over blacks: "There is no evidence of significant
racial bias in Philadelphia's nineteenth century court system, or indeed of those in other northern cities in the same period. In terms of
either the comparative likelihood of conviction or the severity of sentence for a given offense, the two indices that can be measured, justice
was surprisingly color-blind." Although he was talking only about the
North, where blacks made up a much smaller percentage of the total
population, his conclusion is doubtful. Lane does acknowledge some
racial bias within the legal system but says it was not significant,
though I would imagine the black person going to jail would view it as
very significant. And what would make whites in Philadelphia or
elsewhere who discriminated against blacks in every way possible decide that within the legal area they should cast off their prejudices?
Their own rationalization of racial discrimination would undoubtedly carry over to court trials as well.[15]

Just as they decried the number of lynchings in America, black
leaders complained that the American legal system, especially in the
hands of southern whites, discriminated against blacks, ensuring that
they would be found guilty of alleged crimes. Frederick Douglass ob-
served that southern society was totally against the black man and
that he would be punished, whether right or wrong. Going further, he
noted with dismay, "No decent white man in the South will pretend
that in that region there could be impanelled a jury, black, white, or
mixed, which would in case of proof of the deed allow a guilty negro
to escape condign punishment." Francis J. Grimké, a contemporary of
Douglass, agreed: "Another effect of this race hatred is seen in the un-
due severity with which negro criminals are punished by the courts."
No mercy is ever shown them, he concluded. Writing in the early
1900s, the prominent black leader Mary Church Terrell concurred
with the view that black defendants stood little chance of clearing
themselves in court: "Even those who condone lynching do not pretend to fear the delay or the uncertainty of the law, when a guilty
negro is concerned. With the courts of law entirely in the hands of the
white man, . . . a guilty negro could no more extricate himself from
the meshes of the law in the South than he could slide from the devil-

15. Roger Lane, *Roots of Violence in Black Philadelphia, 1860–1900* (Cambridge, 1986).

fish's embrace or slip from the anaconda's coils. Miscarriage of justice in the South is possible only when white men transgress the law."[16]

Ignoring the many blacks who were executed by the state or who received long prison sentences, many whites took an opposite view, saying that criminals manipulated the legal system by having their trials delayed or moved to other locales, and by pursuing an endless number of appeals. For the most part, the people taking part in lynchings wished "ardently to enforce justice," explained North Carolina judge Walter Clark. "The purpose in hanging a man is not to reform him but to deter others. To have that effect the punishment must be prompt and certain whenever guilt is clear beyond all reasonable doubt. This principle which is so often ignored by the courts is the one which instinctively actuates lynching mobs. The principle is in itself right and just, and courts should act upon it and not leave it to be at once as a motive and a plea for the illegal execution of justice." The state's leading paper, the *Courier-Journal*, voiced its opposition in 1895 to the Blair proposal being debated in Congress, which called for a federal investigation into lynchings. This would only be a waste of time and money, according to the paper. "The remedy for this state of things is not obscure. People are pretty generally agreed that the cure lies in a better and more speedy execution of the laws." Members of the legislature could help end lynchings by "regulating criminal proceedings as would permit the conviction of a larger percentage of persons notoriously guilty, but who often contrive to escape conviction. The belief that our laws are constituted to facilitate the escape of criminals is undoubtedly growing."[17]

Edward L. Ayers argues convincingly that rich whites did in fact avoid persecution, but this was not the case for poor whites and, of course, not for Afro-Americans. Judge Clark's comments clearly apply only to rich whites: "Courts are very expensive to the people. Yet in

16. Frederick Douglass, "Lynch Law in the South," *North American Review*, CLV (July, 1892), 19–20; Grimké, *The Lynching of Negroes in the South*, 21; Mary Church Terrell, "Lynching From A Negro's Point of View," *North American Review*, CLXXVII (1904), 853–68.

17. Walter Clark, "The True Remedy for Lynch Law," *American Law Review*, XXVIII (November–December, 1894), 801–807; for an example of an editorial denouncing crime in Kentucky and the failure to punish criminals, see the Lexington *Kentucky Gazette*, January 19, 1878; Louisville *Courier-Journal*, June 14, 1887, January 11, 1895.

most cases if a criminal can procure the services of able and skillful counsel the advantages granted to the prisoner in a trial for a capital offense are such that a verdict for the State is almost impossible no matter how flagrant the offense." The judge then made another point that applied only to whites, since Afro-Americans were systematically excluded from serving on juries: "The sympathy of the jury for a fellow being on trial for his life will always be stronger than the desire to vindicate the outrage upon society, and such sympathy can always be readily appealed to by eloquent counsel."[18]

Despite numerous comments that the law was lenient on criminals, at least 229 people (two of whom were females) were executed by the state of Kentucky between 1872 and 1940. Afro-Americans, composing around 10 percent of the state's population, accounted for 130—fully 57 percent—of the people put to death by the state.[19] The figures indicate that except for the decades of the 1870s, 1890s, and the 1910s, the number of whites and blacks executed was almost identical (Table 6). However, it is extremely important to remember two points when investigating executions in Kentucky. First, no blacks served on juries; every Afro-American executed had been found guilty by an all-white jury. (We will never know, of course, how many times racism worked in favor of whites, when, for example, all-white grand juries refused to indict whites for criminal offenses against Afro-Americans.) Second, since blacks accounted for 57 percent of the executions but for only 10 percent of the population, they were greatly overrepresented in the number of people put to death by the state. Clearly, a black stood a significantly greater chance of being executed in Kentucky than did a white person.

Many of the whites put to death in the late 1800s were convicted of multiple murders. Ellis Craft and William Neal killed several members of the Gibbons family in December, 1881. Before dying on the gallows, Craft maintained his innocence, saying that "two niggers"

18. Ayers, *Vengeance and Justice,* 227; Clark, "The True Remedy for Lynch Law."
19. In the early 1880s when it began citing the number of people lynched, the Chicago *Tribune* also listed the number put to death by the state. On occasion when giving the details of an execution, local newspapers would discuss the last execution that had occurred. A very useful source on executions is "Men Electrocuted in Kentucky since the Electric Chair was installed at the Kentucky State Penitentiary at Eddyville, Kentucky in 1911." The author obtained a copy of this report from the Kentucky Corrections Cabinet, Office of Corrections Training, Louisville.

TABLE 6   Executions by Decade

Decade	Blacks	Whites	Total
1870–79	5	1	6
1880–89	16	16	32
1890–99	24	16	40
1900–1909	13	12	25
1910–19	26	10	36
1920–29	19	18	37
1930–39	27	26	53

TABLE 7   Executions During Three Different Periods

Period	Blacks	Whites	Total
1865–1874	4	1	5
1875–1899	41	32	73
1900–1934	85	66	151

did the crime. In March, 1884, Frank Wolford Slagel was put to death for the murder of three men in Somerset. And on July 31, 1889, Charles Dilger and Harry Smart died on the scaffold in Louisville. Dilger had murdered two policemen and Smart had killed a married couple.[20]

In all probability, more than 229 people were executed in Kentucky. It is highly likely, for example, that the first execution after the Civil War occurred before 1872, though data is unavailable for the earlier years.[21] Richard H. Shuck, a member of an outlaw band responsible for numerous robberies and murders in Owen and Henry counties in the mid-1870s, dictated his confession while awaiting execution. Al-

20. Louisville *Courier-Journal*, October 13, 1883, July 31, August 1, 1889; Maysville *Bulletin*, March 20, 1884.

21. I have taken a conservative approach when attempting to record executions. On occasion, a local history account or a newspaper would mention that an execution had occurred in the area sometime in the past, but no other source could be found regarding the execution. I have not included these in my figures. It is obvious that the Chicago *Tribune* failed to include all of the executions in Kentucky. Also, the records of the state prison at Eddyville fail to cite the ones that were conducted elsewhere in the state.

though no record confirming his death on the gallows could be found, in all likelihood he and a number of other gang members were executed.[22] A lack of court records for many cases further complicates the matter. The blacks accused of committing these crimes, just like those who received the death penalty from the state or the mob, were already tried and convicted in the newspapers and in the eyes of the white public. Many of the cases for which the outcome is unknown involved rape. This fact is surprising, since whites usually demanded quick "justice" for alleged black rapists. In 1885, the *Courier-Journal* reported that Phil Bellmire was on trial for rape and that the woman had made a positive identification of him. Nevertheless, the newspaper failed to show whether the black man was put to death, convicted of a lesser crime, or simply set free. Several years later, a Lexington black, Tom Brown, was arrested and charged with the rape of a four-year-old white girl, but no other details about the incident have been found. Because their trials were held in Lexington and in Louisville respectively, these two black men probably were not lynched, though legal executions of blacks for rape most surely occurred in both cities. According to newspaper accounts, a "pretty little white girl," Allie Brockham, was raped in the Harrodsburg area in 1889. Accused of the crime was John Cunningham, who the paper described as "more brute than man, and who from his appearance, looks to be Darwin's missing link." After being captured, he was taken to jail, over the protest of some of the men in the mob. According to the paper, Allie Brockham and several other girls identified Cunningham, and he confessed to the crime. But even in this case, which is similar to many that ended in lynchings, the outcome is unknown.[23] If these three men were not executed by the state, their relatively light sentences undoubtedly reinforced the view of mob members that they must take the law into their own hands.

As we have seen, whites were quick to respond to incidents in

22. Jesse Fears, *Confessions of Richard H. Shuck, A Member of the Owen and Henry County Marauders of the State of Kentucky* (Frankfort, 1877).

23. Louisville *Courier-Journal*, May 28, 1885, March 20, 1888, September 11, 1889. In the twentieth century, there were several instances of Afro-Americans either being charged with rape or convicted and sentenced to death for rape, yet the outcome of these cases is unknown. See Lexington *Morning Herald*, May 5, 1902, Lexington *Herald*, March 29, August 8, 1906, Hopkinsville *Kentuckian*, April 10, 1909, Henderson *Daily Journal*, March 15, 1915.

TABLE 8   Executions by Region

Region	Blacks	Whites	Total
1. Jackson Purchase	14	3	17
2. Western Kentucky	28	13	41
3. Louisville Metro	27	19	46
4. Central Kentucky	35	18	53
5. Northern Kentucky	12	8	20
6. Eastern Kentucky	12	32	44
7. S. Central Kentucky	1	6	7
County Unknown	1		1

which blacks had murdered whites. On Christmas Day, 1882, Charles Weir killed a white man who attempted to enter a dance being held by blacks. Weir, like many other Negroes found in such a predicament, pleaded self-defense. The outcome of the case is unknown. In February, 1895, governor John Y. Brown signed the death warrant for the March 15 execution of John Young, who had murdered another black. There is no indication of the outcome, even through Governor Brown had demonstrated in the past a willingness to allow executions to happen. Perhaps even more of a puzzle is the case of Johnson Howe, who was charged with killing a police officer in 1897. Nothing can be found to indicate whether Howe was lynched, executed, or found not guilty.[24]

While the vast majority of lynchings took place in western Kentucky, the greatest number of legal executions—30 percent—occurred in Louisville and Jefferson County or Lexington and Fayette County (Table 8). Jefferson County, located in Region 3, had 44 executions; Fayette, in Region 4, had 21. These counties are followed by two other counties with 8 executions each. This is not surprising as whites in urban areas were determined to prevent lynchings and took pride in maintaining law and order. In fact, over the years prisoners from other

24. *History of Daviess County* . . . (Chicago, 1883), 428–29; Louisville *Courier-Journal*, February 9, 1895. In the new century there would be a number of cases of blacks being accused of murder yet the outcome is unknown: Lexington *Morning Herald*, January 16, 1902; Lexington *Herald*, April 12, 1907, November 24, December 1, 1924; Louisville *Courier-Journal*, February 12, 1915.

TABLE 9   Causes for Executions, by Race

Cause	Blacks	Whites	Total
1865–1940			
Rape	25	6	31
Murder	104	93	197
Other	1		1
1865–1899			
Rape	8	1	9
Murder	37	32	69
1900–1940			
Rape	17	5	22
Murder	67	61	128
Other	1		1

areas were rushed to Lexington or Louisville to prevent their being lynched.

Of the 229 people legally executed, 197 were for murder, 31 were for rape, and 1 was for "other causes," which turned out to be armed robbery (Table 9).[25] That relatively few people were put to death for rape, the offense that whites most often associated with blacks, can be accounted for in several ways. Since whites consistently resorted to lynchings to avenge rape of their women, very few blacks accused of assaulting females were tried in the courts, especially during the late nineteenth century. Also, the vast majority of whites convicted of rape were sentenced to prison, not death.

A number of blacks were executed for the deaths of members of

25. In Louisville in the mid-1930s, three blacks, Sam Franklin, Gene Lee, and Arthur Williams, were arrested for armed robbery, "in the perpetration of which they displayed and used a pistol, a deadly weapon." Williams and Lee pleaded guilty and were sentenced to life in prison. Franklin pleaded not guilty and was sentenced to death. He died in the electric chair in March, 1937. See *Franklin* v. *Commonwealth*, 266 Kentucky Reports, 833–39 (1936).

their own race. As a general rule, these involved men, spurned as lovers, who in a fit of anger killed their wives or girlfriends. To be sure, whites were also put to death for the murder of their wives or sweethearts. But because of legal lynchings, trials of blacks were usually disposed of in a hasty manner—not at all like the trials of whites. Indeed, whites could at least hope that the men on the jury would be sympathetic to them. A typical case of a black man killing a woman involved Clarence Williams of Paris. Outraged over seeing his common-law wife, Josie Tillman, talking to another man, Williams shot her three times. Williams's all-white jury deliberated only twenty minutes before finding him guilty and sentencing him to death. On the very same day that Bob Blanks died in Mayfield, another black man, Will Tutt, was executed for the murder of his wife. Tutt killed her for attending a baseball game in another city without his permission.[26]

The events surrounding the execution of George Miller on April 30, 1874, became commonplace until well into the twentieth century. As a reporter for the Louisville *Commercial* explained, "If a stranger had traveled this morning from daylight until noon upon any or all of the roads leading into Springfield, Ky., he would have believed that a greater showman than Barnum had pitched his tent in that village." Somewhere between five thousand and ten thousand people came by buggies, stagecoaches, carriages, horseback, and foot to witness the hanging of Miller, who had been convicted of killing his former master. After being involved in games and fighting for hours, the huge crowd grew silent to hear the black man's last statement. After the hanging, all of the saloons did a booming business, even though many in the crowd had already overindulged before the "main event." The reporter for the *Commerical*, unlike most who would write about such events, was disgusted by the public execution. "Not one person present went home wiser, unless indeed it is wisdom to know that a man in good health, sound in body and mind, weighing 175 pounds, can live just eight minutes when suspended at the end of a rope with a noose around his neck." He ended with a few words for people

26. Cincinnati *Enquirer*, December 11, 1899; Mayfield *Monitor*, April 19, 1899. For other cases of blacks killing their wives or lovers, see the Louisville *Courier-Journal*, May 31, 1887, the Lexington *Transcript*, November 14, 1889, and the Lexington *Morning Herald*, May 22, 1897.

prone to lawless activities: "For a successful hanging, artistically done, I commend all criminals to the ministering officers of Washington county."[27]

Public executions in late-nineteenth-century Kentucky were spectator sports, drawing crowds that rivaled attendance at the Kentucky Derby. All of the newspapers devoted extensive coverage to the executions. (The reporters thoroughly enjoyed writing that the condemned had "expiated" for his crime.) This, of course, was part of the national fascination with death. The newspapers gave details about the last meal, the state of mind of the condemned, and whether or not he confessed his crime to local law officers and God before leaving the cell for the last time. White reporters often spoke with admiration of how blacks faced death. The highly racist Mayfield *Monitor* headlined the execution of Bob Brown, "He Met Death in a Composed and Heroic Manner After an Eloquent Talk to 3,000 Spectators." Brown's "expiation" (for the murder of a white man) "was perhaps the most remarkable hanging witnessed in this county for years and the most successful, as well." According to the paper, Brown acted and looked, as he left the jail, more like a man on his way to a marriage feast than to his own hanging. With the noose around his neck, Brown spoke to the huge throng for more than an hour, advising them "to let whisky, gambling, and down fallen women severely alone." Several years later in Richmond, condemned killer William Taylor spoke for eleven minutes to the crowd, concluding with some words of wisdom:

> My advice to both young and old is to leave whisky alone. My advice to friends that I leave behind is not to follow the steps which lead to where I am going. I am twenty-six years of age and this is the first and only crime that I ever committed. . . . Now that I am about to be ushered into the presence of death by the laws of man, I feel that the laws of society that inflict the death penalty for murder are just, and the penalty I am about to pay is merited. I am going home to die no more.[28]

While executions for murder were on occasion held in carnival-like environments, the execution of a black for rape often drew boisterous crowds determined to lynch the condemned man because they believed that a simple hanging was too mild for such a heinous offense.

27. Louisville *Commercial*, May 3, 1874. The account from the Louisville *Courier-Journal*, May 1, 2, 1874, is detailed but lacks the sarcasm of its rival's version.

28. Mayfield *Monitor*, June 14, 1893; Louisville *Courier-Journal*, January 12, 1895.

In late October, 1878, Charles Webster and George Washington were charged with the rape of a young white girl in Louisville. Even before their capture—much less their trial—the local newspaper had already found them guilty and had called for their execution. Indeed, the paper called Washington "the colored fiend who committed the nameless outrage on the little white girl." Given the uproar and the threat of mob vengeance, it came as no surprise that both men were quickly tried, found guilty of rape, and sentenced to death. Even after the death sentence was handed down, however, the threat of a lynching remained. An estimated twenty thousand people came to Washington's public execution, and a riot nearly developed. The police resorted to force to prevent the mob from seizing and carrying off the black man. In an attempt to maintain control, Louisville authorities decided that Webster would hang in private. On April 2, 1880, Webster and Robert Anderson, a white man convicted of murder, died in the enclosed yard at the Louisville jail with only a few selected people looking on.[29] From that point on, all executions held in Louisville would be done in private, and those who wanted to witness the "event" would need tickets. Before each execution, thousands of people applied for tickets. Some who were turned down resorted to purchasing counterfeit tickets sold by enterprising con men. Lexington eventually joined Louisville in holding private executions, while most of the smaller towns continued public hangings, to the obvious delight of many citizens. But even in the two larger cities, people still desired to witness executions. Thousands of Louisvillians and Lexingtonians of all ages paid for choice positions where they could look over walls or from rooftops and observe the "private hangings."[30]

Many of the trials that resulted in blacks dying on the scaffold were highly controversial, leading to the speculation that race had been the deciding factor in these verdicts. As we have seen when looking at lynchings, the word of a black man meant nothing when he was accused of raping a white woman, especially if the woman identified him as her attacker. Tragically, this mentality carried over to the

29. For the capture of Washington and Webster, see the Louisville *Courier-Journal*, October 22–November 10, 1878. The *Courier-Journal* of April 3, 1880, discusses the execution of Webster and mentions Washington's death.

30. *Ibid.*, July 31, 1889, March 23, 1892; for the execution of a black convicted of rape in Lexington, see the *Morning Herald*, June 2, 3, 1896.

courts, resulting in legal lynchings for rape. Most amazing, however (and most surely reinforcing the significance of race in determining guilt), are the cases in which a black man was sentenced to death for murder even though both he and the victim had drawn their guns. Such was the case of Henry Smith, who died on the gallows in Louisville for the murder of Louis Specht. Smith worked in the saloon and grocery owned by Specht. One evening they had an argument. According to Smith, Specht "came to me and said I was talking too much. He cursed me. He called me a big coward, and said he was going to kill me. He started toward me, and I pulled my pistol and shot him." Specht had reached in his back pocket and pulled out his gun before Smith shot. Totally rejecting Smith's account, the jury decided that for some unprovoked reason, Smith had shot his employer in cold blood. It is highly likely that if the results had been reversed— if Smith had been killed by Specht because he saw the black man reach for his gun—Specht would never have stood trial. Another case in which being black most surely cost the accused man his life was that of James McElroy. On September 29, 1886, a white farmer, Walter Marter, gave a black man a ride in his wagon. Late that evening, Marter was found in the wagon, his head almost severed from his body. Suspicion centered on McElroy, who matched the description of the black last seen with the farmer. At his trial, only one of the five prosecution witnesses identified McElroy as the man in the wagon with Marter, and none of them witnessed the murder nor knew of a motive. McElroy, after nearly being lynched, was found guilty and was executed in Henderson on June 30, 1887.[31]

A murder trial from Lexington shows clearly how race was *the* crucial factor in determining guilt or innocence. On January 13, 1879, John Bush of Lexington was charged with the murder of his employer's daughter. His case, which ultimately took five years and ten months to resolve, also raised the issue of whether or not Afro-Americans were being excluded from serving on juries in Kentucky. In 1878, John Bush and his wife were hired as servants for the Van Meters, a prominent Lexington family. On the day of the killing, Joseph Van Meter returned home intoxicated and accused Bush of spreading false rumors about his wife. According to Bush, Van Meter tried to shoot him but accidentally hit his own daughter, seventeen-

31. Louisville *Courier-Journal*, March 23, 1892, June 30, 1887.

year-old Annie. Upon reaching one of the weapons in the house, Bush tried to return the fire, but Mrs. Van Meter caught hold of the pistol and caused it to go off toward the ground. When the police arrived, Van Meter said that Bush shot Annie in anger over the girl's intention to end her romantic relationship with the black man.[32]

Refusing to believe the word of a black servant over that of his white employer, the police arrested Bush and charged him with murder. Lexington blacks, convinced that Bush was being framed, raised sufficient funds to finance Bush's various trials. Surprisingly, in late May, 1879, the jury failed to agree on a verdict and was discharged. Bush's second trial, however, resulted in a guilty verdict and a sentence of death. Bush's white attorneys successfully appealed the decision and had the case remanded for retrial. The lawyers also filed a petition to have the case moved to the United States Circuit Court on the grounds that Bush had been denied his privileges as a citizen under the Civil Rights Act because no blacks had been included within the pool of jurors. Under sharp examination in the circuit court, the Lexington sheriff acknowledged that no blacks had been considered for jury duty. The court then ordered the indictment against the black man quashed.

Bush's troubles were far from over. He was immediately rearrested. At the start of his next trial, the prosecuting attorney ordered the sheriff to summon a venire of seventy-five persons without any reference to race. Yet no Afro-Americans were selected. Bush's attorneys made another motion to have the indictment set aside on the ground that under Kentucky law, blacks had been prohibited from serving on the grand jury that handed down the original indictment in 1879. This motion was overruled, the trial held, and Bush found guilty. His case was then carried to the Kentucky Court of Appeals, where the ruling of the lower body was affirmed.

Refusing to quit, Bush's attorneys appealed the case to the United States Supreme Court on the grounds that blacks had been excluded from the grand jury. When handing down its decision in October, 1882, the Supreme Court agreed that the omission of blacks from consideration on the grand jury was in violation of the Constitution. The

---

32. *Bush* v. *Commonwealth*, 78 Kentucky Reports, 268 (1882). An excellent account of the entire drama can be found in the Lexington *Morning Transcript*, November 22, 1884. Information in this and following paragraphs has been drawn from this source.

court explained that the case of *Commonwealth* v. *Johnson*, which had been decided by the Kentucky Court of Appeals on June 29, 1880, had said the language limiting jury duty to whites only was unconstitutional: "It was not until after the grand jurors who returned the indictment against Bush had been selected that the highest court of Kentucky, speaking with authority for all the judicial tribunals of that Commonwealth, declared that the local statutes, in so far as they excluded colored citizens from grand and petit juries because of their race, were in conflict with the national Constitution." In reversing the ruling of the Kentucky Court of Appeals in Bush's case, the Supreme Court remanded the case to Fayette County Circuit Court and ordered a new trial.[33]

It would be another year and a half before the final resolution of the case. During the February, 1884, term of the Fayette County Circuit Court, the sheriff was ordered to summon two hundred persons, without regard to race, from whom a jury could be selected. As had happened in Bush's previous trials, only white men were selected for the jury. The trial started on February 12 and ended the next day with the all-white jury reaching a guilty verdict. Once again the case was appealed, and Kentucky's highest court again affirmed the ruling of the lower court. This time, however, the United States Supreme Court refused to review Bush's conviction. The nation's highest court was satisfied that blacks had not been excluded as potential jurors, and in the view of the justices (as stated in the 1879 case of *Virginia* v. *Rives*), the mere absence of blacks from the jury did not mean that a black had been discriminated against.

After having four trials in the Fayette County Circuit Court and having his conviction reviewed by Kentucky's highest court, the United States Circuit Court, and the United States Supreme Court, Bush was out of appeals. His execution was set for November 21, 1884. In his final statement from the gallows, Bush told his version of what happened on the fateful day, January 13, 1879. He shocked the huge crowd with this statement: "Mr. Joseph Van Meter did not tell you he destroyed his infant before its time." According to Bush, Mrs. Van Meter had been forced by her husband to have an abortion. Rumors about the abortion had quickly surfaced in the home of Isaac Van Meter, and Joseph Van Meter had assumed that Bush had told about the killing of the fetus. Bush also denied having an intimate relation-

33. *Bush* v. *Kentucky*, 107 U.S., 110–23 (1882).

ship with Annie Van Meter, stating emphatically that the girl's father concocted the story to cover up the accidental shooting. The doomed black man concluded that he had not been given a fair chance to vindicate himself. A Lexington newspaper disagreed, saying that of the forty-eight men from Fayette County who heard the various cases, forty-seven said Bush should die and only one said he was not guilty. Furthermore, the reporter believed that the jurors had been fair and thorough in their deliberations regarding Bush's fate. The all-white juries "were made up of our best citizens, not likely to be so unanimous in their opinions unless convinced of his guilt," argued the reporter. The whites witnessing the execution were impressed with Bush's composure while facing death, "all saying they never saw such a remarkable exhibition of nerve and coolness in a criminal."

Although race was not the only factor leading to their convictions, two blacks were involved in a highly publicized trial in Louisville in the late nineteenth century. This case clearly shows the phenomenon of legal lynching: The two Afro-Americans were convicted in the minds of the general white public before the trial started. The case also illustrates a morbid fascination that many people of that era had with criminals. About ten o'clock on the morning of April 21, 1887, Mrs. A. Y. Johnson and her two children left home to spend the day visiting relatives. Remaining home to do the chores was their domestic servant, Jennie Bowman, a white woman in her twenties. Almost two hours later, the son returned home to get an item left behind by his mother. After Bowman failed to answer the door, the boy climbed in the window and found the house in total disarray: Furniture was broken and blood was everywhere, and the trail led to a bedroom upstairs where Bowman was found unconscious. Her mouth was tightly bound with a wet towel, and her head and face were badly lacerated. A medical report would show that Bowman's jaw and skull had been crushed. Two items in the bedroom had obviously been used by the young woman and her attacker: "At the head of the bed was found a heavy iron poker, covered with hair and human blood. . . . On the floor was found the stem of a stout glass goblet that had been used by the girl in her desperate struggle."[34]

After talking with several neighbors, the police began a search for

34. From April 22 to July 1, 1887, the Louisville *Courier-Journal* ran stories almost daily about the case. Information in this and following paragraphs has been drawn from these stories.

several white men seen in the area. Late the second evening, Jennie Bowman regained consciousness for a few minutes. A physician asked, "Jennie, who was it that struck you?" She replied, "It was a Negro." Two men had broken into the house, and during the struggle she had cut one of them in the face with the goblet. Police Chief John H. Whallen, a major political boss in Louisville, decided to personally investigate the matter. After obtaining a description of the girl's assailants, he instructed his officers "to thoroughly search from cellar to attic every black saloon, lodging house and dwelling in the city. Sentries were posted at all the depots and steamboat landings in the city and turnpikes." In their sweep through Louisville's black community, the police arrested more than one hundred black men, many of whom only marginally fit the description Bowman had given. One man, William Patterson, "a vicious and desperate negro," was arrested on general principles. The police justified holding Patterson because of his extensive police record. Several days later, the major break in the case occurred. A white woman came forward to say that on occasion she had employed a man to do chores around her house and that she had once again required his services. Upon finally locating his house, she had been shocked to see scratch marks on his face. Within an instant, she said, she realized that he fit the description of Bowman's attacker. The police, strong in numbers, quickly arrested the man, Albert Turner, who also had a police record. Within minutes of being arrested, Turner confessed (newspaper accounts fail to say whether he did so freely or under duress) but refused to name his accomplice. Word leaked out of Turner's arrest, and a mob formed, intent on lynching him. Chief Whallen and a group of officers then secretly took Turner to Frankfort. Before reaching Frankfort, they stopped and questioned Turner once again about his partner. According to the newspaper, Turner, still in a state of fear at the thought of being taken by the mob, agreed to talk and implicated William Patterson. Turner shifted most of the blame to Patterson, explaining that he suggested robbing the house. Once in the house, Turner came up on the girl, who grabbed the goblet and cut him. Turner admitted to the police that he then hit her with the iron poker. But it was Patterson who, upon entering the room where the girl lay unconscious, hit her repeatedly with the poker and wanted to rape her as well. Turner prevented Patterson from raping Bowman by threatening to beat him. Realizing that he was on the verge of solving the case, Whallen had

Patterson brought to Frankfort and placed in a lineup with several other black men. Turner easily identified Patterson as his accomplice.

Stories of the arrest of Turner and Patterson made headlines in the newspapers. The *Courier-Journal*, the most respected newspaper in the state, ran drawings of the men that depicted them as almost animal-like. In a front page editorial, the paper called their crime one that "has few parallels for atrocity in the annals of crime in civilized communities, or elsewhere for that matter." When the paper went to press, Jennie Bowman was still alive and from all accounts had not been raped, but the paper said Louisville citizens wanted, and should get, prompt executions: "The blood of the culprits cannot pay the penalty of their crime." The *Courier-Journal* said it was merely reporting on the people's collective anger over this horrible crime. "The fact that the assault had been committed in the broad light of day, when fathers, husbands and brothers leave their homes unprotected added to the general indignation."

Several days later, police officials returned Patterson and Turner to the Louisville jail. Aware that a mob might rush the jail, Whallen ordered his officers to be on alert. At midnight, a mob of five hundred men, heavily armed and carrying a section of a telegraph pole, marched toward the jail. The police demanded that the mob disperse and arrested ten men when the mob refused to move. Only by charging the mob were the police able to scatter the crowd and end this threat of a lynching. Two hours later, the mob returned but was again dispersed. It is clear that Louisville's leading citizens led the mob, for among those arrested during the second lynching attempt was John Letterie, a member of the state legislature, and Allen McDonald, a leader in the Law and Order Club, which claimed to promote honesty in government. Not arrested, but rumored to be the instigator of the mob, was a well-known physician who had informed the mob that no white woman could rest easily until criminals like Turner and Patterson had been killed. To prevent further trouble, the mayor sent a request to the governor for the militia and additional weapons. The governor responded by sending five hundred men and a Gatling gun. The militia's presence turned out to be vital, for the next evening some ten thousand people gathered in front of the jail and demanded the prisoners. As they had the night before, the police made arrests, this time taking thirty-eight people into custody. After having previously called the attack on Bowman one of the worst incidents in the history of mankind, the *Courier-Journal* now urged the people to avoid a lynching at all cost, saying that they must "stand by the law." Nothing should be done, the paper emphasized, that would ruin Louisville's good name. Turner and Patterson should be made to pay for their crimes, but only within the law. The strong show of force by local and state officials prevented the black men from being lynched, and after several evenings, the mobs completely disappeared.

Newspapers throughout the country applauded Louisville's stand against mob rule. The New York *Times* said a lynching would have been a disgrace to the name of Louisville. On the other hand, the New York *Freeman*, a black newspaper, said that the *Courier-Journal* was largely to blame for the actions of the mob: "Think of a great newspaper like the *Courier-Journal* lending itself to the excitation of mob violence! Surely a man of Mr. Watterson's National reputation cannot afford to have his name coupled to such an infamous business. When the great papers of the South insist . . . that the law shall be allowed to take its course mob violence and infamy will be forced to hide their dirty head." [35]

On May 9, after being unconscious for most of two weeks, Jennie Bowman died. Even before her death, the young woman had become a heroic figure in the eyes of the Louisville media, one who had suffered in ways that no other human being had before: "No pen can portray, no mind can imagine, the agony she endured so long. In her delirium she passed again and again through the awful ordeal of the struggle with the fiends who beat her into insensibility; and during her lucid intervals she was racked with excruciating physical pain, scarcely less horrible than the mental anguish. Only in the unconscious stupor of opium did she find even a poor relief from the terrible torture." In another of its many editorials on Bowman, the *Courier-Journal* said that "in a sense, it may be said that she dies that Justice may live. There can now be no escape for her assailants from the full penalty of their crime."

The trials of Turner and Patterson were held within days of Bowman's death. Because of Turner's confession of guilt, his trial, the deliberation of the jury, and the sentencing took one hour and five

35. A reprint of editorials from other cities can be found in the Louisville *Courier-Journal*, May 3, 1887; New York *Times*, May 1, 2, 1887; New York *Freeman*, May 7, 1887.

minutes. He was sentenced to die on July 1. Patterson pleaded not guilty and was defended by Nathaniel R. Harper, Kentucky's first black attorney and a man of more than fifteen years of legal experience. Patterson denied knowing Turner. Interestingly, Turner refused to testify in court against Patterson, but his statements proved damaging nevertheless. When naming Patterson as his accomplice, Turner said that the blood from the victim could be found on Patterson's undergarments, which the police found. Several whites testified that they saw the two men together on the street the morning of the crime. Patterson's trial lasted three days. The jury, however, deliberated only twelve minutes before finding him guilty and handing down the death sentence. Harper filed for an appeal, which carried an automatic delay until the September term of the court. On November 23, the Kentucky Court of Appeals made known its ruling in Patterson's case. After acknowledging that no testimony had been entered in court that placed Patterson directly at the scene of the crime and that witnesses had said Patterson was with them when the crime occurred, the court said, "We have carefully examined the record in this case, and perceiving no error of law occurring at the trial to the prejudice of the substantial rights of the accused, the judgment must be affirmed."[36]

The weeks leading to Turner's execution witnessed a bizarre spectacle on the part of Louisville whites toward the condemned black man. They seemed to be horrified by, yet attracted to, Turner and his crime against a white woman. Maybe they believed his story that though he had taken part in the incident, he had not administered the repeated blows that killed Bowman and that he had prevented Patterson from raping the woman. That Turner admitted his guilt and seemed willing to accept the punishment due him led to admiration from some Louisvillians. In mid-June, the *Courier-Journal* started counting down the number of days he had left to live. Reporters went on a regular basis to interview Turner. "A talk with this brute is one of the most depressing things that a sensitive person could subject himself to." In the view of this reporter, Turner contradicted every optimistic theory about mankind. "Without being an idiot, without any mental derangement whatever, he is absolutely impervious to a moral idea." It soon became apparent that only a small percentage of

36. *Patterson* v. *Commonwealth*, 86 Kentucky Reports, 313–26 (1887).

the thousands of people desiring to witness Turner's execution would be allowed to do so. Therefore, many people asked the jailer if they could visit with Turner in his cell. In a story headlined "Turner's Last Sunday," the paper applauded the jailer for ignoring the ban on Sunday visitors and for allowing all who wanted to come and see Turner, to observe "how he passed the last Sunday he would ever see in this world."

Deciding that he wanted a large funeral and hoping that his white visitors would pay for it, Turner posted two large placards over the windows of his cell. One said "May God have mercy upon me for my crime"; the other one, "Ladies and Gentlemen: Please Donate Something to help bury me, July 1, 1887." On that final Sunday, 1,538 whites entered his cell. Many of them brought along cameras, and for twenty-five cents they were allowed to have a photograph made of themselves and Turner. The doomed man raised more than $50 in this manner. More than 2,500 whites came through his cell the day before the execution—only one-third of those seeking admission. A majority of these people were women. The newspaper tried to put the best light on the desire of these white females to rub shoulders with the black murderer: "The women were not all, as might be supposed, of the lower elements of society . . . but were in some instances ladies who are sometimes seen in their carriages on Fourth avenue and among the gay assemblages of higher social life, while many were from the middle walks. Let it be said, however, for Louisville womanhood that those of the better classes who came felt keenly the horror of the picture presented, which did not prevent them from being very much ashamed of the step they had been led to take." According to the *Courier-Journal*, which, of course, thoroughly enjoyed keeping the public informed of every minute detail of the doomed man's existence, Turner raised far more than the $75 needed for his funeral. In addition to paying for his funeral expenses, Turner was able to have meals from Louisville's best restaurants brought to him and two friends in jail, to purchase cigars, jelly cakes, and watermelons, and to hire messenger boys to run errands for him. He also left $130 to be divided between his sister and his niece!

Proclaiming that he had made his peace with death and that he wanted to get right to meet God, Turner made a statement at the scaffold. He explained that Stephen Morrill, the black man who had recently been sent to prison for the robbery of a streetcar, was innocent because he, Turner, had committed the crime. Then he added, "Gentlemen, I want all of you to hear what I have got to say. I am going to die with an honest heart and bring no one to the gallows. I am going to die alone. Free the man Patterson. The man was not with me. That is all I have got to say. I am willing to die now." Turner's confession had a positive effect for Morrill, who received an immediate pardon from the governor.

Turner's statement about Patterson, however, was rejected. He died on the same gallows used for Turner but noticeably without the fanfare that surrounded Turner's hanging. The story of Patterson's execution was buried on page six of the *Courier-Journal*. While Turner had entertained only white visitors, a number of prominent black ministers came to see Patterson. Also unlike Turner, Patterson confessed a belief in Jesus Christ and joined the church. Some Louisville whites found justice in the suffering that Patterson endured before dying: He did not die from the fall but slowly suffocated. He spoke from that position for five minutes. The black minister who preached Patterson's funeral reached a different interpretation. "Did you ever hear in the history of creation of a man that God allowed, with a rope around his neck after the drop fell, hanging by the neck, to have breath enough to say: 'Lord receive my soul'? . . . I believe Brother Patterson is sitting around in heaven enjoying himself."[37]

Because of the drama involved in executions and the public's fascination with the gory details surrounding the condemned man's crime and death, legal executions received widescale publicity in Kentucky and elsewhere. But in reality, the form of legal lynching that sent blacks to jail on sham charges had a far greater impact on the state's black citizens. That Afro-Americans accounted for a greater number of the people arrested seemed natural to whites, since they viewed blacks as inferior and prone to committing petty crimes. A cursory reading of the police reports printed in newspapers for any period from the end of the Civil War to the Great Depression reveals that most of the people who were in jail on minor offenses or awaiting trials or who were sent to local workhouses were Afro-Americans. This was true even in Louisville, the most enlightened city in Kentucky and a place where blacks participated in political activities to a degree not found elsewhere in the state. Almost two decades after the

37. Louisville *Courier-Journal*, June 22, 23, July 9, 1888.

Civil War, Kentucky blacks convicted of being vagrants were compelled to work for whites. As the New York *Times* headlined in 1882,
"Negro Sold Into Servitude in Louisville." A state law of 1795, which
had not been overturned, allowed a vagrant to be sold for one year to
the highest bidder. During these same years, Bourbon County black
vagrants received even longer sentences; some of them were required
to labor three years for white landowners. Records in the state archives
entitled "Apprentice Bonds for Freedmen for the years 1877–1886 for
Garrard County Court" indicate that blacks in that county often labored for whites under conditions reminiscent of slavery.[38]

With the end of slavery, the number of blacks within Kentucky's
prison population grew significantly. By January 1, 1868, blacks made
up 38.5 percent of the inmates in the state penitentiary, and over the
next decade they became the majority and remained so until the
middle of the twentieth century. Black females represented 95 percent of the women incarcerated by the state. As a rule, blacks received
longer prison sentences that did whites. For example, at the beginning
of the 1890s, blacks predominated in the groups of men in prison
serving terms of ten to fifteen years, of fifteen to twenty years, and of
twenty to forty years. During this same time, however, of the men
confined for life, whites outnumbered blacks. This, too, is not surprising. Whites often received life sentences for murder or rape, while
Afro-Americans were given death sentences for these same offenses,
especially when they had been committed against whites.[39]

The racial discrimination existing in the larger society carried over
to Kentucky's prisons. Black and white inmates did not eat, work, or
participate in recreational activities together. Worst of all was the
practice of placing Afro-Americans in the upper tiers of the cell houses,
often putting two of them into an extremely small cell. As a result,

38. New York *Times,* June 15, 1882; Elizabeth R. Clotfelter, "The Agriculture History of Bourbon County, Ky., Prior to 1900" (M.A. thesis, University of Kentucky,
1953), 119–20; the material on Garrard County is found in "Offense and Punishment
Register, 1891–1916," in Kentucky Department for Libraries and Archives, Frankfort.

39. Robert Gunn Crawford, "A History of the Kentucky Penitentiary System,
1865–1937" (Ph.D. dissertation, University of Kentucky, 1955), 147–50; Legislative
Document No. 35, *Biennial Report of the Warden of the Kentucky Penitentiary to the
Board of Directors of the Penitentiary, November 30, 1891* (Frankfort, 1892), 7; Blake
McKelvey, *American Prisons: A Study in American Social History Prior to 1915* (Chi-
cago, 1936), 172–88.

scores of blacks died from pneumonia. In a two-year period in the mid-1870s, twenty-three blacks died. The number declined for several years but rose sharply in 1895, when twenty-four inmates died. That year, in a rather matter-of-fact manner, state prison officials noted that only twenty-four prisoners died, all of whom were Negroes. Segregation existed in Kentucky's prisons until well into the twentieth century. Men's control of every aspect of the lives of women prisoners led to numerous instances of sexual abuse. Black women were more often the target of abuse, since they greatly outnumbered white females. Several of the women were, like Laura Brown, "in a family-way" when granted pardons by Governor Blackburn. Despite a vast majority of the inmates being Afro-Americans, officials refused to hire blacks (or women) for jobs within the penal system, even as guards, a position requiring direct contact with the prisoners. One warden expressed in his diary his view toward hiring blacks as guards: "Upon my word, a Black Freeman appeared at the prison gate and requested employment as a Keeper. It is widely known that I bear no malice towards any of the numerous races that comprise humanities total. But this was a bit too much. . . . I sent word to the Freeman that our employment list is full for the remaining part of this century." This was in 1889, yet the warden said no job openings would occur for the next eleven years. In actuality, this policy of not hiring Afro-Americans remained in effect for another ninety years.[40]

Just as they protested lynchings and mob rule, Afro-Americans consistently cried out against public executions and excessive prison terms meted out to members of the race. As explained by black leaders, Afro-Americans, too, favored law and order and punishing criminals; but they were deeply troubled by a legal system that allowed whites to go unpunished for committing crimes against blacks while at the same time severely punishing blacks after denying them the right to fair trials. After the passage of the Civil Rights Act of 1875, Afro-Americans entered lawsuits to challenge the practice of blacks

40. Crawford, "A History of the Kentucky Penitentiary System," 176–77; Legislative Document No. 26, *List of Pardons*, 228–29, 482–85. An important source for information on life inside Kentucky prisons during the late nineteenth century is "Changing Faces, Common Walls: History of Corrections In Kentucky." Within this report is a section entitled "Excerpts from the Journal of Louis Curry, Chief Warden, Kentucky Prison at Eddyville, 1888 to 1896." This long, detailed report can be obtained from the Kentucky Corrections Cabinet, Office of Corrections Training, Louisville.

being tried by all-white jurors. In 1879, in the case of *Strauder* v. *West Virginia*, the United States Supreme Court ruled that West Virginia had denied blacks due process and equal protection of the law in saying that jury duty would be limited to white men only. That same year, the Supreme Court handed down another significant ruling, *Virignia* v. *Rives*, which in reality all but overruled what had been decided in the West Virginia case. Two blacks had been convicted of murder by an all-white jury in Virginia. The Supreme Court ruled that since the Virginia law did not limit court duty to whites, the absence of blacks from a jury did not in itself prove discrimination. The burden of proving discrimination by an all-white jury, the Supreme Court concluded, rested with Afro-Americans.[41]

In spite of actions by the federal government, Kentucky's legislators were intent on prohibiting Afro-Americans from serving on juries. A law of December 1, 1873, disqualified blacks from serving as petit jurors and also "provided that no person shall be qualified as a grand juryman unless he be a white citizen." Another law, which went into effect January 1, 1877, "expressly provided that the selecting, summoning, and impanelling of a grand jury shall be as prescribed in the General Statutes," which limited service to white men. When reviewing the murder conviction of John Bush of Lexington, the United States Supreme Court commented on these two laws: "It thus appears that the legislature of Kentucky, after the adoption of the Fourteenth Amendment and notwithstanding the explicit declaration therein that 'no State shall deny to any person within its jurisdiction the equal protection of the laws,' twice expressly enacted that no citizen of the African race should be competent to serve either as a grand or petit juror."[42]

On June 29, 1880, in the case of *Commonwealth* v. *Johnson*, the Kentucky Court of Appeals ruled unconstitutional the two statutes excluding blacks from serving on petit and grand juries. Fully aware of the decision rendered by the United States Supreme Court in the case from West Virginia, the Kentucky justices noted, "We therefore hold that so much of our statute as excludes all persons other than white

41. *Strauder* v. *West Virginia*, 100 U.S. 303 (1879); *Virginia* v. *Rives*, 100 U.S. 313 (1879). For a discussion of both cases, see Richard Klueger, *Simple Justice: The History of Brown v. Board of Education and Black America's Struggle for Equality* (New York, 1977), 63–66.

42. *Bush* v. *Kentucky*, 116–21.

men from service on juries is unconstitutional, and that no person can be lawfully excluded from any jury on account of his race or color." The justices went to great length to explain, just as the Supreme Court had ruled in *Virginia v. Rives*, that blacks must not be excluded as potential jurors but that it was still constitutional for a black to be tried by an all-white jury: "We do not mean, however, to be understood to say that a negro cannot be lawfully indicted and tried unless the jury is composed in part of persons of his own race. All we decide is, that such persons must not be excluded because of their race."[43]

Despite the rulings of both the Supreme Court and the Kentucky Court of Appeals, the restrictions on blacks as jurors remained in the General Statutes until January 26, 1882, when the word "white" was deleted from the qualifications of grand and petit jurymen. But white Kentuckians clearly understood the law: Blacks must be considered for jury duty, but it was not mandatory that they actually serve. Not surprisingly, during the 1880s blacks served on juries only on a few occasions and usually only in the largest cities of the state. Typically, blacks were selected to hear cases in which members of a black church, unable to work out a disagreement, had turned to the civil authorities to resolve matters. As far as can be determined from existing sources, only in Louisville did blacks sit on grand juries.[44] Richard Klueger, in his massive study *Simple Justice*, points out that the rulings by the Supreme Court that states could not prohibit blacks from serving on juries did not alter the practice of juries being all-white in the South. His argument most surely applies to Kentucky.

> On the face of it, then, the three cases [*Strauder v. West Virginia, Virginia v. Rives*, and *United States v. Cruikshank*] added up to a gain, certainly in rhetoric, for the Negro, but they did little to affect the continuing prevalence of all-white juries. For the Court did not rule that such juries were, by the very fact of their pure whiteness, illegally constituted and

43. *Commonwealth v. Johnson*, 78 Kentucky Reports, 509–13 (1880); see *Haggard v. Commonwealth*, 79 Kentucky Reports, 366–67 (1881). In this instance, the case of a black man was overturned because at the time of the indictment blacks were prohibited from serving on juries. In another case, *Smith v. Commonwealth*, 37 Southwestern Reporter, 825–26 (1896), the death sentence of a black man was upheld even though the three jury commissioners who had assisted with the selection of potential jurors were white.

44. New York *Times*, May 31, September 7, 1880.

that all their acts were therefore void. Barring a challenge, such juries could continue to function. Negroes did challenge them, repeatedly, but probably no constitutional issue would have to be more frequently litigated. The Department of Justice, which could have sought enforcement of the 1875 provision, chose to sit on its law books. And so the Negro, though his rights to a fair jury trial had been confirmed by the Supreme Court, was guaranteed instead, thanks in part to his spreading disenfranchisement throughout the South, state judicial systems composed entirely of white sheriffs, white prosecutors, white juries, and white judges. The practical effect of such an arrangement was greatly to encourage violence by whites against blacks.[45]

At a convention in October, 1885, black leaders denounced the discrimination the race encountered when appearing in court and the way the law consistently allowed white violence upon blacks to go unpunished: "We are tried in courts controlled entirely by white men, and no colored man sits on a Kentucky jury. This seems no mere accident, but a determined effort to exclude us from fair trials and put us at the mercy of our enemies, from the Judge down to the vilest stubborn witness." It was shameful, they argued, that out of the hundreds of lynchings that had occurred since the Civil War not "a single highhanded murderer has been ever brought before a court to answer." In their view, Afro-Americans were sent to prison mainly because of their race, not for criminal violations: "The penitentiary is full of our race, who are sent there by wicked and malicious persecutions and unjust sentences, dealt out by Judges who deem a colored criminal fit only for the severest and longest sentences for trivial offenses." The black leaders vowed to agitate and work until these forms of discrimination had ended.[46]

Within a matter of days after black leaders had voiced these complaints about discrimination in the legal system, attorney Nathaniel R. Harper, long active in various protests, vehemently argued in court that murder charges be dismissed against his client because blacks had been excluded from serving on the grand jury and had also been absent from the jury box. True, Negroes had been excluded from jury duty, the prosecutor responded, but not because of discrimination; none of them had possessed the required qualifications. Indeed, when called to the witness stand, one of the jury commissioners, who under

45. Klueger, *Simple Justice,* 64.
46. Louisville *Courier-Journal,* October 16, 1885.

Kentucky law had selected the men to be chosen to serve on juries, swore that the "only reason why colored men were not placed on the list was because they were not acquainted with any who were qualified."[47] Finding this comment satisfactory, the judge rejected Harper's request, proclaiming that racial discrimination had not occurred. Indignantly, Harper referred to the Louisville city directory, pointing out that there were more than 28,000 Afro-Americans listed in the document. Louisville had, the black attorney informed the judge and the three jury commissioners, a black college, staffed by Afro-American teachers, and scores of black professionals and businessmen. Refusing to yield, the commissioners claimed they knew none of these blacks. Although he failed in Jefferson County Circuit Court, Harper had his efforts rewarded several weeks later when the Ninth Judicial District Court for Kentucky agreed with his contention that blacks had been systematically excluded from the jury process. Jury commissioners were now required to include the names of blacks for service on both grand and petit juries.[48]

The mandate of the district court was largely ignored. For a time, the names of a few prominent black Louisvillians were routinely included within the pool of potential jurors, but only rarely did these men serve on juries, and then only in minor cases. And at all times they were absent from cases in which blacks were accused of crimes against whites. Indeed, given the racial discrimination in the selection of jurymen in Louisville, it would have been inconceivable for blacks to have been selected for the grand jury or as jurors in the trials

47. According to the Kentucky Court of Appeals, jury commissioners (three highly respected citizens in each county who had been appointed by the county court) were not required to select blacks but were prohibited from discriminating against them. In *Haggard* v. *Commonwealth* (1881), the court explained that "the commissioners, and the sheriff when he acts in their stead, are not bound to select negro jurors, simply because they belong to that race, any more than they are bound to select white jurors. And they are not required to select any particular person or class of persons for jury service, as neither race has a *right* to serve on a jury, but it is a *duty* which the state may require of them." Fifteen years later, in *Smith* v. *Commonwealth,* the court explained that jury commissioners were required to select "intelligent, sober, discreet, and impartial citizens" who could then be selected, by chance, to serve as grand and petit jurymen. To demand that blacks be included, the court reasoned, "would be a concession of a privilege to persons of African descent not granted by the constitution of the United States or laws of congress, nor at all conducive to, or consistent with, due and impartial administration of justice under laws of this commonwealth."

48. Louisville *Courier-Journal,* October 17, 24, 31, November 14, 1885.

of Albert Turner and William Patterson for the murder of Jennie Bowman. By the turn of the century, if indeed not earlier, the charade of including the names of blacks had ended entirely. When conducting research in the early 1900s, Gilbert T. Stephenson sent out questionnaires to attorneys general asking if blacks served on juries in their states. The assistant attorney general from Kentucky sent the following reply: "Negro jurors are sometimes selected in various parts of the state, and I presume all over the State. Twenty years ago the custom was more prevalent than at present of putting Negroes on the juries. They were the best class of Negroes." He ended with an incredible statement, one designed to shift the blame onto blacks for their absence from the jury box: "I am reliably informed that in various parts of the State the Negroes themselves requested to be left off the juries, which may account for the fact that the practice seems to have fallen into disuse." Black involvement in the jury process became so rare in Louisville and elsewhere in the state that when Afro-Americans began serving on juries in the 1940s, most Kentuckians, white and black alike, believed blacks were participating for the first time.[49]

During the last quarter of the nineteenth century, black Kentuckians were mostly unsuccessful in their attempts to end legal lynchings and to convince whites that the legal process discriminated against them. It proved far easier to show thoughtful whites that the lynching of a black rapist or murderer was unjust and a threat to society than to convince them that the trial given a black man had been a sham from start to finish and was held in an environment identical to that of a lynching. In the eyes of most whites, sentencing blacks to long prison terms or death had been done "by the book," upholding the laws of the state and the nation. This white belief in the legal system, that all people were treated fairly and had been tried by a jury of their peers, coupled with their unwillingness to acknowledge that the color of a man's skin could be so great an influence in determining guilt or innocence, ensured the continuation of legal lynchings into the twentieth century. If anything, as the number of mob lynchings declined in the next century, whites became even more convinced that their system dealt fairly with Afro-Americans.

49. Gilbert T. Stephenson, *Race Distinction in American Law* (New York, 1910), 258.

EIGHT Color-Coded Justice: Racial Violence Under the Law, 1900–1940

The conviction that Afro-Americans should be severely punished for their perceived and real transgressions was, of course, nothing new, but in the period from 1900 to 1940, white Kentuckians seem to have been more determined than ever that blacks accused of rape or murder be executed. In the new century, more whites acknowledged that mob violence was no longer acceptable, and they demanded, therefore, that the state punish black criminals quickly and firmly. Several executions occurred that were little short of lynchings: Local officials promised the lynch mob that the accused Afro-American would be given a quick trial and sentenced to death.

This happened in July, 1906, in Mayfield, a town, as we have seen, that richly deserved its reputation as a hostile place for blacks. On July 25, Ethel McLane claimed that she had been raped by Allen Mathias. As usual, hundreds of white men joined the police in the search for the Negro. Plans for lynching Mathias were openly discussed. But after capturing their suspect, the police immediately had him taken to Paducah for safekeeping. When they received word that a mob planned on going to Paducah to lynch Mathias, Mayfield authorities had him sent to Louisville.[1]

Usually, with the accused person out of the mob's reach, the prosecuting attorney would take the case before the grand jury, have an indictment issued, and make plans for the trial at a future date. After hearing the many complaints from irate whites that Mathias should be brought back to Mayfield to receive his "just punishment," local officials decided to speed up his return, trial, and execution. They no-

---

1. Information on this incident has been drawn from the Paducah *Weekly News Democrat*, August 2, 1906, and the Lexington *Herald*, August 1, 1906.

tified the police chief in Louisville that the accused rapist would stand trial within the week. Democratic governor J. C. W. Beckham agreed to provide troops to escort Mathias from Louisville to the courthouse in Mayfield. Realizing that the black man would be sentenced to death, the citizens of Mayfield quickly constructed the scaffold—an event that resembled many lynchings for which plans had already been finalized for the execution before the accused had even been caught and returned.

Tuesday morning, six days after the alleged assault, Mathias and his escorts left Louisville. At some point during the long train ride to western Kentucky, he decided to plead guilty. According to the *Courier-Journal*, Mathias, when captured, had been told of the mob waiting to lynch him in Mayfield, and he had become extremely frightened. It is not known if his decision to plead guilty had been done at the urging of the Mayfield officials who accompanied him from Louisville. Even before the train arrived in Mayfield, the sheriff informed reporters that the black man would be executed: "The scaffold is ready. He realizes that this is his last trip on this earth, and is on the verge of collapse from pure terror and dispair [*sic*]." More than ten thousand people witnessed the arrival of the train, perhaps the largest crowd ever assembled in this small community. By all accounts, Mathias' trial and legal execution were the quickest on record in Kentucky. In its story "Justice is Avenged, Death was Penalty," the Paducah newspaper timed the entire proceedings. The train arrived at 6:58 P.M., and it took the guards ten minutes to carry Mathias to the courthouse. Two minutes after arriving in court, Mathias pleaded guilty. The jury was sent out at 7:10 and returned at 7:24. (The jury was out fourteen minutes only because it took time for each man to affix his signature to the verdict.) After reading the jury's decision, the judge ordered that the sentence be carried out immediately—an announcement greeted with loud cheers. Mathias reached the scaffold at 7:40, and the sheriff cut his body down at 8:00. By then the mob, not the authorities, controlled events in Mayfield: "The body of the dead demon was carried through the streets in a coffin." The mob's leader said this would be a warning to other blacks. Then in a move that must have seemed like a replay of events after the December, 1896, lynchings, a number of whites visited several blacks and told them to leave town immediately. As the paper noted, these Afro-

Americans did as commanded: "The four left town quietly and without asking in what manner they had offended."

The *Courier-Journal* tried to put the best light on the execution of Allen Mathias. Some features of the case are to be regretted, the paper wrote. "The fact, however, that Kentucky was saved the mortification of a lynching by an indignant multitude, bent upon avenging the innocent victim of the crime, is a matter for special congratulation." After explaining that for the dignity of the law it would have been better if the trial had been less hasty, the paper frankly admitted that since a Negro had raped a white woman, "no other result could have been reached, however prolonged the trial." The editorial concluded with the customary justification for the legal lynchings of blacks: "Long-drawn out trials followed by appeal with repeated re-trials, do much to weaken the popular confidence in the law as a remedy for crime."[2] The *Courier-Journal's* editorial clearly reveals that legal lynchings were the norm for blacks accused of certain crimes. A guilty verdict in a rape case did not automatically carry the death sentence, unless, of course, the accused was black. Also, in justifying the prompt execution, the paper all but acknowledged that the state was doing the bidding of the mob. Although the *Courier-Journal* and other commentators expressed some displeasure over the way in which Mayfield authorities had conducted Mathias' "trial," they failed to note that in actuality his execution—which had been planned before the court heard any evidence—was as much a violation of the law they so piously claimed to treasure as was a lynching. Because the execution occurred immediately after the trial, Mathias was denied his right to appeal to a higher court, and he was prevented from seeking clemency from the governor. And in all likelihood, the black youth had been tried and found guilty without the benefit of counsel to represent and advise him.

Mathias was far from being the only Afro-American to experience a speedy trial before a hostile white mob. George Yantis of Lancaster was arrested on the charge of attempted rape of Mrs. Clayton Marse in March, 1920. A mob threatened to lynch Yantis, so the authorities decided to move quickly. The very next day, the grand jury handed down an indictment. Realizing that it would take far more time and evi-

2. Louisville *Courier-Journal*, July 31–August 2, 1906.

dence to convict Yantis of attempted rape, the prosecutor urged the court, and it agreed, to sentence him to seven years in state prison for burglary. Less than twenty-four hours after his arrest, Yantis was on his way to prison. The outcome of a speedy trail proved to be much worse for another black. A fight in the eastern Kentucky community of Lynch resulted in the death of the white man involved and the arrest of Leonard Griffin. Determined to end the matter quickly, Lynch officials immediately tried Griffin for murder. Only at the start of the trial did Griffin confer with an attorney. Not surprisingly, the all-white jury found him guilty of murder and handed down the maximum sentence. With a tip from the authorities, or more likely with its own knowledge of how the legal system worked against blacks, the local newspaper printed stories about Griffin's guilty verdict and death sentence within minutes after the trial ended. The NAACP, believing that an obvious injustice had occurred, intervened on behalf of the doomed man. Members of the organization obtained an audience with the governor and gave what they thought was strong evidence that Griffin had acted in self-defense and that, in any event, a fair trial would have been impossible in Lynch because of intense racial hatred. "It is believed that if his trial had taken place after a reasonable period of time had elapsed between the crime and the conviction, the penalty would not have been so severe," stated the NAACP's memorandum. Although promising a thorough review of the case, Governor William J. Fields refused to commute the sentence, and on March 20, 1925, only three months after his day in court, Griffin died in the electric chair.[3]

That Griffin lived several months after being sentenced to death was partly a result of a law passed after the execution of Mathias. The 1906 law mandated a thirty-day "cooling off" period between sentencing a person to death and carrying out the execution. On November 3, 1909, a white woman was allegedly raped in the small town of Dry Ridge. Seventeen-year-old Earl Thompson was arrested, charged with the rape, and taken to Lexington for safekeeping. On December 6, a special grand jury returned an indictment against him for rape, and a jury was empaneled to hear the case. Meanwhile, a mob gathered at

3. Maysville Bulletin, April 1, 1920; Louisville Leader, December 13, 1924. In the NAACP Papers, see "Memoranda In the Case of Leonard Griffin," prepared by Edward E. Underwood, of the Frankfort NAACP, December 1, 1924, and NAACP press release, December 5, 1924.

the train depot awaiting Thompson's return. Fearing a lynching, the circuit judge addressed the crowd, promising that if a lynching was avoided, Thompson would be found guilty and sentenced to death. The judge also assured the mob that Thompson would not go back to Lexington but would remain in jail in Williamstown until the sentence could be carried out. The word of the circuit judge—his promise that the black teenager would die on the gallows—satisfied the mob. Thompson pleaded not guilty, which meant that the charade of a trial had to take place. The length of the trial, almost five hours, upset some of the spectators. At one point, a man holding a knife rushed toward Thompson saying, "Damn him, I will cut his head off." After deliberating for less than an hour, the jury sentenced the black teenager to death. The announcement of the verdict to the women and young children, who had not been permitted to attend the trial but had been forced to remain outdoors, resulted in a prolonged shout of approval. Some of the men inside the courtroom became wild with rage and were determined to hang him immediately. Thompson was pushed out of a window and carried back to jail, which was quickly surrounded by the mob. Once again the circuit judge pleaded with the mob, saying Thompson would die in exactly thirty days, on Friday, January 7. Thompson's court-appointed attorney, a member of the community, said he would not appeal the conviction. This seemed to satisfy the mob that "justice" would be done. As promised, Thompson's execution took place on January 7, the very first day allowed by the law.[4]

Public hangings, just like speedy trials, satisfied mob opinion that criminals should not be coddled by the state. The activities that seem to be a part of nineteenth-century executions—the large, frenzied crowds, the vendors selling hot dogs, cotton candy, and souvenirs, and the news reporters writing about every trivial step taken by the condemned man—remained a part of public executions in the new century. All along, a number of citizens urged the elimination of the carnival-like atmosphere, claiming that it made light of one of the most serious functions performed by the state. In 1910, a bill was in-

4. Louisville *Courier-Journal*, December 8, 1909, January 8, 1910; Owensboro *Inquirer*, January 7, 1910. When commenting on the promise of the circuit court judge that Thompson would be executed, the Boston *Guardian*, December 18, 1909, expressed hope that this would result in the black youth's case being reviewed by a higher court.

troduced that called for using the electric chair instead of the scaffold for executions. Supporters of the bill added another feature to the law, one clearly designed to end the rowdy behavior that occurred during executions: "All executions of the death penalty by electrocution shall take place within the walls of the State penitentiary, . . . and such inclosures as will exclude public view thereof." This bill, which had the support of Governor Willson, was signed into law on March 20, 1910.[5]

Eventually, however, the practice of hanging condemned rapists in the county where they had been tried and convicted was reinstituted in Kentucky. In an attempt to have Will Lockett quickly convicted and returned to state prison, Lexington officials decided to indict him only with the murder of Geneva Hardman, even though evidence existed that she had been sexually assaulted as well. Although elated that "justice" had been meted out to Lockett, a number of Lexington whites expressed a belief that the electric chair was much too humane for such a heinous crime, that Lockett should have been made to suffer by dying at the end of a rope.[6] Quickly responding to these intense feelings, lawmakers amended the death penalty law, adding a feature that was clearly designed to appeal to the will of the mob: "Except in cases where the accused has been adjudged to suffer a death sentence for the crime of rape or attempted rape, in which event sentence shall be executed by hanging the condemned in the county in which the crime was committed, that such an execution shall be within an enclosure to be provided by the county and admittance to said enclosure be limited to 100 persons."[7]

In clear defiance of this provision to limit the number of people witnessing a hanging, white authorities returned to executing Afro-Americans in front of huge, boisterous crowds numbering in the thousands. In June, 1932, Sam Jennings was executed in Hardinsburg for the alleged attack of a white woman. According to a black newspaper, "The hanging of the colored man . . . attracted such a throng of men, women, and children as might have caused P. T. Barnum of circus fame to hide his face in shame. It took Jennings seventeen

5. *Acts of the General Assembly of the Commonwealth of Kentucky* (Louisville, 1910), 111–13; newsclip from the Willson Collection.

6. See, for example, the Lexington *Herald* and *Leader* for March, 1920.

7. *Acts of the General Assembly Commonwealth of Kentucky, 1920* (Louisville, 1921), 693–94.

minutes to die, to the delight of the crowd who enjoyed every second of the event." The public hanging of Rainey Bethea in Owensboro on August 14, 1936, hastened the end of the practice. Two months earlier, the body of Mrs. Elza Edward had been found in her apartment. The woman had been raped and her apartment burglarized. Found among Edward's possessions was a ring that a police officer recognized as the type made by prisoners in Eddyville. That led police to Rainey Bethea, a former convict, who confessed to the murder and assault and told the police where they could recover the woman's missing items. At his trial in Owensboro, the jury deliberated less than five minutes before sentencing him to death by hanging.[8]

Adding interest to Bethea's execution was the possibility that the hanging would be carried out by a woman sheriff who had been appointed to serve the remaining term of her deceased husband. Although expressing a strong desire to see Bethea die, Florence Thompson decided not to perform the chore. No matter. As the city's historian noted, thousands of people came to Owensboro by horseback, automobiles, excursion trains and buses, and even airplanes during the days leading up to the execution. The Chicago *Tribune* made much of the fact that many of the people coming were "women with babes in arms." The usual vendors arrived in Owensboro to profit from the black man's impending execution. Many citizens held "hanging parties," inviting out-of-town friends to Owensboro. Others held impromptu barbecues and engaged in sporting activities. Some twenty thousand people attended the hanging even though it took place at 5:30 in the morning. (The story in the New York *Times* said thousands of white people, "some jeering and others festive, saw a prayerful black man put to death on Daviess County's pit and gallows.") National newspaper accounts (which carried every detail for the folks back home) depicted the people at the hanging as being uncivilized. They told of how people rushed to the gallows to rip off Bethea's

8. Louisville *Leader*, June 25, 1932. For an excellent account of the Bethea case, see Lee A. Dew, "The Hanging of Rainey Bethea," *Daviess County Historical Quarterly*, II (July, 1984), 51–59. The Owensboro Public Library has several sources and newsclips on Bethea. See, for example, "Executive Order from Governor Keen Johnson to Owensboro Sheriff," setting the date of execution. From August 14 to 16, 1936, nearly every major newspaper in the country carried stories and pictures of the hanging. See also the Lexington *Herald-Leader* of August 14, 1986, which did a story entitled "Public hanging 50 years ago bad memory in Owensboro."

clothes, as well as the hangman's hood, for souvenirs. The editor of the newspaper in nearby Henderson had some criticisms of the hanging as well: The hour of the execution, he wrote, should have been more convenient—perhaps about 2:00 in the afternoon—so more people could have attended. And it should have been conducted at the high school so that everyone "could sit and be comfortable and see the ghastly spectacle."

Rainey Bethea's execution drew nationwide attention to Kentucky as the last state in which public hangings were conducted. Not surprisingly, several organizations, concerned about the state's image, lobbied for an end to the practice. As the execution of John Pete Montjoy approached in August, 1936, the ASWPL and the *Courier-Journal* urged the governor to have the execution moved to Eddyville. They achieved a partial victory when Covington officials agreed that Montjoy would die in private, though the execution would still take place on the gallows. In reaching his decision, the judge expressed concern about the Roman Holiday atmosphere that had occurred in Owensboro. Because of appeals, Montjoy's execution was delayed until December 17, 1937. Several months later, on June 3, 1938, Harold Van Venison, also a Covington Afro-American, died on the gallows after being convicted of rape. Within a month after his death, the new law went into effect, calling for "all executions of the death penalty by electrocution . . . [to] take place within the walls of the state penitentiary, . . . and in such enclosure as will exclude public view thereof."[9] While white reformers were pleased that they had ended a particularly gruesome practice, they never questioned that for more than two decades virtually all of the men who had died on the gallows were blacks who had been convicted by all-white juries.

This willingness to publicly execute alleged black rapists under-

9. See the Louisville *Courier-Journal*, December 12, 1937, for an article, "To Hang in Private," in the Sunday magazine; see also the paper's editorial of June 6, 1938, and its praise of the ASWPL. Efforts of the organization to end hangings have also been praised in Wilma Dykeman and James Stokley, *Seeds of Southern Change: The Life of Will Alexander* (New York, 1962), 146. *Acts of the General Assembly of the Commonwealth of Kentucky* (Frankfort, 1938), 640–41. Information on the execution of Venison was obtained from Perry T. Ryan, *A Legislative History of Hangings in Kentucky* (Frankfort, 1988). I am grateful to Mr. Ryan, an assistant attorney general for the State of Kentucky, for sharing his research with me.

scores the high emotions with which whites regarded this crime and their belief that Afro-Americans were prone to commit this assault despite the severe punishment awaiting them. For all their proclamations about a strong belief in American law, whites denied blacks their fundamental rights when a charge of rape or attempted rape was made. Even in Louisville and Lexington, the newspapers maintained their tradition of convicting blacks of rape even before they had been captured or given the chance to defend themselves in court.[10] In October, 1921, Mildred Sorrell, an eleven-year-old, told of being attacked by an "unidentified negro" in Lexington's Duncan Park. Numerous "suspicious" blacks were sharply questioned by the police. The newspapers spoke in harsh terms of the "black brute" and applauded the actions of the circuit court judge and the grand jury in issuing a "John Doe" indictment for the black rapist. Several days later, Mildred Sorrell identified Harry Mitchell, a fifty-three-year-old white man known to her, as the attacker. She had hidden the truth because Mitchell had threatened to kill her. Earlier that same year, a Louisville white woman was assaulted, allegedly by a black man. For several weeks while the woman lay in bed, the police brought scores of black men to her home for her to identify, and fortunately for them, she exonerated all of them. According to a black newspaper, the evidence pointed to a white man having committed the crime; but the police persisted in arresting blacks, and the Louisville white newspapers railed daily at blacks for the crime. The ultimate outcome of the case is unknown. The very next year, a young white girl told her parents she had been raped by a black man. This provoked the Louisville newspapers to resume their calls for the adoption of drastic steps to remove the black rapist from the streets. Several days later,

---

10. Attorneys often complained that their black clients could not receive fair trials because of the negative stories that had appeared in the local newspapers, stating that the defendants were considered guilty even before any evidence had been given in court. The Kentucky Court of Appeals ruled that the actions of the newspapers alone were not enough to prevent a black from having a fair trial: "While newspaper articles are admissible and may be considered on a hearing of application of change of venue, there must be other evidence tending to show such a condition of public sentiment in the county as would prevent the applicant from having a fair and impartial trial." See *Holmes* v. *Commonwealth*, 241 Kentucky Reports, 573–87 (1931), the quotation comes from p. 582.

the young girl confessed to concocting a tale of being assaulted by a Negro after her parents had refused to have her hair cut. Obviously, the young girl lived in an environment in which blacks were talked of as bogeymen, and she knew that to gain sympathy all one needed to do was claim to have been attacked by a black man.[11]

In addition to the cases of Allen Mathias and Earl Thompson, other controversial rape trials of blacks have occurred in Kentucky during this century. The age of the alleged black rapist mattered little to the emotional whites seeking revenge: James Pearsall was eighteen when he died on the scaffold in Lexington in July, 1906, and Earl Thompson was only seventeen when he died in Williamstown in January, 1910.[12] James White of Middlesboro was sixteen when he was charged with the criminal assault of a fourteen-year-old white girl in 1909. On the advice of his court-appointed attorney, White, described as being mentally incapable of understanding the charges against him, pleaded guilty. His attorney had reasoned that a guilty plea was the only thing that might save White from hanging. Nevertheless, he was sentenced to death, a verdict appealed on his behalf. He would be given two additional trials; both resulted in death sentences. Interestingly, in early January, 1911, Kentucky's attorney general, after carefully reviewing the entire case, expressed grave doubts about the validity of the trials and, specifically, about how White's attorneys had chosen to defend him. He also reached the conclusion that White did not understand the charges made against him. The attorney general appealed to Governor Willson to commute the sentence from death to life in prison.[13]

Having Willson determine White's fate was probably viewed as a positive sign by the many people calling for leniency for the black teenager. More than other governors, and rivaled at best only by fellow Republicans William O. Bradley and Edwin P. Morrow, Willson

11. For stories on the rape of Mildred Sorrell in Lexington, see the Lexington *Herald,* October 17–21, 1921; Louisville *Leader,* January 22, 1921; the Tuskegee Clippings, Reel 223, Frame 92, has a story from the Louisville *News,* April 29, 1922, discussing the false accusation.

12. The Lexington *Herald,* July 1–7, 1906, devoted extensive coverage to Pearsall, showing a strong fascination with his life and impending death.

13. *White* v. *Commonwealth,* 140 Kentucky Reports, September 21, 1910, 9–11; Louisville *Courier-Journal,* January 19, 1910, January 31, 1911.

had consistently denounced mob violence against Afro-Americans, had taken steps to prevent lynchings, and had pardoned dozens of blacks sent to prison who had been tried in hostile environments clearly dominated by the mob. On the recommendation of the attorney general, he granted a stay of execution for White from January 16 to January 30 in order to make a final ruling on the case. One week later, Willson carefully explained that he wanted to avoid making a decision that would "furnish any just ground for fear that the guilty can escape" execution or give "any excuse for mob law or lynch law." Going further, the governor forcefully argued, "The certainty of punishment takes away the only plausible excuse for mobs and lynching, the fear that the guilty will escape." Complicating this highly charged rape case, however, was the fact that the defendant was clearly retarded. The governor had received information showing that White's father had died in an insane asylum and that his mother was physically deformed with a large hump on her back. James White, the governor noted, was abnormally small for a man nearing his twenties; he was no bigger than an average twelve-year-old. The governor then made a most remarkable statement:

> The history of the birth of this boy of parents physically and mentally imperfect, is simply one more instance of the really wicked policy which permits such people to marry and bear children, physically, mentally, and morally defective, dangerous to the community, a heavy charge on the State and subject to life long sorrow, sin, shame, distress and suffering. Our system is wickedly wrong. Such people should be by law prohibited from marriage or subjected to any operation which would prevent offspring. This boy is one of the victims of that system, but he is none the less dangerous to society, and his case, if not punished by death, is dangerous to the whole state.

Willson approved the execution of White because he was a danger to society, a person who should have never been born. Undoubtedly, the governor made his decision with white lynch mobs very much in mind. Although committed to ending lynchings, he did not want to be considered "soft" on criminals, thereby encouraging mobs to take the law into their own hands. He, therefore, like other governors, gave in to the will of the mob, though it had clearly been demonstrated by the attorney general that White, like most blacks accused of rape in small towns, had not received adequate counsel or a fair trial, and

though Willson himself admitted that James White was mentally retarded. On January 30, 1911, White was put to death in Middlesboro,
before the usual huge crowd that witnessed public hangings.[14]

A highly publicized rape trial occurred in Madisonville in 1926.
A number of robberies and assaults had taken place on the highway
between Earlington and Madisonville in the early months of 1926. In
late March, an automobile carrying three young white women stalled,
and if the young women are to be believed, three unidentified black
men suddenly appeared and raped them. The police, as usual, arrested
dozens of black men but released all of them when no evidence could
be found linking them to the crime. This should have suggested to the
police that additional questioning of the young women might lead
to new evidence in the case or to the discovery that no rapes had
taken place. Into the controversy came the Hopkins County Ku Klux
Klan, condemning lawlessness and calling for the protection of white
women: If the police were unwilling to enforce the law strictly and
crack down on Afro-Americans, they would. In early April, the Klan
held a parade through the streets of Madisonville in support of law
and order. Carrying a large flag, the marchers stopped at every church,
and the klansmen made a cross formation and knelt for a few mo-
ments of silent prayer. Several days later, another white woman, Neil
Catherine Breithaupt, told the police that she, too, had been raped by
three unidentified black men. Fearing that the Klan would take the
initiative, the local police conducted an all-out search, promising that
this time the guilty would be brought to justice.[15]

The case was broken in a most unlikely manner. While spending
time with a prostitute, a white man found a picture of a black man
and letters showing that he was intimately involved with the white
prostitute. Offended that a white woman would be romantically in-

14. In the Governor Willson Papers, see "Respite of James White," January 14,
1911; see also a telegram from Willson to Sheriff Robert Van Bever of Middlesboro,
January 14, 1911. In the Willson Collection are a number of newspaper clippings concerning James White. The views expressed by Willson and the quote come from a story
entitled "James White to Pay Penalty of Death: Governor Refuses to Commute to Life
Term."

15. Starting with the report on a KKK service on January 1, 1926, through May,
1927, the Madisonville *Daily Messenger* has extensive coverage on the alleged crime
wave in the area. Louisville's two black newspapers, the *Leader* and the *News*, gave
thorough coverage as well. Additional information on the case can be found in the
many newsclips and papers in the records of the Louisville NAACP.

volved with a Negro, he took the materials to the police, who then arrested the woman. Under brutal interrogation by the police, Mabel Bumpass admitted that she had dated Columbus Hollis and that her close friend, Lucille Davenport, also a prostitute, was intimately involved with two black men. The police reasoned that if black men were having sex with white women, they would, to satisfy their lust, attack other white women. They arrested Hollis, and once confronted with the evidence of his association with Bumpass, he broke down. He told the police that he would confess to being an accomplice in the assault of Neil Breithaupt but that he had not raped her. Hollis identified as the rapists the two men already known to the police as lovers of Lucille Davenport: Bunyan Fleming and Nathan Bard. With the black men in jail, the authorities ordered the two prostitutes to leave town, warning them that if they remained in Madisonville, the grand jury would take up the case of white prostitutes associating with black men.

The police hustled the black men off to Louisville. From the perspective of the local white newspaper, the arrests of the three blacks meant that the case had been solved. Even a Louisville newspaper joined in: The *Herald-Post* referred to Bunyan Fleming as a "monkeyman" and as the leader of the group. In hopes of preventing yet another legal lynching, the Louisville NAACP sent newspaper editor William Warley to investigate the charges against the black men. Despite receiving little encouragement from local black residents—who were afraid of offending whites—he concluded that the men were innocent and that Hollis had been coerced into lying about the incident. The Louisville branch raised funds to assist in the defense of Fleming and Bard. The three men went on trial in late April in Madisonville; both the white establishment and the Ku Klux Klan called for their execution. Only the presence of five hundred guardsmen prevented a lynching. Nevertheless, an editorial in the Madisonville *Daily Messenger* expressed confidence in the all-white jury to give the men a fair trial. The paper praised circuit court judge Ruby Laffoon (who would serve as governor of Kentucky from 1931 to 1935) as the ideal person to preside over the cases: "While there is no doubt in the minds of most people of the guilt of the negro trio, and *The Messenger* concurs in the belief, that the right ones are being accused, there is not one among us who should not take pride in the fact that they will receive a fair and impartial trial."

Bunyan Fleming was tried first. Given the weak evidence presented by the prosecution, "reasonable doubt" would have been a logical decision had Fleming been white. But he was not. Hollis, after admitting that the jailers had given him money for candy and cigarettes after he agreed to testify against the other men, said that he held down Neil Breithaupt while Fleming and Bard raped her. Once on the witness stand, the woman had a difficult time identifying Fleming as one of her attackers. Nevertheless, Fleming's jury was out only nine minutes before sentencing him to death. Nathan Bard received a similar fate. The jury, believing the story told by Hollis and appreciative of his testimony against the others, was lenient toward him, handing down a sentence of twenty years in prison. Tragically, at the conclusion of the trials, Madisonville's black leaders placed a statement in the white newspaper affirming their strong commitment to law and order, implying that the black men had received fair trials.

Although they were given an execution date, Bard and Fleming did not die in 1926. After several delays and appeals, a new date was set for April 8, 1927, after the Kentucky Court of Appeals refused to rehear the case. Yet on the day prior to the execution, another stay was granted. Federal Judge Charles I. Dawson issued a writ of habeas corpus, saying he wanted to make sure that the men had received fair trials. At the hearing in Louisville on April 26, their lawyers argued that the mob had dominated the trial despite the presence of five hundred troops. No juror could vote for acquittal and hope to continue living in Hopkins County, they explained. Furthermore, the lawyers said, they had been denied sufficient time to speak with their clients before the trial started. Finally, in what they hoped would be their most convincing point, they argued that their request for a change of venue had been turned down because two black Madisonville citizens had been unwilling to sign an affidavit saying that racial hostilities in the community would make it impossible for a fair trial to take place. Judge Laffoon, the prosecuting attorney, and other Madisonville whites simply argued that the trials had been fair. A week later, the federal judge made known his ruling. It was unfortunate, Dawson pointed out, that the Hopkins County Circuit Court had rushed the start of the trials. In a statement that seemed to suggest sympathy for the condemned men, the judge said, "It has been testified here by a lot of people that the crowd at Madisonville was a regular 'Sunday' crowd, but I have had much experience with criminal practice and I know there was intense feeling there." The judge dismissed the claim of the attorneys that it had been impossible to get two black citizens to request a change of venue: "Under a new Kentucky law, counsel can file a motion for change of venue supported by the affidavit of the defendant to the effect that he is in danger of mob violence. This was not done in the case." Judge Dawson upheld the death sentences for Bard and Fleming. But he gave their lawyers thirty days to appeal his decision.[16]

The United States Sixth Circuit Court of Appeals decided that the controversial case demanded additional investigation, which led to a further delay. Reaching its decision at the end of June, the court said Bard and Fleming would hang on July 15 unless granted a stay by the United States Supreme Court.[17] Justice Louis Brandeis then issued the men a short stay. After finally receiving the go-ahead from the Supreme Court, Governor William J. Fields selected July 29 as the date for the execution but then settled on November 25 to give the attorneys enough time to exhaust the appeals process. Satisfied that the men were guilty and that the sentence should have already been carried out, state attorney general Frank Daugherty expressed his displeasure over the four-month delay: "To the delays and uncertainties of procedure in the courts will be added another instance tending to encourage lawlessness and criminal acts and these, in turn, will provoke the slumbering tendency of mob violence."

All along, the Louisville NAACP and the national office in New York had provided legal advice and the much-needed funds to fight the death sentences. Immediately after the governor granted the four-month delay, James Weldon Johnson prevailed upon Louis Marshall of the NAACP's legal defense department to review the transcripts of the case one last time. Marshall concluded that nothing could be done to save the two men. He and Johnson then agreed that the national office should withdraw from the case because of the organization's philosophy of not "sponsoring doubtful cases, cases in which there is not a fair fighting chance and which do not involve some important principle or some outstanding act of prejudice and injustice." In recognition of the gallant effort of the Louisville NAACP on behalf of the

16. For details on the hearing before the federal judge, see the Madisonville *Daily Messenger*, April 7, 26, May 7, 1927.

17. *Bard* v. *Chilton, Warden et al.*, and *Fleming* v. *Same*, 20 Federal Reporter, 906–907 (1927).

doomed men, Johnson did contribute $250, even though he knew the case was lost.[18]

The legal opinion expressed by the NAACP and its subsequent withdrawal from the case foreshadowed the end for Bard and Fleming. In early November, the United States Supreme Court refused to review the case. On Wednesday, November 23, both the governor and Judge Dawson agreed to a one-week stay to make certain that all the necessary papers arrived in Madisonville. Fearful of a further delay in the case, Madisonville officials sent the sheriff to Cincinnati to pick up the papers and hand-deliver them to the jailer. The governor rescinded the stay, and the next day the long-delayed execution of Bard and Fleming occurred. The *Daily Messenger* printed an extra edition headlined "XTRA: 2 RAPISTS HANG." The front page carried a large picture of Neil Catherine Breithaupt, the "beautiful daughter of Mr. and Mrs. Leo Breithaupt." A front page editorial denounced once again the hideous crime Bard and Fleming were executed for committing. The paper also applauded the "orderly crowd of 7,000" (estimates by other newspapers put the crowd at close to 20,000). In a second editorial, the newspaper discussed the "facts" of the entire case and how the Ku Klux Klan had been a positive influence in solving the crime. "Stormy indeed was this period in the history of Hopkins County, so stormy that no citizen who passed through it would ever wish to see it duplicated. And yet, through it all, there was the manifest desire of the public in general to see the law take its course, the willingness to let the courts . . . handle the case without any attempt at violence without due trial." An editorial from the Louisville *Times* also supported the hangings, going to great lengths to explain that Bard and Fleming had received fair trials.

Unfortunately, highly controversial rape trials did not end with the 1920s. On two occasions in the 1930s, Covington, the largest city in northern Kentucky, witnessed rape trials during which white mobs first threatened lynchings, then demanded that the blacks be quickly tried and sentenced to death. On March 6, 1930, a white woman in the small community of Crescent Springs, in Kenton County, said she had been raped by a black man. Arrested almost immediately was Anderson McPerkins, a native of Georgia who had just arrived in the

18. James W. Johnson to Louis Marshall, July 19, 1927; see also the numerous letters and clippings in the Bard-Fleming File. In NAACP Papers.

area after jumping from a freight train and who had been seen begging for food in the vicinity of the woman's home. At the trial two months later, McPerkins, described as not "mentally deficient, just ignorant," was found guilty and sentenced to death, a verdict upheld by the Kentucky Court of Appeals on December 5, 1930.[19]

His life was ultimately saved because of the efforts of several groups and individuals in Covington and Cincinnati. After visiting McPerkins in jail, members of the Cincinnati branch of the International Labor Defense (ILD) wrote letters to local newspapers, hoping to arouse public concern over the arrest of the black youth. To the credit of this organization, instead of using McPerkins' troubles to promote their own causes, and realizing that many people found them highly suspect, the ILD encouraged other groups to assist in the fight for the youth's life. Mary D. Brite, the secretary of the Cincinnati chapter of the American Civil Liberties Union, was contacted, and she wrote to William Pickens of the national office of the NAACP, informing him about the case and seeking support. Because the Covington NAACP was inoperative, the national office urged officials of the Cincinnati branch to investigate the case. From the start, the Reverend David M. Jordan, pastor of the Ninth Street Methodist Episcopal Church in Covington, had been interested in the case. Using his church as a rallying place for supporters of McPerkins, Jordan raised money for the attorney and for carrying the case to the Kentucky Court of Appeals. With McPerkins awaiting death in 1931, J. Max Bond, of the Kentucky Commission on Interracial Cooperation, became interested in the case. The turning point in the case occurred when Bond traveled to Kenton County and was able to confirm information he had received about the "disreputable character" of the woman. As he noted in a letter to Mary Brite: "On February 28 I had a conference with the Governor Flem Sampson. I believe I presented evidence that proved this boy's innocence. The result of our conference was McPerkins will not die neither will he get life. As to the exact status of the boy at this present time I am in no position to state." Although he had evidence that nothing had occurred between McPerkins and the woman,

19. *McPerkins* v. *Commonwealth*, 33 Southwestern Reporter, 2nd Series, 622–25 (1930). The Cincinnati branch of the NAACP worked on behalf of McPerkins. Numerous letters and newsclippings concerning the case can be found in Box 1–55, Series G, Group I, NAACP Papers; information on the trial can be found in the Cincinnati *Enquirer*, May 30, 31, 1930.

Sampson failed to act on the case for several months. After receiving a number of letters from members of the ACLU, Sampson finally contacted Bond on July 15, promising to "conclude the consideration of the McPerkins case before long and to take some definite action therein." By the end of the month, McPerkins' one-and-a-half year ordeal had ended with his release from prison.[20]

On the other hand, the case of John Pete Montjoy concluded in the more usual and tragic manner of a black accused of raping a white female. Indeed, as noted previously, his death on the gallows would be one of the last hangings in Kentucky. On March 23, 1935, Mrs. Irene Cummings claimed that she had been robbed by two black men and that one had also raped her. Interestingly, she knew the names of both men, and they were therefore captured that same evening. After being in jail for six days, Willie Black and Montjoy finally signed confessions, saying that they had robbed the woman and that Montjoy had committed rape after Black had left the scene. In court, the prosecutor, fearing that the jury might not condemn Montjoy to death, resorted to racism. He referred to the teenager as "a slimy, greasy, black ape" who, if not executed, would return "to rape another white woman if given only a prison sentence." Unlike most juries considering the case of a black man charged with raping a white woman, this one deliberated for more than three hours before the jurors informed the judge that they needed additional materials before making a decision. The judge responded harshly that "unless a verdict was returned within ten minutes the jury would be locked up for the night." With the mandate from the judge ringing in their ears, the jurymen returned within a matter of minutes with a guilty verdict and a death sentence for Montjoy.[21]

20. Numerous letters give details of the efforts of various groups and individuals to save McPerkins' life. See the first letter from Mary D. Brite to William Pickens, of the national office of the NAACP, April 3, 1930. There would also be more than a dozen letters between Brite and members of the national office. See also the various letters between David M. Jordan and the national office. Especially see his letter to Robert W. Bagnall, of the national office, June 10, 1930. In 1931, a series of letters to the national office concerning the case would come from J. Max Bond. See also copies of letters from Bond to Mary D. Brite. Especially see Bond to Brite, February 6, 1931, and Bond to Brite, undated but in early March, 1931. All of the letters cited here can be found in the NAACP Papers.

21. *Montjoy* v. *Commonwealth*, 262 Kentucky Reports, 426–36 (1935); Theodore M. Berry, of the Cincinnati NAACP, to Walter White, of the national office, May 29,

Just as they had in the McPerkins case, the NAACP, the ACLU, and the ILD joined hands in an attempt to save Montjoy. Their investigation produced a startling revelation: A relationship had existed between Montjoy and Mrs. Cummings prior to the alleged rape. For several months, he had been providing the white woman with an illegal commodity, something called "muggle" cigarettes. On the night of the alleged rape, the pair argued over the amount of money Cummings was to pay for the cigarettes, and Montjoy, perhaps in a fit of anger, took money from the woman's pocketbook as partial payment and requested sex as payment for the final amount. At this point, Willie Black fled the scene. As explained by Mary Brite in a long memorandum to the NAACP:

> In her evidence Mrs. Cummings testified that after Montjoy had "driven" her into the alley he discussed his intention with her, and when she became convinced that she "was in for it," she requested him to go up the alley to ascertain if any one was there. In other words, she sent him to see if any witnesses were around while she waited for him to return and rape her. Why did she not run from that alley if she knew what was going to happen and wished to avoid it? No, she saw in this situation, which she may have welcomed, a means of . . . ridding herself of Montjoy and his relations with her.[22]

When appealing Montjoy's death sentence before Kentucky's highest court, attorney William E. Wehrman raised three major issues, any one of which, he contended, should result in the conviction being struck down. Like other lawyers defending blacks during the 1930s, he argued that the case should be overturned because of the continued exclusion of Afro-Americans from the jury panel. Wehrman argued forcefully that the "confessions" of both black youths had been made under duress and that their original hand-written statements had not been introduced into the court as evidence but had been replaced with typed copies. After their arrest, Black and Montjoy were placed in solitary confinement for six days. Black broke first, telling the police officers that Montjoy had taken Mrs. Cummings' money but that

1935, Berry to Charles H. Houston, of the national office, January 13, 1936, both in NAACP Papers. This collection contains an entire file, with numerous letters and newspaper clippings, on the Montjoy case.

22. Mary D. Brite's memorandum, "The Case of John Montjoy: A Sample of Justice for a Negro" (written in February, 1936), was eventually published in *Crisis*, XLIII (April, 1936), 105, 114.

he could not verify whether the woman had been raped or not. With Black's statement in hand, the police went to Montjoy's cell between 3:30 and 4:00 in the morning and questioned him at length until he confessed. As his attorney informed the justices, not only had Montjoy been kept in solitary confinement and denied adequate sleep for six days, he had been brutally beaten by the police before signing the confession. Wehrman, trying to show that local authorities had worked to prevent the truth about the incident involving the black man and white woman from being known, pointed out that Black was held in custody for nearly a year without being charged with any crime, when released was warned not to discuss the case with anyone, and was then escorted out of town by the sheriff. Unfortunately, efforts to locate Black to testify in behalf of Montjoy had proved fruitless, the attorney revealed. The final argument for overturning the conviction centered on the physical condition of the alleged rape victim after the incident. Unlike most women in a similar situation, Cummings was completely unruffled, in appearance and demeanor, after the attack. More significant, however, she refused to be examined by a physician. Indeed, only on the day before the start of Montjoy's trial—four weeks later—did Cummings consent to an examination. Members of the Kentucky Court of Appeals made short work of Wehrman's arguments, rejecting all of them. No proof had been entered showing that blacks had been discriminated against in the jury selection process. The mere fact that none had ever served on a trial in Kenton County was not sufficient evidence of a racial bias, the justices stated emphatically. In response to Wehrman's assertion that the confessions had been made under duress, they concluded: "Admitting, for the sake of discussion, that the facts are as contended, their cumulation does not amount to duress or force. In nowise do they come within the condemnation of section 1694b-1 et seq., Ky. Stats. commonly known as the 'anti-sweating' act."[23]

The efforts of concerned citizens had saved the life of McPerkins but had failed in the case of John Pete Montjoy. Why? In the first case, it was clearly demonstrated that no relationship existed between the black man and white woman. Montjoy, however, had placed himself in a situation that given the racism of the day, he could not

23. *Montjoy* v. *Commonwealth*; see also a letter in *New Masses*, XVI (July 9, 1935), 21, signed by representatives of the NAACP, the ACLU, and the IDL.

win. Ultimately, it made no difference whether evidence could be obtained to show that Mrs. Cummings was, like the white woman in the McPerkins case, also a woman with a disreputable character. All that mattered was that Montjoy had an illicit relationship with her; whether Cummings had agreed to sexual intercourse or had been forced into it by the black man carried the same weight in the eyes of the white jury. Mary Brite, whose efforts had resulted in Anderson McPerkins escaping the gallows, concluded regarding Montjoy's case:

> With the white light of truth thrown upon the case, it is neither wholesome nor pleasant to consider. Reduced to its simplest elements, it is an instance whereby the unsupported statement of a white woman linked with bitter prejudice is sufficient to condemn a black man to the death penalty. From a legal point of view it contradicts every principle of administering justice in criminal cases. From a social point of view, the case is an example by which race hatred and ill will is fostered and fomented. It appears that officers of the law and officers of the court closed their eyes to principles of fair-play and simple justice in order to conform to concepts of race hatred. Hence a challenge exists to all fair-minded citizens of the Commonwealth of Kentucky and American citizens in general to voice a protest against this manner of administering justice. All that could be requested for Montjoy is a new trial where he would be afforded the opportunity of a hearing of all the facts, free from rancor, passion and prejudice. That is the least that should be required of the courts which are the instruments of the people and exist to preserve to every man equal, fair, and unprejudiced justice.[24]

In the continuation of another trend from the nineteenth century, hostile whites packed the courtrooms as Afro-Americans were sentenced to death for the murder of whites. Even in cases with circumstantial evidence or facts suggesting that Afro-Americans had acted in self-defense, they stood little chance of winning acquittal from all-white juries.

On July 26, 1906, Martha Broughton was murdered in Knox County. Suspicion centered on her black domestic servant, Annie Henson, and Henson's male companion, Jesse Fitzgerald. Robbery was thought to be the motive. No solid evidence could be found linking them to the woman's death; but Barbourville officials concluded that the black couple had the opportunity, and Fitzgerald had been linked with the

24. Brite, "The Case of John Montjoy," 3.

deaths of two white women in Alabama, though this allegation proved to be false. While in jail awaiting their indictment from the grand jury, the two were almost lynched by a mob. After having Henson and Fitzgerald secluded in jail in another community, authorities made plans for the trial. The governor sent two companies of state troops and a Gatling gun to ensure that the mob would not interfere with the court proceedings. But as the *Courier-Journal* candidly stated, "No effort is expected to be made to lynch the negroes if speedy trials are given." The paper failed to mention the obvious, that the speedy trials would certainly result in guilty convictions and death sentences.[25]

Fitzgerald and Henson were brought back to Barbourville on the evening of August 9. After being taken off the train, they were hand-cuffed and placed in the center of the 120 troops and marched to jail. A large, angry crowd jeered them every step of the way and were held back from attacking the Afro-Americans only by the troops' sharp bayonets. The next morning, the defendants appeared in the packed courtroom. Indeed, at the start of the trial each morning, people rushed madly to secure one of the six hundred seats. Once these seats were taken, the remaining people were forced to stand outside. Only after Fitzgerald and Henson were seated in court did the judge select two well-known attorneys, F. D. Simpson and James M. Gilbert, to represent them. Despite being community leaders, both lawyers feared the mob. "These attorneys stated they would not have taken the case for any money consideration, but being appointed to defend the prisoners, they would devote every energy to the cases and defend the negroes as they would anyone else." Both lawyers asked for a delay to have sufficient time to prepare a defense. The judge agreed, saying that the trial would begin three and a half hours later, after lunch. The attorneys also asked for a change of venue, a request denied by the judge.

However, for unexplained reasons, several changes took place right before the start of the trial. The court granted a two-day delay and decided to try the defendants separately. And in a move that suggested that Fitzgerald and Henson could not receive a fair trial from the citi-

25. Extensive coverage of the trials can be found in the Lexington *Herald*, August 1–20, 1906, and the Louisville *Courier-Journal* for the same dates; quotations in the next three paragraphs come from these sources. The quote here comes from the *Courier-Journal*, August 3, 1906.

zens of Knox County and Barbourville, the court brought in jurors from Whitley County to hear both cases. The state tried Fitzgerald first. A surprise witness against him turned out to be the jailer of Stanford, where Fitzgerald had been taken to avoid the mob. (It is interesting how often white jailers testified that blacks had willingly confessed to them, pouring out all of the details of their crimes.) According to jailer W. J. Herring, Fitzgerald had gone to the Broughton home to see Henson. While talking with the woman, Fitzgerald had been ordered by Broughton to leave. "This made him angry and he returned later in the night, forced an entry, got into the woman's room where she was asleep and plunged his knife into her throat. He then stole $36 and fled." Fitzgerald's lawyers, who had already expressed their displeasure at being chosen as his counsel, made no case for the black man, directing only a few questions to the various witnesses for the state and putting only two witnesses for the defense on the stand. After deliberating for less than an hour, the jury handed down the death sentence. The Lexington reporter was surprised by Fitzgerald's lack of concern about the verdict: "He seems indifferent to his fate. He spent today tying small nooses from twine which the soldiers gave him and handed them out as souvenirs. He does not seem to realize the enormity of his crime."

The court started the second trial immediately. Throughout the proceedings, the prosecution failed to produce any evidence showing that Annie Henson had assisted Fitzgerald in the crime. Nevertheless, the county attorney asked for the death penalty. After more than twelve hours of deliberation, the jury found Henson guilty but sentenced her to fifteen years in prison instead of to the gallows. Described as a "light verdict" by the newspaper, the decision almost led to her lynching by the mob. Although the execution was initially scheduled for exactly thirty days after Fitzgerald's conviction, the death sentence was delayed several times. As far as can be determined, his conviction was not reviewed by the state's highest court. He died on the gallows February 15, 1907.

In their attempt to appease the mob, Lebanon officials conducted a murder trial in May, 1911, within a matter of days after the crime had been committed. Police officer John A. Robey ventured into the black community to end a disturbance around 2:00 A.M. on Sunday, May 8. Later, his body was found, and the medical report showed that he had been stabbed nineteen times. After questioning all of the residents in the neighborhood where Robey died, the police began a search for two black teenagers, Jessie Smith and James Buckner. That same morning, the city council held an emergency meeting and offered a $200 reward for their arrests. By evening, the suspects had been captured, and the police found Robey's .45 Colt on Buckner.[26]

The police rushed the two youths to Louisville, where they remained for only a few days. Back in Lebanon, events moved quickly; the county prosecutor and court officials agreed to start the trial on Saturday, May 13, only five days after the murder of the policeman. They could not have selected a worse day for the trial if they wanted to avoid violence: People were off from work, and Lebanon would be crowded with Marion County residents in town on business. Buckner and Smith were returned as scheduled with the customary group of heavily armed guards protecting them. As had become common whenever a murder or rape trial took place, every seat in the courtroom was taken, and more than a thousand people, under the watchful eye of the troops, hovered outside the courthouse. Expressing sympathy for the white crowd, a reporter explained that the people were threatening "only in that they demanded a life for a life." Before the trial started, the judge, the sheriff, and the county attorney openly expressed their fears of a riot if the jury failed to return verdicts of first degree murder and death sentences. The four attorneys appointed by the court to defend the black youths asked to be excused. After their requests were denied, one lawyer expressed his distaste for the assignment. Buckner was tried first, since the police believed that he had committed the stabbings. Although it was late in the afternoon before the jury, made up of farmers and townspeople, had been selected, the trial began at once and ended quickly. When the jury retired to deliberate, the mob made rumblings that suggested an attempt on Buckner's life might occur, but the threat quickly ended when the jury returned after less than five minutes. The jury, of course, sentenced him to death. "When the news was spread through the crowd there was a mighty grunt of satisfaction—that and nothing more." By now dark-

26. The Louisville *Courier-Journal*, which prided itself on being a state newspaper, gave extensive coverage to the entire case. See the paper from May 8–15, 1911, for the information and quotations in this and the following paragraph. Unfortunately, no paper from Lebanon or Marion County could be found.

ness had come, and the court decided to postpone Smith's trial until Monday, to the obvious displeasure of many in the crowd who would be unable to attend. In the second trial, the only clear point established by the prosecution was that Smith and Buckner were close friends. Although he had probably witnessed the stabbing of Robey, Smith had not, as it had been contended, assisted Buckner in any manner. Nevertheless, his jury deliberated for thirty minutes before finding him guilty of voluntary manslaughter and handing down a sentence of twenty-one years in prison.

Buckner became the first person to die in the electric chair in Eddyville. Aware of the public's continued interest in how condemned men would die, the *Courier-Journal* sent a reporter to give all of the details on how the execution would happen: "The first shock to be administered to the victim will last ten seconds and will consist of 1,700 volts; the second shock will be a repetition with 300 voltage added, and the third and last shock will convey the full voltage power of the apparatus." At sunrise on July 8, 1911, two months after his conviction of murder, Buckner died. A black teenager had become the first victim of the electric chair, and as the paper pointed out, the next two people scheduled to die were also blacks. Indeed, of the seven men put to death in 1911, all were Afro-Americans.[27]

A case similar in some respects to the events in Lebanon occurred in Paducah several years later. Like Lebanon, Paducah had been visited by racial violence: Two blacks had been lynched in October, 1916, and whites were angry about what they perceived as the militant response by blacks to the incident. While attempting to arrest several men outside of a club in the black community, policeman Will F. Romaine was shot and killed with his own gun in August, 1917. After conducting a thorough search of the neighborhood and making dozens of arrests, the police named Jim Howard, "a bad type of negro," and his friend Harry Porter as their leading suspects. Reputedly, Howard had a grudge against the officer for having given him a speeding ticket in his automobile. In hopes of avoiding further racial violence, Paducah's black teachers, physicians, and business-

27. *Ibid.*, July 7–9, 1911; in the Governor Willson Papers, see "Respite of James Buckner sentenced to be electrocuted on the 9th day of June, 1911, respited unto the 8th day of July, 1911" and "Men Electrocuted In Kentucky Since the Electric Chair was Installed at the Kentucky State Penitentiary at Eddyville, Kentucky in 1911."

men passed a resolution to show the white community that they, too, stood for law and order and the punishment of criminals. Black employees of the Illinois Central Railway expressed, in a resolution, their regret over the officer's death and offered their assistance in bringing to justice the blacks responsible. Howard and Porter remained at large for almost six weeks before their capture on a train in Maysville in northern Kentucky. Within a week, Paducah authorities had returned the men to stand trial, refusing their request for a change of venue, despite all of the violence that had happened in the area. The trial of the two men was quick; the jury was out for less than two hours. Howard, accused of pulling the trigger, was given the death sentence, and Porter, his accomplice, received a life sentence. After delays for more than a year, Howard died in Eddyville on June 6, 1919.[28]

Very little change occurred over the next two decades. Blacks on trial for the murder of whites still had to be escorted by heavily armed guardsmen; whites still flocked to see the "event" and let it be known that if the jury did not have the stomach to fully punish the accused blacks, they would. Three blacks were tried for murder in Elizabethtown on April 28, 1931, in a courtroom filled, as usual, with hostile whites. They had been arrested for the murder of a white farmer during a crime spree through Illinois, Indiana, and Kentucky. Much of the mob's anger was directed toward one of the defendants, Walter Dewberry, because he chose C. Eubank Tucker, a black civil rights activist from Louisville, as counsel instead of one of the white attorneys appointed by the court. During the court's recess for lunch, Tucker was physically attacked by a group of white men; one of the assailants struck him repeatedly in the face with brass knuckles. Several guardsmen took Tucker to a doctor and then back to the courthouse and remained with him for the duration of the trial. Upon returning to court, Tucker "filed a change of venue upon the grounds that no justice could be given in a Court where the State Militia was needed to guard the prisoners and where the defense attorney narrowly escaped death at the hands of an angry mob." The judge ignored the request and ordered the trial to continue. The all-white jury found Tucker's client guilty of murder after deliberating for thirteen minutes. Charles Rodgers and Walter Holmes also received the death penalty.

28. *Jim Howard and Harry Porter* v. *Commonwealth*, 178 Kentucky Reports, 844–48 (1918); Paducah *News-Democrat*, August 12–15, September 26, 1917.

As had become routine, appeals and delays lasted for almost a year, but eventually the three men died in the electric chair: Rodgers and Holmes on April 29, 1932, and Dewberry almost eighteen months later on November 10, 1933.[29]

Given how easily many blacks were convicted of murder and sentenced to death or to long prison terms, it is surprising to discover that on several occasions they succeeded in challenging their convictions or in having their sentences commuted by the governor. Several such cases occurred in Lexington in the first decade of the 1900s. On Sunday, November 20, 1904, a fight occurred in a saloon between a group of whites and three blacks, John Taylor, Ed Taylor, and James Garfield Smith. During the struggle, a pistol was fired three or four times; one of the shots proved fatal to William Moore, a white man. In the chaos immediately after the shooting, most of the whites left the saloon, including the man the blacks said was responsible for the incident. The police, upon arriving, arrested the three blacks and charged them with murder. Although tried separately, each man received a death sentence. One of the jurors in the trial of James Garfield Smith told a reporter that "a verdict could have been reached without the jury leaving their seats." The attorney for John Taylor had asked the court to overturn the indictment on the ground that "the jury commissioners had discriminated against negroes in their selection of names from which the grand jury was drawn."[30]

The Kentucky Court of Appeals overturned the death sentences and ordered new trials. But in doing so, the court refused comment on the failure of the judge to grant a change of venue or on the continued exclusion of Afro-Americans from the jury selection process. Instead, the justices said that errors had been made in how the men were

29. The account of Tucker's beating comes from the Louisville *Leader,* May 2, 9, 1931. When calling upon the state's highest court to uphold the death sentence of Dewberry, the prosecutor said that Tucker had not requested a delay or a change of venue because he had been attacked by a mob, a view substantiated by the judge. When making its ruling, the Kentucky Court of Appeals said that the statements made by the whites, and not those of the Negro lawyer, were correct. The appeals for the three men were heard separately by the court but decided on the same day. See 241 Kentucky Reports (1931) for *Holmes* v. *Commonwealth,* 573–87, *Rogers* v. *Commonwealth,* 593–94, and *Dewberry* v. *Commonwealth,* 726–38.

30. Lexington *Herald,* November 22–December 4, 1904, and for all of January and February, 1905; at the Kentucky Department for Libraries and Archives, see *Fayette County Circuit Court Judge Criminal Dockets, 1899–1905* (December 14, 1904), 506.

charged. First of all, the prosecutor, unable to determine which man had allegedly fired the gun, had charged all three with murder. Then the judge, by instructing the jurors to consider whether or not the men had been involved in a conspiracy to murder William Moore, had also erred: "This instruction was an invitation to the jury to give free rein to their imagination or suspicion, and to convict the defendant of a conspiracy with parties whose names the grand jury did not know, and which the evidence failed to disclose to the court." Finally, the judge failed to instruct the jury that Moore might have been killed by accident.[31]

To avoid the charge that the men could not receive a fair trial in Fayette County, the circuit court ordered that a jury be selected from Woodford County for the retrials in June, 1906. Also, in an attempt to comply with the ruling of the appellate court, the prosecution charged each defendant with complicity, not conspiracy, in the death of William Moore. The all-white jury found the men guilty and sentenced them to life in prison, probably the harshest punishment the Kentucky Court of Appeals would have allowed in the case. On several occasions, Republican governor Willson proved sympathetic to Afro-Americans convicted in controversial cases and commuted their sentences. Whether he did so in this case is unknown, but clearly the three men had avoided the gallows.[32]

Another shooting occurred in a Lexington saloon just before the start of the second trial of the three men. The account published in a Lexington white newspaper said that Aaron McCabe, "crazed by whisky and bent on wreaking vengeance against members of the white race, for whom he is alleged to have had an intense hatred," went into the saloon and for no reason shot and killed the barkeeper, Martin Clark. After being arrested, however, McCabe gave a different

31. *John Taylor* v. *Commonwealth*, 90 Southwestern Reporter, 581–84 (1906); see also *Ed Taylor* v. *Commonwealth*, 90 Southwestern Reporter, 584–85 (1906). Two months later in another case, *Smith* v. *Commonwealth*, the Kentucky Court of Appeals addressed the issue of blacks being excluded from the jury. A black man convicted of murder in Hardin County and sentenced to death stated that the jury commissioners failed to select blacks even though they accounted for 20 percent of the voters in the county. The court made the usual ruling, that the absence of blacks did not mean that racial discrimination had occurred. See *Smith* v. *Commonwealth*, 91 Southwestern Reporter 742 (1906).

32. Lexington *Herald*, April 30, June 14, 15, 1906.

version. Upon entering the saloon, he had ordered a drink of a "good whisky." After finishing the drink, McCabe asked how much he owed for the drink, and the bartender said fifteen cents. McCabe then challenged the white man, saying that it was a whisky of poor quality, worth no more than a dime. McCabe's bold words led to a confrontation, and the bartender warned him to "pay me fifteen cents or I'll kill you, and I saw him reach for his revolver. After he fired two shots at me I shot at him." In court, one of the whites testifying for the state did admit that Clark fired first and fired several additional shots before dying. Nevertheless, McCabe's all-white jury quickly gave him the death sentence. The case was appealed and a new trial was ordered. Several months later, McCabe was found guilty again but this time was given a life sentence. Like the other Lexington blacks, he, too, had avoided a legal execution. But his case had a tragic ending. While awaiting transfer to state prison, McCabe, according to the version released by the police and other officials, strangled himself to death in his jail cell.[33]

In rural Fayette County on June 29, 1907, Robert Hocker killed Newton D. Veal, a white farmer, after an argument over wages. Hocker's death penalty was upheld by the Kentucky Court of Appeals. At the last moment, with the gallows already erected and Hocker transported to Lexington for execution, Governor Willson commuted the sentence to life in prison. In explaining his decision, the governor expressed a strong disbelief in the story told by whites in court; almost all of their testimony for the prosecution had been contradictory. No doubt Hocker had shot Veal to death, Willson explained, but no motive for the shooting had been established in court. Perhaps, in the final analysis, Willson commuted the black farm laborer's death sentence because of a sincere belief that "all lawyers realize that there is often a lack of the great care in the trial of [Negroes] which a high-minded fulfillment of the solemn duty should secure, especially in cases where they kill white men."[34]

33. *Ibid.*, April 30, July 6–9, October 13, 1906; for mention of McCabe's death, see *ibid.*, December 3, 1908.

34. Concerning the actions of Willson in commuting sentences, see various newspaper clippings in the Willson Collection; *Hocker* v. *Commonwealth*, 111 Southwestern Reporter, 676–81 (1908); see the Lexington daily newspapers from December 1–10, 1908. Especially see the *Herald*, December 6, for a statement by the governor and for comments by the newspaper saying that too many murderers had escaped the

These same years witnessed another court case involving a black farm laborer charged with the murder of a white landowner. Rufus Browder shot and killed James Cunningham on July 13, 1908, in Logan County, an act that led to the tragic lynching of four innocent black youths. In August, the grand jury indicted Browder for murder. After being turned down by attorneys in Russellville and in Logan County, Browder finally secured the services of James C. Sims, a prominent lawyer from Bowling Green. Sims had been involved in controversial cases before, having served as one of the attorneys for Bob Harper, the innocent black youth charged with rape who died at the hands of a lynch mob in Bowling Green in 1892. Determined to save his client's life instead of just going through the motions, Sims argued for a change of venue, which the judge denied, and exhausted his preemptive challenges before a jury was selected. Surprisingly, the trial ended in a hung jury: Nine jurors voted for the death penalty; two, for a life sentence; and one, for twenty-one years in prison.[35]

Browder's second trial took place in February, 1909. Logan County whites again flocked to the courtroom but were visibly upset that many blacks attended the trial as well. This time the jury agreed on the death sentence for Browder, setting April 16 as the date. In the eyes of the jury, the most damaging evidence against the black man was the testimony of Cunningham's widow, who stated that Browder had fired first. Russellville's correspondent for the *Courier-Journal* said that Browder had received a fair trial at the hands of the all-white jury: "Comment is universal here upon the dignity, quietness and deliberation that marked the trial." In finding Browder guilty, the jury had demonstrated no racial prejudices. "There was a saneness, calmness pervading the trial that the law-abiding element here point to as indicating a better future in the criminal element of Logan County."[36]

Irene Cunningham's statement that she saw Browder shoot her husband is highly questionable. A coroner's inquest was held at the Cunningham home immediately after the shooting. Justice of the peace J. W. Riley, a neighbor of Cunningham's, presided over the hearing and took extensive notes on the testimony of the widow. Upon

---

gallows in Lexington. The Harrodsburg *Democrat*, December 8, 1908, was outraged by Willson's decision to commute Hocker's death sentence.

35. Louisville *Courier-Journal*, October 6-8, 1908.

36. *Ibid.*, February 9, 12, 1909.

the conclusion of the inquest, Riley returned home, recopied his notes, and mailed a formal report of the incident to the office of the circuit court clerk. In his report, Riley quoted Irene Cunningham as saying that she did not witness the beginning of the trouble between her husband and Browder, that she arrived at the door only after the first shot had been fired. Yet at the trial, the following exchange took place between attorney Sims and Mrs. Cunningham:

Q. Did you or not in your testimony at that time before the coroner's jury make the statement in substance or form of words, that you did not see the beginning of the trouble—knew that James Cunningham had gone to buggy house to put buggy in it, heard a pistol fire, run to the door, saw Jim Cunningham fall to his knees and throw one hand to his breast, saw him pull pistol from his pocket while on his knees and fire at Rufus—Rufus run off by the time I got there and Jim Cunningham had fallen on face, saw he was dying, and run back to the telephone and called for doctor, and thought I heard four shots fired?
A. I did not.
Q. Didn't make that either in form of words or substance?
A. I did not.

Later in the trial, attorney John B. Rodes, who assisted Sims in the defense of Browder, questioned Riley about Mrs. Cunningham's statement during the inquest.

Q. I will get you to state whether or not she said on that occasion at that coroner's inquest, in substance, that she did not see the beginning of the trouble, knew that Jas. Cunningham had gone to buggy house to put buggy in it—heard a pistol fire and ran to the door?
A. That is my best recollection now.[37]

When ruling on Browder's case, the Kentucky Court of Appeals first addressed the question of the lower court's refusal of the defense request for a change of venue. Under Kentucky law, the court declared, "when it appears that the defendant can not have a fair trial in the county where the prosecution is pending, the judge shall . . . order the trial to be held in the most convenient county in which a fair trial can be had." The motion for the change of venue had been filed on August 1, the day after the four young men had been killed and after

37. *Commonwealth of Kentucky* v. *Rufus Browder,* Logan Circuit Court (1909). A complete copy of the transcript of the case can be found in the Governor Willson Papers.

whites had threatened violence on the entire black community of Russellville. Furthermore, the court noted with dismay, at the start of Browder's trial, the two men who had signed the affidavits for moving the trial had been told by the mob, "We will get you next." The justices pointed out that the existence of racial prejudice led to the indictment and conviction of Browder. Usually when overturning the convictions of Afro-Americans, members of the Kentucky Court of Appeals failed to comment on, or acknowledge the pervasiveness of, racial discrimination in the state. But in a most significant statement in the Browder decision, one that clearly applies to numerous other convictions of Afro-Americans, the court clearly discussed the issue:

> If the defendant had killed a negro, or if he were a white man, and had killed a white man, we might look at the case differently; but we can not shut our eyes to the fact that here was a case of race prejudice excited to the white heat. A prominent white man had been shot by a negro laborer working for him. The mob wished to execute the negro summarily the night he was placed in jail. Being balked in that attempt, . . . they wreaked their vengeance on four innocent negroes whose only offense was that they were friends of his. . . . To say the defendant could have a fair trial in Russellville under such circumstances is to shut our eyes to the conditions which must have prevailed when such things as we have detailed took place.

The justices firmly believed that Browder could not receive a fair trial in Russellville. They pointed out that all of the members of the local bar, fearing the wrath of their fellow citizens, had staunchly refused to take part in the defense of the black man. An indication that racial prejudice existed was the total rejection by the judge and prosecutor of the defendant's plea that he shot in self-defense; they ignored his life as an exemplary citizen with no criminal record. The court ended with a telling point: "When the public mind is excited by race hostility the feeling may smolder, but though not apparent on the surface, it does not soon die out, on the contrary often the sentiment spreads and strengthens."[38]

Rufus Browder was tried once again, this time in Franklin, Simpson County. He was found guilty and sentenced to life imprisonment. Browder arrived in state prison in July, 1910. Almost immediately, a number of black citizens from Logan County sent petitions to Willson,

38. *Browder* v. *Commonwealth*, 136 Kentucky Reports, 45–54 (1909).

urging him to release Browder from prison. Hoping that the bitter feelings generated by Cunningham's death and the lynchings of the four youths would ease in time, Willson refused to make any ruling on Browder's case for a year. In the fall of 1911, however, he informed the residents of Logan County of his intention to review Browder's conviction. Numerous letters, both for and against pardoning Browder, were sent to the governor. Many whites, referring to themselves as leading citizens, called for the release of Browder. After a thorough review of the case, Governor Willson informed Sims, a man he greatly respected, of his dilemma: "I am not able to reach a conclusion to the exclusion of a doubt that the verdict and judgment in Rufus Browder's case is wrong." Sims responded immediately: "This being true ought you not resolve that doubt in behalf of Browder, which seems to be the rule in all criminal proceedings? Can you not see your way clear to commute his sentence from life to 10 years, which would be ample punishment even if the recrod [sic] shows that he is guilty of voluntary manslaughter." Willson agreed, and two days later he informed the public of his decision to "commute the sentence to a sentence of ten years in the penitentiary with the usual allowance for good time." Ultimately, Rufus Browder, who was twenty years old when arrested for killing James Cunningham, was never released from prison. In a letter written more than three decades after the governor reduced the sentence from life to ten years, attorney Rodes explained that Browder had died of unknown causes during his seventh year of incarceration.[39]

In view of the many legal lynchings that occurred in the Bluegrass State, Browder's being sent to prison was a victory of sorts. Yet after the strong statements made by the justices of the Kentucky Court of Appeals, it must have been surprising to him and his attorneys that he was made to stand trial again. The court had clearly said that Browder had not received a fair trial and had left the implication that it would be difficult for any black charged with such an offense to have a fair hearing from an all-white jury. To be sure, Governor Willson reduced the sentence, but this seemed like a token gesture

39. Willson to James C. Sims, December 5, 1911, Sims to Willson, December 7, 1911, the governor's official statement concerning the pardon, dated December 9, 1911, and dozens of other letters concerning whether or not a pardon should be granted, can be found in the Governor Willson Papers. See the letter from Rodes to Mary Helm, July 29, 1944, in Rodes Manuscript.

when considering the clear fact that Browder had defended himself. That he died without ever regaining his freedom concluded the tragedy; indeed, being in jail might have hastened his demise.

As mentioned previously, in 1908, the very same year that Browder killed Cunningham, a shootout in Dixon resulted in the death of one white and the arrest of eleven blacks. The men were charged in the usual court setting that included whites demanding "justice." With the prosecution unable to determine who had fired the fatal shots, the jury gave each defendant a "light sentence" of seven years in prison for participating in the "race riot." On November 23, 1910, after the eleven men had spent almost a year and a half in jail, Governor Willson acted favorably on their petitions for pardons and released the men from prison.[40] "It is a sorrow to every man who honors and loves Kentucky that such a story as this could be true." That Jacob McDowell, the father of one of the men sent to prison, was lynched after his son and the other black men had been arrested, proved, in the eyes of the governor, that the men were justified in making plans to guard the jailhouse. Contrary to the accounts published in white newspapers, Willson explained, the white man killed and the one seriously injured were not just "traveling along" but were members of the lynch mob, making them guilty of a felony when shot. "No person in this mob is entitled to any sympathy or consideration. On the contrary, every person in it was guilty of a felony and ought to be in the penitentiary." Instead, the honest, hardworking black men "who had gone to Dixon on a call of humanity . . . were indicted and sent to the penitentiary." When considering that the men were tried in a hostile environment, the "light sentence," the governor noted, indicated that the men were innocent. "If they had been guilty as charged the verdict would have been death or imprisonment for life." Willson

40. The Governor Willson Papers contains considerable information relating to the eleven black men and their requests for pardons. See their Prisoner's Records, which in every case described them as ideal inmates. Numerous Webster County whites wrote favorable letters on their behalf. W. J. Nisbet, the president of Providence Mining Company, informed the governor that one of the young men had been an excellent employee: "If you could conscientuously [sic] release this boy I will grately [sic] appreciate the favor[.] I will furnish him clothes and transportation from prison and will give him a good job[,] and I will assure you [that he] will not be caught out in bad company again." Nisbet to Willson, July 27, 1910. See the letter from C. W. Bennett, Webster County prosecuting attorney, to Willson, December 26, 1908, with the names of seventy-seven people opposing the pardons, also in Governor Willson Papers.

commented on the number of blacks who had been sentenced to prison by all-white juries for doing nothing more than protecting themselves and their families from white aggression. At one point he said, "All men of ordinary sense know that negroes do not band together in such a county as this to mob white men."[41]

These five cases, from the murder trial of the three Lexington blacks in 1905 through that of the Webster County blacks for "rioting," resulted in total or partial court victories for Afro-Americans accused of killing whites. Clearly the actions of Governor Willson challenging the verdicts of all-white juries had been influential. The Kentucky Court of Appeals had also played a significant role, overturning death sentences and ordering trials moved from the communities where the shootings had occurred. Yet Kentucky blacks still had reason to be concerned that the legal system discriminated against them, for these same years, as well as the next two decades, witnessed a succession of Afro-Americans found guilty by all-white juries in front of hostile white mobs. Also, a great majority of blacks on trial in small towns experienced quick trials in which they were denied the opportunity to confer with counsel or to locate potential defense witnesses. Two significant cases, the first in 1918 and the other two decades later, challenged the practice of having speedy trials for blacks and the continued exclusion of blacks from juries.

Although ignoring the issue when reviewing the numerous convictions of blacks in the past, the justices of the Kentucky Court of Appeals, in the case of a black teenager, finally addressed the repeated instances of hasty trials for Afro-Americans. On April 22, 1918, Bradley McDaniel shot and killed Dee Spears in the small community of Smith's Grove, Warren County. Local authorities carried the youth to Louisville for safekeeping after a mob attempted without success to spring him from the jail. They would try again, one member of the mob candidly told law officers, because Mrs. Spears had pleaded with them to "bring that negro back with you and hang him in front of my window, so that I can witness his death." On Sunday night, May 12, the black youth was taken to Bowling Green to stand trial. Believing as usual that a black shooting a white was an "open

---

41. The governor's official statement concerning the pardon is a three-page untitled letter dated November 23, 1910, in Governor Willson Papers; Louisville *Courier-Journal*, July 21, 1908, November 26, 1910; Madisonville *Hustler*, April 24, July 21, 1908; *Crisis*, I (February, 1911), 6.

and shut case," officials had McDaniel indicted by the grand jury, put on trial, found guilty, and sentenced to death—all on Tuesday.[42]

The Kentucky Court of Appeals issued a detailed opinion of the case on October 29, 1918. Without a doubt, the justices explained, McDaniel had shot the white man, but the evidence was not clear about whether or not Dee Spears was charging McDaniel with a large piece of lumber when he was shot and killed. Regardless, they noted, "we have reached the conclusion that the judgment appealed from should be reversed and the defendant granted a new trial, and this, upon the sole ground that his motion for a continuance should have been sustained." Clearly, the lower court had erred (the justices called it "a prejudicial error") when compelling the black youth to go on trial the very same day that the murder indictment had been returned.

The court of appeals next condemned the whites of Warren County for the procedures involved in the "trial" of McDaniel. In the eyes of the justices, the mob—not the authorities—had controlled events in Bowling Green. That the black youth received the death sentence was no surprise; the mob had "presented a petition to the county attorney demanding that the defendant be placed upon trial immediately at a special term of the court, and unless he was given the death sentence they would take the law into their own hands and see that he was executed." The justices agreed with the defense attorney's contention that at the start of the trial the courtroom was crowded with mob members who had attempted to lynch McDaniel and that at least six of these men were placed on the jury.

The defense counsel has an important responsibility when his client faces the death penalty, the court explained. Therefore, regardless of how brilliant or experienced an attorney might be, he needs sufficient time to prepare an adequate defense. Toward the end of their ruling, the justices emphasized that for the sake of public confidence, trials should be held without unnecessary delays. They stressed this point, however: "Notwithstanding the clamor for speedy trials, we believe that trials may be too speedy, and thus do more harm than good to the body politic by lessening in place of increasing respect for law." The outcome of McDaniel's new trial resulted in another guilty

---

42. *McDaniel* v. *Commonwealth*, 181 Kentucky Reports, 766–81 (1918). Quotations in following paragraphs are taken from this source.

verdict and a death sentence. Although a final ruling on the case is unknown, the black youth avoided death in Kentucky's electric chair. In all likelihood, the governor commuted the sentence to life in prison. Even this, of course, can be viewed as a form of legal lynching, considering that the killing of Dee Spears was probably done in self-defense.[43]

A challenge to the continued exclusion of blacks from juries was made in a case in Paducah, and when it was rejected by the Kentucky Court of Appeals, it was carried to the United States Supreme Court. On the night of August 18, 1935, W. R. Toon, white, was found in the black community slumped over in his car. He had been stabbed three times, and he died two hours later in the hospital. The police investigation revealed that Toon had been driving through the community, probably trying to pick up black women, and had twice unsuccessfully approached Eugenia Hale. Several people came forward and mentioned that they had seen Joe Hale, the brother of Eugenia, go near Toon's car. And Eugenia made a damaging statement to the police that tied her brother to the murder. When he returned to the house after talking with Toon, she asked him what had happened, and he said, "That man went up on Ohio Street and parked in the dark and I gigged him a time or two and told him to quit stopping these colored girls." She then pointedly asked if he had hurt the white man, and he replied, "No, I just gigged him a little."[44]

With the assistance of the NAACP, Hale's attorneys argued for a change of venue and also asked that the indictment be thrown out because blacks had been excluded from both the grand and petit jury pools. In support of their motions, the attorneys submitted materials showing that 8,000 of the county's 48,000 citizens were black and that at least 700 of these blacks were eligible for jury duty under the laws of Kentucky. Nevertheless, of the almost 600 people selected by the jury commissioners for jury service in 1936, none had been Afro-Americans. To show that the exclusion of blacks in 1936 was a typical practice, an affidavit was submitted showing that blacks had not

43. Warren County Circuit Court Order Book (January Term, 1919), 385, in Kentucky Department for Libraries and Archives. Unfortunately, no Bowling Green newspaper could be located for the period from October, 1918, through January, 1919.

44. A full account of the case can be found in *Hale* v. *Commonwealth*, 269 Kentucky Reports, 743–52 (1937), and *Hale* v. *Commonwealth* 108 Southwestern Reporter, 2nd Series, 716–20 (1937).

served on juries in McCracken County since 1906. (The attorneys would have argued that the practice had gone on even longer but they lacked the evidence to document previous years.) In short, Hale's lawyers argued that "a long continued, unvarying and wholesale exclusion of Negroes from jury service in this County on account of their race and color" had occurred. Ignoring the well-documented evidence, the judge refused to drop the charges against Hale and denied his request for a change of venue. The all-white jury found Hale guilty of murder and handed down the death sentence.

In its June, 1937, ruling, the Kentucky Court of Appeals agreed that no blacks had served on juries in McCracken County; yet it said that Hale's attorneys had presented no evidence that showed a systematic exclusion of blacks because of their race. Relying on legal jargon to dismiss Hale's contention that discrimination against blacks had taken place over the years in the county, the justices noted, "We therefore have a case where the proof might be regarded as sufficient to sustain the ground upon which the motion was evidently made, but there is wanting in the record a sufficient statement of those grounds to permit the introduction of that proof." Carrying their argument further, the justices concluded, "The failure so pointed out is analogous . . . to a case where there is proof without pleading, and the rule is that 'pleading' without proof or proof without pleading are each unavailable." In the view of the members of Kentucky's highest court, the McCracken County court had acted properly in overruling the motions to stop the indictment and to discharge the jury panel.[45]

Charles H. Houston of the national NAACP office argued Hale's case before the United States Supreme Court on March 29, 1938. The prominent black attorney was confident of winning because the case was similar to one from Oklahoma that had been decided three years earlier. Hale's Kentucky lawyers had done such a thorough job of investigating the exclusion of blacks from juries in McCracken County that Houston merely presented their data and added a few remarks concerning court decisions about blacks and the jury process. Almost two weeks later, the court announced its unanimous decision. In an extremely short, three-page opinion, the Supreme Court said, "We are of the opinion that the affidavits, which by the stipulation of the State

45. *Hale* v. *Commonwealth*, 748, 752.

were to be taken as proof, and were uncontroverted, sufficed to show a systematic and arbitary exclusion of Negroes from the jury lists solely because of their race or color, constituting a denial of the equal protection of the laws guaranteed to petitioner by the Fourteenth Amendment." The court ordered a new trial for Hale.[46]

In response to the Supreme Court's ruling, the commonwealth attorney said that blacks would serve on the jury at Hale's next trial. Exactly one year later, Hale pleaded guilty to murder and was given a life sentence by the jury that contained several Afro-Americans. The ruling by the Supreme Court led to blacks serving on juries elsewhere in the state. By the end of 1939, blacks in Lexington and Louisville were being empanelled on grand and petit juries. And by the mid-1940s, the names of blacks were included within the pool of jurors in most of the smaller counties in Kentucky.[47]

Although black leaders proclaimed *Hale* v. *Kentucky* an important victory, the case did not ensure that blacks would receive equal treatment in court. Just as it is extremely difficult to prove in every instance when a legal lynching occurred, it is likewise difficult to prove when and if race quit being a factor in the conviction of black defendants. Also, it must be remembered that the Supreme Court ruled that blacks had to be included in the pool of potential jurors; the court did not rule that the absence of blacks from a particular jury— even when a black was the defendant—meant that discrimination had obviously occurred. Many Kentucky blacks would still be convicted of murder or rape and sentenced to death by all-white juries. Of the twenty-four men put to death between 1940 and 1962, fifteen were Afro-American. Since 1940, no whites have been executed for rape, while five blacks have died in the electric chair for this offense. As far as can be determined, the fifteen blacks were sentenced to death by all-white juries, and no whites received death sentences for crimes against blacks. Since the Hale case, a new pattern of discrimination had become part of the legal system in the state: When a black is accused of petty crimes, blacks can serve on the jury; when a black commits rape or murder against a white, the jury will be all-white;

46. *Hale* v. *Kentucky*, 303 U.S., 613–15 (1938).

47. Paducah *Sun-Democrat*, April 12, 1938, ran the story about the court's decision on page 2; Louisville *Courier-Journal*, April 12, 1938; Louisville *Leader*, April 16, 1938, May 6, 1939, December 2, 1939; *Crisis*, XLV (May, 1938), 149.

and when a white is accused of a crime, the jury will be all-white, and this is especially true if the victim is black.[48] While there may have been progress in challenging the convictions of Afro-Americans sentenced to death, it is difficult to determine how much headway was made in the legal lynching of Afro-Americans for "lesser" crimes. Often in a matter-of-fact manner, the white newspapers documented the large number of blacks who were "doing time" in city and county jails or who were in jail awaiting the start of circuit court. Indeed, in white newspapers all over the state, blacks were mentioned most often when circuit court was in session. A story from Scottsville in July, 1905, reported that Myrtle Sanders, a black woman, had been charged with robbery and several counts of arson. In all, nine blacks had been arrested on a variety of charges. With circuit court ready to convene, the blacks would be given speedy trials to prevent further trouble in Scottsville, the reporter predicted. In Madisonville, a black woman was convicted of malicious cutting with intent to kill and sentenced to two years in prison. "This makes five negroes that have received penitentiary sentences, and the first week of court has just been finished." Willie Smith of Paducah was sent to prison for the murder of a black in 1927. His conviction, the local paper noted, "makes the third man to receive a penitentiary sentence since the court convened. All are negroes."[49]

In Kentucky and elsewhere, some offenses were viewed as "Negro crimes." Writing in 1910, Gilbert Stephenson pointed out how certain legal statutes, though not mentioning the Negro, "are thought by many to have peculiar application to him." In his view, Kentucky had passed a law directed at blacks in 1904. Popularly called the "chicken-thief law," the ordinance read, "That if any person shall steal chickens, turkeys, ducks, or other fowls of the value of two dollars, or more, he

<hr/>

48. For the most part, blacks have been excluded from jury duty despite the law mandating their inclusion in the pool of juries. On April 30, 1986, in *James Kirkland Batson* v. *Kentucky*, 106A U.S., 1712–45, the U.S. Supreme Court in a 7–2 decision "barred prosecutors from disqualifying potential jurors solely because of their race." This involved the case of James K. Batson of Louisville, who had been convicted of burglary by an all-white jury in Jefferson County Circuit Court. See the Louisville *Courier-Journal*, May 1, 1986.

49. Louisville *Courier-Journal*, July 1, 1905; Madisonville *Hustler*, February 11, 1908; Madisonville *Daily Messenger*, February 10, 1927. According to the Louisville *Leader*, blacks were not only sent to jail on far more occasions than were whites but

shall be confined in the penitentiary not less than one nor more than five years." Considering that early in this century defendants in most minor cases had no lawyers and that blacks were usually tried in very hostile environments, the chicken-thief law might have had an awful effect on them, especially in small isolated communities. In March, 1930, the American Civil Liberties Union wrote to Walter White about a Paris black being sentenced to life in prison for stealing six chickens. The circuit court justified such a harsh sentence by saying that the black man was a habitual criminal. The national office of the NAACP contacted William Scroggins, a black leader in Paris, and asked him to investigate the matter. His intervention proved beneficial. Within a week, the court set aside the verdict and ordered a new trial for the convicted black. He was then given four years in jail.[50]

Burglary was another criminal offense that whites associated with Afro-Americans. A burglary conviction always carried the possibility of a stiff prison sentence, and this became even more likely after the Kentucky legislature passed a statute in 1922 that said, "Every person guilty of burglary shall be punished with death or confinement in the penitentiary for life, in the discretion of the jury."[51] Two years later, Alex Gibson, age sixty-four, broke into the home of R. W. Thompson of Lexington. Upon being discovered in the house by Lucien Thompson, Gibson attempted to shoot him with a shotgun, but fortunately for Thompson the weapon was not loaded. In a struggle with Gibson, Thompson sustained several severe knife wounds; he was hospitalized for seven weeks. In court, the elderly black man confessed to entering the house, saying that he was hungry and wanted some food. He denied trying to shoot Thompson and claimed he had cut the white man in self-defense. The jury deliberated only an hour before handing down the death sentence. They gave Gibson the maximum sen-

---

also received higher fines. Robert Owsley, a "prominent Chauffeur," was fined three hundred dollars in Jefferson County Circuit Court for cutting a white man who had attacked him. He was fined, the paper stated, for being an "impudent Negro." See the *Leader,* January 25, 1930.

50. *Acts of the General Assembly, 1904* (Louisville, 1904), 47–48; Stephenson, *Race Distinction in American Law,* 275; ACLU to Walter White, March 13, 1930, White to William Scroggins, March 14, 1930, Scroggins to White, March 17, 1930, all in NAACP Papers.

51. *Acts of the General Assembly, 1922* (Frankfort, 1922), 48.

tence after learning that he had served two fifteen-year sentences for burglary.[52]

The Kentucky Court of Appeals concluded that a sentence of death was appropriate because burglars like Gibson were perhaps the most desperate men in society: "Nothing will prevent the consummation of their design, not even the necessity of taking human life. Indeed, the fact that Thompson is alive today, we firmly believe, is due to the fact that this gun was not loaded, or to the appellant's failure, in his stabbing of Thompson, to reach a vital spot." In the opinion of the justices, Kentucky's legislators had the right to make the conviction of burglary punishable by death. Shortly after the ruling by the state's highest court, members of the Lexington NAACP met with Governor William J. Fields, urging him to spare Gibson's life. Although appalled by Gibson's criminal career, the governor agreed to commute the sentence to life in prison.[53]

Believing that blacks were prone to criminal acts, white city fathers on occasion adopted measures that would have been totally unacceptable if they had been directed at whites. In the view of Henderson whites, blacks were responsible for a crime wave in 1915. Early in the year, a black teenager, identified on one occasion as James Blackwell and on another as Willie Blackburn, was arrested and charged with the theft of a gun and a suit of clothing. His crimes, which were not that uncommon, received coverage in the newspaper for several days. The paper also made much of the arrest of two black men who had been caught in bed with two white prostitutes. Ignoring the women, the court fined the black men fifty dollars each plus court costs and gave them one hour to leave town. Meanwhile, another black had been arrested and held over to the circuit court for the attempted rape of a seven-year-old white girl. On the heels of the alleged criminal assault came the account of two young white girls being followed for five blocks by an unidentified black man. "The negro's acts indicated that he was only waiting for the young ladies to separate." The young

52. *Gibson* v. *Commonwealth,* 204 Kentucky Reports, 748–65 (1924); New York *Times,* February 21, 1924.

53. *Gibson* v. *Commonwealth.* See the letter from the national office of the NAACP to Mrs. Lizzie B. Fouse, a member of the Lexington NAACP, February 25, 1924, Fouse to Walter White, April 10, 1925, A. A. Balitz, a Lexington attorney, to the Reverend J. T. Morrow, February 29, 1924, all in NAACP Papers.

women met a white man who agreed to walk with them, and the black man quickly left the scene. "The many lawless acts committed by negroes during the past few weeks," the paper reported, "have so enraged the whites and the better class of colored citizens, that something is likely to happen at any time."[54]

For the police, the tipping point occurred when George Powell struck Mrs. Lizzie Branson, his landlady. According to the authorities, Branson had asked Powell to pay his rent, and the black man responded by striking her repeatedly in the face. Branson received numerous bruises and a deep gash. Fearing that a mob might attempt to lynch the black man, the police had him moved to another city. Within a day of this latest episode, police chief Posey Bailey declared war on "bad negroes": "I am determined to put a stop to the rowdyism and trouble from the belligerent portion of the negro population of the city." Police officers working the streets received orders to arrest all intoxicated blacks. The police chief also instructed his men to break up crowds of boisterous and rowdy blacks. Too often, he said, groups of blacks pushed whites off sidewalks into gutters. In addition to being bothered by these alleged criminal acts, whites also seemed to have been troubled by blacks asserting themselves. In other words, though claiming that their efforts were directed at "bad negroes," whites were in reality saying that all blacks must be compelled to respect the rights of whites on the streets in Henderson. As the chief pointed out, a number of white people had "complained to him that negroes refused to even walk to the side of the pavement in order to give room to pass on the sidewalks." Chief Bailey promised them that things would soon return to normal.

The *Daily Journal* fails to clearly spell out how the police brought the crime wave to an end. They probably resorted to random arrests of blacks and the running of some undesirables out of town. The actions of the police led to numerous unsubstantiated charges against Afro-Americans, which tended to fuel the belief that blacks were involved in criminal acts. About a month after the police chief declared his intention to crack down on black criminals, Roscoe Jewell, a young

---

54. See the Henderson *Daily Journal* for most of January through March, 1915. Especially see March 14–21. Quotations in the next paragraph also come from this source.

white man, was struck in the head, knocked unconscious, and robbed of two dollars and his watch. Although he had been surprised and stunned by his unidentified assailant, Jewell instinctively knew that "it was a negro who struck him, [though] he is unable to give any description of the thief."[55]

The bias of the police in viewing blacks as criminals led to tragic consequences on at least one occasion. In Lexington on Tuesday, March 31, 1925, Gertrude Boulder, while walking toward her house, fell to the ground, suffering from a severe attack of indigestion. A police officer found Boulder and arrested her on a charge of public intoxication. Throwing the woman in a cell, the police ignored her screams for a physician. Boulder died early the next morning. Once word was released of how she died (the police at first stated emphatically that she was drunk, only to be disproved by a medical examiner), the black community strongly expressed its disapproval and called for an investigation. Led by Mrs. Lizzie Fouse, a woman long active in various causes, dozens of churches and clubs expressed their shock that such a thing could happen to a civic-minded, church-going woman like Boulder. A petition sent to the mayor said, "Inasmuch as there were no signs of intoxication as certified to by the coroner, no disorderly conduct, no scars to indicate quarrel, coupled with the fact that she was neatly dressed, we feel that either our colored police woman, probation officer, city physician or trained nurse might have been called in to identify her since so few of our best citizens are known by the white policemen." After the white newspapers joined the call for an investigation, the mayor and the police chief felt moved to respond. Their report acknowledged that Boulder was a woman of "unimpeachable character," interested in the well-being of the community. Every attention was paid to Boulder with the exception of calling a physician, they claimed. But because of the tragic circumstances of her death, in the future "it will be the duty of officers in charge of police station, when any one is brought to the station in an unconscious condition, that such person be immediately taken to one of the hospitals or a physician called at once to give medical attention to the case."[56] Despite the promise of the mayor and the police chief

55. *Ibid.*, April 20, 1915.
56. See both the Lexington *Herald* and the *Leader* from April 1 to 17, 1925. Also

that such an incident would not happen again, the death of Gertrude Boulder was a result of whites treating all blacks as criminals.

Interestingly, in the many cases of "legal lynchings" that occurred in Lexington, black leaders refused to speak out—or if they did, it was to endorse the actions of the authorities. To be sure, the case of Gertrude Boulder was a blatant example of racial prejudice, but so too were the arrest, the prosecution, and the execution of many other blacks in the city. In 1905, after three black men had been charged with the murder of a white man in a saloon and after other blacks had been accused of a number of unsolved crimes, Afro-American leaders formed the Good Citizens League to work with the police. Fearing that the misdeeds of a few might reflect negatively on the entire black community, they expressed a desire to assist the police in any manner. The leaders urged the mayor to enforce the law and close many dives and saloons that were ruining the youth. As one spokesman explained, "There are more of our colored boys annually going to the penitentiary than attend our colleges." In 1913, after the shooting of the police chief by Joe Smith, "the Southern Negro who wandered into Lexington and will put the State to the expense of caring for him for some time because of his criminal misconduct," leading black citizens thought it necessary to condemn the act and remind whites that blacks, also, stood for law and order. That black leaders were unsympathetic to Smith pleased the editor of a local white newspaper: "It was scarcely necessary for the colored citizens who constituted this mass meeting to take this means of assuring the community that the conduct of this man Smith met with their emphatic disapproval. It is well known that there is in Lexington a large body of colored citizens who are faithful to all of the rules of good citizenship, who condemn lawlessness in every form, and who contribute freely to the betterment of the moral tone of the community." Black leaders also expressed approval of the quick trial and the death sentence meted out to Will Lockett in February, 1920. Likewise, in 1926, after Ed Harris was convicted and sentenced to death, Lexington blacks applauded this action. Harris told a reporter, "The white people have been mighty good to me but there hasn't [been] a single one of my own color . . . to

see a letter about the incident from Lizzie Fouse to Walter White, April 10, 1925, in NAACP Papers.

see me or written to me or anything." Consistently, blacks all over the state condemned the crimes attributed to members of their race, but rarely—at least in the newspapers—did they question whether the accused blacks had received fair trials before all-white juries in courthouses packed with hostile whites.[57]

Black leaders, however, were quick to complain, and did so consistently, that the police and the courts were lenient toward white lawbreakers, especially when they were accused of committing crimes against blacks. Considering the documented cases in which a white was actually charged with a crime against a black and found innocent by an all-white jury, how many other times did the authorities refuse to press charges against whites for violating the rights of Afro-Americans? One can only speculate what it must have been like for blacks in rural areas who knew that to protest to the authorities would probably result in additional problems for themselves instead of the possible prosecution of the accused whites.

The early 1900s witnessed a number of blatant attacks by whites on blacks. Many of these brutal incidents occurred in the state's largest cities, not just in isolated hamlets. One such incident happened in Lexington on October 2, 1900, and involved Robert Charles O'Hara Benjamin, a man active in civic affairs in the black community. Throughout his life Benjamin worked as a lawyer and a journalist. He edited newspapers in several southern cities beginning in the 1880s and authored a number of books, including *Southern Outrages: A Statistical Record of Lawless Doings*, which strongly denounced lynchings. Benjamin arrived in Lexington in the mid-1890s and became a partner with W. D. Johnson in the operation of the *Standard*. To the dismay of some whites, Benjamin quickly became involved in local politics. On the morning of October 2, an argument broke out between Benjamin and Michael Moynahan over the white man's continued harassment of blacks who wanted to register to vote. Moynahan, obviously unaccustomed to being challenged by a black man, struck Benjamin several times with his revolver. Benjamin had Moynahan arrested on assault charges. Within an hour of being taken into custody, Moynahan posted bond and was released from jail.[58]

57. Lexington *Herald,* January 23, 1905; newsclip from the Lexington *Leader,* 1913, in the Willson Collection; New York *Times,* February 11, 1920, March 16, 1926.

58. Biographical data on Benjamin can be found in W. D. Johnson, *Biographical Sketches of Prominent Negro Men and Women of Kentucky* (Lexington, 1897). At

That evening, Moynahan stationed himself in an alley near Benjamin's home, waiting to confront the black man again. When Benjamin approached the area, he saw Moynahan and quickly realized that his life was threatened. He immediately turned and began running but was brought down in a hail of gunfire as Moynahan shot him six times in the back. Benjamin, a black man who had denounced lynchings and had called upon the South to live up to the American creed, died at the hands of violence. Upon the arrival of the police, Moynahan simply stated, "I surrender." At his examining trial several days later, he pleaded not guilty by reason of self-defense. Moynahan's lawyer told the court that Benjamin had been the aggressor, that one round had been fired from his gun. When the police had examined the deceased black man, they had found a gun in his pocket with one chamber empty. It was unclear when the gun had been fired, but since the weapon was still in Benjamin's pocket, not his hand, it had certainly not been fired during the encounter with Moynahan. Two hours after the hearing started, the judge dismissed the case on the grounds that Moynahan had acted in self-defense. This led, of course, to the usual outcries of injustice from blacks and, to their surprise, from the white local newspaper as well. In a story headlined "He Shot Benjamin From Behind in Self-Defense," the *Morning Herald* said that Moynahan's testimony was unbelievable and that officials should have filed formal murder charges against him. The newspaper followed with an editorial saying that something had to be done to protect blacks from whites. In addition to the tragic murder of Benjamin, two other black men had been killed in Lexington by whites within the past week "under circumstances that have excited a not unnatural feeling of unrest among the negroes" and a feeling also that they are not accorded full protection of the law. As far as can be determined, none of the whites accused in the shooting deaths of Afro-Americans stood trial.

Another case that received considerable attention and comment as to whether or not the law vigorously prosecuted whites for killing blacks occurred in Louisville. On April 13, 1920, the son of William J. James was slightly injured by an automobile driven by Joseph Lowe,

---

present, the author is writing a biography of Benjamin as an example of a "forgotten" black leader. For information on the incident involving Benjamin and Moynahan, see the Louisville *Courier-Journal,* October 3, 1900, and the Lexington *Morning Herald,* October 3–10, 1900. Information in the following paragraph also comes from these sources.

the personal chauffeur for the owner of Wolf Confectionery. Lowe promptly informed his employer of the accident, who in turn called James, telling him that he would pay any medical bills and damages. James was a former officer in the Spanish-American War and an expert with a revolver, and he had killed a black burglar in the 1890s. He was outraged over his son's injury. Armed with two automatic revolvers and a Bowie knife, James went to Wolf Confectionery, confronted the black chauffeur, and shot him dead, saying, "Well, my conscience is clear." Repeated protests from the black community eventually led the authorities to arrest James and charge him with murder. Just as the Lexington paper had called for the conviction of Benjamin's killer, the *Courier-Journal* expressed dismay over the possibility that James might not be fully prosecuted. In a lengthy editorial called "Erase the Color Line," the paper said: "Everyone with an elementary sense of justice will be glad that James . . . was held without bail." The editorial added that everyone believing in fair play will commend the police judge for rebuking and fining the defense attorney for introducing the race question at the examining trial. "The issue is one of guilt or innocence, not one of color. Should the trial be aborted by introduction of the color line it would blacken the records of the court, disgust the community and reflect upon the civilization often proclaimed, proudly, 'a white man's civilization.'"[59]

The NAACP hired a prominent lawyer to help with the prosecution of James. Convinced that the sheriff and the deputies guarding James had become too friendly with him and allowed him special privileges, they demanded, though unsuccessfully, that new officers be assigned to the jail. James went on trial almost two months after the death of Joseph Lowe. A large crowd of blacks were on hand "to witness the trial of a white man charged with murder of one of their race." James pleaded self-defense and asked for a continuance, which was granted until October 21. James's lawyer proved adept in delaying the trial even further, having it eventually postponed until December. But in a dramatic turn, the case came to a sudden end on November 5. Taking advantage of the lax attitude of the guards, James's wife smuggled a knife into his cell. James took the knife and plunged it into his heart, killing himself instantly.[60] White Louis-

59. Louisville *Courier-Journal*, April 12, 22, 1920.

60. *Ibid.*, April 27, June 9, July 2, November 6, 1920. Lee Brown, of the Louisville NAACP, to James W. Johnson, November 11, 1920, in NAACP Papers.

villians would cite this case as an example of the law being color-blind. It must be remembered, however, that if justice was served, it was mainly because of the persistence of blacks in demanding that James be made to stand trial for killing Joseph Lowe.

Just as race was a primary consideration for white jurors passing judgment on blacks accused of murdering whites, so it was a factor for white jurors deciding the fate of white defendants. At the end of the 1920s, Tom Crawford killed a black man for allegedly attacking Crawford's daughter. The Louisville police arrested Crawford only after learning that his daughter had not been assaulted and that the person Crawford killed was not the man who had been accused of the crime. Found guilty, he received twenty-one years in prison. "Had Crawford been a Negro and the innocent victim white he would have gotten nothing short of the electric chair," the Louisville *Leader* said with open contempt for the verdict. Crawford's successful escape from jail only compounded the miscarriage of justice, in the view of the black newspaper.[61] Several months later, W. R. Morgan, a white veterinarian, stood trial in Lebanon for the murder of two blacks. One Sunday morning, Morgan had ventured into the black community to purchase some liquor. After sharing a drink with two black men, Morgan testified, he was struck on the head with a plank as the men attempted to rob him. Pulling out his gun, Morgan shot one of his assailants and then pursued the second one into the house of a neighbor. Not taking any chances, Morgan wildly fired a number of shots inside the house, one of which struck and killed Cordelia Adams. In court, the state offered no evidence to dispute Morgan's claim of self-defense, even in the death of the black woman. The all-white jury deliberated less than five minutes before reaching its not-guilty verdict. "When it was read there was a loud applause in the court room which the judge was unable to stop for several minutes." The NAACP was upset about the manner of the trial and the makeup of the jury, which contained a number of friends of the doctor.[62]

On a few occasions, whites were charged with raping black females. As noted, no white man in Kentucky died on the gallows or in the electric chair for the rape of a black woman. Usually the charges, if not dismissed outright, were reduced in court to detaining a woman

61. Louisville *Leader*, November 16, 1929.
62. A copy of the Lebanon *Enterprise*, May 2, 1930, containing Morgan's entire testimony as well as the events of the shootings, can be found in the NAACP Papers.

against her will. Afro-Americans lashed out at the hypocritical practice of sentencing blacks to death or to long prison terms while showing complete sympathy toward whites charged with the same crime. In Louisville, some whites were charged in court with raping black females. That more assault charges were filed in Louisville probably indicates an aggressiveness on the part of blacks that was lacking in smaller towns. In 1914, Mary Woodridge, aged sixteen, claimed that she had been raped by a white census taker and that he had threatened to kill her if she told the police. A physician confirmed that the girl had been raped. Nothing seems to have come from her charges. This may have been because the census taker had prominent relatives. The black press complained that unlike the widespread coverage given alleged attacks on white women by blacks, "a peculiar feature of the case is that nothing concerning the affair, although it occurred on Wednesday, has appeared in the daily papers." Six years later, Edwin Harding was convicted of assault on a black woman only after the prosecutor agreed to reduce the charge to disorderly conduct. Instead of being sent to jail, Edwin Harding was fined twenty dollars. The *Leader* voiced its complaint: "Can you beat that for adhering to the principles of law and order. Imagine Harding being a Colored man and Miss Carter a white woman, and ponder a minute to whether he would have been promptly sentenced and punished by the mob or turned over to the authorities to be sent to Frankfort for ninety-nine years and one dark day." A year later, Louis Hembaugh, a painter, was left alone in the house with five-year-old Mary McElroy while her aunt went to a nearby grocery store. When the aunt returned, Hembaugh rushed out of the girl's bedroom, and his actions indicated that something had occurred. An examination by a white doctor revealed that the girl had been sexually violated. In court, despite the testimony of the girl and the physician, the grand jury dismissed Hembaugh. Once again, the *Leader* expressed the outrage of blacks: "It doesn't take a Philadelphia lawyer to tell what would have been the results had the five year old girl been white and the brute black."[63]

Attacks on black women continued in Louisville. In the summer

63. Details on the 1914 incident can be found in the Amsterdam (N.Y.) *News*, April 17, 1914, which reprinted the story from the Louisville *News; Crisis*, VIII (June, 1914), 64; Tuskegee Clippings, Reel 221, Frame 247, and Reel 222, Frame 623; Louisville *News*, January 29, February 5, 1921, September 2, 9, 1922; Louisville *Post*, September 4, 1922; Louisville *Leader*, February 5, 1921, October 28, 1922.

of 1925, two white men, disguised as police officers, stopped a black woman for no reason. One man watched while the other one allegedly raped her. After finally capturing the men, the police charged them with detaining a female, not with rape. The court sentenced W. O. Metcalf, whom the woman identified as the rapist, to two years in prison, while the other man, Mike Miller, was given a year in prison. The sentences were much too mild, police court judge Eugene Daily said; the warrants for the two men should have been for rape. If detaining a female was the only charge, why did the jury give one of the defendants a longer sentence, he asked.[64] In November, 1926, Charles Falone, a man with a long record of brutal crimes, was charged with the rape and beating of a black woman. In April, 1927, his first trial ended in a hung jury. A month later, Falone was found guilty of rape, fined one thousand dollars, and sentenced to five years at hard labor. The black press proclaimed it a fair decision, "but had the criminal been black and the victim white—well." Although Falone was a hardened criminal and was imprisoned for a crime for which blacks were usually executed, he was paroled on February 23, 1928, after serving less than a year of his sentence.[65]

A controversial case began in Lexington on Sunday evening, February 28, 1926, when Charles Merchant forced at gunpoint two sisters, Evelyn and Sarah Jones, into a commercial laundry. He tore the clothes off both girls and raped Evelyn, the younger one. Next, Merchant forced the nude girls to walk outside with him and they were seen by several blacks. Susie Brown approached them. Merchant threatened her, but she managed to escape. She successfully persuaded several black men to return with her in an attempt to apprehend Merchant and free the girls. When he saw them coming toward him, Merchant fled but was eventually overtaken by the group. The team of white and black doctors selected to examine the younger girl found evidence that she had been sexually assaulted. At the police station, both girls easily identified Merchant. The rape and assault on the Jones sisters occurred while Lexingtonians were anxiously awaiting the execution of Ed Harris for the rape and murder of a white woman and were hoping

64. Louisville *News*, June 20, 27, November 28, 1925.

65. Louisville *Leader*, February 19, March 26, April 2, May 14, 1927, January 7, 1928. The NAACP was concerned that Falone would not stand trial for rape. See a letter from Bessie Etherly, secretary of the Louisville branch, to Robert W. Bagnall, December 22, 1926, in NAACP Papers.

to avoid any racial outburst. Fayette County's prosecuting attorney tried to calm the fears of blacks that Merchant would go unpunished. Justice would be served, he proclaimed. He would work just as hard for Merchant's conviction as he had for the death sentence for Harris. Upon learning that Merchant was a member of a prominent family and would have four attorneys, black leaders began raising money to help in the prosecution. The Reverend James W. Gibson, pastor of Main Street Baptist Church and a member of the NAACP, held a meeting at his church that raised $750. Several other groups held rallies and raised another $400. The Lexington NAACP wrote to the national office for advice. James Weldon Johnson told them to call upon their white friends for "justice" for whites just as they had for Harris and other blacks accused of crimes. Immediately after the examining trial, in which Merchant was formally charged with the rape of Evelyn Jones and the detaining of her sister, the national office issued a press release. In it, the NAACP pointed out that a white man had just been charged with rape, and no troops had been needed to protect him from a lynching; yet whenever a black is charged with rape, a lynching becomes a real possibility.[66]

Merchant's trial started on Monday, April 5. It took an entire day for both sides to agree on the twelve white men who would decide the case. After two days of testimony, the trial came to a sudden and dramatic end: Merchant was found insane and sentenced to a mental hospital. William Warley, editor of Louisville's other black newspaper, the *News*, wrote an editorial entitled " Color and Crime." Warley reminded his readers of the trial of Ed Harris in Lexington: The courthouse had been completely surrounded by armed guardsmen and the entire trial had lasted less than twenty minutes. By contrast:

> Merchant was given a trial by a jury of his peers and it took three days, not seventeen minutes, to find him insane. Merchant thereby does not dangle

66. Information on the case can be found in Lexington's white newspapers from March through April 17, 1926. See, for example, the *Herald*'s editorial of March 5, urging local officials to press for a conviction of rape against Merchant. The Louisville *Leader* also devoted considerable time to the issue. See, for example, the *Leader*, April 17, 1926; Louisville *Times*, March 1, 1926; letter from James Weldon Johnson to Lizzie Fouse, March 9, 1926, Fouse to Johnson, March 15, 1926, James W. Gibson to J. E. Spingarn, of the national office, March 26, 1926, Johnson to Gibson, April 6, 1926, NAACP press release, "White Kentuckian Attacks Negro Girls, No Troops Needed to Prevent Lynching," March 12, 1926, all in NAACP Papers.

from the end of a murderous rope, but is committed to an institution for the insane and we have no doubt his sanity will soon be restored and he will be permitted to go scot-free while Ed Harris lies rotting under the bluegrass of Kentucky and the two little violated girls of dusky hue can find no balm in Gilead for their defiled bodies. It will take a weird imagination to reconcile these two flagrant cases. To Kentucky and the South, however, a philosophy is ever-present that can explain those matters with surprising simplicity. Harris was black and Merchant was white. It is not a matter of crime but a matter of color.[67]

It is highly likely that Charles Merchant was insane. Were Will Lockett and Ed Harris mentally capable of standing trial? This question had not been raised at their trials. No motive was given for their crimes. In the eyes of whites, blacks like Lockett and Harris had no motives but were merely depraved human beings. Furthermore, many whites of the early 1900s believed that most black people acted in ways that were far from normal anyway, so an insanity plea was an option not available to them. Black leaders, embarrassed by the crimes committed by Lockett and Harris and hoping to show whites that not all blacks were rapists and murderers, wanted the trials resolved quickly and were not about to ask for anything that looked like leniency for either man.

Lockett clearly seems to have been deranged. Shortly before being put to death, he confessed to several other assaults and murders. Explaining that his real name was Petrie Kimbrough, he had fled the community of Pembroke in Christian County after an unsuccessful assault on a white woman in 1905. He killed a white woman in Illinois in either 1912 or 1913, a black woman in Indiana in 1917, and a woman, whose color he could not determine, while stationed in Louisville in the United States Army during the war. At the time of

67. Louisville *News,* April 17, 1926; Louisville *Leader,* April 17, 1926; Tuskegee Clippings, Reel 224, Frame 785. On another occasion, two black Lexington women were allegedly raped by a gang of eight white men. On the evening of June 11, 1928, the women were in a car with two black men when the whites, posing as revenue officers, forced them to stop and get out of the car. The whites beat and robbed the black men and then drove off with the women. Found on different county roads, each woman said she had been taken to an isolated area and assaulted. A month later, two of the men were arrested and charged with robbery after being identified by the four blacks. Ignoring the protest of the women and local NAACP officials, police authorities refused to press charges of rape against the men. Lexington *Morning Herald,* June 12, July 12, 1928; Houston *Informer,* July 21, 1928.

Lockett's death in 1920, editor William Warley wrote an editorial suggesting that the horrible acts committed by Lockett and his insanity were logical by-products of living in America's racist society:

Will Lockett was a product of his environment. Born and reared in a state where lawlessness was rampant, where mobs intimidated judges and juries, where justice was a mockery. Having no rights himself that anyone was bound to respect, he soon reached that malevolent stage of human depravity wherein he lost all regard for the rights of others. . . . He began to feel malice against all mankind—against the white race, for thus brutalizing the Negro and against the black race for his submission to brutality. So long as the Negro is treated as he has been treated will there be Will Locketts.[68]

Legal lynching was only a part of the racial violence experienced by Afro-Americans in Kentucky. Clearly, however, legal lynching, because it made a complete mockery of the law and tended to destroy the respect citizens had for their legal process, proved to be far worse than the horrible acts of the mobs that ran blacks out of town or. lynched them. These acts were illegal and no clear-thinking citizens suggested otherwise. On the other hand, the overwhelming majority of white Kentuckians believed that their legal system was fair, that even though blacks were denied equal access to most places in society, they were dealt with fairly in court. Therefore, they simply ignored the omission of blacks from juries and the obvious discrimination they faced in court, whether they were there as the defendant or the victimized party. With such an attitude so firmly embedded in white society, blacks clearly and consistently faced discrimination before the law.

The racial violence discussed in this study has ended for the most part. Steps taken by concerned government officials and by black and white civic leaders have proven over time to be sufficient to eradicate the acts of mobs. Even though they still lack total equality before the law, black Kentuckians are no longer tried in courthouses where white mobs are clamoring for the death penalty and heavily armed soldiers surround the building, closely checking each person entering the courtroom. Their trials last much longer than an hour, and jurors take longer than five minutes to render verdicts. The mental state of

68. New York *Times*, March 9, 1920. The quote from Warley's paper can be found in the Tuskegee Clippings, Reel 221, Frame 173.

the accused is also considered. All of this can be viewed as progress; we as a nation no longer allow people to be lynched inside or outside the courtroom. We as Americans tend to applaud ourselves for doing the "right thing," for extending to the accused person the right to defend himself and to challenge fully his accusers in court. Many people do not want to be reminded of a time when racial violence was rampant; they think this is too negative and dwells on only the worst aspects of society. Regardless, it is extremely important to remember that Kentuckians and Americans consistently went to great extremes to deny blacks their most fundamental rights. Centuries of judicial prejudice and mob violence are not erased quickly. Within our society the dangers still remain, dormant perhaps, but present nevertheless. If we understand the past evils, and are reminded of them, perhaps such evils will stay as they should be, behind in the past.

Victims of Lynchings

NAME	RACE	CITY/COUNTY	DATE	REASON
1. "Bertraud"	B	Paris Bourbon County	March, 1866	rape
2. Charles	B	Frankfort Franklin County	May, 1866	attempted rape
3. ———	B	Louisville Jefferson County	May, 1866	rape
4. "Tom"	B	Owensboro Daviess County	May, 1866	rape
5. ———	B	Paris Bourbon County	September, 1866	attempted murder
6. Clem Crowders	W	Lebanon Marion County	November, 1866	robbery
7. William Goode	W	Lebanon Marion County	November, 1866	robbery
8. Thomas Stephens	W	Lebanon Marion County	November, 1866	robbery
9. Al McRoberts	B	Danville Boyle County	December, 1866	attempted murder
10. Trowbridge	B	Danville Boyle County	February, 1867	stealing
11. Thomas Carvier	W	Parksville Boyle County	February, 1867	———
12. Adam Smith	B	Nicholasville Jessamine County	April, 1867	murder
13. "Boz"	B	Nicholasville Jessamine County	April, 1867	murder
14. John Devine	W	Harrodsburg Mercer County	June, 1867	———
15. Nathan Lawson	W	Cornishville Mercer County	August, 1867	———
16. ———	B	Mackville Washington County	August, 1867	———

NAME	RACE	CITY/COUNTY	DATE	REASON
17. ——	B	Mackville Washington County	August, 1867	——
18. Joseph Sutherland	W	Harrodsburg Mercer County	August, 1867	rape
19. Robertson	——	Harrodsburg Mercer County	November, 1867	——
20. Leake Hicks	W	Danville Boyle County	1867	——
21. Jim Macklin	B	Frankfort Franklin County	January, 1868	rape
22. Sam Davis	W	Harrodsburg Mercer County	May, 1868	——
23. George Rogers	W	Bradsfordsville Marion County	June, 1868	stealing and counter- feiting
24. ——	B	Columbia Adair County	July, 1868	rape
25. William Pierce	B	Christian County	July, 1868	——
26. James Parker	B	Pulaski Pulaski County	August, 1868	——
27. William Gibson	B	Washington County	August, 1868	——
28. John Gibson	B	Washington County	August, 1868	——
29. Cabe Fields	B	Keene Jessamine County	August, 1868	——
30. John Montfort	W	Woodford County	August, 1868	——
31. William Glasgow	B	Warren County	September, 1868	——
32. Cummins	B	Pulaski County	September, 1868	——
33. Cummins' daughter	B	Pulaski County	September, 1868	——
34. Adams	——	Pulaski County	September, 1868	——
35. Crasban	——	Cornishville Mercer County	September, 1868	——
36. Terry Laws	B	Nicholasville Jessamine County	October, 1868	——
37. James Ryan	B	Nicholasville Jessamine County	October, 1868	——
38. ——	B	Richmond Madison County	November, 1868	——
39. ——	B	Union County	December, 1868	——
40. ——	B	Union County	December, 1868	——
41. ——	B	Morganfield Union County	December, 1868	——

NAME	RACE	CITY/COUNTY	DATE	REASON
42. Albert Bradford	B	Scott County	January, 1869	——
43. George Bratcher	B	Garrard County	March, 1869	——
44. Thomas Lancaster	W	Brownsville Edmondson County	April, 1869	murder
45. John Perry	B	Nevada Mercer County	May, 1869	——
46. George Bolling	B	Harrodsburg Mercer County	July, 1869	——
47. James Crowders	B	Lebanon Marion County	August, 1869	——
48. Cash	B	Lincoln County	September, 1869	——
49. Coffey	B	Lincoln County	September, 1869	——
50. John Mosteran	B	Lincoln County	September, 1869	——
51. Wiley Gevens	——	Dixon Webster County	October, 1869	——
52. George Rose	B	Madison County	October, 1869	——
53. Frank Searcy	B	Richmond Madison County	November, 1869	murder
54. ——	B	Boydsville Graves County	December, 1869	rape
55. ——	B	Boydsville Graves County	December, 1869	rape
56. ——	B	Richmond Madison County	December, 1869	——
57. Jim Sims	B	Richmond Madison County	January, 1870	——
58. Chas Fields	B	Fayette County	January, 1870	——
59. ——	B	Springfield Washington County	January, 1870	——
60. ——	B	Springfield Washington County	January, 1870	——
61. Simms	W	Kingston Madison County	January, 1870	——
62. R. L. Byrom	B	Richmond Madison County	February, 1870	——
63. William Hart	——	Clark County	April, 1870	——
64. Hyatt	B	Lincoln County	April, 1870	——
65. Perry	B	Lancaster Garrard County	April, 1870	——
66. Sam Lambert	B	Mercer County	April, 1870	——

NAME	RACE	CITY/COUNTY	DATE	REASON
67. ———	B	Greenville Muhlenburgh County	May, 1870	———
68. Daniel Parker	W	Laurel County	May, 1870	murder
69. Pleasanton Parker	W	Laurel County	May, 1870	murder
70. Willis Parker	W	Laurel County	May, 1870	murder
71. William Sheldon	W	Laurel County	May, 1870	murder
72. Simpson Grubbs	———	Montgomery County	August, 1870	———
73. ———	B	Harrodsburg Mercer County	August, 1870	———
74. ———	B	Harrodsburg Mercer County	August, 1870	———
75. ———	B	Harrodsburg Mercer County	August, 1870	———
76. ———	B	Harrodsburg Mercer County	August, 1870	———
77. James Parker	B	Versailles Woodford County	August, 1870	being a Re- publican
78. William Turpin	B	Versailles Woodford County	August, 1870	being a Re- publican
79. Frank Timberlake	B	Flemingburg Fleming County	August, 1870	———
80. Mrs. John Simes	B	Henry County	September, 1870	husband was a Re- publican
81. Oliver Williams	B	Richmond Madison County	September, 1870	———
82. Jesse Crowe	W	Irvine Estill County	November, 1870	murder
83. Murrell Tyree	W	Mount Sterling Montgomery County	December, 1870	murder
84. George	B	Cynthiana Harrison County	December, 1870	rape
85. ———	B	Fayette County	December, 1870	———
86. ———	B	Fayette County	December, 1870	———
87. ———	B	Mayfield area Graves County	1870	———
88. ———	B	Mayfield area Graves County	1870	———
89. ———	B	Mayfield area Graves County	1870	———

NAME	RACE	CITY/COUNTY	DATE	REASON
90. ——	B	Mayfield area Graves County	1870	——
91. ——	B	Mayfield area Graves County	1870	——
92. ——	B	Mayfield area Graves County	1870	——
93. ——	B	Lexington Fayette County	January, 1871	——
94. Harry Johnson	B	Frankfort Franklin County	August, 1871	rape
95. Henry Washington	B	Frankfort Franklin County	August, 1871	murder
96. ——	B	Morganfield Union County	August, 1871	rape
97. ——	W	Morganfield Union County	August, 1871	rape
98. John Nevil	W	Metcalf County	August, 1871	murder
99. Abijah Gridley	W	Warsaw Gallatin County	October, 1871	murder
100. George Duncan	B	Brookville Bracken County	December, 1871	murder
101. Richard Taylor	B	Crab Orchard Lincoln County	1871	extortion of evidence
102. ——	B	Franklin County	1871	——
103. Leonard Stough	W	Richmond Madison County	February, 1872	murder
104. Sam Bascom	B	Owingsville Bath County	October, 1872	arson
105. Samuel Hawkins	B	Fayette County	November, 1872	being a Re-publican
106. Hawkins' wife	B	Fayette County	November, 1872	being a wife of a Repub-lican
107. Hawkins' daughter	B	Fayette County	November, 1872	being a daughter of a Re-publican
108. John Wadlington	B	Madisonville Hopkins County	November, 1872	being a Re-publican
109. Ross Branson	B	Blaudville Ballard County	November, 1872	rape
110. ——	B	Minerva Mason County	April, 1873	rape

NAME	RACE	CITY/COUNTY	DATE	REASON
111. Bob Curd	B	Harrodsburg Mercer County	April, 1873	rape
112. Lewis Wilson	B	Gratz Owen County	July, 1873	———
113. Dudley White	B	Muhlenburg County	January, 1874	murder
114. Ed Shields	B	Taylorsville Spencer County	April, 1874	rape
115. Robert Becket	W	Harrison County	June, 1874	murder
116. ———	B	Jessamine County	August, 1874	rape
117. Lewis Franklin	B	Nicholasville Jessamine County	September, 1874	rape
118. Jim Tarpin	B	Danville Boyle County	April, 1876	rape
119. Ben French	B	Warsaw Gallatin County	May, 1876	murder
120. Mrs. Ben French	B	Warsaw Gallatin County	May, 1876	murder
121. Williams	B	Burlington Boone County	June, 1876	murder
122. Washington Lee	W	Vanceburg Lewis County	July, 1876	murder
123. James Anderson	W	Hickman Fulton County	July, 1877	depredations upon farms
124. George Stark	W	Point Oliver Allen County	July, 1877	rape
125. Jim Simmons	W	Owen Henry County	September, 1877	member of Simmons gang
126. Bob Goodrich	W	Owen Henry County	September, 1877	member of Simmons gang
127. Sam Goodrich	W	Owen Henry County	September, 1877	member of Simmons gang
128. Joe Goodrich	W	Owen Henry County	September, 1877	member of Simmons gang

NAME	RACE	CITY/COUNTY	DATE	REASON
129. ———	W	Owen Henry County	September, 1877	member of Simmons gang
130. Stiver	B	Lexington Fayette County	January, 1878	murder
131. Tom Turner	B	Lexington Fayette County	January, 1878	knowl-edge of a murder
132. Edward Claxton	B	Lexington Fayette County	January, 1878	knowl-edge of a murder
133. John Davis	B	Lexington Fayette County	January, 1878	knowl-edge of a murder
134. George Williams	B	Lagrange Oldham County	November, 1878	rape
135. Kilburn	W	Breathitt County	1878	member of a gang
136. ———	B	Breathitt County	1878	taking food to Kilburn
137. Peter Klien	W	Newport Campbell County	March, 1879	rape
138. John Breckinridge	B	Nicholas County	July, 1879	rape
139. Jack Williams	B	Union County	June, 1880	murder
140. Sam Ramey	B	Owingsville Bath County	1880	murder
141. John Winn	W	Paris Bourbon County	April, 1881	murder
142. Bob Sarver	B	Franklin Simpson County	March, 1882	attempted rape
143. William Courts	W	Brooksville Bracken County	April, 1882	murder
144. Bradford Courts	W	Brooksville Bracken County	April, 1882	murder
145. George Ellis	W	Cattlesburg Boyd County	June, 1882	rape
146. Jim Mitchell	B	Mt. Sterling Montgomery County	June, 1882	rape
147. William Ritter	B	Henderson Henderson County	July, 1882	rape
148. "Dish" Emberton	W	Glasgow Barren County	August, 1882	rape

NAME	RACE	CITY/COUNTY	DATE	REASON
149. Richard Spearman	W	Glasgow Barren County	August, 1882	rape
150. ———	B	Hanson Hopkins County	May, 1883	rape
151. Henry Colbert	B	Hickman Fulton County	June, 1883	attempted rape
152. Nelson Cooper	B	Russellville Logan County	October, 1883	murder
153. Henry Kilburn	W	Jackson Breathitt County	April, 1884	murder
154. William Strong	W	Jackson Breathitt County	April, 1884	murder
155. Charles Dickerson	B	Burlington Boone County	May, 1884	burglary
156. Miles Petty	B	Hardin County	May, 1884	rape
157. Richard May	B	Owensboro Daviess County	July, 1884	rape
158. John Martin	W	Farmers' Station Rowan County	December, 1884	murder
159. Sambo Bailey	B	Russellville Logan County	1884	———
160. John Stapleton	W	Magoffin County	January, 1885	accessory to murder
161. Sam Scales	B	Burlington Boone County	September, 1885	rape
162. Calvin Simpson	B	Henderson Henderson County	January, 1886	murder
163. Handy Woodward	B	Russellville Logan County	March, 1886	attempted rape
164. ———	B	Auburn Logan County	March, 1886	attempted rape
165. ———	B	Auburn Logan County	March, 1886	attempted rape
166. ———	B	Auburn Logan County	March, 1886	attempted rape
167. Meredith Jones	B	Auburn Logan County	April, 1886	attempted rape
168. ———	W	Elliot County	July, 1886	arson
169. ———	W	Elliot County	July, 1886	arson
170. William Cornish	W	Springfield Washington County	January, 1887	murder
171. ———	W	Falmouth Pendleton County	March, 1887	murder
172. John Thomas	B	Union City Madison County	July, 1887	rape

NAME	RACE	CITY/COUNTY	DATE	REASON
173. John Vanderford	B	Fulton Fulton County	July, 1887	rape
174. Charles Coleman	B	Flemingsburg Fleming County	September, 1887	attempted rape
175. Tom Doss	B	Franklin Simpson County	December, 1887	attempted murder
176. Samuel Price	W	Clinton Hickman County	February, 1888	murder
177. Bill Reams	B	Clinton Hickman County	February, 1888	attempted murder
178. Henry Skinner	B	Hopkinsville Christian County	March, 1888	murder
179. Eli Nary	B	Hickman Fulton County	March, 1888	arson
180. Thomas Reney	B	Rich Pond Warren County	May, 1888	poisoning horses
181. ——	W	Smith's Mills Henderson County	July, 1888	murder
182. Joe Thornton	B	Wickliffe Ballard County	May, 1889	rape
183. Tony Cravasso	W	Pineville Bell County	June, 1889	murder
184. Tony Cravasso's brother	W	Pineville Bell County	June, 1889	murder
185. Charles Ardell	W	Shepherdsville Bullitt County	June, 1889	murder
186. Jim Kelly	B	Paris Bourbon County	July, 1889	rape
187. David Malone	B	Covington Kenton County	July, 1889	rape
188. ——	B	Somerset Pulaski County	September, 1889	rape
189. O. A. Smith	W	Elkton Todd County	November, 1889	murder
190. Jack Turner	B	Greensburg Green County	December, 1889	murder
191. Dock Jones	B	Owensboro Daviess County	December, 1889	murder
192. Samuel Moody	B	Auburn Logan County	April, 1890	murder
193. John Henderson	B	Midway Woodford County	August, 1890	murder
194. Ernest Humphries	B	Princeton Caldwell County	October, 1890	murder

NAME	RACE	CITY/COUNTY	DATE	REASON
195. Will Skapp	B	Bowling Green Warren County	April, 1891	murder
196. John Wilcox	W	Sandy Hook Elliot County	May, 1891	rape
197. Hy Wilcox	W	Sandy Hook Elliot County	May, 1891	rape
198. Sam Pulliam	B	Shelbyville Shelby County	July, 1891	rape
199. John Grange	B	Franklin Simpson County	July, 1891	making threats
200. James Dudley	B	Georgetown Scott County	August, 1891	murder
201. Harvey Gilland	W	Somerset Pulaski County	September, 1891	murder
202. Joe Gilland	W	Somerset Pulaski County	September, 1891	murder
203. Lee Gibson	B	Owenton Owen County	January, 1892	murder
204. Nick Willis	B	Campbellsville Taylor County	May, 1892	rape
205. Austin Porter	W	Grayson Carter County	June, 1892	murder
206. Charley Hill	B	Paducah McCracken County	June, 1892	attempted rape
207. John Redfern	W	Franklin Simpson County	July, 1892	murder
208. Lee McDaniels	B	Oaks Crossing McCracken County	July, 1892	attempted rape
209. Logan Murphy	B	Mount Sterling Montgomery County	August, 1892	murder
210. John Wilcoxson	B	Edmonton Metcalf County	September, 1892	murder
211. James Bond	B	Guthrie Todd County	December, 1892	rape
212. Bob Harper	B	Bowling Green Warren County	December, 1892	rape
213. Edward Moorman	B	Guston Meade County	January, 1893	murder
214. Richard Moorman	B	Guston Meade County	January, 1893	murder
215. James Collins	W	Sherman Grant County	May, 1893	horse stealing
216. C. J. Miller	B	Bardwell Ballard County	July, 1893	rape
217. Felix Poole	W	Owensboro Daviess County	August, 1893	rape

NAME	RACE	CITY/COUNTY	DATE	REASON
218. Charles Walton	B	Morganfield Union County	August, 1893	murder
219. ——	B	Paducah McCraken County	August, 1893	rape
220. Leonard Taylor	B	Newscastle Henry County	August, 1893	murder
221. Judge McNeal	B	Cadiz Trigg County	September, 1893	attempted rape
222. William Arkinson	B	McKinney Lincoln County	September, 1893	rape
223. Phil Evans' wife	B	Bardstown Nelson County	November, 1893	revenge on Phil Evans
224. Phil Evans' daughter	B	Bardstown Nelson County	November, 1893	revenge on Phil Evans
225. Phil Evans' mother	B	Bardstown Nelson County	November, 1893	revenge on Phil Evans
226. Henry Givens	B	Nebo Hopkins County	December, 1893	poisoning stock
227. M. G. Gumble	B	Jellico Whitley County	January, 1894	rape
228. Len Tye	B	Harlem Harlan County	March, 1894	——
229. Archie Haines	B	Mason County	June, 1894	horse stealing
230. Burt Haines	B	Mason County	June, 1894	horse stealing
231. William Haines	B	Mason County	June, 1894	horse stealing
232. Cabel Gadley	B	Bowling Green Warren County	June, 1894	attempted rape
233. Marion Howard	B	Scottsville Allen County	July, 1894	rape
234. Edwin Traughber	W	Adairville Logan County	July, 1894	a bad man
235. Louis Lafordette	W	Burlington Boone County	July, 1894	murder
236. William Tyler	B	Nicholas County	July, 1894	attempted rape
237. Marshall Boston	B	Frankfort Franklin County	August, 1894	rape
238. Rich Berry	W	Marion County	October, 1894	robbery
239. Al Richardson	W	Irvine Estill County	October, 1894	rape

NAME	RACE	CITY/COUNTY	DATE	REASON
240. Oscar Morton	W	Beattyville Lee County	October, 1894	murder
241. Willis Griffey	B	Princeton Caldwell County	October, 1894	rape
242. Gabe Nalls	B	Blackford Webster County	November, 1894	incendiarism
243. Ulysses Nalls	B	Blackford Webster County	November, 1894	incendiarism
244. Thomas Blair	W	Mount Sterling Montgomery County	January, 1895	murder
245. ——	B	Fulton Fulton County	February, 1895	attempted rape
246. George Ray	B	Jensonton Washington County	April, 1895	troublesome
247. John Howeston	W	Marion Crittenden County	May, 1895	rape
248. Claude Thompson	B	De Koven Union County	May, 1895	attempted rape
249. Abithal Colston	W	Trigg County	July, 1895	murder
250. Mollie Smith	B	Trigg County	July, 1895	rape
251. Robert Huggard	B	Winchester Clark County	July, 1895	rape
252. Harrison Lewis	B	Springfield Washington County	August, 1895	murder
253. William Butcher	B	Hickman Fulton County	September, 1895	murder
254. ——	B	Henderson Henderson County	November, 1895	rape
255. ——	B	Henderson Henderson County	November, 1895	rape
256. ——	B	Calvert Marshall County	November, 1895	train wrecking
257. William Dever	W	Marion County	December, 1895	improper relations with Mrs. T. J. West
258. Mrs. T. J. West	W	Marion County	December, 1895	improper relations with William Dever
259. Fount Martin	B	Monticello Wayne County	February, 1896	arson
260. ——	B	Fulton Fulton County	May, 1896	murder

NAME	RACE	CITY/COUNTY	DATE	REASON
261. Thomas White	B	Aurora Fulton County	September, 1896	——
262. Arch Proctor	W	Russellville Logan County	December, 1896	murder
263. Dink Proctor	W	Russellville Logan County	December, 1896	accessory to murder
264. Bill Proctor	W	Russellville Logan County	December, 1896	accessory to murder
265. Henry Finley	B	Mayfield Graves County	December, 1896	attempted murder
266. Jim Stone	B	Mayfield Graves County	December, 1896	rape
267. Alfred Holt	B	Owensboro Daviess County	December, 1896	murder
268. Robert Morton	B	Rockford Warren County	February, 1897	insulting a white woman
269. ——	B	Rock Springs Henderson County	March, 1897	stealing
270. William Braydee	W	Middlesboro Bell County	April, 1897	murder
271. Ephraim Brinkley	B	Madisonville Hopkin County	July, 1897	bad repu- tation
272. George Wilson	B	Meyers Nicholas County	August, 1897	——
273. Eleany Sullivan	W	Williamsburg Whitley County	August, 1897	rape
274. Raymond Bushrod	B	Hawesville Hancock County	September, 1897	attempted rape
275. Richard Allen	B	Mayfield Graves County	February, 1898	robbery
276. Tom Holmes	B	Mayfield Graves County	February, 1898	murder
277. Gams Calls	B	Glasgow Barren County	June, 1898	rape
278. George Scott	B	Russellville Logan County	June, 1898	rape
279. Arch Bauer	B	Tompkinsville Monroe County	October, 1898	attempted rape
280. Pleas Goin	W	Middletown Jefferson County	December, 1898	murder
281. Walter Holland	W	Meyers Nicholas County	December, 1898	rape
282. Henry Stevens	W	Fulton Fulton County	June, 1899	robbery

NAME	RACE	CITY/COUNTY	DATE	REASON
283. Richard Coleman	B	Maysville Mason County	December, 1899	rape
284. Fraten Warfield	B	Elkton Todd County	October, 1900	attempted rape
285. George Carter	B	Paris Bourbon County	February, 1901	rape
286. Frank Howard	B	Wickliffe Ballard County	September, 1901	murder
287. Sam Reed	B	Wickliffe Ballard County	September, 1901	murder
288. Ernest Harris	B	Wickliffe Ballard County	September, 1901	murder
289. Jimbo Fields	B	Shelbyville Shelby County	October, 1901	murder
290. Clarence Garnet	B	Shelbyville Shelby County	October, 1901	murder
291. Silas Esters	B	Hodgenville Larue County	October, 1901	rape
292. Jim Mays	B	Springfield Washington County	January, 1902	attempted rape
293. Tom Brown	B	Nicholasville Jessamine County	February, 1902	rape
294. Duly Bell	B	Fulton Fulton County	February, 1902	robbery
295. Elijah Drake	B	Madrid Bend Breckenridge County	March, 1902	stealing
296. James Stewart	B	Madrid Bend Breckenridge County	March, 1902	stealing
297. Thomas Blambard	B	Fulton Fulton County	April, 1902	attempted murder
298. Ernest Dewley	B	Brandenburg Meade County	May, 1902	attempted murder
299. Josh Anderson	W	Owensboro Daviess County	July, 1902	murder
300. Harlan Buckles	B	Elizabethtown Hardin County	November, 1902	murder
301. William Thacker	W	Flemingburg Fleming County	July, 1903	murder
302. Thomas Hall	B	Kevil Ballard County	October, 1903	murder
303. Lewis Radford	B	Guthrie Todd County	January, 1904	murder
304. Marie Thompson	B	Lebanon Junction Bullitt County	June, 1904	murder
305. ——	B	Stephensport Breckinridge County	July, 1904	murder

NAME	RACE	CITY/COUNTY	DATE	REASON
306. Lon Beard	B	Normandy Spencer County	July, 1905	attempted rape
307. Frank Leavell	B	Elkton Todd County	October, 1905	attempted rape
308. Virgil Bowers	B	London Laurel County	October, 1905	murder
309. Ernest Baker	B	Cadiz Trigg County	January, 1906	attempted rape
310. William Clifford	B	Maple Grove Trigg County	August, 1907	rape
311. Tom Weaver	B	Trigg County	March, 1908	killed by Night Riders
312. Jacob McDowell	B	Dixon Webster County	May, 1908	attempted murder
313. Virgil Jones	B	Russellville Logan County	August, 1908	approved of a murder
314. Robert Jones	B	Russellville Logan County	August, 1908	approved of a murder
315. Thomas Jones	B	Russellville Logan County	August, 1908	approved of a murder
316. Joseph Riley	B	Russellville Logan County	August, 1908	approved of a murder
317. David Walker	B	Hickman Fulton County	October, 1908	swearing at a white woman
318. Walker's wife	B	Hickman Fulton County	October, 1908	wife of Walker
319. Walker's child	B	Hickman Fulton County	October, 1908	child of Walker
320. Walker's child	B	Hickman Fulton County	October, 1908	child of Walker
321. Walker's child	B	Hickman Fulton County	October, 1908	child of Walker
322. Walker's child	B	Hickman Fulton County	October, 1908	child of Walker
323. Walker's child	B	Hickman Fulton County	October, 1908	child of Walker
324. Elmer Hill	W	Monticello Wayne County	December, 1908	————
325. Bennie "Booker" Brame	B	Flat Lick Christian County	April, 1909	attempted rape

NAME	RACE	CITY/COUNTY	DATE	REASON
326. John May	B	Frankfort Franklin County	June, 1909	murder
327. Wallace Miller	B	Cadiz Trigg County	August, 1909	attempted rape
328. Eugene Marshall	B	Shelbyville Shelby County	January, 1911	murder
329. Wade Patterson	B	Shelbyville Shelby County	January, 1911	detaining a white woman
330. Will Porter	B	Livermore McLean County	April, 1911	attempted murder
331. ——	B	Germantown Bracken County	August, 1913	——
332. ——	B	Germantown Bracken County	August, 1913	——
333. Joe Richardson	B	Leitchfield Grayson County	September, 1913	rape
334. Houston Underwood	W	Irvine Estill County	February, 1915	——
335. Thomas Tinker	W	Mayfield Graves County	February, 1915	murder
336. Arthur Bell	B	Princeton Caldwell County	June, 1915	rape
337. Peter Hart	B	Ohio County	August, 1915	——
338. Claude Johnson	W	Princeton Caldwell County	September, 1915	rape
339. Ellis Buckner	B	Henderson Henderson County	November, 1915	rape
340. Brock Henley	B	Paducah McCracken County	October, 1916	rape
341. Luther Durrett	B	Paducah McCracken County	October, 1916	approving of Henley's act
342. William Sanders	B	Maysville Mason County	March, 1917	theft, self-defense
343. Lawrence Dempsey	W	Fulton Fulton County	May, 1917	attempted rape
344. Charlie Lewis	B	Hickman Fulton County	December, 1918	attempted murder
345. Grant Smith	B	Paris Bourbon County	March, 1920	rape
346. Richard James	B	Versailles Woodford County	March, 1921	murder
347. "Kid Shannon"	B	Floyd County	November, 1924	murder

NAME	RACE	CITY/COUNTY	DATE	REASON
348. Jim Evans	B	Jellico Creek Whitley County	April, 1925	murder
349. Primus Kirby	B	Guthrie Todd County	June, 1926	murder
350. Leonard Woods	B	Whitesburg Letcher County	December, 1927	murder
351. Chester Fugate	W	Breathitt County	December, 1929	murder
352. Walter Merrick	W	Princeton Caldwell County	June, 1932	dynamit- ing a store
353. Rex Scott	B	Hazard Knott County	January, 1934	murder

Names of People
Legally Executed

NAME	RACE	COUNTY TRIED IN	DATE	REASON
1. John Ryan	W	Graves	May, 1872	murder
2. Thomas Guthrie	B	Boyle	July, 1872	murder
3. Will Carter	B	Fayette	August, 1872	murder
4. Thomas Smith	B	Jefferson	March, 1873	murder
5. George Miller	B	Washington	May, 1874	murder
6. George Washington	B	Washington	October, 1878	rape
7. Charles Webster	B	Jefferson	April, 1880	rape
8. Robert Anderson	W	Jefferson	April, 1880	murder
9. John Major Hicks	B	Kenton	February, 1882	murder
10. John Bridges	B	Trigg	June, 1882	murder
11. Isaac Turner	B	Fayette	July, 1882	murder
12. William Austin	B	Garrard	October, 1882	murder
13. Daniel Timberlake	B	Fayette	July, 1883	rape
14. Samuel Bulgar	B	Mason	September, 1883	rape
15. Ellis Craft	W	Carter	October, 1883	murder
16. Frank Slagel	W	Pulaski	March, 1884	murder
17. Rude Fitzpatrick	W	Adair	March, 1884	murder
18. Champ Fitzpatrick	W	Adair	March, 1884	murder
19. Washington Fletcher	B	McCracken	October, 1884	murder
20. John Bush	B	Fayette	November, 1884	murder
21. Tim Bugler	B	Mason	1884	rape
22. Tim Sexton	W	Knox	March, 1885	murder
23. William Neal	W	Carter	March, 1885	rape
24. Augustus Finley	W	Floyd	April, 1885	murder
25. Moses Canton	W	Union	May, 1885	murder
26. Jordan Taylor	B	Christian	June, 1885	murder
27. Floyd Williams	W	Wolfe	September, 1885	murder
28. Robert Fowler	W	Union	April, 1886	murder

NAME	RACE	COUNTY TRIED IN	DATE	REASON
29. Grandville Prewitt	W	Wayne	January, 1887	murder
30. James Marcum	W	Lawrence	April, 1887	murder
31. Albert Turner	B	Jefferson	July, 1887	murder
32. James McElroy	B	Henderson	July, 1887	murder
33. Tucker Agee	W	Fayette	November, 1887	murder
34. William Patterson	B	Jefferson	June, 1888	murder
35. James Ross	B	Meade	February, 1889	murder
36. Monroe Wilkinson	B	Washington	March, 1889	murder
37. Charles Dilger	W	Jefferson	July, 1889	murder
38. Harry Smart	W	Jefferson	July, 1889	murder
39. Ellison Mounts	W	Pike	February, 1890	murder
40. Thomas O'Brien	W	Fayette	February, 1890	murder
41. Mrs. Wiginton	W	Montgomery	March, 1891	murder
42. Levi James	B	Fulton	June, 1891	murder
43. Jesse Brown	B	McCracken	January, 1892	murder
44. William Puckett	W	Estill	February, 1892	murder
45. Robert Charlton	B	Henderson	February, 1892	murder
46. Spring Bush	W	Power	February, 1892	murder
47. Henry Smith	B	Jefferson	March, 1892	murder
48. Oscar Jones	B	Bath	November, 1892	murder
49. Dennis McCarthy	W	Jefferson	December, 1892	murder
50. Stephen Hite	W	Jefferson	December, 1892	murder
51. Nelson Lewis	B	Jefferson	December, 1892	murder
52. Grant Thomas	B	Jefferson	December, 1892	murder
53. Robert Brown	B	Graves	June, 1893	murder
54. Henry Hale	W	Pulaski	August, 1893	murder
55. George Armstrong	B	Spencer	December, 1893	murder
56. Robert Marlen	B	Bell	December, 1893	murder
57. Philip Evans	B	Nelson	January, 1894	murder
58. Beverly Adams	B	Christian	September, 1894	murder
59. Robert Marter	W	Bell	February, 1894	murder
60. William Taylor	B	Madison	January, 1895	murder
61. George McGee	B	Franklin	March, 1895	murder
62. John Johnson	B	Montgomery	August, 1895	murder
63. James Dewitt	W	Carter	May, 1896	murder
64. Henry Mitchell Smith	B	Fayette	June, 1896	rape
65. Burford Overton	B	Bell	October, 1896	murder
66. Robert Laughlin	W	Bracken	January, 1897	murder
67. Scott Jackson	W	Campbell	March, 1897	murder

NAME	RACE	COUNTY TRIED IN	DATE	REASON
68. Alonzo Walling	W	Campbell	March, 1897	murder
69. George H. Weston	B	McCracken	November, 1897	murder
70. Thomas Hayden	B	Ohio	June, 1898	murder
71. Clarence Vinegar	B	Scott	June, 1898	murder
72. Manual Morris	W	Madison	October, 1898	murder
73. William Miller	B	Oldham	February, 1899	rape
74. John Franklin	W	Barren	March, 1899	murder
75. Robert Brown	W	Barren	April, 1899	murder
76. Robert Blanks	B	Graves	April, 1899	rape
77. Will Tutt	B	Graves	April, 1899	murder
78. Clarence Williams	B	Bourbon	December, 1899	murder
79. Thomas Cole	W	Hickman	April, 1901	murder
80. Reuben Quinn	W	Boyle	December, 1901	murder
81. James Black	B	Jefferson	May, 1903	murder
82. Claude O'Brien	W	Fayette	July, 1903	murder
83. Earl Whitney	W	Fayette	July, 1903	murder
84. Custer Gardner	W	Hart	July, 1904	murder
85. John Hathaway	B	Clark	January, 1905	murder
86. J. W. Bess	W	Fayette	January, 1905	murder
87. Roy Green	B	Daviess	February, 1905	murder
88. Robert Mathley	W	Daviess	July, 1905	murder
89. George Holland	B	Christian	July, 1905	murder
90. William Vandalsen	W	Jefferson	January, 1906	murder
91. Garth Tompkins	B	Hopkins	March, 1906	murder
92. James Hanna	B	Fayette	March, 1906	murder
93. James Pearsall	B	Fayette	July, 1906	rape
94. Cornelius Johnson	B	Jefferson	July, 1906	murder
95. Allen Mathias	B	Graves	August, 1906	rape
96. Joseph Johnson	B	Jefferson	August, 1906	murder
97. Thomas Stout	B	Fayette	November, 1906	murder
98. Jesse Fitzgerald	B	Knox	February, 1907	murder
99. Benjamin Huffaker	B	Lyon	February, 1907	murder
100. Guy Lyon	W	Logan	February, 1907	rape
101. W. R. "Polk" Fletcher	W	Logan	February, 1907	rape
102. Harrison Alexander	W	Muhlenburg	August, 1907	rape
103. Clarence Sturgeon	W	Jefferson	January, 1908	murder
104. Earl Thompson	B	Grant	January, 1910	rape
105. Floyd Frazier	W	Letcher	May, 1910	murder
106. Charles Howard	B	——	January, 1911	murder
107. James White	B	Bell	January, 1911	rape

NAME	RACE	COUNTY TRIED IN	DATE	REASON
108. Roger Warren	B	McCracken	May, 1911	murder
109. James Buckner	B	Marion	July, 1911	murder
110. Sandy Penman	B	Lincoln	August, 1911	rape
111. Oliver Locks	B	Jefferson	August, 1911	murder
112. Mathew Kelly	B	Jefferson	September, 1911	murder
113. Charles Howard	B	Franklin	January, 1912	murder
114. Willard Richardson	W	Carlisle	April, 1912	murder
115. Cal Miracle	W	Bell	August, 1912	murder
116. James Smith	B	Mason	September, 1912	murder
117. Charles Smith	B	Mason	September, 1912	murder
118. James Ellis	W	Pulaski	November, 1912	murder
119. Silas Williams	B	Woodford	March, 1912	murder
120. William Wilson	B	Jefferson	March, 1913	murder
121. John Bowman	W	Marion	April, 1913	rape
122. Isom Tolferras	B	Todd	April, 1913	rape
123. Jim Brown	B	Clark	April, 1913	murder
124. Thomas Martin	B	Shelby	June, 1913	murder
125. Thomas Lawson	B	Shelby	June, 1913	murder
126. General May	W	Laurel	June, 1913	murder
127. Turner Graham	W	Hardin	July, 1915	murder
128. William Lane	B	Bell	July, 1915	murder
129. Wallace Smithers	B	Clark	September, 1915	rape
130. John Henry	B	Boyd	November, 1915	rape
131. James H. Blue	B	Jefferson	January, 1916	murder
132. Harry Garrison	B	Campbell	November, 1916	rape
133. John H. Blue	B	Jefferson	August, 1917	murder
134. Melvin Collins	W	Kenton	July, 1918	murder
135. James Lawlwe	W	Kenton	February, 1919	murder
136. Pat Carney	W	Kenton	February, 1919	murder
137. Jim Howard	B	McCracken	June, 1919	murder
138. Lennis Hones	B	Calloway	June, 1919	murder
139. Lube Martin	B	Calloway	July, 1919	murder
140. Charles Music	W	Boyd	March, 1920	murder
141. Will Lockett	B	Fayette	March, 1920	murder
142. Lee Ellison	B	Hopkins	January, 1921	murder
143. Dave Brown	W	Pike	November, 1922	murder
144. Tom Nichols	B	Christian	January, 1923	murder
145. Benny Bibbs	B	Christian	January, 1923	murder
146. Henry S. Banks	B	Scott	May, 1923	murder
147. James Power	W	Kenton	June, 1923	murder

NAME	RACE	COUNTY TRIED IN	DATE	REASON
148. Will Chambers	B	Barren	March, 1924	murder
149. Frank Thomas	W	Jefferson	May, 1924	murder
150. George Weick	W	Jefferson	May, 1924	murder
151. Charles Miller	B	Breckinridge	May, 1924	murder
152. Sid Davis	B	Fayette	March, 1925	murder
153. Leonard Griffin	B	Harlan	March, 1925	murder
154. Elmer Hall	W	Bourbon	June, 1925	murder
155. Richard Newhouse	W	Bourbon	June, 1925	murder
156. George Farrell	W	Bourbon	June, 1925	murder
157. Harry Armond	B	Jefferson	July, 1925	murder
158. Ray Ross	B	Fayette	August, 1925	rape
159. Ed Harris	B	Fayette	March, 1926	murder
160. Edward Lake	W	Jefferson	May, 1926	murder
161. Elisha Sloan	W	Perry	May, 1926	murder
162. John Baker	B	Jefferson	May, 1926	murder
163. Roger Brannon	W	Fayette	December, 1926	murder
164. Smokey Harry	B	Christian	December, 1926	murder
165. Raymond Davis	W	Fayette	September, 1927	murder
166. Bunyan Fleming	B	Hopkins	November, 1927	rape
167. Nathan Bard	B	Hopkins	November, 1927	rape
168. Charles P. Mitra	W	Jefferson	July, 1928	murder
169. Red Seymoure	W	Jefferson	July, 1928	murder
170. Hascue Dockery	W	Harlan	July, 1928	murder
171. Milford Lawson	W	Knox	July, 1928	murder
172. Willie Moore	B	Jefferson	July, 1928	murder
173. James Howard	B	Jefferson	July, 1928	murder
174. Clarence McQueen	B	Jefferson	July, 1928	murder
175. Carl Hoard	W	Jefferson	September, 1929	murder
176. Ivan Hutsell	W	Oldham	September, 1929	murder
177. Ballard Ratcliffe	W	Jefferson	June, 1930	murder
178. Richard Edmonds	B	Jefferson	June, 1930	murder
179. A. B. Cooksey	B	Hopkins	April, 1932	murder
180. Charles Rodgers	B	Hardin	April, 1932	murder
181. Walter Holmes	B	Hardin	April, 1932	murder
182. Sam Jennings	B	Breckinridge	June, 1932	rape
183. Jeff Covington	B	Madison	December, 1932	murder
184. Frank Carson	W	Nelson	April, 1933	murder
185. Sam McGee	B	McCracken	April, 1933	murder
186. Kermit R. Pope	B	Jefferson	April, 1933	murder
187. Richard Gaines	B	Caldwell	April, 1933	murder

NAME	RACE	COUNTY TRIED IN	DATE	REASON
188. John Young	W	Jefferson	April, 1933	murder
189. Wm. "Bad Bill" Waters	B	Montgomery	November, 1933	murder
190. Ishmael Scott	W	Floyd	November, 1933	murder
191. Harve Buton	W	Elliott	November, 1933	murder
192. Walter Dewberry	B	Hardin	November, 1933	murder
193. Will Chaney	B	Jefferson	August, 1934	murder
194. George W. Tincher	W	Scott	August, 1934	murder
195. Francis Glenday	W	Scott	December, 1934	murder
196. Wiley Graves	B	Fayette	February, 1935	murder
197. Charlie Williams	B	Christian	March, 1935	murder
198. Willard T. De Boe	W	Livingston	April, 1935	rape
199. James Smith	B	Fayette	June, 1935	murder
200. Bill Young	W	Harlan	June, 1935	murder
201. Eulie Lotheridge	W	Carroll	December, 1935	murder
202. Neal Bowman	W	Mercer	January, 1936	murder
203. Calvin Tate	W	Jefferson	January, 1936	murder
204. Willard Hall	W	Jefferson	January, 1936	murder
205. James Matthews	W	McCreary	January, 1936	murder
206. Bennie Lee	B	Bell	February, 1936	murder
207. Erleon Whitehead	W	Barren	March, 1936	murder
208. Roy Simmons	B	McCracken	May, 1936	murder
209. Alfred Drake	B	Jefferson	May, 1936	murder
210. James Russell Woodford	B	Fayette	May, 1936	murder
211. Homer Young	B	Bell	June, 1936	murder
212. Rainey Bethea	B	Daviess	August, 1936	rape
213. George B. Underwood	W	Bullitt	February, 1937	murder
214. Sam Franklin	B	Jefferson	March, 1937	armed robbery
215. Arnold Clift	W	Laurel	July, 1937	murder
216. Perry Marion	W	Laurel	November, 1937	murder
217. John Montjoy	B	Kenton	December, 1937	rape
218. Troy Triplett	W	Letcher	May, 1938	murder
219. Harold Van Venison	B	Kenton	June, 1938	rape
220. Parkie Denny	W	Madison	September, 1938	murder
221. Leonard "Sank" Mosley	B	Meade	October, 1938	murder
222. Sylvester Warner	W	Casey	February, 1939	murder
223. Arnold Powell	W	Estill	March, 1939	murder
224. Bonnie Griffin	W	Estill	March, 1939	murder

NAME	RACE	COUNTY TRIED IN	DATE	REASON
225. Willie Waters	B	Jefferson	March, 1939	murder
226. Arvil Rice	W	Bell	July, 1939	murder
227. Charles H. Smith	W	Lyon	July, 1939	murder
228. Jack Davis	W	Leslie	July, 1939	murder
229. Edward Higgins	B	Mercer	July, 1939	rape

Selected Bibliography

PRIMARY SOURCES

Manuscript Collections

Association of Southern Women for the Prevention of Lynchings. Papers. Special Collections and Archives, Woodruff Library, Atlanta University.

Bradley, William O. Papers. Kentucky Department for Libraries and Archives, Frankfort.

Bradley, William O. Scrapbooks. Division of Special Collections and Archives, University of Kentucky, Lexington.

Bureau of Refugees, Freedmen, and Abandoned Lands. Record Group 105. National Archives, Washington, D.C.

Commission on Interracial Cooperation. Papers. Special Collections and Archives, Woodruff Library, Atlanta University.

Kentucky Governors' Papers, 1792–1926. Pardons and Rejected Petitions. Kentucky Department for Libraries and Archives, Frankfort.

Morrow, Edwin P. Papers. Division of Special Collections and Archives, University of Kentucky, Lexington.

National Association for the Advancement of Colored People. Papers. Manuscript Division, Library of Congress, Washington, D.C.

Rodes, John B. Manuscript. Kentucky Library, Western Kentucky University, Bowling Green.

Stanley, Augustus O. Papers. Kentucky Department for Libraries and Archives, Frankfort.

Stanley, Augustus O. Papers. Division of Special Collections and Archives, University of Kentucky, Lexington.

Willson, Augustus E. Papers. Kentucky Department for Libraries and Archives, Frankfort.

Willson, Augustus E. Papers and Scrapbooks. Filson Club, Louisville.

Legal Cases

Bard v. *Chilton, Warden et al.,* and *Fleming* v. *Same,* 20 Federal Reporter 2nd 906 (1927).

Batson, James Kirkland v. *Kentucky,* 106A United States 1712 (1986).

Blanks v. *Commonwealth,* 48 Southwestern Reporter 164 (1898).

Bowman v. *Commonwealth,* 143 Southwestern Reporter 47 (1912).

Browder v. *Commonwealth,* 136 Kentucky Reports 45 (1909).

Bush v. *Commonwealth,* 78 Kentucky Reports 268 (1882).

Bush v. *Kentucky,* 107 United States 110 (1882).

Commonwealth v. *Johnson,* 78 Kentucky Reports 509 (1880).

Commonwealth of Kentucky v. *George Dinning,* Simpson Circuit Court (1897).

Commonwealth of Kentucky v. *Rufus Browder,* Logan Circuit Court (1909).

Commonwealth of Kentucky v. *Tom Croe and Others,* Webster Circuit Court (1908).

Dewberry v. *Commonwealth,* 241 Kentucky Reports 726 (1931).

Ed Taylor v. *Commonwealth,* 90 Southwestern Reporter 584 (1906).

Franklin v. *Commonwealth,* 266 Kentucky Reports 833 (1936).

Gibson v. *Commonwealth,* 204 Kentucky Reports 748 (1924).

Haggard v. *Commonwealth,* 79 Kentucky Reports 366 (1881).

Hale v. *Commonwealth,* 269 Kentucky Reports 743 (1937).

Hale v. *Commonwealth,* 108 Southwestern Reporter 2nd 716 (1937).

Hale v. *Kentucky,* 303 United States 613 (1938).

Hocker v. *Commonwealth,* 111 Southwestern Reporter 676 (1908).

Holmes v. *Commonwealth,* 241 Kentucky Reports 573 (1931).

Jim Howard and Harry Porter v. *Commonwealth,* 178 Kentucky Reports 84 (1918).

John Taylor v. *Commonwealth,* 90 Southwestern Reporter 581 (1906).

McDaniel v. *Commonwealth,* 181 Kentucky Reports 766 (1918).

McPerkins v. *Commonwealth,* 33 Southwestern Reporter 2nd 622 (1930).

Martin v. *Commonwealth,* 178 Kentucky Reports 540 (1917).

Martin v. *Commonwealth,* 199 Southwestern Reporter 603 (1917).

Montjoy v. *Commonwealth,* 262 Kentucky Reports 426 (1935).

Patterson v. *Commonwealth,* 86 Kentucky Reports 313 (1887).

Rogers v. *Commonwealth,* 241 Kentucky Reports 593 (1931).

Smith v. *Commonwealth,* 37 Southwestern Reporter 825 (1896).

Smith v. *Commonwealth,* 91 Southwestern Reporter 742 (1906).

Public Documents

Acts of the General Assembly, 1897. Louisville, 1897.

Acts of the General Assembly, 1904. Louisville, 1904.

Acts of the General Assembly of the Commonwealth of Kentucky. Louisville, 1910.

Acts of the General Assembly, 1922. Frankfort, 1922.

Acts of Kentucky, 1902. Louisville, 1902.

Kentucky Acts of General Assembly for the Year 1920. Frankfort, 1920.

The Kentucky Statutes, Containing All General Laws. Louisville, 1915.

Legislative Document No. 26. *List of Pardons, Etc., Granted By Governor Luke P. Blackburn.* Frankfort, 1882.

Legislative Document No. 29. *Report of the Adjutant General State of Kentucky to the Commander-in-Chief, for the Years 1882–83.* Frankfort, 1883.

Legislative Document No. 35. *Biennial Report of the Warden of the Kentucky Penitentiary to the Board of Directors of the Penitentiary, November 30, 1891.* Frankfort, 1892.

U.S. Census Bureau. *Bulletin 8, Negroes in the United States.* Washington, D.C., 1904.

———. *Fifteenth Census of the United States, 1930.* 6 vols. Washington, D.C., 1932.

———. *Fourteenth Census of the United States, 1920.* 11 vols. Washington, D.C., 1923.

———. Manuscript Census of Henry County, 1870.

———. *Negro Population in the United States, 1790–1915.* Washington, D.C., 1918.

———. *Negroes in the United States, 1920–1932.* Washington, D.C., 1935.

———. *Seventeenth Census of the United States, 1950.* 5 vols. Washington, D.C., 1952.

———. *Twelfth Census of the United States, 1900.* 10 vols. Washington, D.C., 1901.

Newspapers and Periodicals

American Law Review, 1894, 1900

Arena, September, 1906

Boone County *Recorder,* July, 1894, January 9, 1895

Chicago *Tribune,* 1882–1936

Cincinnati *Commercial,* 1869, 1877

Cincinnati *Enquirer,* January, February, 1895, December, 1899, May, 1930

Corbin *Times,* October 31, November 7, 1919

Crisis, 1911–1938

Earlington *Bee,* January 15, 1911

Elliott County *News,* January 1, 1988

Frankfort *State Journal,* March 23, 1920

Georgetown *Times,* August 26, September 2, 1891

Hampton's Magazine, February, March, April, 1909
Harper's Weekly, July 31, 1858, February 8, 1908
Harrodsburg *Democrat*, December 8, 1908
Henderson *Daily Journal*, January–April, 1915
Hickman *Courier*, June, July, 1892, May, 1897
Hopkinsville *Kentuckian*, May, November, 1897, April, 1909, January, March, 1911
Indianapolis *Freeman*, January 12, February 2, 1895, May 20, 1899
Jessamine *Journal*, February 7, 1902
Lexington *Herald*, 1904–1908, 1921–1925
Lexington *Kentucky Gazette*, November, 1872, January, 1878
Lexington *Leader*, 1924–1926
Lexington *Morning Herald*, 1896, 1897, 1900–1905, 1926, 1928
Lexington *Morning Transcript*, November 22, 1884
Louisville *Commercial*, 1870–1902
Louisville *Courier-Journal*, 1868–1938, 1986
Louisville *Leader*, 1921–1939
Louisville *News*, 1922–1927
Louisville *Post*, September 4, 1922
Louisville *Times*, March, April, 1926, January 25, 1934
McClure's Magazine, January, February, 1905, October, 1922
Madisonville Daily *Messenger*, January, 1926–May, 1927
Madisonville *Hustler*, 1908
Mayfield *Monitor*, 1893–1899
Maysville *Bulletin*, March 20, 1884, April, 1920
Mount Sterling *Advocate*, January, February, 1895
Mount Verna *Signal*, February 15, 1901
New York *Freeman*, July 25, November 7, 1885, May 7, 1887
New York *Times*, 1866–1936
North American Review, July, 1892
Outlook, February 29, 1908
Owensboro *Messenger*, September, 1910, June 15, 1926
Paducah *Evening Sun*, August, 1915, March, 1920
Paducah *News-Democrat*, 1906–1917
Paducah *Sun-Democrat*, April 12, 1938
Shelby *News*, October 3, 1901, February 2, 1911
Tuskegee Institute Newspaper Clippings
World's Work, February, 1909

Pamphlets

Ames, Jessie Daniel. *The Changing Character of Lynching.* Atlanta, 1942.
Benjamin, Robert C. O. *Southern Outrages: A Statistical Record of Lawless Doings.* N.p., 1894.
Bruce, John Edward. *The Blood Red Record: A Review of the Horrible Lynchings and Burnings of Negroes by Civilized White Men in the United States.* Albany, 1901.
Coleman, J. Winston. *Death at the Court House.* Lexington, 1952.
Grimké, Francis J. *The Lynching of Negroes in the South: Its Cause and Remedy.* Washington, June, 1899.
Hobson, Will. *About The Hanging of Robert Harper, By A Mob, Wednesday, December 28, 1892, at Bowling Green, Ky.* N.p., n.d.
The Jake McDowell Tragedy. N.p., n.d.
Kentucky State Colored Education Convention Held at Benson's Theatre, Louisville, Kentucky, July 14, 1869. N.p., n.d.
Lynchings Go Underground. Atlanta, n.d.
National Association for the Advancement of Colored People. *Thirty Years of Lynchings in the United States.* New York, 1918.
Proceedings of the State Convention of Colored Men, held at Lexington, Kentucky, in the AME Church, November 26, 27, 28, 1867. N.p., n.d.
State Inter-Racial Conference for Kentucky, July 23d and 24th, 1920. Louisville, 1920.

Interviews with Author

Butner, Lillian, January 30, 1987, London.
Clark, Thomas D., March 18, 1988, Frankfort.
Hurst, Walter, November 15, 1984, Lexington.
Klotter, James, March 25, 1988, by telephone.
Reed, Tip, April 1, 1987, Mayfield.

SECONDARY SOURCES

Books: Local and State Histories

Ardery, Julia S., ed. *Welcome the Traveler Home: Jim Garland's Story of the Kentucky Mountains.* Lexington, 1983.
Coffman, Edward. *The Story of Logan County.* Nashville, 1962.
Collins, Lewis, and Richard H. Collins. *Collins' Historical Sketches of Kentucky.* Rev. ed. 2 vols. Covington, Ky., 1882.
Connelley, William E., and E. Merton Coulter. *History of Kentucky.* Edited by Charles Kerr. 5 vols. Chicago, 1922.

Coulter, E. Merton. *The Civil War and Readjustment in Kentucky.* Chapel Hill, 1926.

Crawford, John Leland. *A Tale of One City: Some Highlights in the History of Corbin.* Chicago, 1981.

Cunningham, Bill. *On Bended Knees: The Night Riders Story.* Nashville, 1983.

Ellis, William E., H. E. Everman, and Richard D. Sears. *Madison County: 200 Years in Retrospect.* Richmond, Kentucky, 1985.

Hayes, William Foster. *Sixty Years of Owensboro, 1883–1943.* Owensboro, 1943.

History of Union County, Kentucky. Evansville, Indiana, 1886.

Houchens, Mariam Sidebottom. *History of Owen County, Kentucky.* Owenton, Ky., n.d.

Howard, Victor. *Black Liberation in Kentucky: Emancipation & Freedom, 1862–1884.* Lexington, 1983.

Jillson, Willard Rouse. *Edwin P. Morrow–Kentuckian.* Louisville, n.d.

Johnson, W. D. *Biographical Sketches of Prominent Negro Men and Women of Kentucky.* Lexington, 1897.

Kramer, Carl E. *Capital on the Kentucky: A Two Hundred Year History of Frankfort and Franklin County.* Frankfort, 1986.

Marrs, Elijah P. *Life of Reverend Elijah P. Marrs.* Louisville, 1885.

Miller, John G. *The Black Patch War.* Chapel Hill, 1936.

Montell, William L. *Killings: Folk Justice in the Upper South.* Lexington, 1986.

Perrin, W. H., J. H. Battle, and G. C. Kniffin. *Kentucky: A History of the State.* Louisville, 1888.

Richards, John A. *An Illustrated History of Bath County, Kentucky, With Historical and Biographical Sketches and Notes and Anecdotes of Many Years.* Yuma, Ariz., 1961.

Rives, Hallie Erminie. *Smoking Flax.* 2nd ed. New York, 1897.

Robertson, Archibald Thomas, ed. *Life and Letters of John Albert Broadus.* Philadelphia, 1910.

Starling, Edmund L. *History of Henderson County, Kentucky.* Henderson, Ky., 1887.

Tapp, Hambleton, and James Klotter. *Kentucky: Decades of Discord, 1865–1900.* Frankfort, 1977.

Van Hook, Joseph O. *The Kentucky Story.* 4th ed. Norman, Okla., 1959.

Webb, Ross A. *Kentucky in the Reconstruction Era.* Lexington, 1979.

Work Projects Administration. *In the Land of Breathitt.* Northport, N.Y., n.d.

Wright, George C. *Life Behind A Veil: Blacks in Louisville, Kentucky, 1865–1930.* Baton Rouge, 1985.

Books: General

Alexander, Roberta Sue. *North Carolina Faces the Freedmen: Race Relations During Presidential Reconstruction, 1865–67.* Durham, 1985.

Ayers, Edward. *Vengeance and Justice: Crime and Punishment in the 19th Century American South.* New York, 1984.

Chadbourn, James Harmon. *Lynching and the Law.* Chapel Hill, 1933.

Cutler, James Elbert. *Lynch Law: An Investigation into the History of Lynching in the United States.* 1905; rpr. Montclair, N.J., 1969.

Dykeman, Wilma, and James Stokley. *Seeds of Southern Change: The Life of Will Alexander.* New York, 1962.

Eller, Ronald D. *Miners, Millhands, and Mountaineers: Industrialization of the Appalachian South, 1880–1930.* Knoxville, 1982.

Foner, Philip, ed. *The Life and Writings of Frederick Douglass.* 4 vols. New York, 1955.

Hall, Jacquelyn Dodd. *Revolt Against Chivalry: Jessie Daniel Ames and the Women's Campaign Against Lynchings.* New York, 1979.

Hofstadter, Richard, and Michael Wallace, eds. *American Violence: A Documentary History.* New York, 1970.

Klueger, Richard. *Simple Justice: The History of Brown v. Board of Education and Black America's Struggle for Equality.* New York, 1977.

Lewis, Ronald L. *Black Coal Miners In America: Race, Class, and Community Conflict, 1780–1980.* Lexington, 1987.

Litwack, Leon. *Been in the Storm So Long: The Aftermath of Slavery.* New York, 1979.

McGovern, James R. *Anatomy of a Lynching: The Killing of Claude Neal.* Baton Rouge, 1982.

McKelvey, Blake. *American Prisons: A Study in American Social History Prior to 1915.* Chicago, 1936.

Pleck, Elizabeth. *Domestic Tyranny: The Making of Social Policy Against Family Violence from Colonial Times to the Present.* New York, 1987.

Rabinowitz, Howard. *Race Relations in the Urban South, 1865–1890.* New York, 1978.

Rable, George C. *But There Was No Peace: The Role of Violence in the Politics of Reconstruction.* Athens, 1984.

Raper, Arthur. *The Tragedy of Lynching.* Chapel Hill, 1933.

Shapiro, Herbert. *White Violence and Black Response: From Reconstruction to Montgomery.* Amherst, 1988.

Singletary, Otis A. *Negro Militia and Reconstruction.* Austin, 1957.

Spero, Sterling D., and Abram L. Harris. *The Black Worker.* New York, 1931.

Stephenson, Gilbert T. *Race Distinction in American Law.* New York, 1910.

Trelease, Allen W. *White Terror: The Ku Klux Klan Conspiracy and Southern Reconstruction.* New York, 1971.
Wells, Ida B. *Southern Horrors: Lynch Law In All Its Phases.* New York, 1892.
Wells-Barnett, Ida. *A Red Record: Lynchings in the United States, 1892–1893–1894.* Chicago, 1895.
Williamson, Joel. *The Crucible of Race: Black and White Relations in the American South Since Emancipation.* New York, 1984.
Zangrando, Robert L. *The NAACP Crusade Against Lynching, 1909–1950.* Philadelphia, 1980.

Articles

Carpenter, John A. "Atrocities in the Reconstruction Period." *Journal of Negro History,* XLVII (October, 1962), 234–47.
Cutler, James E. "Proposed Remedies for Lynchings." *Yale Review,* XXII (August, 1904), 194–212.
Dew, Lee A. "The Hanging of Rainey Bethea." *Daviess County Historical Quarterly,* II (July, 1984), 51–59.
Harlan, Louis R. "Booker T. Washington in Biographical Perspective." *American Historical Review,* LXXV (October, 1970), 1581–99.
Holmes, William F. "Whitecapping: Agrarian Violence in Mississippi, 1902–1906." *Journal of Southern History,* XXXV (May, 1969), 165–85.
Klotter, James. "Feuds in Appalachia: An Overview." *Filson Club History Quarterly,* LVI (July, 1982), 290–317.
Lawson, Hughie G. "Geographical Origins of White Migrants to Trigg and Calloway Counties in the Ante-bellum Period." *Filson Club History Quarterly,* LVII (July, 1983), 286–305.
Waldrep, Christopher. "Planters and the Planters' Protective Association in Kentucky and Tennessee." *Journal of Southern History,* LII (November, 1986), 565–88.
Wright, John D. "Lexington's Suppression of the 1920 Will Lockett Lynch Mob." *Register of the Kentucky Historical Society,* LXXXIV (Summer, 1986), 263–79.

Dissertations and Theses

Clotfelter, Elizabeth R. "The Agriculture History of Bourbon County, Ky., Prior to 1900." M.A. thesis, University of Kentucky, 1953.
Crawford, Robert Gunn. "A History of the Kentucky Penitentiary System, 1865–1937." Ph.D. dissertation, University of Kentucky, 1955.
Dudley, Julius Wayne. "A History of the Association of Southern Women for the Prevention of Lynching, 1930–1942." Ph.D. dissertation, University of Cincinnati, 1979.

Meals, Claude L. "The Struggle of the Negro for Citizenship in Kentucky Since 1865." M.A. thesis, Howard University, 1940.

Ramage, Thomas W. "Augustus Owsley Stanley: Early Twentieth Century Democrat." Ph.D. dissertation, University of Kentucky, 1968.

Taylor, Marie. "Night Riders in the Black Patch." M.A. thesis, University of Kentucky, 1934.

Volz, Harry A. "The Administration of Justice By the Freedmen's Bureau in Kentucky, South Carolina, and Virginia." M.A. thesis, University of Virginia, 1975.

Index